Visit us at

www.syngress.com

Syngress is committed to publishing high-quality books for IT Professionals and delivering those books in media and formats that fit the demands of our customers. We are also committed to extending the utility of the book you purchase via additional materials available from our Web site.

SOLUTIONS WEB SITE

To register your book, please visit **www.syngress.com**. Once registered, you can access your e-book with print, copy, and comment features enabled.

ULTIMATE CDs

Our Ultimate CD product line offers our readers budget-conscious compilations of some of our best-selling backlist titles in Adobe PDF form. These CDs are the perfect way to extend your reference library on key topics pertaining to your area of expertise, including Cisco Engineering, Microsoft Windows System Administration, CyberCrime Investigation, Open Source Security, and Firewall Configuration, to name a few.

DOWNLOADABLE E-BOOKS

For readers who can't wait for hard copy, we offer most of our titles in downloadable e-book format. These are available at **www.syngress.com**.

SITE LICENSING

Syngress has a well-established program for site licensing our e-books onto servers in corporations, educational institutions, and large organizations. Please contact our corporate sales department at corporatesales@elsevier.com for more information.

CUSTOM PUBLISHING

Many organizations welcome the ability to combine parts of multiple Syngress books, as well as their own content, into a single volume for their own internal use. Please contact our corporate sales department at corporatesales@elsevier.com for more information.

SAP Security Configuration and Deployment

The IT Administrator's Guide to Best Practices

Leslie Wun-Young Technical Editor
Joey Hirao

Jeanmarie Hirao
Mimi Choi
Perry Cox
Steven L. Passer

Unique Passcode

84730685

PUBLISHED BY
Syngress Publishing, Inc.
Elsevier, Inc.
30 Corporate Drive
Burlington, MA 01803

SAP Security Configuration and Deployment
The IT Administrator's Guide to Best Practices

Printed and bound in the United Kingdom

Transferred to Digital Print 2011

ISBN 13: 978-1-59749-284-3

Publisher: Laura Colantoni
Acquisitions Editor: Andrew Williams
Technical Editor: Leslie Wun-Young
Developmental Editor: Gary Byrne
Page Layout and Art: SPI
Copy Editor: Christina Solstad
Indexer: SPI
Cover Designer: Michael Kavish

For information on rights, translations, and bulk sales, contact Matt Pedersen, Commercial Sales Director and Rights, at Syngress Publishing; email m.pedersen@elsevier.com.

Library of Congress Cataloging-in-Publication Data
Application Submitted

Technical Editor

Leslie Wun-Young is a senior SAP security specialist. She has conducted several SAP full life-cycle implementations and delivered superior solutions in high-pressure environments with tight timelines for companies such as the Walt Disney Company, IBM, and NBC Universal. Her specialties include security architecture, strategy, and design, plus SOD evaluation and GRC management. Leslie's background includes positions as a senior developer for the American International Group, Inc. (AIG) and as a technical team lead for the Science Applications International Corporation (SAIC).

Leslie holds a master's degree in computer science and information systems from City College of New York/CUNY, and she is a member of the Multicultural Radio Broadcasting Association.

Lead Author

Joey Hirao (SAP Technical Certified Consultant; SAP NetWeaver Certified Consultant Enterprise Portals; Oracle OCP 8i,9i,10g; SUN Certified Solaris Administrator, Microsoft MCSE) is a senior Basis consultant for Group Basis (www.groupbasis.com), a firm specializing in SAP Basis and security solutions. He has over 11 years' experience providing SAP Basis solutions for customers worldwide. Joey is the author of *SAP R/3 Administration for Dummies* (IDG Books Worldwide Inc., 1999). He has also presented at SAPAdmin and written many articles for SAPtips.com.

I dedicate this book to my fabulous duo, Julianna and Sofia. They make every day brighter and more beautiful.

Contributing Authors

Jeanmarie Hirao (CPA) is a senior SAP consultant with Group Basis. She has over 10 years of SAP experience, ranging from system auditor to project management. Her background includes positions as an external auditor for a Big Four accounting firm, an internal auditor for a multinational computer distribution company, and a consultant on SAP internal audits and FICO projects. She holds a master's degree in accountancy from San Diego State University, California.

I dedicate this book to my amazing husband, who is the reason for my happiness.

Mimi Choi is a Basis consultant with over 7 years' experience in SAP Basis. She currently works as a freelance consultant and provides technical consulting to a variety of large enterprise customers. Mimi previously worked as an advisory SAP technical consultant within the IBM Business Consulting Services team in Sydney, Australia. She is a certified SAP technology consultant. Mimi holds a bachelor's degree in commerce from the University of New South Wales, Australia. She is currently based in London, U.K.

Perry Cox is the managing partner of P.W. Cox Consulting, L.P. with over 25 years' experience in the IT industry, including three years as an adjunct faculty member teaching both undergraduate and graduate business students about IT. He has specialized in SAP security solutions for the past 12 years, implementing SAP for clients and instructing them on how to maintain their own SAP security environment.

He is currently associated with Group Basis as a senior security consultant and holds an MBA from Indiana Wesleyan University.

Steven L. Passer is a senior manager in Accenture's SAP Consulting Practice. He recently joined Accenture from NASA, where he was the lead SAP systems architect responsible for operations and engineering on the program. While with NASA Steve was responsible for the technical services revolving around NASA's implementation, including SAP NetWeaver, new releases, landscape, capacity planning, performance, and operations across all NASA instances, including SAP NetWeaver Portal, SAP Contract Management, SAP Business Information Warehouse, SAP Service and Asset Management, and SAP Solution Manager. Steven has over 14 years of SAP implementation experience in pharmaceutical, automotive, and federal organizations.

Contents

Chapter 1

Introduction

Solutions in this chapter:

- NetWeaver Web Application Server
- ABAP WEB AS 7.0
- J2EE WEB AS 7.0
- Backend UNIX/Oracle
- Governance, Risk, and Compliance (GRC)

☑ Summary

☑ Solutions Fast Track

☑ Frequently Asked Questions

Introduction

When you consider the changes in SAP over the years, it's an evolution that is both amazing and inspiring. The vision of R/3 back in 1993 compared to where it is today, 15 years later, highlights its initial purpose. That purpose was to enable business to be more efficient, effective, and integrated. Those of us that studied process engineering and realized that the decentralized information technology (IT) culture and islands of automation we had in the 1980s and early 1990s were ineffective in helping business evolve, understood this need for an integrated enterprise solution.

Rudy Puryear[1] of Accenture Consulting discusses the evolution of IT systems from the 1970s to today. He describes three phases of an electronically driven economy. These phases are about how organizations develop and execute business strategy enabled by IT. The first era was data processing, next came information systems, and finally knowledge management. One sees how this evolution aligns with SAP's continuous improvement program. The desired outcome for IT to improve business efficiency has stayed consistent through the years. However, the delivery of value-producing systems has not been easy to achieve until we finally reached this knowledge management era. The state of art at the time R/3 was being developed was not in keeping with that early vision.

Now, we fast forward to today and can see that our vision goes beyond enabling business and sees IT as an almost equal partner in effecting business efficiency. Today's worker is now a knowledge worker enabled by Web-based flexible tools and technologies. These tools provide nearly instant information about the business problems they are working with. But with the incredible efficiency SAP can provide comes a heavy burden on infrastructure complexity. The systems requirements for SAP are significant in terms of IT architecture, development architecture, and security infrastructure. In fact, I would maintain that embedded into every aspect of the infrastructure is now a component of security specification that must be addressed. Unfortunately, we still see many occasions where security is the appendix of the infrastructure plan. Security is often relegated to an after-thought that only gets emergency attention when an event occurs, a question of senior management is asked, or an audit drives a specific change. It is the rare organization that has an embedded active security-thinking culture.

Security infrastructure as an embedded part of the IT culture has yet to be recognized in the mainstream. However, when you consider the initiatives being addressed in corporations, institutions, and governments throughout the world, you begin to understand the strategic intent in evolving security. In nearly every conference on technology in the SAP and out of the SAP space there is a topic on security. And, now, SAP NetWeaver technology has evolved to include the major SAP components necessary to implement the full life cycle of security infrastructure. While IT enables business, security enables IT, and hence security is the underlying foundation to the business enablement.

With IT organizations yet to adapt to this mind-set, the challenges are even greater. Most IT organizations are classically stove-piped and hence the skills and training associated with these stovepipes are yet to evolve. Even worse, often an organization creates project teams that may tax the stove-piped security group with a part-time representative. When I speak with young engineers across the organization, however, they seem to realize the change that's happening and are struggling to help their leaders make the right investments and reorganize to face the change. I challenge management to bring these facets out in the open and create enabling organizations that put the security mind-set at the forefront. It's no longer a cliché to say that security is everyone's responsibility. SAP has laid a foundation for this. In each aspect of SAP's NetWeaver use-case scenarios lies a security layer. SAP describes these as usage types, which determine the intended purpose of a system or sub-system. They are available by installing and configuring collections of software components.

Figure 1.1 presents NetWeaver as a collection of components that meet different needs up and down the integration stack.[2] It is important to recognize that today SAP NetWeaver is more than just a collection of components; it is an open technology platform which offers a comprehensive set of technologic capabilities that are natively integrated to support the needs of IT organizations worldwide. By reviewing the full gamut of capabilities one arrives at IT Scenarios and IT Practices that I refer to as use-cases.

Figure 1.1 SAP NetWeaver Usage Type Component Collection

IT Practice	IT Scenarios			
Enabling User Productivity	Enterprise Portals, Enabling Collaboration, Dashboards	Business Workflow	Mobilization	Enterprise Knowledge Management
Unification of Data	Master Data Synchronization	Master Data Consolidation	Central Data Management	Enterprise Data Warehousing
Business Support	Enterprise Reporting	Business Planning	Analytical Modeling	Enterprise Data Warehousing
Process Fulfillment	Enabling Business Workflows	Enabling eCommerce	Business Process Management	Business Workflow
Customized Development	Application Development	Applications Test & Delivery	Application Integration	Enabling Platform Interoperability
Unified Life-Cycle Management	Software Lifecycle Management	Systems Development Lifecycle	Solution Management Framework	SAP NetWeaver Operations & Design
Governance and Security	Authentication and Single Sign-On	Integrated User and Access Management	Segregation of Duties	Risk Management
Consolidation	Enabling Platform Interoperability	SAP NetWeaver Operations & Design	Master Data Consolidation & Unification	Enterprise Knowledge Management
Enterprise Services	Enabling Services	Open Standards	SAP NetWeaver Operations & Design	Solution Management Framework

IT Scenarios identify how one uses SAP NetWeaver to solve specific business problems. This is accomplished through deployment of the integrated IT scenarios in a way that does not disrupt existing business operations. IT practices look at the overall SAP NetWeaver platform as a strategic investment. One views the usage framework vertically and determines the options to focus on critical business issues rather then specific business problems addressed by tactical scenarios. This flexibility is the power of SAP NetWeaver.

SAP recommends that each practice be broken into one or multiple IT scenarios, providing organizations with a process-oriented approach to making best use of NetWeaver. By implementing IT scenarios, customers can adopt core functionality of SAP NetWeaver in incremental phases. The aim of IT scenarios is to help customers, partners, and independent software vendors (ISVs) install and operate SAP NetWeaver, to run business applications (custom-built and packaged applications), or to implement a defined IT goal like migrating to the services architecture. Focusing on the flow of activities rather than on the nature of the involved components, IT scenarios are collections aimed at resolving specific business area challenges.

The best way to see these IT practices and IT scenarios is with the SAP NetWeaver Technology Map.[3]

The SAP NetWeaver Technology Map

In Figure 1.1, each IT practice is on the left, with its associated IT scenarios to the right. Usage types describe how installations of SAP NetWeaver are used, and which capabilities each offers to the overall IT landscape. By providing installation and basic configuration support for SAP NetWeaver systems, usage types provide the groundwork to run IT and business scenarios. Usage types make system landscape planning easier by determining how capabilities provided by SAP NetWeaver can be deployed and activated in a SAP NetWeaver system. In addition, configuration will be simplified by offering configuration templates for usage types and IT scenarios. Usage types were introduced with SAP NetWeaver 7.0. Each scenario or practice has a security implication. Each instantiation comes with its own unique set of questions, technologies, and considerations for implementation and architecture.

As an organization implements a new component or scenario, the development cycle used to design, create, test, and deploy must adopt their design and testing methodology to ensure compliance. There are a host of tools and processes available for this. This book, then, is to be a model for highlighting the SAP technologies available for implementing and institutionalizing security into the technology plans and implementations throughout the industry.

Security can no longer be the afterthought for implementations. I contend that as an afterthought, it is more costly to implement and retrofit. But as a key component in the early planning of any implementation security, security considerations are an equal partner in the design. A simple example of this shift is the following. Let's take a mythical company, Superior Marbles Inc. Superior Marbles has successfully deployed SAP and is using the system to manage its assets. A key aspect to many assets in a firm is location. And, with assets that are used by the average worker, tracking can be quite difficult. Every two or three years an asset such as a PC or cell phone may need to be replaced or upgraded. Also, work or home office locations for these devices must be tracked. Finally, when an employee leaves of the assets must be collected and accounted for. So, in this example, let us consider the Superior Marbles sales team. The sales force often has a personal data assistant (PDA), a laptop, a printer, and so on. So in a firm with 50 sales people we are quickly dealing with at least 150 line items to track.

The capital acquisition is an easy entry into SAP by the purchasing/receiving organizations, but when the asset is delivered it is no longer easy to track. Typically, inside SAP the tracking is at a cost center/departmental level. But, with a useful kiosk through the Web, enabling the sales team to self manage the assets would prove extremely useful. So, an extension from the SAP database to an applet available to end-users (the sales people) over the Web will be our project. Many technologies are in play for this project. How will they securely log in? What will be presented to them and how will the data exchange occur back into SAP?

One can envision tackling the project via the typical analysis/requirements development process. But where are the security considerations determined and discussed with the user? They often aren't. It's left to IT network people, IT architects, and the developers to build on the basic requirements and ensure security. Even worse, there are times when audit concerns are missed until an actual audit, which can reveal additional shortcomings. So, the corrected approach is to address with the users the complete life cycle for the application and secure the application and its data. Having proper requirements specifications for the development team removes the ambiguity. And, better still, during audits these specifications are part of the development record and often this kind of data serves an important purpose as part of the catalog of documents used in building the application. So, then, what are the technologies that one must be concerned with in deploying an application within the SAP framework?

There are three key underlying concepts to all of the security infrastructure layers. These are data integrity, user access, and user authorization. Simply put, how is the data in the system ensured, how do users gain access, and what can users do with that access? The concepts associated with securing the infrastructure and applications will address these three key areas.

Scope

The scope of this discussion will be focused on four overlying security technologies that specifically encompass SAP. There are a host of certified for NetWeaver non-SAP, such as Microsoft's BizTalk framework that complement SAP; however, these are out of scope for this book. It is hoped that through a study of the components and considerations of the SAP technologies extension to the non-SAP is possible. The same considerations will be consistent across the infrastructure independent of the specific technology. Thus, we will focus on both ABAP and Java Web Application Server 7.0, Governance, Risk and Compliance (GRC) and the typical backend infrastructure foundations UNIX/Oracle. We do not mean to exclude specific, relevant technologies such as SQL Server or Linux, but we believe extensibility is appropriate and we also find in the main that UNIX/Oracle still appear to have the lion's share of systems in an SAP installation. Thus, if you are working in a heterogeneous landscape the concepts outlined here will still apply.

NetWeaver Web Application Server

SAP NetWeaver 7.0 provides an open integration and application platform and facilitates the implementation of Enterprise Services Architecture (see Figure 1.2). Both ABAP and Java are fully supported in SAP. Sizing considerations and architecture plans should be considered in order to determine the best model for implementing these stacks. While integrated ABAP/JAVA Web AS on the same server is possible, it is recommended to have separate hardware (application server) in either virtual or physical modes for the ABAP Web AS and the JAVA Web AS. Highlighted in the following sections is an overview of the J2EE Web AS and the ABAP Web AS feature, functions, and security insights.

Figure 1.2 NetWeaver Application Server Architecture

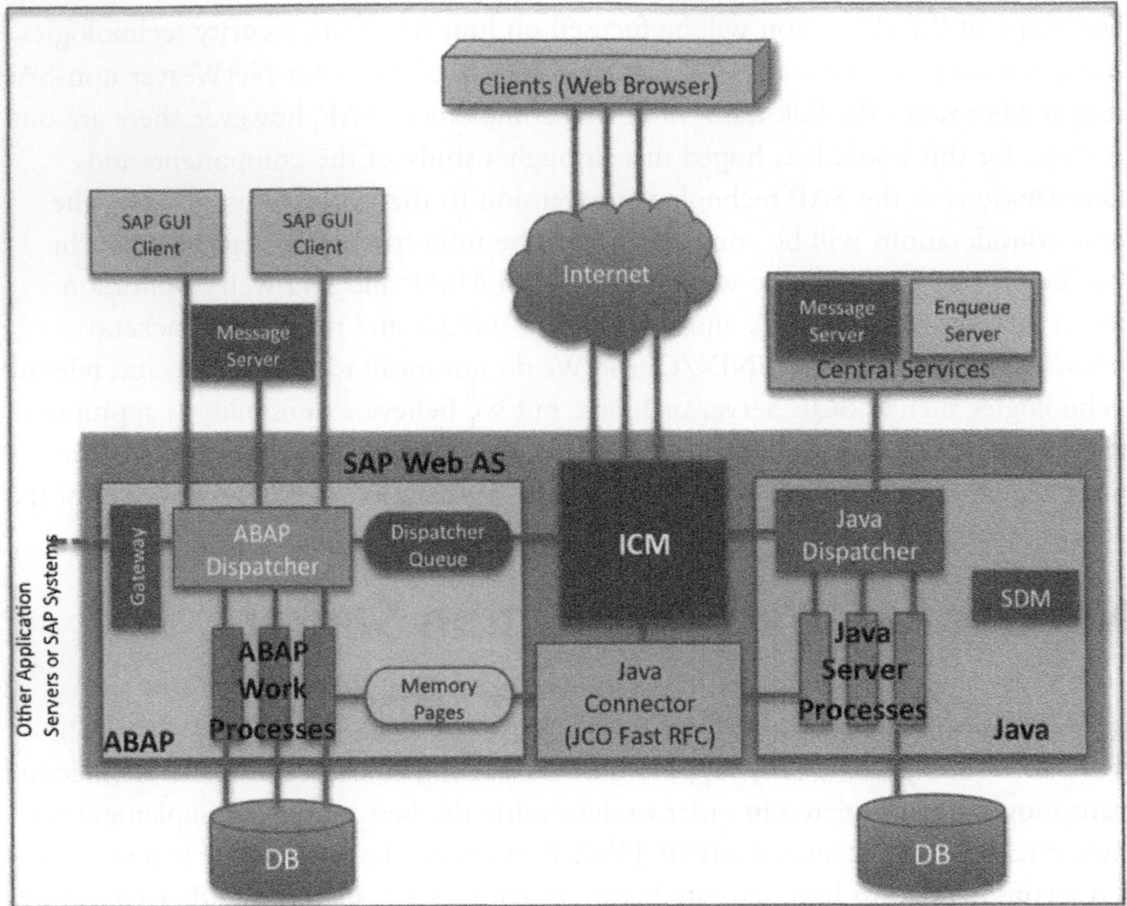

Figure 1.2 describes the combined ABAP and Java Web Application Architecture. Yellow Represents ABAP components and Green is Java. As mentioned previously, if you can afford it, the advantages to installing separate Java and ABAP engines outweigh the cost. For example, the technical patch requirements are more complicated and if patching one or the other service is necessary, with separate installations the other stays up while one is being patched. The Internet Communication Manager (ICM) is independent from the ABAP and JAVA stack but is installed with the ABAP application server. The ICM determines how to forward Web traffic requests. Each engine has a dispatch queue and the Java connector shown is an independent component but a function of the Java engine. It enables communication between ABAP and Java.

Client options are SAP GUI or Web Browser. The ICM is the Internet Communication manager which sets up the connection to the Internet for browser-based communications. The ICM process uses threads to parallelize the load that come through it. It can process both server and client Web requests. It supports the protocols Hypertext Transfer Protocol (HTTP), Hypertext Transfer Protocol Secure (HTTPS), and Simple Mail Transfer Protocol (SMTP). The dispatcher distributes the requests to the work processes. If all the processes are occupied the requests are stored in the dispatcher queue.

The ABAP work processes execute the ABAP code and the Java Server processes the Java code.

The Gateway makes the Request for Comments (RFC) interface between the SAP instances available within an SAP System and beyond system boundaries. Message servers exchange messages and balance the load in an SAP System.

ABAP WEB AS 7.0

System security functions that apply specifically for SAP Web AS ABAP are Trust Manager and Security Audit Log. Trust manager is the tool to use when using public-key technology with the SAP Web AS ABAP server. Use the Security Audit Log to keep track of security-related events on the SAP Web AS ABAP server. Events such as unsuccessful log-on attempts, starting of transactions or reports, or changes to user master records can be recorded and analyzed. Secure storage is part of the SAP Web Application Server ABAP and is used by SAP applications to store the passwords used for connecting to other systems. The passwords are stored encrypted. As a result they cannot be accessed by unauthorized users.

Establishing solid trust relationships is vital to the success of business processing. This becomes paramount with today's mobile knowledge worker that transcends corporate bounds and works from anyplace. Therefore, many applications in SAP Systems rely on the use of public-key technology to establish the trust infrastructure that is necessary for successful business relationships.

SAP Systems support the use of an external security product using the Secure Store and Forward (SSF) mechanism. By using SSF, applications can support the use of digital signatures and document encryption in their processing. At start-up, each SAP System is supplied with a public-key pair, which includes a public-key certificate that is stored in its own system Personal Security Environment (PSE). The SAP System can therefore produce its own digital signatures using the public-key information contained in its system PSE. Other systems can then verify the system's digital signature, which guarantees the integrity and authenticity of a document that has been digitally signed by the system. With the SAP Web AS, a single login by a user enables the system to authenticate the user through other subsystems using the digital signature provided with the log-on ticket. Lastly, The SAP Web AS supports the Secure Sockets Layer (SSL) protocol, which provides for authentication between communication partners and encrypted communications. In this case, the application server must also possess a public and private key pair to use for the SSL communications.

The Security Audit Log is designed for security and audit administrators who wish to have detailed information on what occurs in the SAP System. By activating the audit log, you keep a record of those activities you consider relevant for auditing. You can then access this information for evaluation in the form of an audit analysis report.

The SAP Web AS ABAP communicates with its communication partners using various protocols. The primary protocols used are Dialog (DIAG), RFC, and HTTP. The security mechanism for managing these protocols is either Secure Network Communication (SNC) or SSL.

J2EE WEB AS 7.0

SAP NetWeaver 7.0 provides an open integration and application platform and facilitates the implementation of the Enterprise Services Architecture. The Java SAP Web Application Server provides complete user management services called a User Management Engine or UME, the Universal Description Discovery and Integration or UDDI and data base integration facilities. By default, UME is set upon install.

The purpose of the UME is to provide central user administration for all applications developed using Java. The UME is completely integrated into SAP Web Application Server Java as a service and is used as the default user store. The UME itself administers users and uses databases, directory services, or the SAP ABAP user administration to store the data. In the UME, the words *data sources* are used to refer to repositories for user data.

To display the active user store, select a Server in the Visual Administrator. In the Security Provider service, select **Runtime → User Management**, and choose

Manage Security Stores. If it is grayed out, you have to go to **Change Mode**. If Activate User Store is inactive for a user store, this means that the user store that you have just chosen is already active. If you want to use UDDI instead of the default user store UME, you can use the described method to change this by choosing **Activate User Store** for the UDDI user store.

UME Installation Options

During the installation of an SAP Web Application Server (SAP Web AS), you can select the following options for setting up the UME:

- **SAP Web AS Java (without ABAP)** The UME can be configured so that the ABAP user management of another SAP Web Application Server ABAP is used. The UME can be configured so that the database of this SAP Web Application Server Java is used to store user data.
- **SAP Web AS ABAP + Java** The UME is configured so that the ABAP user management of this SAP Web Application Server is used. By default, you have read-only access to the user data in ABAP user management from the UME.

The communication between the UME and the ABAP user management is performed with the SAPJSF user. After an installation, this user has the ABAP role SAP_BC_JSF_COMMUNICATION_RO, which provides read access from the UME to the ABAP user management. You can obtain write access by adding the role SAP_BC_JSF_COMMUNICATION. SAP recommends the role SAP_BC_JSF_COMMUNICATION_RO for this user. You can only configure the use of a directory service as the data source later. In this case, it is recommended that you use the database as the data source for user data during the installation Administration of Users (UME with ABAP User Management as data source) ABAP Users: transaction SU01, ABAP authorizations and roles: transaction PFCG, Java authorizations and roles (UME roles, security roles): Visual Administrator and UME administration console. If you are using an SAP Enterprise Portal in this environment, the user administration is controlled using the portal.

The Java dispatcher receives the client request and forwards it to the server process with the lowest capacity usage. If there is already a connection to the client, the request goes to the server process that processes this client (see Figure 1.3).

Figure 1.3 Java Web Application Server Architecture

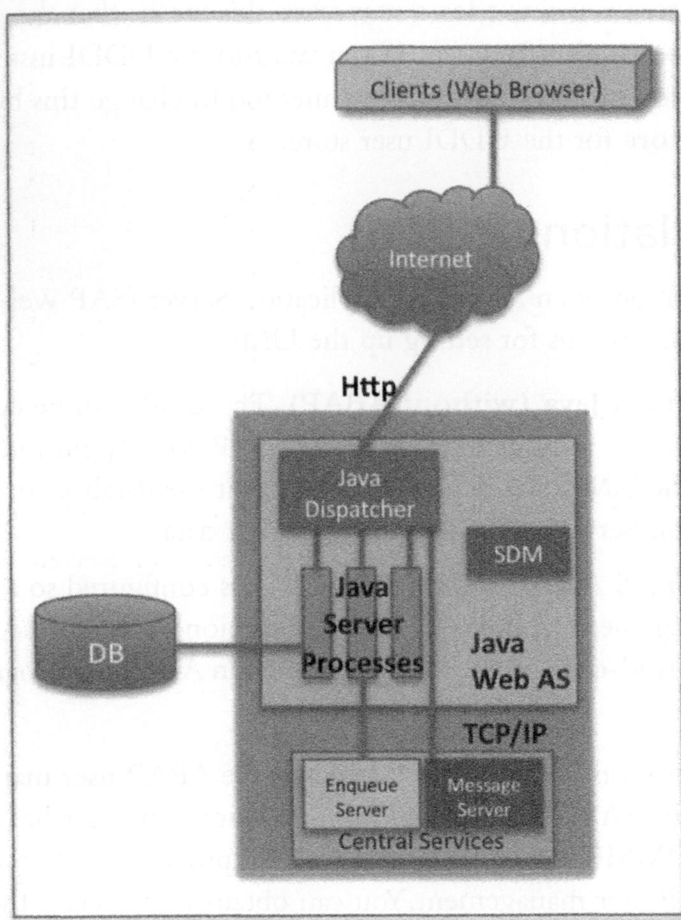

To operate the J2EE Engine, the following services must be active in the HTTP service tree (transaction SICF):

- **/sap/public/icman:** The ICM uses this service to forward requests to the J2EE Engine.
- **/sap/public/icf_info** supplies the Web Dispatcher the details of log-on groups, server load, and so on.

These services must be activated so that the SAP Web dispatcher and the ICM can forward the request correctly. If these services are not active, you have to activate them in transaction SICF.[4]

The Web Dispatcher is the central access point from the Internet into the SAP System. The Web dispatcher has to decide to which SAP Web AS it will send each incoming request. For each incoming HTTP request, the ICM must decide whether it should forward the request for processing to the ABAP engine or to the J2EE engine. This decision is made using the URL prefix. A separate protocol is used for the communication between the ICM and Java Dispatcher. The ICM can be set up so that the communication with the J2EE Engine is SSL-encrypted. If the ICM receives an HTTPS request, it decodes it. If it determines from the URL that the request should go to the J2EE Engine, there are various communication options. You can set whether the request should be SSL-encrypted, before it is forwarded to the J2EE Engine. You can do this in the following ways:

- Do not encrypt the request: The request is sent to the J2EE Engine with the protocol described above via TCP sockets.
- Encrypt the HTTPS request again: All requests that arrived as HTTPS at the ICM are SSL-encrypted again, before they are sent to the J2EE Engine.
- Encrypt all requests: Regardless of whether the request was HTTP or HTTPS, it is SSL-encrypted, before it is sent to the J2EE Engine.

The ICM is configured for communicating with the J2EE Engine using an icm profile parameter.[5]

The Software Deployment Manager (SDM) is an integrated directory of SAP software components in the library. The SAP Web AS engine includes the Universal Description, Discovery and Integration (UDDI) Business Registry. This is a global, public, online directory that gives businesses a uniform way to describe their services, discover other companies' services, and understand the methods necessary to conduct e-business with a particular company. As a key element of the framework that makes Web services a reality, the UDDI Business Registry is an implementation based on the UDDI Specifications.[6]

UDDI has been around for several years initially driven by IBM and SAP adopted it in 2001. Unfortunately, the incredible power of UDDI offers significant concerns in the security and change management space. It's vital to have a test program that actively manages in this arena. Today's Java development world still lacks rigorous change control and tracking. As a result, while Java development projects facilitate rapid delivery through component reuse and ease of programming, it can be a two edged sword. Its important to understand the building blocks and risks associated with these in order to have an active program that certifies use of programs and components.

The J2EE Engine can communicate with its communication partners using several different protocols. The primary protocol used is HTTP, however, P4, which is the protocol to use for RMI, as well as the protocols LDAP, ODBC, and telnet are also supported. SAP documents the protocols and security methods in the online documentation. Table 1.1 lists this information.

Table 1.1 Protocols and Security Methods

Protocol	Security Mechanism	Comment
HTTP	SSL	SSL provides for authentication, integrity, and privacy protection.
P4	SSL	P4 is the transfer protocol for RMI and when using the Visual Administrator. P4 supports HTTP tunneling and can also be used with proxies.
LDAP	SSL	You can use an LDAP directory server as the persistency layer for the UME user store.
RFC	SNC (Secure Network Communications)	SNC is a SAP-proprietary layer used with the NI protocol.
ODBC	driver-dependent	Used to connect to the database.
Telnet	Virtual Private Network	You can use telnet for remote administration.

Additional system security functions for SAP Web AS Java include Key Storage service, Managing protection domains, Secured Web service, Application specific secured storage, File System secured storage, and Managed log-in sessions.

The Key Storage service of the J2EE Engine enables you to manage certificates and credentials on the server; you can also use it to generate keys and certificates. Application specific secured storage is related to this area. These keys and certificates can be used for encrypting, identification, and verification. The Key Storage entries are stored in a distributed database and can be assigned particular access rights. The service is compatible with the Java Cryptography Architecture.[7]

Protection domains enable you to manage system resources. This enables you to make access control decisions. You can add new categories of permissions that are supported by the J2EE Engine.

With secured Web services a user (or other client) sends a document to a server using the Simple Object Access Protocol (SOAP), which is then sent over the network using the HTTP protocol. Therefore, to secure this communication, one can use the SSL protocol, which is supported by the J2EE Engine. What you must ensure is that you secure the transmission and have proper authorizations for processing such documents. There are several mechanisms available on the J2EE Engine, which include securing the communications, authenticating the client, and providing for authorizations. The J2EE Engine implements the *Java Authentication and Authorization Service (JAAS)* standard to support various authentication methods. This enables you to choose the required authentication mechanisms for your applications.

Applications running on the J2EE Engine can either use declarative or programmatic authentication. Both types of authentication rely on the same underlying technology: log-in modules and log-in module stacks. Programmatic authentication additionally uses authentication schemes. SAP ships log-in modules and authentication schemes to support various authentication mechanisms.

Protection domains enable you to manage system resources. This enables you to make access control decisions. You can add new categories of permissions that are supported by the J2EE Engine.

The SAP Web AS Java stores security-relevant information encrypted in a file in the file system. Because the cryptographic software needs to be deployed after the installation, you first need to activate the secure storage in the file system to have this information stored in encrypted form. Alternately, the information is encoded using 64 bit encoding.

J2EE Engine associates a security session object to the thread of control of each authenticated user for a login. The security session is recognized by the cluster element it is created in. It is also has an associated signed certificate by the cluster element that identifies the security session. It can be transferred by protocols that cannot or do not want to maintain client sessions on their own.

Backend: UNIX/Oracle

Today's SAP infrastructure offers incredible flexibility. From single-system landscapes to multisystem heterogeneous environments, SAP has the capability to manage and execute in these frameworks. Any landscape planning must take into account the intended purpose for the initial and postproduction architecture. As well, the organizations hardware familiarity and strategic plans are also critical to successful planning. Finally, a maintainable environment that can be understood and managed by all IT administrators is also a priority.

Infrastructure team resources are given a lot of work today. And, often this work comes with conflicting priorities. The flexibility for choosing the right backend technology offers another project for consideration by the already over-worked infrastructure team. It is important, therefore, to select a maintainable infrastructure to minimize additional burden on the infrastructure team. But, with the right level of planning and documentation selecting a maintainable infrastructure should be easy. A key to making the decision on backend infrastructure is sizing. SAP together with its partner vendors and ISVs can offer a good deal of help in the sizing and planning for the infrastructure decision. With the onset of the NetWeaver usage type Scenarios, it is important to develop an adaptable infrastructure that can be extended at the lowest cost. Initial hardware costs often pale in comparison to the actual operating costs and impacts to administrators. There are new tools available from Oracle that aid in system management. As of basis release 7.00 SP12, DBACOCKPIT is the new central database administration tool. It is a representative monitoring transaction. This now offers a Unified framework with a consistent look and feel for all SAP supported DB/OS platforms. DBACOCKPIT contains former ST04 (for Performance), DB02 (for Space), and planning calendar (DB13) functions and includes several new monitors (particularly for Oracle 10g) with RAC monitoring now embedded. Monitoring and administration of remote Oracle and non-Oracle databases (both ABAP and non-ABAP systems) is also possible via DB MultiConnect. The former transactions ST04, DB02, DB13 (for Jobs), and others are still available but have been renamed to ST04OLD, DB02OLD, DB13OLD, etc., and will become unnecessary in future releases.

When connecting to the database, the J2EE Engine and the applications deployed on it authenticate themselves by means of a user name and a password. They are specified only once, when the DataSource that is used to provide the database connection is created. The DataSource is initialized with the supplied credentials and uses them for the authentication of all physical connections that it provides.

You can use one of two options for database connectivity. You can use the default DataSource. With this source you can connect to the system database in which the J2EE Engine stores its information. Alternately, you can register a new DataSource to connect to another database that your application uses.

Governance, Risk, and Compliance (GRC)

In 1982 the Defense Science Board (DSB) Task Force examined why the **Department of Defense** (DoD) continued to experience significant cost overruns and schedule delays on major weapon system acquisitions. The resulting DSB report identified a lack of a systematic approach to managing technical risk as the primary cause of system cost overruns and deployment delays.

The DSB noted that although cost overruns and schedule delays often manifested themselves during full-scale production, the origin of most production problems stemmed from design risks.[8] As a result, the DSB recommended that the DoD develop a systematic approach for identifying, understanding, and managing technical risk throughout a weapon system's life cycle, with specific emphasis on managing design risk.

While initially developed for Weapons System, the documentation from the DoD has been extended through the years and applied to a plethora of technical systems development outside those on which the DoD initially focused.

The outcome of the 1982 DSB study was the issuance of DoD 4245.7-M, "Transition from Development to Production,"[9] in September 1985. DoD 4245.7-M decomposes each phase of a weapon system's developmental life cycle into discrete steps, and, in template form, identifies potential risks and provides recommendations for reducing those risks. Another critical work product from the DoD is the "Risk Management Guide for DoD Acquisition."[10] In government projects these documents often go hand in hand.

The focus of other DoD risk discussions and articles on the subject go on to marry contracts with risk assessment, that is, how government contract types are determined and used in control and management of risks. It is not our intent to discuss the issues and options of Federal Accounting Regulations (FAR) supplements or practices as they relate to risk. But, rather it is our intent to create a framework to apply in and out of the government and on projects both large and small. It is up to the user to determine the risk framework. That framework can be the foundation for assessing and scoping the risk program in the project and the design process and decisions for what to implement and how. I hope to provide a solid foundation for understanding risk science. As it relates to the overall subject of security in general, I will propose an alternate means for thinking about risk. As in determination of security implications up front in design, risk determination, too, should be made up front in program or project planning. They go hand in hand.

Establishing a risk-conscious culture can lead to far better quality systems implementations and cost control.

The Risk Management Guide states that each risk has three components. These components are:

- A future root cause
- The probability of the future root cause occurring
- The consequence/impact if the root cause occurs

In distinguishing between risk management and issue management risks are events yet to happen. They have future consequences, and can be "closed" only after successful mitigation through avoiding, controlling, transferring, or assuming the risk. Issues are current problems and/or challenges with real or near real-time consequences, and can be closed within shorter windows as they complete. Often risk closure is only possible at the end of a project or program when all mitigations are proven or in force.

At NASA we use the DoD risk management process, as outlined in the DoD "Risk Management Guide for DoD Acquisition" referred to above for many of our programs and we are additionally involved in further improvement of the science of risk management. In 2000 NASA commissioned the University of Virginia's Center for Risk Management of Engineering Systems, directed by Dr. Yacov Y. Haimes, to develop a five-year roadmap that identifies the activities required to meet NASA's long-term corporate goals. The purpose of the Capstone effort was to locate and analyze different methodologies that could be incorporated into this plan. The plan was presented in 2001.[11]

Several disasters in NASA's past caused a top to bottom assessment of how to improve the culture at NASA. As a result of the many identified improvement recommendations a better focus on risk management was created. This risk management process includes risk planning, assessment (identification and analysis), handling, and monitoring steps with feedback from risk monitoring and documentation for all process steps as illustrated in Figure 1.4.

Figure 1.4 A Typical Risk Management Process

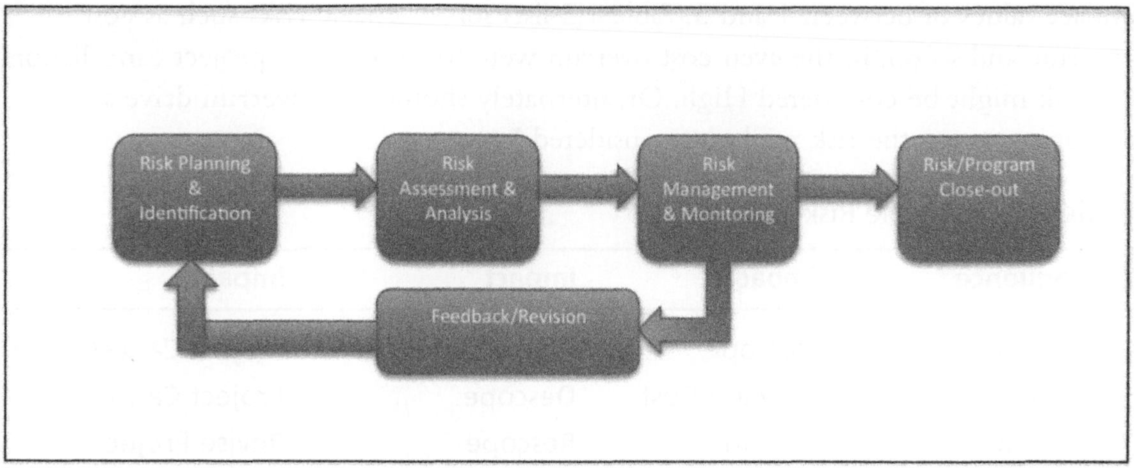

Risk Planning & Identification involves developing and documenting a systematic and comprehensive strategy and methods for identifying and analyzing risk issues, developing and implementing risk handling plans, and documenting the overall risk management process. The identification piece is the initial examination of all program/project areas for potential risks to be fed to the next phase for formal documentation and mitigation management.

Risk Assessment & Analysis involves examining each identified risk issue and validates its applicability in scope for the program/project. Each risk level is identified as well.

Risk Management & Monitoring involves the continuous tracking of active risks and potential additional risk during the program. Levels are continuously assessed and validated (up or down) and closure recommendations can also be made.

Risk/Program Close-out involves the closure of individual risks as appropriate; when the program is complete a risk close-out is conducted for all remaining open items in the event the program is moved to operation/maintenance.

Feedback/Revision involves the continuous improvement of the process and extension of new risks as they are identified for proper documentation.

In getting a program or project started, the critical task in *Risk Planning & Identification* is agreeing on the risk plan and methodology. Determining risk items and scope is covered in this arena. As the general requirements of the technical challenge to be implemented unfold, a thorough analysis must be made. A risk matrix is the proper place to start once consequences and impacts are determined. Typically the probability for an item's occurrence is factored against the consequence to yield impact values of between 1 and 5. Table 1.2 lists some generic risks such as cost overrun, and so on. In the even cost overrun were to likely cause project cancellation, the risk might be considered High. Or, alternately should cost overrun drive a descoping event, the risk might be considered Low.

Table 1.2 A Sample Risk Matrix

Consequence	Impact	Impact	Impact
Cost Overrun	Descope	Extend Schedule	Project Cancellation
Schedule exceeded	Increase Cost	Descope	Project Cancellation
Requirement mismatch	Replan	Rescope	Revise Project

It is in collecting and discussing how to rank these impacts against a consequence that the science of risk management is at its best.

On a typical project, a comprehensive risk evaluation might be used to both screen and tailor the items included on each piece of documentation. Several inputs can be used to perform risk identification, including the following:

- The project organization
- The project budget
- The project schedule
- Lessons learned from other projects
- Project performance requirements
- Information about key business processes and rules
- Auditability requirements
- Initial segregation of duty and execution requirements

For each discussion comes mitigations aimed at ensuring the risks are fully understood, well managed, and mitigated. In SAP's GRC offering on security we have a product that enables administrators and users to define policies or rules, and enforce these policies through the provisioning of services. SAP GRC Access Control delivers a comprehensive, cross-enterprise set of Access Control facilities that enables agencies and companies alike to define and monitor SOD enforcement, role and profile management, and compliance. The GRC tools from SAP were formerly known as the Virsa Access Control product suite prior to the acquisition. This toolset offers a complete suite of tools to control and manage risk.

One should ensure the definition of Segregation of Duties (SOD) is fully understood and consistent in the organization. SOD is a policy for controlling responsibilities in a business organization. As a security practice the main objective is to prevent fraud and errors. These can be systematic or manual business processes. Successful segregation of duties is accomplished by separating tasks among multiple users or departments. For example, the person responsible for performing payment processing in accounts payable should not also be responsible for inventories, operating expenses or other expenses. This would create a conflict of duties. If a person could modify inventory levels and also make payments to replenish inventory, they could be allocating inventory for their own use and hence misappropriating company assets. This example highlights the importance of SOD as a means of maintaining checks and balances.

The SAP GRC Access Control includes the Compliance Calibrator application for SAP, the Role Expert application for SAP, the Firefighter application for SAP, and the Access Enforcer application for SAP. When deployed together, they provide an end-to-end Access Control solution that addresses risk detection, risk remediation, reporting, and prevention. In SAP's risk detection module, SAP applications for Access Control detect access and authorization risks across SAP and non-SAP applications, providing protection. The application focused on risk remediation enables mitigation of access and authorization risks through automated workflows and collaboration between all users. The reporting component delivers comprehensive reports and role-based dashboards needed to monitor the performance of compliance initiatives and to take action as needed. And, finally, risk prevention is where, once access and authorization risks have been remediated, only SAP applications for Access Control can prevent new risks from entering a production system. By empowering business users to check for risks in real time and by automating user administration, the applications make risk prevention a continuous, proactive process.

Summary

We've discussed a variety of topics to be covered in depth in the chapters in this book. The topics cover the change in mind-set needed to better design security and consider GRC up front in the project planning phases to detailed implementation considerations for security planning on SAP application services and databases. These topics are discussed at nearly every SAP conference and workshop in industry today. Finally, you have a publication that can give you the details and case information needed to change your organization into a security and risk aware culture.

Solutions Fast Track

NetWeaver Web Application Server

☑ SAP NetWeaver 7.0 provides an open integration and application platform and facilitates the implementation of Enterprise Services Architecture.

☑ Both Java and ABAP are supported in either standalone or integrated modes with standalone being the preferred approach.

☑ Client options are SAP GUI or Web Browser.

ABAP WEB AS 7.0

☑ Trust manager is the tool to use when using public-key technology with the SAP Web AS ABAP server.

☑ Use the Security Audit Log to keep track of security-related events on the SAP Web AS ABAP server.

☑ By using Secure, Store and Forward Mechanism (SSF), you enable applications to support the use of digital signatures and document encryption in their processing.

☑ The SAP Web AS ABAP communicates with its communication partners using various protocols. The primary protocols used are Dialog (DIAG), RFC, and HTTP. The security mechanism for managing these protocols is either SNC or SSL.

J2EE WEB AS 7.0

☑ The Java SAP Web Application Server provides complete user management services called a User Management Engine or UME, the Universal Description Discovery and Integration or UDDI, and database integration facilities.

☑ When a user connects to the database, the J2EE Engine and the applications deployed on it authenticate themselves by means of a user name and a password.

☑ You can use one of two options for database connectivity. You can use the default DataSource. With this source you can connect to the system database in which the J2EE Engine stores its information. Alternately, you can register a new DataSource to connect to another database that your application uses

☑ The J2EE Engine can communicate with its communication partners using several different protocols. The primary protocol used is HTTP; however, P4, which is the protocol to use for Remote Method Invocation (RMI), as well as the protocols Lightweight Directory Access Protocol, Open Database Connectivity (LDAP, ODBC)[define] and telnet are also supported.

Backend: UNIX/Oracle

☑ Select a maintainable infrastructure to minimize additional burden on the infrastructure team.

☑ Proper Sizing and consideration for the existing infrastructure is another factor in determining the right solution.

☑ You can use one of two options for database connectivity. DataSource is the default or, alternately, you can register a new DataSource to connect to another database that your application uses.

Governance, Risk, and Compliance (GRC)

- ☑ Risk Planning & Identification involves developing and documenting a systematic and comprehensive strategy and methods for identifying and analyzing risk issues, developing and implementing risk handling plans, and documenting the overall risk management process.
- ☑ When you are getting a program or project started, the critical task in Risk Planning & Identification is agreeing on the risk plan and methodology.
- ☑ SAP GRC Access Control delivers a comprehensive, cross-enterprise set of Access Control facilities that enables agencies and companies alike to define and monitor SOD enforcement, role and profile management, and compliance.
- ☑ By empowering business users to check for risks in real time and automating user administration, the applications make risk prevention a continuous, proactive process.
- ☑ Proper monitoring and reporting are critical success factors in GRC.

Frequently Asked Questions

Q: How has SAP shaped the IT culture through the years?

A: SAP has been part of a software life cycle evolution. While helping integrate islands of automation in the early 1990s they began moving toward delivering on the true promise of IT, by providing the tools to enable business. Today SAP is delivering through open standards and a usage type model that allows customers to choose what is right for their environment with solid products that deliver on the vision for IT.

Q: What is the state of SAP technology today?

A: Today SAP has technology solutions the cover most areas driven by business needs. With recent acquisitions of Business Objects and Virsa the technology offerings are robust enough to handle most of the business requirements on the minds of key stakeholders throughout the enterprise.

Q: What are the considerations a company must factor in determining the Application Server architecture needed to implement ABAP or Java?

A: Landscape optimization and solution decisions are key drivers in determining the application server model. It is always best to separate Java from ABAP servers when possible. There are trade-offs and specific support requirements that impact operational efficiency when these are combined on a single hardware platform.

Q: What is the purpose of the User Management Engine and what are the installation options?

A: The purpose of the UME is to provide central user administration for all applications developed using Java. UME is fully integrated into SAP's WEB AS as a service. The User Management Engine (UME) provides central user administration for all Java applications. The UME is completely integrated into SAP Web Application Server Java and is used as the default user store. The UME is integrated into SAP Web Application Server Java as a service. The UME itself administers users and uses databases, directory services, or the SAP ABAP user administration to store the data. In the UME, the words data sources are used to refer to repositories for user data.

Q: What are the critical success factors for a risk program?

A: Risk planning, risk identification, risk remediation, and risk reporting are all critical to a successful risk program.

Q: How does an organization perform risk identification?

A: Several inputs can be used to perform risk identification, including project organization, budget, schedule, lessons learned from prior events, performance expectations, compliance needs, and initial segregation of duties requirements, as well as reporting.

Q: How has risk management evolved through the years?

A: Risk management was often a back office operation or, for IT projects, was an afterthought driven by audit findings. Today risk management is an integral part of project planning that must be accommodated up front prior to an audit in order to ensure successful implementations.

Q: What are the key components in risk?

A: Among the key factors in considering risk one must include Risk Planning & Identification, Risk Assessment & Analysis, Risk Management & Monitoring, Risk/Program Close-out, and Feedback/Revision.

Q: How does an organization differentiate between risks and issues?

A: In distinguishing between risk management and issue management, risks are events yet to happen. They have future consequences, and can be "closed" only after successful mitigation through avoiding, controlling, transferring, or assuming the risk. Issues are current problems and/or challenges with real or near real-time consequences, and can be closed within shorter windows as they complete. Often risk closure is only possible at the end of a project or program when all mitigations are proven or in force.

Q: What are the SAP offerings in GRC?

A: SAP's GRC offerings include SAP GRC Access Control which delivers a comprehensive, cross-enterprise set of Access Control facilities that allow organizations to define and monitor SOD enforcement, role and profile management, and compliance. GRC Access Control includes the Compliance Calibrator application for SAP, the Role Expert application for SAP, the Firefighter application for SAP, and the Access Enforcer application for SAP. When deployed together, they provide an end-to-end Access Control solution that addresses risk detection, risk remediation, reporting, and prevention.

Notes

1. "Information Technology Consulting," by Rudy Puryear from *Management Consulting, A Complete Guide to the Industry*, 2002, Sugata Biswas and Daryl Twitchell.
2. http://help.sap.com. Choose: Documentation, then SAP NetWeaver, select your language, then "IT Scenarios at a Glance"
3. https://www.sdn.sap.com/irj/sdn/netweaver
4. See Activating ICF Services in the SAP documentation.
5. See profile parameter icm/HTTP/j233_<xx> in the SAP documentation.
6. See OASIS Web reference.
7. See Deploying the SAP JAVA Cryptographic Toolkit in the SAP documentation.
8. "UnderstandingRisk Management in the DoD – Tutorial", *Acquisition Review Quarterly*, Spring 2003, by Mike Bolles.
9. "Transition from Development to Production. Solving the Risk Equation", September 1985, Department of Defense.
10. "Risk Management Guide for DoD Acquisition" (Sixth Edition, Version 1.0), August 2006, Department of Defense.
11. NASA Risk Assessment and Management Roadmap, 2001, University of Virginia, Jacob Burns, Jeff Noonan, Laura Kichak, and Beth Van Doren.

Chapter 2

Concepts and Security Model

Solutions in this chapter:

- ABAP
- J2EE
- GRC
- Backend: UNIX/Oracle

☑ Summary

☑ Solutions Fast Track

☑ Frequently Asked Questions

Introduction

While somewhat of a hot topic lately, security is increasingly becoming one of the key issues many organizations have to address. In the broadest sense, organizations have to ensure security issues such as provisioning, access control, data protection and privacy, and regulatory compliance are addressed properly. In order to protect the enterprise information asset stored in their systems, organizations must address these security issues with appropriate security measures together with sound security policies.

As an important aspect to any SAP implementation, SAP NetWeaver security infrastructure is based on market standards with various security technologies and mechanisms available to protect business data privacy and integrity from unauthorized access. This chapter introduces you to security concepts surrounding the SAP NetWeaver security infrastructure.

In this chapter, we will take a look at the approach SAP takes in providing security solutions for SAP NetWeaver technologies such as SAP Web Application Server (AS) ABAP; SAP Web AS J2EE; Governance, Risk, and Compliance (GRC); as well as backend systems (based on UNIX and Oracle).

Specifically, the next sections will explain the security concepts and mechanisms available for user authentication such as user ID and password, Secure Network Communication (SNC), Secure Sockets Layer (SSL), X.509 certificates for Internet connections, and SAP log-on tickets for Single Sign-On (SSO) solutions.

Additionally, this chapter includes the explanation on the authorization concepts, benefits of role-based access controls, significance of integrating user management, user and role management options, as well as other security measures available for protecting and encrypting data exchange to set up private communication channels and increase content security.

The chapter then provides sections explaining available options for governance, risk, and compliance with the SAP GRC solution, such as access control, process control, and risk management.

ABAP

Gone are the days when security for SAP ABAP systems only addressed security issues on an application layer and implementing authorizations and roles was enough. With the introduction of the SAP NetWeaver technology platform, SAP solutions are now based on a more open, Web-based and multitiered client/server architecture that integrates many different components, applications, or systems across business and technology boundaries. Data/information can be exchanged and integrated seamlessly between components, applications, and systems. However, this poses a data vulnerability security problem at each integration point where data/information is exchanged between components, so it needs to be addressed on the transport layer.

For these reasons, security for SAP Web AS ABAP is addressed on the presentation, application, and transport layers; all of the security aspects are based on restricting access at each level to authorized users or systems only. This should form part of your overall SAP security strategy.

- The *Presentation* layer represents various forms of front-end applications (for example, SAP graphical user interface [GUI] for Windows) or Web clients (for example, Web browsers) used to access the SAP Web AS ABAP. As data is exchanged over exposed networks (for example, Internet), it introduces risks to the security of the communication to the AS ABAP system. To ensure communication is protected, users must be authenticated successfully before they are allowed into the system; this security mechanism is called user authentication.
- The *Application* layer represents the application logic within the AS ABAP system. Because important and sensitive data can be accessed in the AS ABAP system, significant business risks are introduced if access control is not properly managed. To prevent unauthorized access, access control is based on the authorization concept and user management. Sensitive and arbitrary data can be further protected using the Secure Store and Forward (SSF) mechanism.
- The *Transport* layer supports the necessary communication for the whole system landscape. Data that is exchanged over an unsecured network is not protected; it becomes a huge risk to data integrity and privacy protection, and creates other security threats. To ensure data is communicated securely, security protocols such as Secure Network Communication (SNC) and Secure Sockets Layer (SSL) can be used.

Authenticating Users

User authentication is the process of attempting to verify the identity of the users, programs, or services and only allow access onto the system based on a successful authentication. Authentication is important because various security threats such as viruses, worms, and information and identity theft are on the rise. Any of these attacks can cause hours of lost productivity from running virus scans to applying security patches on the client applications.

User Authentication protects the Presentation layer of the SAP Web AS ABAP systems. The standard user ID and password is the default authentication mechanism supported by all SAP NetWeaver products. While simple password authentications cannot completely prevent security attacks, you can make sure your systems are further protected through the use of stronger authentication methods, such as external security products that support encryption or client certificates that are signed by a trusted Certificate Authority (CA). Limitations may arise due to the legal export rules of different countries for encryption software and algorithms; in these cases you can use SNC.

SAP Web AS ABAP supports a number of user authentication mechanisms to authenticate and keep unauthorized parties from accessing secure information. The following sections introduce you to these user authentication mechanisms and a quick walk-through on how they work.

Using Secure Network Connection

Secure Network Connection (SNC) integrates an external security product with the SAP system to provide additional security functions not directly available with SAP systems. The external security product must be certified by the SAP Software Partner Program. SNC can provide various levels of authentication (verification of the identity), integrity protection (detects any changes of the data which may have occurred during the communication), and privacy protection (provides encryption of the message), depending on what the external security product can provide.

You can use SNC to provide secure authentication for protecting the communication between various client and server components of the AS ABAP system that use the Dialog (DIAG) and Remote Function Call (RFC) protocols.

For SNC authentication with client components (for example, SAP GUI for Windows), you are required to integrate with an external security product that has been certified for use by SAP. For authentication between server components (for example, connection between ECC and BW systems), the default security product you can use is called SAP Cryptographic Library (SAPCRYPTOLIB). Cryptographic algorithms from the security product ensure the privacy protection of communication by encryption.

Some additional security measures may be necessary for certain security products to ensure that security is not compromised. For example, if the security product uses public-key technology (for example, client certificates), then you need a Public-Key Infrastructure (PKI). In this case, appropriate security procedures must be put in place for generating and distributing the keys and certificates for the users and system components. You must also ensure that the private keys are stored in a secure location, by means of crypto boxes or smart cards, and that the public keys are signed by a trusted CA.

It is also important to note that some countries have various restrictions on the use of encryption in software applications.

Using Secure Sockets Layer

Secure Sockets Layer (SSL) is a cryptographic protocol that provides secure communications over the Internet. SSL can provide data encryption, server-side authentication (the server identifies itself to the client), client-side authentication (the client identifies itself to the server), and mutual authentication. It provides data confidentiality over the network. The SSL protocol uses public-key infrastructure to provide its protection.

You can use SSL to provide secure HTTP connections between client and server components of the SAP Web AS ABAP system.

For SSL authentication, the server must have a public-private key pair and public-key certificate. It must possess one key pair and a certificate to identify itself as the server component, and another key pair and certificate for identifying a client component. These key pairs are certificates which are stored in the server's Personal Security Environment (PSE).

Using User ID and Password

As mentioned earlier, user ID and password is the default authentication mechanism supported by all SAP NetWeaver products. In order for the user to log on to the SAP system, he or she must enter the correct user ID and password. When the user enters the user ID and password, the system performs some checks to see whether the user can actually log on with a password logon, not locked by the administrator, and that the password is indeed correct.

If the password is set to initial, expired, or reset by the administrator, the user must set a new password. This password must meet SAP predefined and custom-defined password rules, as well as security-related profile parameter settings. For example, if the user enters an incorrect password, he or she can repeat the log-on attempt until the permissible number of log-on attempts (set by profile parameter *login/fails_to_user_lock* and *login/fails_to_user_session_end*) is exhausted. When one parameter limit is reached, then the user ID locks or the session ends.

Using X.509 Client Certificate

X.509 client certificate is basically a digital identification card or key. Using this security mechanism, users need to have their X.509 client certificates as part of a Public-Key Infrastructure (PKI).

Any user who tries to access the AS ABAP system needs to present a valid certificate to the server using the SSL protocol. The server then decrypts the log-on request using its private key; only the server can decrypt this log-on request. If the authentication is successful and the server can indeed map the user's Distinguished Name in the certificate with a valid user ID on the AS ABAP system then the user can log on to the system. The authentication takes place in the underlying SSL protocols. Hence, no user ID and password entries are necessary.

To ensure that certificates are issued from a trusted source, it is recommended that you use certificates that are signed by a trusted CA. This means the chosen CA becomes the designated on the AS ABAP system (the private key) and user who access the AS ABAP system must possess a valid certificate signed by the chosen CA (the public key). The corresponding user's private-key must be stored in a secure location (for example, password-protected or use smart cards).

In addition to protecting the Presentation layer, this security mechanism can also be used to protect the Transport layer, specifically for protecting the Hypertext Transfer Protocol (HTTP) connections between various client and server components of the AS ABAP system.

Using SAP Logon Tickets and Single Sign-on

SAP Logon Ticket provides authentication for protecting the communication between various client and server components of the AS ABAP system. The user is authenticated using the Logon Ticket as the authentication token. The user only needs to be authenticated once (for example, using a valid user ID and password) and the system can issue a Logon Ticket to the user. With this Logon Ticket, the user can access subsequent systems (SAP and non-SAP systems) without the need to re-enter his or her user ID and password.

SAP Logon Tickets are used in the Single Sign-On (SSO) solution. This security mechanism is highly beneficial in a complex SAP system environment where there are many different types of SAP systems in the system landscape, users have multiple passwords to access different applications, and keeping track of passwords creates predictable problems (for example, forgetting passwords) which results in more help desk calls and increased administration costs.

For SAP Logon Ticket authentication with client components (for example, SAP GUI for Windows), users must have the same user ID in all of the systems they need to access and their Web browsers must accept cookies.

For authentication between server components, both the accepting systems and issuing server must have synchronized system clocks. The issuing server must possess a public and private key pair so that it can digitally sign the Logon Ticket. And the accepting systems must be placed in the same Domain Name Server (DNS) domain as the issuing server and the systems must have the public key certificate to verify the digital signature on the log-on ticket.

It is recommended that you identify one system in your system landscape as the ticket-issuing system before you configure other systems to accept tickets from this system. By default, the Personal Security Environment (PSE) is used to store the certificates. You can configure the AS ABAP system to issue log-on tickets by setting profile parameter *login/create_sso2_ticket* to 2.

In order for the AS ABAP system to accept Logon Tickets from another AS ABAP system, you need to install the SAP Security Library (or SAP Cryptographic Library) and set profile parameter *login/accept_sso2_ticket* to 1. Use transaction **SSO2** (Single Sign-On Wizard) to automatically establish the appropriate configuration for the accepting system.

If the AS ABAP system needs to accept Logon Tickets from a J2EE Engine, then you must implement the SAP Cryptographic Library and set the same profile parameter on the AS ABAP system. In addition, you also need to manually import the J2EE Engine's public key certificate into the PSE using transaction **STRUST** or **STRUSTSSO2** (Trust Manager). Use transaction **STRUSTSSO2** or edit table *TWPSSO2ACL* to add J2EE Engine's system ID and its Distinguished Name to the access control list. You must maintain the PSE for SSO with Logon Ticket only in client 000.

Authorization Concept

Authorization concept for SAP AS ABAP involves the provision of SAP access to users using a role-based identity management approach while preventing unauthorized access to ensure protection of important and sensitive data within the SAP security infrastructure.

When a user logs into the SAP application, the system authenticates that user and sets access controls by checking authorization objects assigned to the user.

This ensures the user can only execute those transactions, programs, and services to which he or she has been granted access.

In order to execute a transaction in SAP, the user needs to have a series of authorization objects allocated to his or her user master record. These authorizations are then combined into a position-based role with corresponding authorization profiles to represent a logical combination of transactions for performing a specific function or task (for example, maintaining HR data). A combination of these roles, or a composite role, defines access for a specific position within an organization (for example, personnel administrator). Composite roles can be a group of single or derived roles or both. The corresponding roles are then assigned directly to the users in the user master record. The diagram below in Figure 2.1 illustrates the hierarchical relationship between user, composite/single role, transaction, authorization object, and authorization fields.

Figure 2.1 Relationship between User, Simple/Composite/Derived Roles, Transaction, Authorization Object, and Authorization Fields

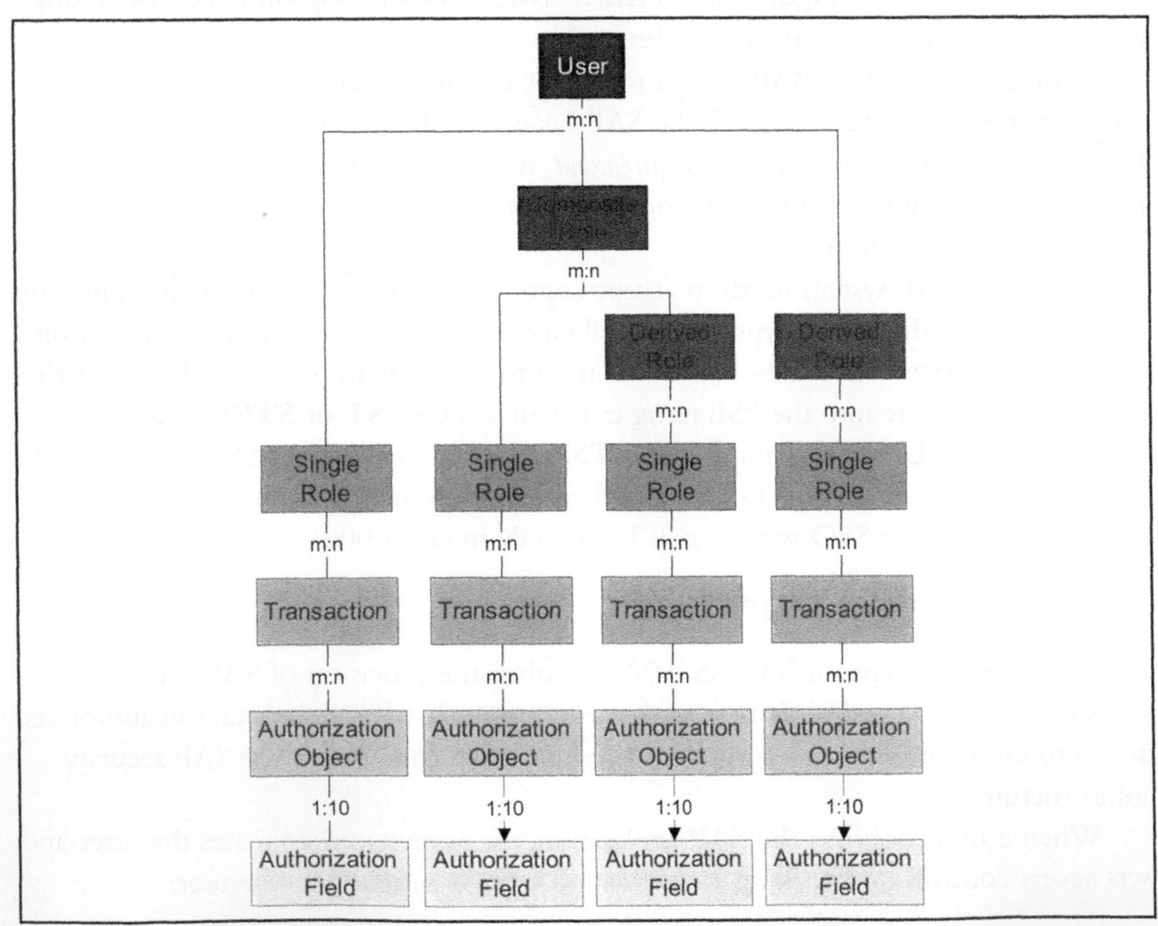

User Master Record

The user master record stores all the information regarding the user, including authorizations and other user settings. Once the user administrator creates a user in the user master record, this enables the user to log on to the SAP system and access the functionalities within the limits of the authorization profiles assigned from the roles.

You can create new users using transaction **SU01** (Create/Maintain Users). To maintain a large number of users, you can use transaction **SU10** (Mass Maintain Users).

Roles and Profiles

Each role type represents a logical combination of SAP transactions required to perform a specific function or task. You can create roles using transaction PFCG (the profile generator). There are several types of roles, namely single, composite, and derived:

Single role contains all the authorization data and the log-on menu structure that consists of transactions assigned to the role. Users who are assigned to the role will inherit the menu structure and transactions.

Composite role, unlike single role, does not contain authorization data. It is merely a reference point to group related single roles. Users who are assigned to a composite role are automatically assigned to the corresponding single roles during a user comparison.

Derived role refers to roles that already exist; it inherits the menu structure and transactions from the referenced role. Default values may be passed on; however, the organization values and user assignments are not passed on. Derived roles are suitable for maintaining roles where functionalities are the same but organization levels may be different. The inherited menus cannot be changed in the derived roles. It is possible to remove the inheritance relationship; however, once this is removed, the inheritance relationship can only be reestablished by reassigning the reference role by doing the following steps:

1. Go to Derived role, Remove all transactions from Menu, **SAVE**, Exit.
2. Go to Derived role, Reenter Derive from role, **SAVE**
3. Generate it from the template role (Derive from role, the bequeathing role)

Authorization Objects and Field Values

An *authorization* object is what SAP uses to assign authorization and enable complex checks of an authorization to determine what access is allocated to users. An authorization object consists of authorization fields and it can group up to 10 authorization fields which are checked in an AND relationship.

The authorization fields within an authorization object are considered as system elements to be protected and relate to data elements stored with the ABAP Dictionary. The authorization field can be a number of single values or value ranges for a field. These value sets are called *authorizations*. You can allow all values or allow an empty field as a permissible value. The system checks these value sets authorizations in OR relationships. In order for an authorization check to be successful, all field values of the authorization object must be maintained accordingly in the user master.

For example, lets take a look at authorization object *F_KNA1_BUK* (Customer: Authorization for Company Codes), this requires authorization fields *ACTVT* (Activity) and *BUKRS* (Company Code). In order to allow a master data administrator to create a customer master record, the security administrator needs to create the authorization by assigning the user authorization object *F_KNA1_BUK* with the authorization field *Activity* set to 01 and authorization field *Company Code* set to 3129.

From an operational standpoint, authorization may be categorized as general authorization, functional authorization, and organization authorization. General authorization specifies the function a user may perform, that is, authorization object *F_KNA1_BUK* has been assigned for creating customer master records. The system checks for the user's authorization to create customer accounts (that is, Activity 01) in at least one company code. Then the system checks whether the user is allowed to create accounts for the specified organizational unit (that is, Company Code 3129) and overall whether the user has the required functional authorizations.

Authorization Checks

When the user attempts to start a transaction from the Menu or by entering a Command, the system performs various checks. The first of these checks is on table TSTC to see whether the transaction code is valid and whether the transaction is locked. The system then checks whether the user has authorization to start the transaction by checking authorization object *S_TCODE*; this contains the authorization field *TCD* (Transaction Code). The user must have an authorization with the value of the selected transaction code.

If you create a new transaction in transaction SE93, you can assign an additional authorization to this transaction. This is particularly useful when you want to protect a transaction with a separate authorization. For transactions where additional authorization is entered via transaction SE93, the user also requires the defined authorization object TSTA, which is stored in table *TSTCA*. Alternatively, you can consider using other methods to protect the transaction, such as at a program level with command *AUTHORITY-CHECK*.

Indirectly called transactions are not included in this transaction start check. For complex transactions where other transactions are called, additional authorization checks are performed.

Next, the system checks whether the selected transaction is assigned to an authorization object. If this is the case, a check is made to see whether the user has authorization for this authorization object. You can use transaction **SU24** (Edit Authorization Object) and click on the Check Indicators button to see what other authorization objects are assigned to this transaction.

You should note that the system does not perform any authorization checks in the following cases:

- If you have deactivated the check indicator of the authorization object for the specific transaction in transaction SU24. Keep in mind that you cannot deactivate the check indicators for SAP pre-defined authorization objects from the SAP NetWeaver and Human Resource areas.
- If you have globally deactivated authorization objects for all transactions with transaction SU24 or transaction SU25.
- If profile parameter *auth/no_check_in_some_cases* for the deactivation is set to Y.

And finally, the user can start the transaction when all of the checks above are successful; otherwise the system will return an appropriate message.

Authorization Groups

An authorization group can be defined as an authorization field to protect tables and programs. For example, you can protect tables with table authorization groups by defining authorization groups in table TBRG and assigning the relevant authorization group to the tables you want to protect in table TDDAT for table authorization group. An authorization group can be assigned to one or more tables. A table can only be assigned to one specific authorization group. Alternatively, you can use transaction **SE11** under Utilities | Table Maintenance Generator to maintain the table authorization group assignment for individual tables. With this security mechanism, you can prevent users from accessing the tables using transactions such as **SE16** (Display Table) or **SM30** (Table Maintenance). To access the protected table, the user requires authorization to both the authorization group defined in table TDDAT and the authorization object S_TABU_DIS with authorization field DICBERCLS containing that authorization group. This is particularly useful when you want to protect customized tables. Standard SAP tables are generally protected; however, you can manually change the authorization group assignment if required.

Similarly you can define program authorization group in table TPGP and assign the relevant authorization group to the programs you want to protect in table TPGPT. An authorization group can be assigned to one or more programs. A program can only be assigned to one specific authorization group. Alternatively, you can assign the program authorization group in the program attribute using SE38. This prevents users from accessing the program using transactions such as **SE38** and **SA38** (Execute Program). To access the protected program, the user requires authorization to authorization object S_PROGRAM with authorization field P_GROUP containing that authorization group.

User Management

User Management is a core function to the business. For many organizations, the *provisioning* process is typically initiated by access request forms. Whether it is a new access request, change in access request, or request for emergency access; the access request form must be approved by the employee's manager to ensure the access being requested is valid. Some consideration must be given to the overall impact on access to information including any potential issues regarding segregation of duties. If the level of access requested is deemed to be inappropriate, then the form is returned to the originator with comments outlining reasons why the request was denied. Only when the form has been appropriately amended is business approval given and access authorized. The user is notified when he or she has been granted access to the system. When notice of employee termination is received from the HR department, the security administrator should eliminate all access for the user by locking the user ID, changing the user license type, and entering the appropriate end date in the log-on data tab of the user master record. This *deprovisioning* process will both eliminate all access for the user and exclude the user from future licensing audits.

It is not uncommon for new access request forms to take up to two weeks to fulfill as it involves complex coordination and integration with human resources, waiting for the appropriate business approvals, and the actual provisioning of access. This complicated process can leave new employees unproductive for days or weeks waiting for their access and can become a provisioning problem for the organization.

Effective user management should also streamline the process for adjusting access rights when users get promoted or leave the organization. By shortening the time and complexity of user provisioning, it can reduce the number of help desk calls, increase employee productivity and frequently is a source of cost savings.

As more organizations are realizing the need to manage individual user identities across different environments, there is a risk involved with managing multiple identities for users.

For example, if an employee quits, then theoretically all access to systems should be revoked; however, there is an element of risk where an administrator may have missed revoking the user's access to the SAP Enterprise Portal system, in which case the user may still be able to access the system. The simplest way to mitigate this risk is to integrate user management and use a centralized user store that other systems must synchronize with. This means the user's access is deactivated in one system and triggered in all other necessary systems.

It is very important to implement a proper design early on in the project, as it can make or break any User Management deployment.

Integrating User Management

Integration of user management is the consolidation of user and authorization data across multiple systems into a centralized user store. All user management data is maintained centrally in one system.

This can not only help to make user administration easier, but also reduce data redundancies and management overhead, increase transparency, and improve security privacy.

When you are dealing with SAP Web AS ABAP systems, there are two user management options you can use depending on your system landscape:

- Central User Administration (CUA) integrates user management data of multiple ABAP-based systems into one system.
- Lightweight Directory Access Protocol (LDAP) synchronization integrates user management data of multiple systems (SAP and non-SAP) into one system.

Using Central User Administration

Central User Administration (CUA) is an embedded feature in SAP AS ABAP systems, with which you can integrate user management for multiple ABAP-based systems in one system. The system where CUA resides is defined as the Central system and all the other systems to which CUA distributes user data are defined as *Child* systems. Any changes to user management information (for example, name, email address, role assignments, license data) must be maintained in the CUA Central system and the changes are distributed asynchronously to the Child systems using Application Link Enabling (ALE) technology.

With the implementation of CUA, you can streamline your user management for multiple AS ABAP systems. It makes it easier for administrators to maintain users and role assignments, and the users receive their access control changes faster.

Let's take a look at a scenario where there are three AS ABAP systems (for example, ECC, BW, CRM) in the system landscape. Each of these AS ABAP systems has the four-tiered system architecture (that is, Development, Test, Production, and Training). As user master records are client-specific, user management is required for every client in all of the systems. User Management can become quite complex and hard to manage properly and efficiently. In the example shown in Figure 2.2, the CUA Central system is split for the Productive and non-Productive systems. The *Production* Solution Manager system maintains user management for the Production systems, while the *Development* Solution Manager system is used to maintain user management for non-Productive systems. By separating user management for Productive and non-Productive system, you can manage system maintenance activities and coordinate system downtimes without affecting the Productive systems.

You can use transaction **SCUM** to configure the user data distribution parameters.

Figure 2.2 Integrating User Management Using CUA

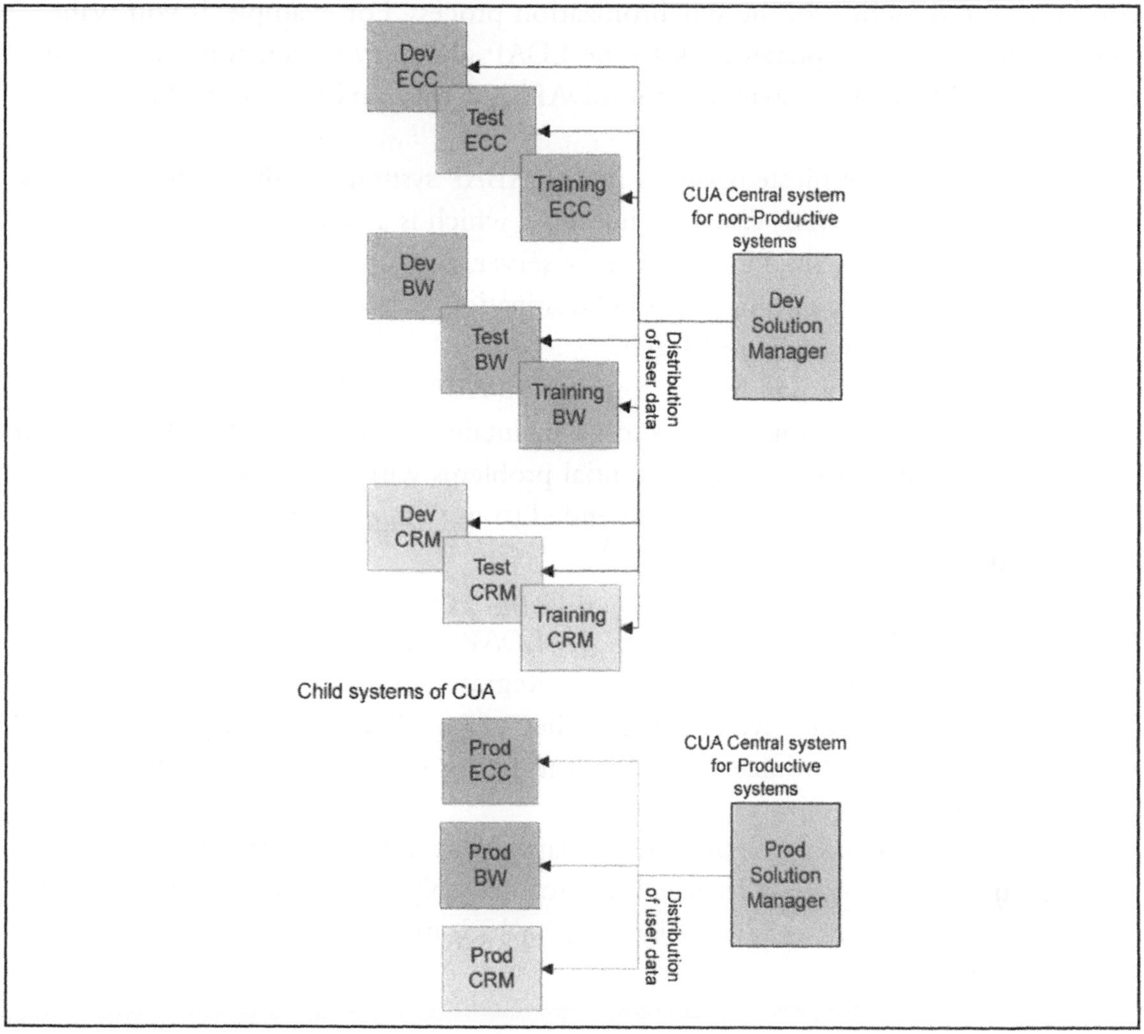

Using Lightweight Directory Access Protocol Synchronization

With Lightweight Directory Access Protocol (LDAP) synchronization, you can integrate user management as several systems (SAP and non-SAP) can synchronize with the LDAP directory service for user information.

The synchronization process enables you to exchange user information to/from the LDAP directory server in your system landscape. For example, you can make use of employees' personnel information stored in a corporate LDAP directory and copy the user data (for example, address, phone number, email address) into the AS ABAP system.

Depending on the custom settings on the LDAP directory server, you can configure the direction of the synchronization process. For example, if you want to send any user data updates back to the LDAP directory server, communication between the AS ABAP system and the LDAP directory server uses the LDAP protocol.

In order to communicate between the AS ABAP system and the LDAP directory server, you need the *LDAP Connector* interface, which is a collection of function modules used to access the LDAP directory server. You can enable the LDAP Connector interface by creating an RFC destination called LDAP and make the necessary settings in transaction **LDAP**.

The password is not transferred from the AS ABAP to the LDAP directory during the synchronization, so it has to be maintained in both the AS ABAP system and the LDAP directory. To avoid potential problems with duplicate passwords and synchronization problems, it is recommended to use Single Sign-On (SSO) for accessing the systems.

Following on from the scenario given in the previous section, you can also integrate the CUA Central system with the LDAP directory as shown in Figure 2.3. This is usually a good idea if you want to integrate your user data with a LDAP directory server and you have a large number of AS ABAP systems, as it means you only need to synchronize once with the LDAP directory server to the CUA central system.

By integrating your user management data with the LDAP directory server, you can streamline your user management for not only your AS ABAP systems but also other external systems in your landscape which may also integrate with the LDAP directory.

Figure 2.3 Integrating User Management Using LDAP

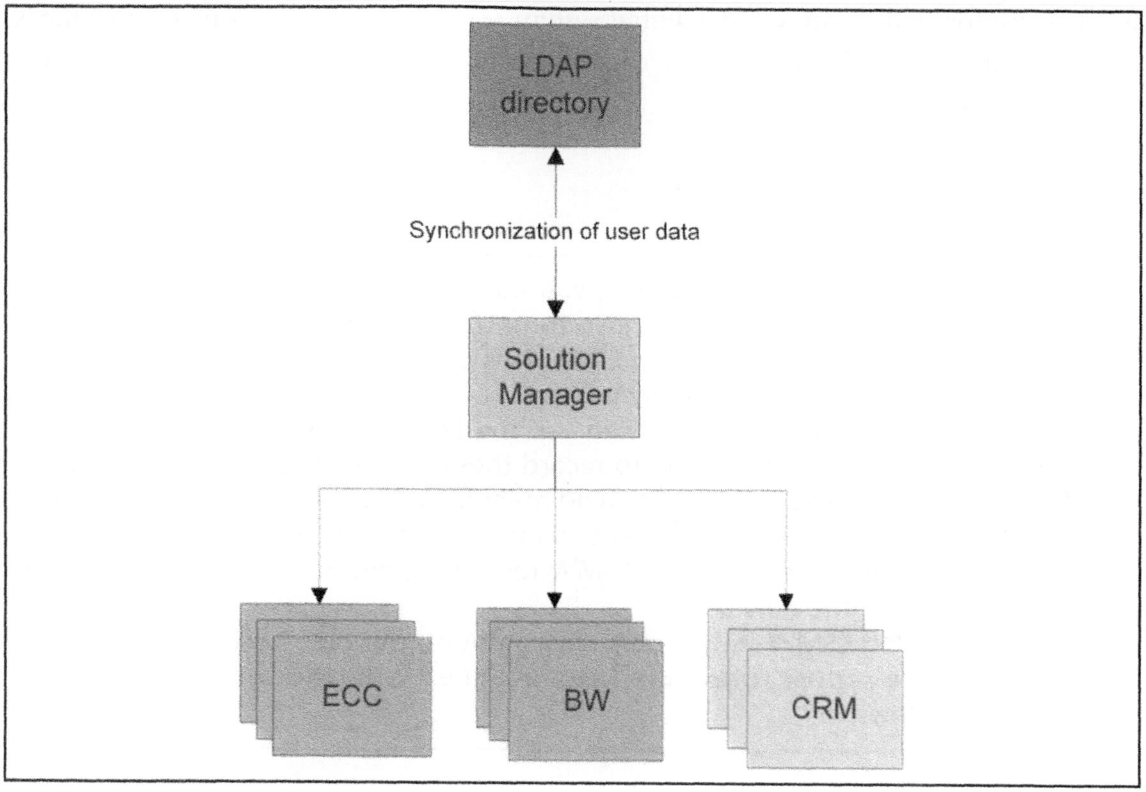

User Maintenance

User maintenance involves creating, changing, deleting, locking user master records. You can use transaction **SU01** to maintain user master records. Some functions of this transaction include the ability to:

- Create, edit, copy, delete and lock user ID.
- Set, change, and generate passwords.
- Assign one or more roles to the user.
- Maintain user defaults such as default printer, user parameters, time zones, etc.
- Maintain other settings such as user type, email address, user valid date to/from, user group, SNC, license data, etc.

To maintain a large number of users in one system, you can use transaction **SU10** (Mass User Changes), where you can change user master records relating to log-on data, defaults, parameters, roles, and profiles.

For multiple AS ABAP systems where CUA is implemented, user maintenance must be performed in the CUA Central system so that any user information changes are distributed according to the user data distribution settings in transaction **SCUM** to the CUA Child systems.

TIP

During an implementation project, you may need to create a large number of new users. For this task, you have to perform the same repetitive action for each new user in transaction **SU01.** This can be quite time-consuming and the task can become mundanely boring.

To save you some time, you can use the Legacy System Migration Workbench (transaction **LSMW**) to record these repetitive actions in transaction **SU01** and define all the necessary field mappings. Then you create a batch file containing all the new user data you want to create, format it to correspond to the field mappings defined in LSMW recording, and run a batch session from LSMW to create the new users.

When using LSMW in the CUA environment, double check the user master file to ensure proper roles have been assigned with the corresponding logical systems.

Role Maintenance

Role maintenance involves creating, changing, assigning, and deleting a role. You can use transaction **PFCG** (Profile Generator) to maintain roles. Some functions of this transaction include the ability to:

- Create, edit, copy, delete, and transport Single role.
- Create roles as templates.
- Create Composite and Derived roles.
- Maintain a default Menu structure for the role.
- Generate authorization profiles for the role automatically.
- Assign authorization objects to the role.
- Adjust authorization objects and authorization values.
- Assign one or more user ID to the role and perform a user comparison to transfer authorizations to user master records.

In terms of roles and responsibilities for Role Maintenance, the SAP Security Administrator typically creates and maintains the roles while the user administrator assigns the role to the users, and sometimes the help desk resets and changes the passwords.

Analyzing Authorization

When you are creating new roles, maintaining existing roles, or troubleshooting an authorization denial error, it is quite useful to use transaction **SU53** for analyzing missing authorizations. To generate the missing authorization report, you have to execute the transaction **SU53** or **/nSU53** directly after the authorization denial error message displays. With this report, you can analyze what authorization object was checked for a particular transaction. You can also use transaction SU56 to display a list of all authorizations in your user master.

Alternatively, you can use the system trace by executing transaction **ST01**. Make sure the check box **Authorization** is checked before activating a trace session. As this is a system wide trace, the information recorded in the trace is also system wide. You can limit the trace session by the user ID, transaction, or profile name. Remember to **Deactivate** the trace session once it is no longer required.

TIP

When it comes to assigning authorizations to roles, use the *less is more* pragmatic approach. Start with only the authorization objects that you think you need, use the authorization trace to find the necessary authorization object and values; and build the role by gradually adding the necessary authorization objects. Otherwise it may become a case of assigning too much access to the role and it would later require another process to analyze which authorization object needs to be taken out.

The same approach can be used for assigning roles to users.

Logging and Monitoring

Logging and Monitoring enable earlier detection of any weaknesses or vulnerabilities in the SAP system as the administrator can pro-actively monitor security-related activities, address any security problems that may arise and enforce security policies appropriately.

The tools you can use include Security Audit Log, the Audit Info System (AIS), security alerts within CCMS, and the Users Information System (SUIM).

Using Security Audit Log

Security Audit Log (transaction SM19 and SM20) is used for reporting and audit purposes. It monitors and logs user activity information such as:

- Successful and unsuccessful log-on attempts (Dialog and RFC)
- Successful and unsuccessful transaction and report start
- RFC call to function module
- Changes to the user master records
- Changes to the audit configuration

Using Audit Info System (AIS)

The Audit Info System (AIS) is an auditing tool that you can use to analyze some security aspects of your SAP System. You can access AIS using transaction **SECR**. The following functions are available:

- Auditing procedures and documentation
- Auditing evaluations
- Audit data downloads

Security Alerts in Computing Center Management System (CCMS)

When the Security Audit Log records security events, it can trigger a corresponding security alert in the Computing Center Management System (CCMS) alert monitor. The security alerts that are created correspond to the audit classes of events as defined in the Security Audit Log. You can access CCMS alerts using transaction **RZ20**.

Using the User Information System

The User Information System is a reporting and monitoring tool used by security administrators to provide an overview of authorizations and users in the SAP system, and is particularly useful when collating information for monitoring and audit purposes.

To access the User Information System, you can use transaction **SUIM** or from the SAP menu, choose **Tools | Administration | User Maintenance | Information System.** The list reports you can produce using User Information System include:

- Display users by complex selection criteria
- Display users by critical combination of authorizations at transaction start
- Display users by log-on date and password change
- Display users with critical authorizations
- Display roles and profiles by complex selection criteria
- Comparison of different roles and users
- Display the transactions contained within a role
- Display change documents for users, roles, profiles, and authorizations
- Create where-used lists for roles, profiles, and authorizations

As an alternative, you can also use transaction **SE16** to browse security-related tables as shown in Table 2.1 to get similar information for monitoring and audit purposes.

Table 2.1 Security-Related Tables for Monitoring and Auditing Purposes

Table	Description	Use in SUIM reports
USR02	User data (log-on data)	Used in conjunction with table AGR_1016 to provide report RSUSR020 for profiles by complex selection criteria
USR04	User master authorization	
UST02	User profiles	
USR10	Authorization profiles	
UST10C	Composite profiles	
USR11	Text for authorization profiles	
USR12	Authorization values	Provides authorization values for report RSUSR030, that is, authorizations by complex selection criteria

Continued

Table 2.1 Continued. Security-Related Tables for Monitoring and Auditing Purposes

Table	Description	Use in SUIM reports
USR13	Short text for authorization	
USR40	Table for illegal passwords	
USGRP	User groups	
USGRPT	Text table for USGRP	
USH02	Change history for log-on data	
USR01	User master records (runtime)	
USER_ADDR	Address data for users	
AGR_1016	Name of the activity group profile	Used in conjunction with table USR02 to provide report RSUSR020 for profiles by complex selection criteria
AGR_1016B	Name of the activity group profile	
AGR_1250	Role object, authorization, field, and values for the activity group	
AGR_1251	Role object, authorization, field, and values for activity group	Provides authorization data for report RSUSR040, that is, authorization objects by complex selection criteria
AGR_1252	Organization elements for authorizations	
AGR_AGRS	Roles in composite roles	
AGR_DEFINE	Role definition	Provides role definitions for report RSUSR070, that is, roles by complex selection criteria
AGR_HIER2	Menu structure information	
AGR_HIERT	Role menu texts	

Continued

Table 2.1 Continued. Security-Related Tables for Monitoring and Auditing Purposes

Table	Description	Use in SUIM reports
AGR_OBJ	Assignment of menu nodes to role	
AGR_PROF	Profile name for roles	
AGR_TCDTXT	Assignment of roles to transaction codes	
AGR_TEXTS	File structure for hierarchical menu	
AGR_TIME	Time stamp for role: including profile	
AGR_USERS	Assignment of roles to users	
USOBT	Relation transaction to SAP authorization objects	
USOBT_C	Relation transaction to customized authorization objects	
USOBX	Check table for table USOBT	
USOBXFLAGS	Temporary table for storing USOBX/T* changes	
USOBX_C	Check table for table USOBT_C	
TSTCA	Transaction codes, object, field, and values	

Securing Transport Layer for SAP Web AS ABAP

From a data integrity and privacy protection standpoint, it is important to protect the network infrastructure as it supports the necessary communication for your business. SAP Web AS ABAP uses various protocols to protect the communication with its communication partners.

The mechanism used for the transport layer security and encryption depends on the protocols used.

- For SAP protocols, such as DIALOG and RFC, you can use Secure Network Communications (SNC). By using SNC, you can strengthen communication to your SAP system by implementing additional security measures that SAP systems do not directly provide (for example, client certificates or smart cards authentications).
- For Internet protocols, such as HTTP, you can use the Secure Sockets Layer (SSL) protocol to protect communication. By using Hypertext Transport Protocol Secure (HTTPS) in the URL instead of HTTP, it directs the communication to a secure port number rather than the default Web port number of 80. The user session is then managed by the SSL protocol.
- Directory access protocols, such as LDAP, also use SSL. By using SSL, you can ensure that data exchange (for example, user ID and password, user data) between the Directory and the SAP system is secure.

A well-defined network topology can prevent security threats such as computer viruses, denial-of-service attacks, eavesdropping, and theft of enterprise information. It is highly recommended to use a demilitarized zone (DMZ) to establish network infrastructure as shown in Figure 2.4 DMZ adds an additional layer of security to an organization's local area network (LAN) as an external attacker only has access to the equipments in the DMZ rather than the whole of the organizational network.

This means by placing your SAP systems such as SAP Web AS ABAP systems (both the database and application servers) in the Intranet zone, you increase access protection and optimal security level of your systems. As the systems are within a secured LAN that is protected with a firewall, you can operate securely without the need to use SNC (that is, setting profile parameter *snc/r3int_rfc_secure to the value 0*).

Other intermediary devices such as SAP Web dispatcher, Application gateway, and SAProuter can be placed in the inner DMZ to provide access to the Internet.

Figure 2.4 Transport Layer Security for SAP Web AS ABAP Systems

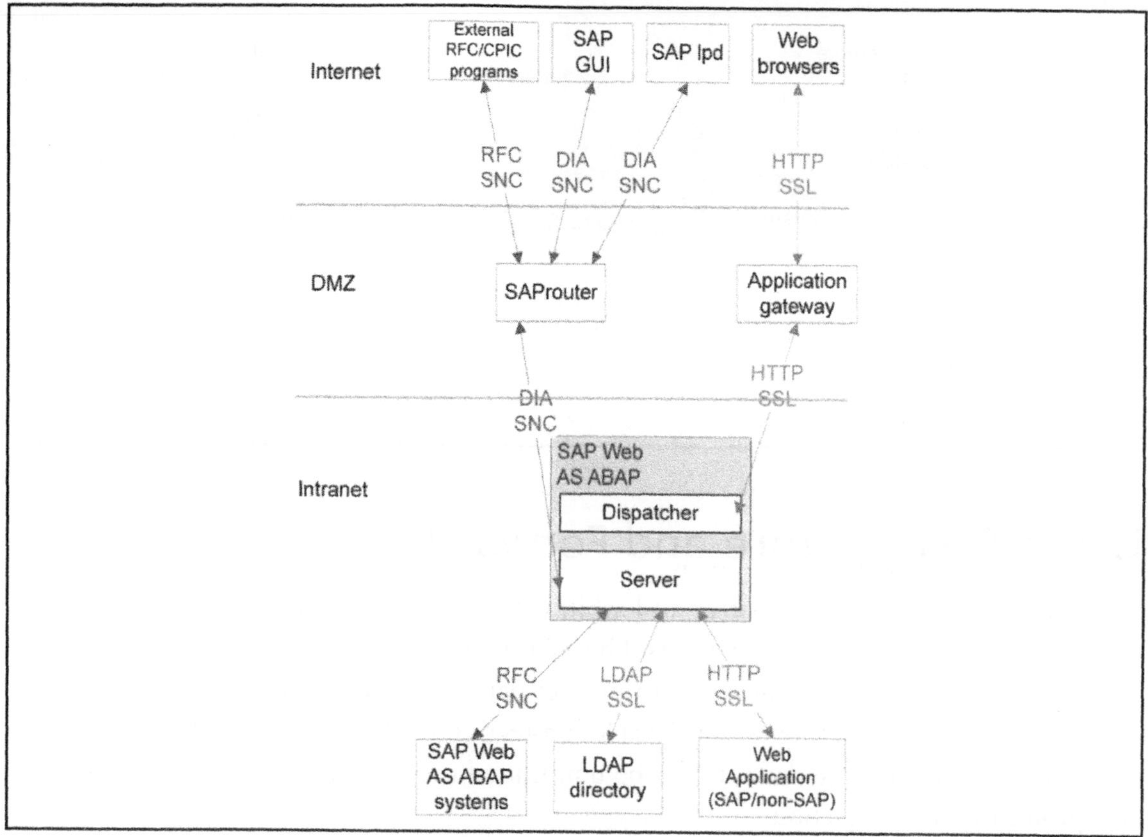

For additional security measures, you can protect each zone with firewalls, as shown in Figure 2.5. The firewall is a device that is configured to permit or deny data traffic between different security domains. Provided that the firewall is equipped with a SAProuter and the SNC interface, a Secure Tunnel can be established between two networks using SNC.

Figure 2.5 Establishing a Secure Tunnel Using SAProuters and Firewalls

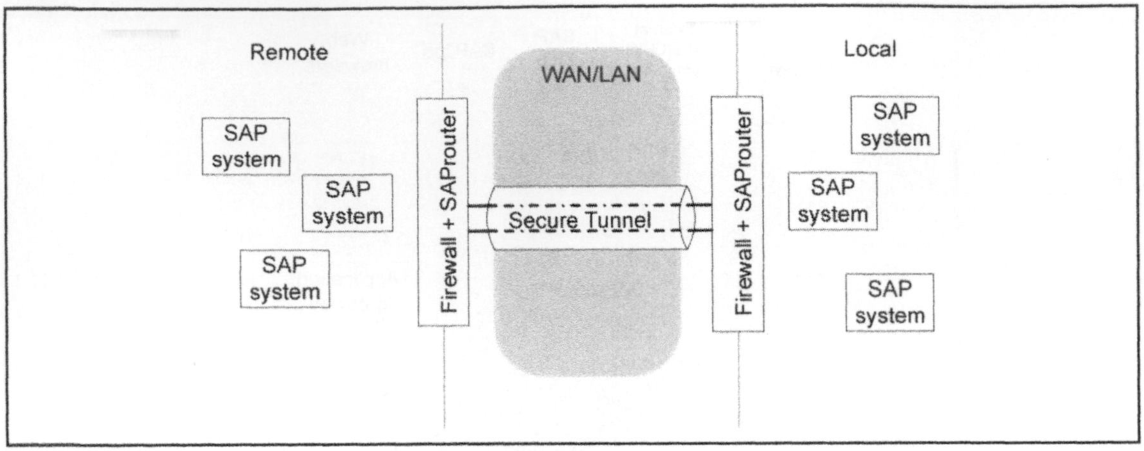

Using Secure Store and Forward

It is important to protect sensitive and arbitrary data stored in the SAP system and prevent data from unauthorized access. The SAP Web AS system uses a mechanism called *Secure Store and Forward (SSF)* to protect data and documents using digital signatures and digital envelopes. This enables protection of the data even when it leaves the SAP System, meaning the data can be transmitted over communication paths without compromising the protection.

Similar to what a handwritten signature is for a paper document, a digital signature uniquely identifies the individual that signs the digital document and guarantees that the individual is really who he or she claims to be. The digital signature also protects the integrity of the signed data, meaning that if the data is changed in any way or form then the signature is invalid. A digital envelope makes sure the contents of the data are visible only to the intended recipient.

By default, SAP Web AS ABAP already has SAP Security Library (or SAPSECULIB) for digital signatures. Alternatively, you can use SAP Cryptographic Library, which supports digital envelopes and crypto hardware, or another SAP-certified external security product.

Each participant using the digital signatures and envelopes needs to own a key pair (that is, public and private key). It is particularly important that security measures are in place to protect the keys from unauthorized access and misuse. The private keys must be stored in a secured location and you can either store the private keys using smart cards, crypto boxes, or password protection. For public keys, you must ensure the certificates are from a trusted source and are signed by a trusted certification authority (CA).

Similarly for the AS ABAP server, there is a public and private key pair. The private key is stored in the system Personal Security Environment (PSE) in a file called *SAPSYS.pse*, which is located in the subdirectory sec of the directory specified by the profile parameter *DIR-INSTANCE*. This directory is only accessed by system administrators and must be secured to ensure the private key is not compromised. The public key can either be self-signed (where the receiver needs to validate the certificate) or CA-signed (where verification is automatic because the receiver trusts the CA).

Using Virus Scan Interface

Due to the open structure of the SAP NetWeaver technology, there is a risk of viruses, Trojans, adware, spyware, or other malware attacks each time an external file upload takes place. For example, supplier documents and interface files (for example, data exchanged between an SAP system and legacy system) which are externally uploaded are susceptible to contain viruses, Trojans, or other malwares.

You can use the Virus Scan Interface (VSI) in the SAP landscape to the increase the content security of your systems by scanning files or documents that are processed by your applications for viruses. It supports both the AS ABAP and J2EE Engine as shown in Figure 2.6.

The VSI solution consists of the VSI and an antivirus product from a certified vendor. A list of the certified vendors for the interface (VSI) is available in the SAP Service Marketplace.

Figure 2.6 Protecting Content Security Using Virus Scan Interface

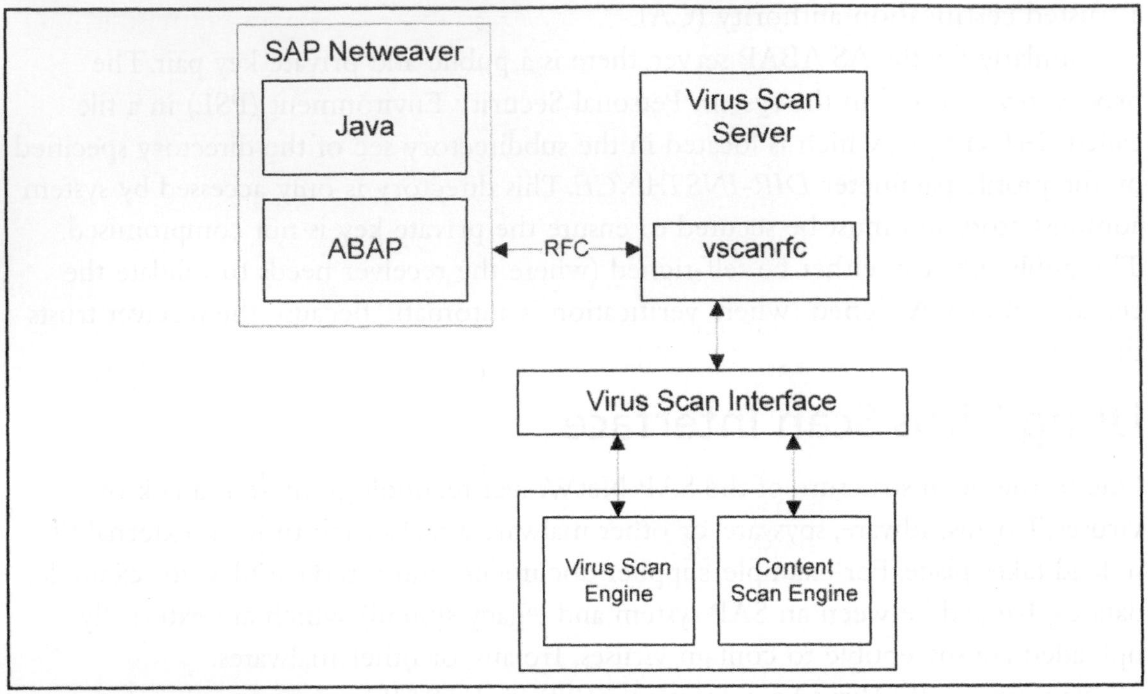

Enforcing Security Policies

It is imperative that you have a framework of security policies under which the maintenance and administration of security is conducted within your SAP environment. A well-defined security policy with a defined set of protocols can support the organization in mitigating any potential security risks and ensures that there is a consistent approach for all relevant parties. Here is a list of suggested security policies:

- Restrict sensitive transactions (for example, PA20, PA30, PPOME, F110) as well as sensitive authorization objects (for example, P_ORGIN, P_ORGXX, P_PERNR, P_TCODE) to only authorized users.
- Protect System Administration transactions (for example, DB13, SE16, SM01, SM36, SM49, SM59, SE06, SCC4, SU01 and PFCG) so they are restricted to System Administrators only.
- Ensure the SE06 and SCC4 settings are set correctly in Production system (that is, system is not opened for change).

- Restrict access to system critical objects on the Operating System (for example, profile parameters, transport files, authentication keys, batch input files) to System Administrators only.
- Define a Provisioning procedure for handling Access Control Requests (for example, new user request) and ensure an appropriate approval process take place. Incorporate into this procedure the process for handling access change for employee promotions and emergency changes in the Production system to ensure that appropriate business approvals and risk/impact analysis take place. Additionally, include the employee termination process as part of the de-provisioning procedure to ensure user access is properly revoked in a timely and accurate manner.
- Define a Change Management procedure to ensure access to the Transport Management System is restricted to the Administrators only and that change is controlled by Change Management (for example, Change Control forms, Release Management) and propagated across the systems accordingly (for example, approved change is implemented in the Development system where it is unit-tested, and the change is further tested in the Test or Quality Assurance system before it is moved into the Production system and finally moved to the Training system).
- Protect the name of the SAPConnect user (that is, by not using the user ID in the Name field in transaction SU01) from being disclosed to external parties.
- Prevent sensitive list downloads by restricting authorization object *S_GUI* or use customer exit SGRPDL00 to add additional restriction by user group or authorization object.
- Activate table logging in the Production system to ensure change documents are recorded for all critical tables.

J2EE

The SAP NetWeaver technology platform is based on an open, Web-based and multitiered client/server architecture that integrates many different components, applications, or systems across business and technology boundaries. As of SAP Web Application Server 6.20, SAP provides a J2EE-compliant Java Application Server, the J2EE Engine. Understanding SAP's approach to security for the J2EE Engine begins with understanding the J2EE specification and some basic principles of J2EE Security.

This section gives you an overview of the J2EE Application Concept including J2EE terminologies that will be helpful to Security teams looking to secure their J2EE-based programs using the SAP Web AS platform.

Security for the SAP Web AS Java system is addressed on the presentation, application, transport layers; all of the security aspects are based on restricting access at each level to authorized users or systems only. This should form part of your overall SAP security strategy. Here is an introduction to each of them; these will be covered further in the later sections:

- The *Presentation* layer represents various forms of front-end applications (for example, SAP GUI for Java, SAP GUI for HTML) or Web clients (for example, Web browsers) used to access the SAP Web AS Java. As data is exchanged over exposed networks (for example, Internet), it introduces risks to the security of the communication to the SAP Web AS Java system. To ensure communication is protected, users must be authenticated successfully before they are allowed into the system; this security mechanism is called user authentication.
- The *Application layer* represents the application logic within the SAP Web AS Java system. As important and sensitive data can be accessed in the system, significant business risks are introduced if access control is not properly managed. To prevent unauthorized access, access control protection is based on the authorization concept and user management.
- The *Transport layer* supports the necessary communication for the whole system landscape. Data that is exchanged over an unsecured network is not protected; it becomes a huge risk to the data integrity, privacy protection, and other security threats. To ensure data is communicated securely, security protocols such as Secure Network Communication (SNC) and Secure Sockets Layer (SSL) can be used.

The Enterprise Portal (EP) uses the SAP Web AS Java system as its underlying application server, so the security concepts for the EP system are based on the same fundamental security concepts as the SAP J2EE Engine.

J2EE Application Concept

The Java 2 Enterprise Edition (J2EE) specification is a Java platform for development of highly scalable and secure enterprise applications in a thin-client tiered environment. It is the foundation or standard for developing, deploying, and running enterprise applications.

There are two types of J2EE applications, with security for each handled differently. The first type is an enterprise application that uses a Web application as an entry point. The second type uses enterprise java beans (EJBs) or RMI-P4/RMI-IIOP Remote Objects that are requested from RMI-P4, RMI-IIOP, or CORBA clients.

The next section gives you an overview and some security approaches for Web applications and Remote Objects.

Web Applications

Web applications are applications that are accessed via the Intranet or Internet. They consists of Web components (for example, Java Server Pages, servlets), Web Dynpro, static files (for example, Hypertext Markup Language pages, image files), filters, JavaBeans, Java classes and other components defined by the J2EE specification.

Users use Web-based clients (for example, Web browser) to communicate with a Web application by sending a HTTP request. The Web application converts this request into an *HTTPServletRequest* object and sends the object to the Web component. Depending on the request, the Web component interacts with the database or other JavaBeans components to generate the dynamic content. The Web component then creates an *HTTPServletResponse* object and passes this to the J2EE Web application, which converts it into a HTTP response before returning it to the client.

User authentication occurs at the Web containers. Authentication methods such as security session IDs (JSESSIONID), log-on tickets and Security Assertions Markup Language (SAML) supports SSO for Web applications, which enables the security principals of the authenticated user to be propagated to other containers and the user is allowed to access the EJB and database.

Authorizations for Web applications use a *role*-based approach where authorizations are assigned to users based on their job positions.

Communication between the Web clients and the Web applications uses the HTTP protocol. Web applications use SNC and SSL protocols to protect and encrypt the communication with its communication partners. The interaction between a Web client and J2EE Web application is illustrated in Figure 2.7.

Figure 2.7 Interaction of Web Client to the J2EE Web Application

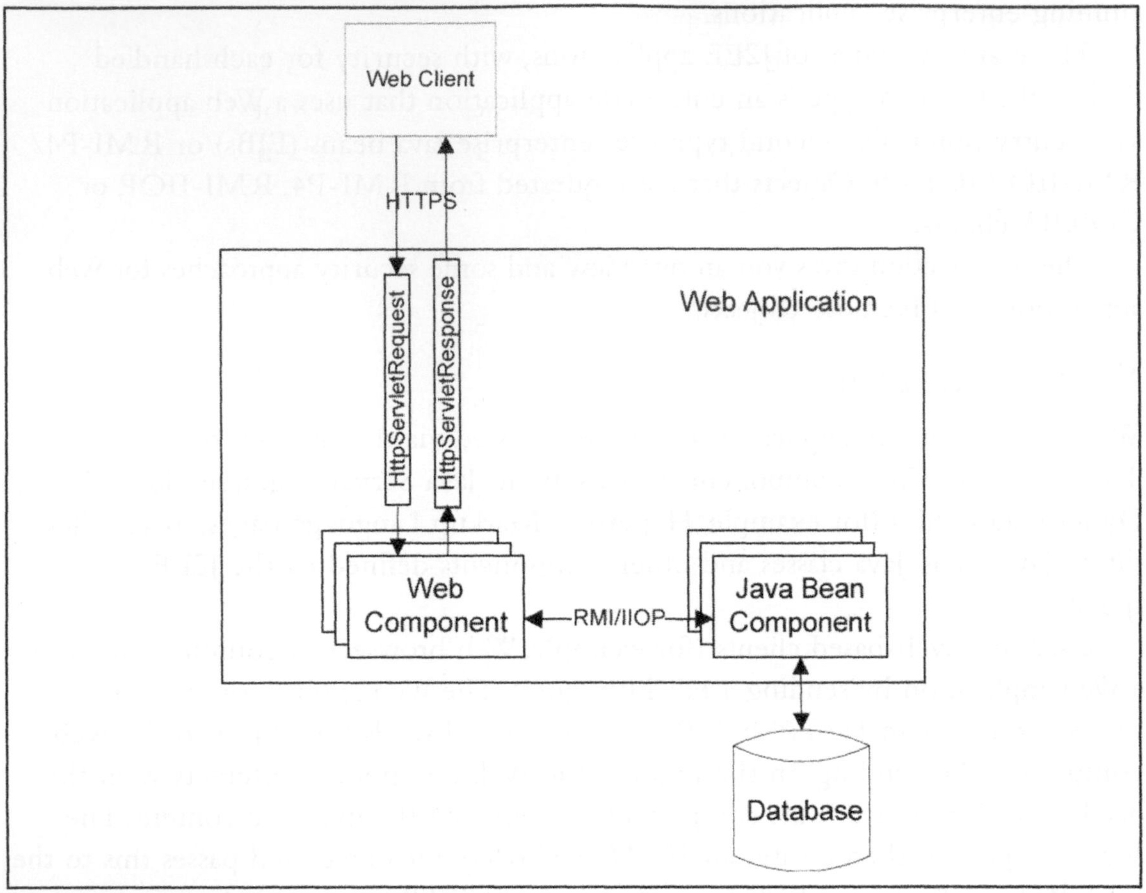

Web Components

Servlet is a Java programming language class that process requests and constructs responses dynamically. It can handle control functions of a Web application such as setting request parameters, dispatching requests, and handling nontextual data.

Java Server Page (JSP) is a text-based document that executes as a servlet. It is also referred to as a HTML or Extensible Markup Language (XML) page with embedded Java code. JSPs can add dynamically generated content from other resources to a static Web page. JSP generates other text-based markup such as Scalable Vector Graphics (SVG) and Wireless Markup Language (WML).

A JSP is compiled by the Web Container, either at first request or when the application starts depending on how you have configured your Web Container Service.

JSP technology allows Web developers to rapidly develop and easily maintain, information-rich, dynamic Web pages that leverage existing business systems. It also enables rapid development of Web-based applications that are platform independent. JSP technology separates the user interface from content generation enabling designers to change the overall page layout without altering the underlying dynamic content.

Web Container

Web container is the runtime environment for Web component. It serves as an entry point of most client requests to J2EE applications that are running on the J2EE Engine. It provides services such as request processing, authenticating the users, authorizing users to access certain resources, concurrency, and life-cycle management. It also gives Web components access to Application Programming Interfaces (API) such as naming, transactions, and email.

SAP J2EE Engine implements the Java Authentication and Authorization Service (JAAS) specification to support various authentication methods including user ID and password, SSL, and X.509 client certificates.

Remote Objects

Remote Object is based on the *Remote Method Invocation* interface where the methods are invoked from a client located in a remote Java Virtual Machine (JVM). The three types of Remote Objects are enterprise java beans (EJB), RMI-P4, and RMI-IIOP. These Remote Objects are called by RMI-P4, RMI-IIOP, and CORBA clients by P4 or IIOP provider services, as shown in Figure 2.8.

User authentication is handled by P4 or IIOP provider services and the authentication mechanism is user ID and password. Authorization for Remote Objects is based on a descriptive *role*-based approach. Remote Objects use SSL protocol to protect and encrypt data communication.

Figure 2.8 Interaction of RMI-P4, RMI-IIOP, and CORBA Clients with J2EE Web Application

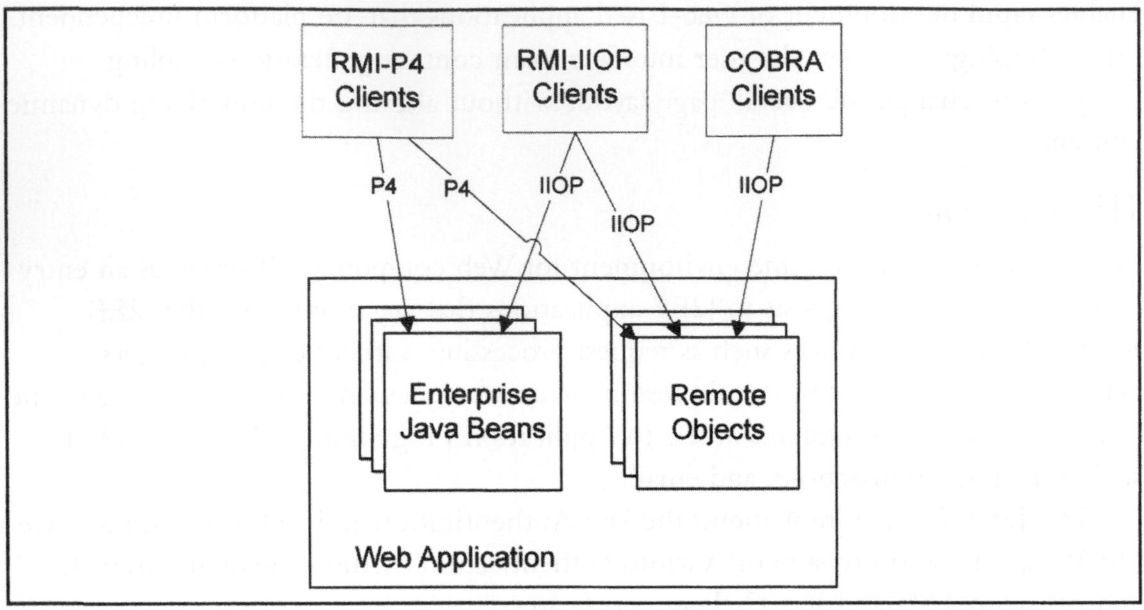

Authentication Concept

User Authentication is the process of attempting to verify the identity of the users, applications, or services and only allow access onto the system based on a successful authentication. Authentication is important because various security threats such as viruses, Trojans, worms, and information and identity theft are continuing to rise. Any of these attacks can cause hours of lost productivity from running virus scans to applying security patches.

User Authentication protects the Presentation layer of the SAP Web AS Java systems. The standard user ID and password is the default authentication mechanism supported by all SAP NetWeaver products. While using standard password authentications alone simply cannot prevent security attacks, you can make sure your systems are further protected through the use of various stronger authentication methods.

For instance, you can use an external security product that supports encryption and client certificates that are signed by a trusted Certificate Authority (CA). When using encryption software, you should note that there may be some limitations of use due to the legal export rules of different countries for encryption software and algorithms, in which case you can use Secure Network Communication (SNC) for authentication.

SAP J2EE Engine supports various user authentication approaches/mechanisms used to control user access and keep unauthorized parties from accessing secure information. It is based on the Java Authentication and Authorization Service (JAAS) specification. An authentication has three properties:

- Authentication *approach* describes where the user authentication takes place in the application.
- Authentication *scheme* describes how the authentication is presented to the user.
- Authentication *mechanism* describes what security mechanism is used to authenticate the user.

The following sections introduce you to these user authentication properties and how they work.

Authentication Approaches

There are two types of authentication approaches that applications running on the SAP J2EE Engine can use.

Declarative authentication is also referred to as container-based authentication. As the name suggests, the authentication and all access control decisions occur within the Web container (that is, J2EE Engine). The application deployment descriptor (for example, *web.xml*) defines how the application should be deployed with specific configuration requirements such as which login module stack to use and role mappings to the security roles that are defined on the target J2EE Engine. The authentication process is triggered when a protected resource is accessed. There are benefits with using declarative authentication as it requires minimal programming and changes can be made without any recoding efforts.

Programmatic authentication is also known as UME authentication. Applications running on the J2EE Engine authenticate directly against the User Management Engine (UME) using the UME API. The application explicitly triggers authentication and the whole process is controlled by the authentication framework. Applications that use Programmatic authentication are associated with an authentication scheme file (*authschemes.xml*) that contains settings for login module stack (by standard, this is set to *default*) and user interfaces.

J2EE Web applications can use either Declarative or Programmatic authentication depending on which the developer decides to use. Web applications in Enterprise

Portal, for example, Web Dynpro applications and Portal iViews, use the Programmatic authentication.

Authentication Schemes

J2EE specification defines four compulsory schemes for Web application user authentication: Basic, Form, Digest, and Client-Cert.

- *Basic* authentication is where the user ID and password-based authentication takes place in a browser-generated input screen.
- *Form* authentication performs the user ID and password-based authentication in a form page which requires the user's input.
- *Digest* authentication also uses the user ID and password-based authentication; however, the user ID and password is sent a checksum.
- *Client-Cert* authentication is where the authentication is performed using digital certificates.

You can define your own "pluggable" authentication scheme to suit the security architecture of your Web application by developing a JAAS-based login module (or by developing several login modules and configuring them into a stack). To use your login module, you need to register your login module in the Security Provider Service on the J2EE Engine and set your application as the corresponding login modules using its *web-j2ee-engine.xml* additional descriptor.

For Programmatic or UME user authentication, applications are associated with an authentication scheme file (that is, *authschemes.xml*) that contains the settings for login module stack (by standard, this is set to *default*) and user interfaces.

You can change the *authschemes.xml* file using Config Tool of the SAP J2EE Engine in the property **cluster_data | server | persistent | com.sap.security.core.ume.service**. However, it is recommended that if you edit the file, you should download the file to a local directory to edit it, and upload the edited file into a new node in the configuration tree so that the original version of the file is not overwritten.

Authentication Mechanisms

Authentication mechanisms are the security mechanisms that the SAP J2EE Engine uses to authenticate users and keep unauthorized parties from accessing secure information.

The authentication process is based on the concept of a login context object plugged with a configured stack of login modules called the *login module stack*. These are part of the JAAS standard. The login context stores information about the authentication status (that is, success or failure) and the authenticated users. The login modules can check the authentication against different sources of user information and declare the strength of the authentication (for example, required, sufficient or optional). For a required authentication status, the login module is required to succeed. Whether it succeeds or fails, the authentication process continues to proceed down the login module stack. For a sufficient status, the login module is not required to succeed. If authentication is successful, the control function returns to the application and the authentication process does not proceed any further. If authentication fails, the authentication process continues down the login module stack.

With this flexible authentication process, you can define a wide range of authentication policies using different combinations of authentication mechanisms for the applications running on the SAP J2EE Engine. It is very much a technology choice, dependent on the resources you want to protect and on each organizational environment.

For instance, a stand-alone system (for example, internal system) using user ID and password and client certificate may be sufficient. For an integrated access to multiple systems (for example, Single Sign-On), logon tickets or client certificates may be a better option. When accessing from external systems, you can consider using SNC, Kerberos authentication, header variables for authentication, or SAML assertions.

The following sections provide you with an overview on the different combinations of authentication mechanisms with some explanations on how each scenario works.

Using User ID and Password

This is a standard method for authentication whereby the user provides a valid user ID and password for authentication. By default, SAP J2EE Engine uses the basic authentication for applications that can use either basic or form authentication. Both authentications use the login module *BasicPasswordLoginModule*.

With *basic* authentication, the user's information is passed onto the server over the HTTP connection in a header variable as a base-64 encoded string.

With *form* authentication, however, the information is passed in the URL as an URL parameter.

For example, you can use the user ID and password authentication mechanism for setting up Single Sign-On (SSO) in an Enterprise Portal (EP) system. By default, EP system uses the basic authentication. In this case, the administrator needs to map the portal user data to the user data on the external system (for example, LDAP or database). This enables the EP system to connect to the external system using the user's credentials. If you want to SSO to a non-SAP system via an iView in EP, you must use Java APIs to map the user data. The user's credentials are passed over the network and it is highly recommended that you use SSL protocol (for example, SAP Java Cryptographic Library toolkit) to secure the Transport layer and prevent unauthorized access. This is only useful if your EP system cannot accept or verify SAP logon tickets; otherwise, the SAP logon ticket for SSO is a stronger authentication option.

Using X.509 Certificate on SSL

X.509 client certificate is a digital identification card or key. Using this security mechanism, users need to have their X.509 client certificates as part of a Public-Key Infrastructure (PKI). Any user who tries to access the SAP J2EE Engine needs to present a valid certificate to the server using the SSL protocol for authentication. This means the Transport layer is secured. Given that SSL can be configured on the SAP J2EE Engine with or without an intermediary gateway proxy server (for example, SAP Web Dispatcher), this determines where the user authentication actually takes place.

If the user accesses the SAP J2EE Engine *directly*, authentication can take place on the SAP J2EE Engine provided that it is configured to accept client certificates. If the authentication is successful and the server can map the user's Distinguished Name in the certificate with a valid user ID on the SAP J2EE system, then the user is allowed onto the system. User authentication takes place in the underlying protocols. Hence no user ID and password entries are necessary.

If the user accesses the SAP J2EE Engine via an *intermediary* server (for example, SAP Web Dispatcher), authentication can take place either on the intermediary server or J2EE Engine depending on the proxy settings used. When a user connects to the SAP J2EE Engine via a SAP Web Dispatcher, the SAP Web Dispatcher terminates the connection so the user's client certificate with SSL cannot be used for authentication on the SAP J2EE Engine, as shown in Figure 2.9. In this case, authentication takes place on the SAP Web Dispatcher as it establishes a new connection and passes the user's client certificate to the SAP J2EE Engine in a header variable (this requires the parameter *icm/HTTPS/forward_ccert_as_header* set to true).

If the SAP Web Dispatcher possesses the public key to establish SSL with SAP J2EE Engine, the SAP J2EE Engine can accept this certificate based on its trust relationship with the SAP Web Dispatcher. In this case, the user is authenticated end-to-end without the intermediary server terminating the connection as shown in Figure 2.9.

When the user accesses the SAP J2EE Engine via the Internet Communication Manager (ICM), the user's client certificate is passed using the protocol between the ICM and the SAP J2EE Engine. In this case, the authentication takes place on the SAP J2EE Engine.

Figure 2.9 Scenarios When Using SSL with an Intermediary Server

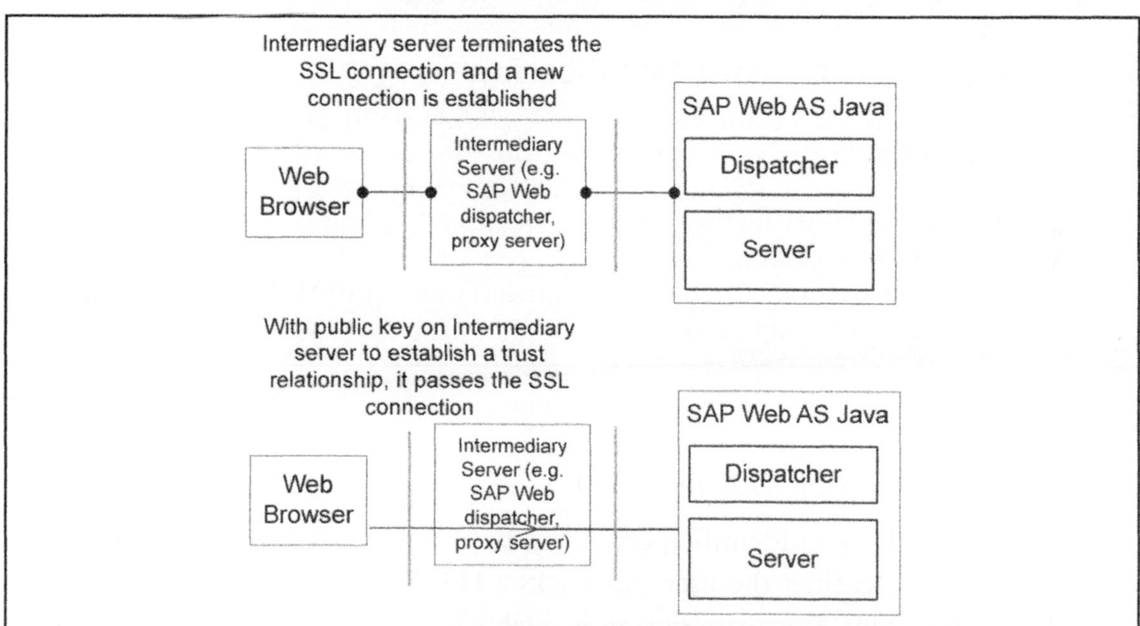

Users can use their client certificates for secure access to other intranet or Internet services. It is recommended that you use certificates that are signed by a trusted CA. This means the chosen CA becomes the designated certificate authority on the SAP J2EE system (the private key) and the user who accesses the SAP J2EE system must possess a valid certificate signed by the chosen CA (the public key). The corresponding user's private key must be stored in a secure location (for example, password-protected or using smart cards).

In addition to protecting the Presentation layer, this security mechanism can also be used to protect the Transport layer, specifically for protecting the HTTP connections between various client and server components of the SAP J2EE system.

Tools & Traps...

Logging off with Client Certification

As logon is not required for systems using client certificate authentication, a navigation problem can arise when the user tries to log off from the system. This is due to the fact that when a user logs off from the system, by default he or she is redirected back to the log-on screen, making it impossible for the user to log off from the system.

To fix this problem, you need to maintain the log-off URL on your system and redirect it to another page.

Using Security Session IDs for SSO

Security Session ID is an identifier, generated by the SAP J2EE Engine's Web container, which identifies the user and tracks a HTTP session. When a user logs onto the J2EE system, a security session is established and the information relating to the user's identity and actions performed with the Web application are stored into a non-persistent cookie called JSESSIONID.

Using this mechanism, session-related information is exchanged between the user and the server over HTTP using the session cookie or URL rewriting and SSO is enabled between applications in one system. Some examples of JSESSIONID:

- Cookie looks like: Cookie:JSESSIONID=12345
- URL rewrite looks like: http://www.example.com/index.html;jsessionid=12345

The restriction with using this mechanism is that the user authentication is non-persistent and it cannot be migrated to other systems.

Using Logon Tickets for SSO

SAP Logon Ticket provides authentication for protecting the communication between various client and server components of the SAP J2EE system. The user is authenticated using the Logon Ticket as the authentication token. The user only needs to be authenticated once (for example, using a valid user ID and password) and the system can issue a Logon Ticket to the user. With this Logon Ticket, the user can access subsequent systems (SAP and non-SAP systems) without the need to reenter his or her user ID and password.

For SAP Logon Ticket authentication with client components (for example, SAP GUI for Java, SAP GUI for HTML), users must have the same user ID in all of the systems they need to access and their Web browsers must accept cookies. The user's ticket is stored as a non-persistent cookie within the user's Web browser. This cookie stores all the information necessary to log the user on to subsequent systems without having to provide an explicit password authentication. To prevent the SAP Logon Ticket from being manipulated during transfer, you should protect the communication by using HTTPS (Hypertext Transfer Protocol over Secure Sockets Layer) between Internet-enabled components.

Furthermore, due to the nature of cookie technology, the Logon Ticket is sent to all servers within the same DNS domain or where the ticket-issuing server is located. To protect the Logon Ticket from being sent to servers that should not receive it, it is recommended to use a separate domain for your Productive systems.

For authentication between server components, both accepting systems and the issuing server must have synchronized system clocks. The issuing server must possess a public and private key pair so that it can digitally sign the Logon Ticket. And the accepting systems must be placed in the same DNS domain as the issuing server and the systems must have the public key certificate to verify the digital signature on the Logon Ticket. It is recommended that you identify one system in your system landscape as the ticket-issuing system and configure all other systems to accept tickets from this system. The Logon Ticket is stored as a non-persistent cookie called *MYSAPSSO2*, which contains the user ID and is digitally signed by the ticket-issuing server.

You specify the use of Logon Tickets in the logon module stacks by setting the properties in the **Security Provider** service on J2EE Engine. *CreateTicketLoginModule* and *EvaluateTicketLoginModule* modules are used to create and verify Logon Tickets with the UME or DBMS user stores. You can then import the public key certificate onto the issuing server using the Visual Administrator, and use the Trusting Systems SSO Wizard to configure the accepting J2EE servers to accept Logon Tickets.

An example where you can use this authentication mechanism is when setting up SSO in an EP system. In this scenario, the administrator needs to map the portal user data in the UME with the user data in the LDAP directory. This enables the EP system to connect to the LDAP directory using the user's credentials. Although the user ID is encrypted in the UME, it is not encrypted in the LDAP directory. To prevent unauthorized access to user data, you must ensure no unauthorized users have write-access to the LDAP directory. It is also recommended that the EP system is the ticket-issuing system since the EP system should be a user's single point of access to all applications.

Using Security Assertion Markup Language (SAML) Assertions for SSO

When using Security Assertion Markup Language (SAML) Assertions, a user is authenticated using an external authentication system (SAML authority). If the user is authenticated, he or she receives an SAML Assertion. The assertion is a statement from the SAML authority that authenticates the user and confirms some attributes about the user before granting or denying authorization. Because SAML only provides the message format, SSL must be used.

In a SAML SSO scenario, the user initiates the SAML communication by logging onto the source site (for example, using user ID and password). When the user authenticates and requests a resource (for example, a URL) at the destination site, the source site contacts the destination site's artifact receiver (for example, applications on the SAP J2EE Engine) and sends the requested URL along with the assertion artifact, which is an identifier for the user's assertion. The artifact receiver then passes the assertion on for evaluation by the SAML login module. The login module determines the source site and requests from it the user's authentication assertions using SOAP (protocol for exchanging XML messages) over HTTP binding of the SAML protocol. The source site's responder then acts as the SAML authority and sends the user's assertions (that is, user ID or SAML principal). The login module evaluates the assertions, authenticates the user, and the destination site directs the user to the requested destination. The process flow of the SAML Assertion authentication is shown in Figure 2.10.

Figure 2.10 Process Flow of the SAML Assertion Authentication

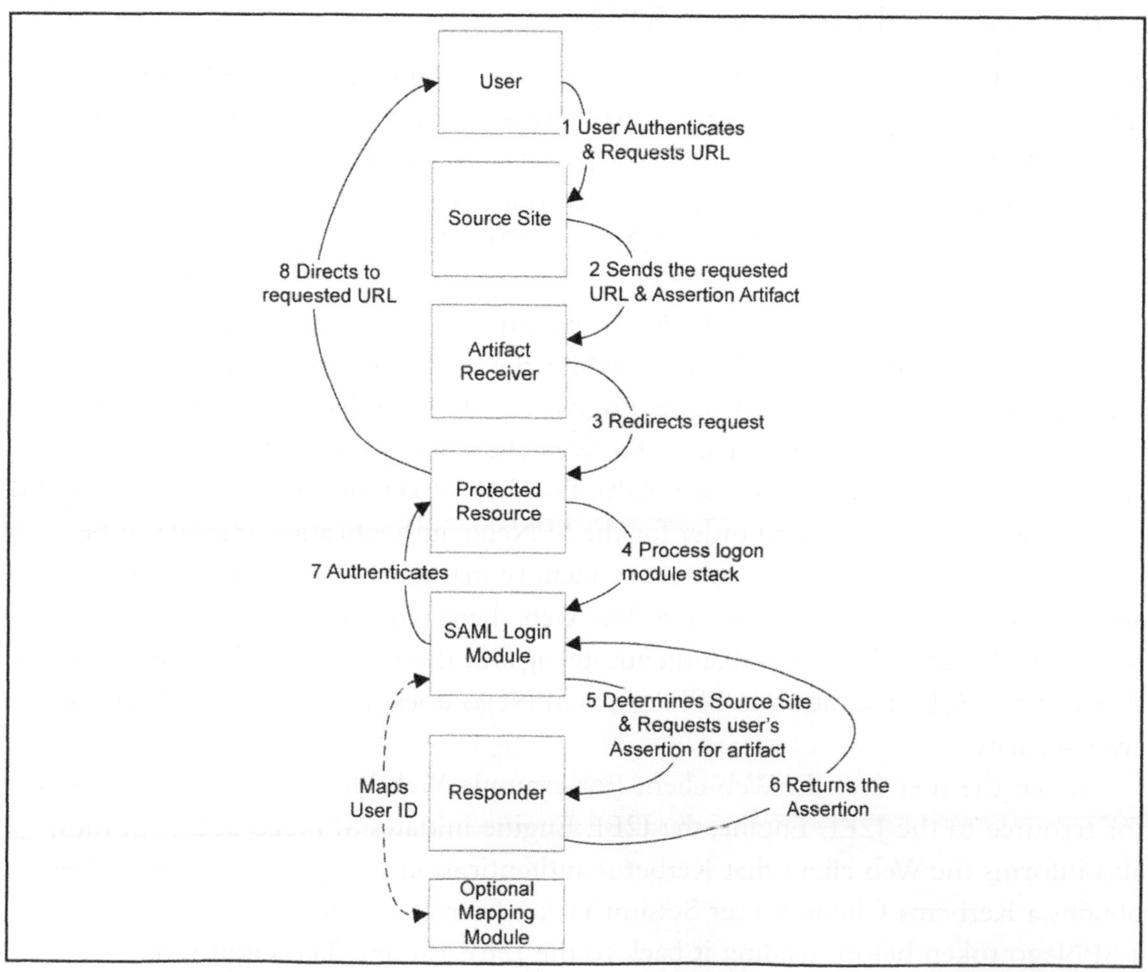

In cases where the user ID as provided by the SAML authority is *not* identical to the user ID at the destination site, the destination site must provide some sort of user mapping mechanism for authentication. You can create a mapping module either using a mapping table in a database, or a hard-coded mapping or use table entries within a directory server.

To use SAML, you configure the *PartnerInbound* parameters using the Configuration Adapter. You also need to check whether login module *SAMLoginModule* exists in the active user store and add it to the login module stack. Once the application is configured to accept SAML assertions, you have the option to either access the application directly by transferring the SAML artifact as a URL parameter, or use the generic SAML receiver (or *sap.com/tc~sec~app* application) on the SAP J2EE Engine by using the */saml/receiver* path in the URL.

Using Kerberos Authentication SSO

SAP J2EE Engine enables the use of the Simple and Protected GSS-API Negotiation (SPNego) mechanism for Kerberos authentication with Web clients. This is supported as of SAP NetWeaver Application Server Java Release AS Java 640 SP 15. To use SPNego authentication, you are required to configure several systems including the Kerberos Key Distribution Center (KDC), the J2EE Engine and its UME, as well as the Web client.

The main function of the KDC is to authenticate the user and grant Kerberos Client/Server Session Tickets that are used for the communication between the J2EE Engine and the Web client. SAP J2EE Engine, on the other hand, provides access to the resources or services requested by the Web client using Generic Security Service Application Program Interface (GSS-API). The Web server also needs to be configured to allow anonymous access in order for the SPNego authentication module to be operational. UME provides the necessary identity management information for authenticating with the Kerberos user. The Web client requests resources or services from the SAP J2EE Engine and authenticates against the KDC. It is highly recommend that you use SSL in addition to SPNego, as SPNego does not provide any transport layer security.

When the user uses the Web client (for example, Web browser) to send a request for resource to the J2EE Engine, the J2EE Engine initiates SPNego authentication and informs the Web client that Kerberos authentication is required. The Web client obtains a Kerberos Client/Server Session Ticket from the KDC, and wraps it as a SPNego token before sending it back to the J2EE Engine. The login module

SPNegoLoginModule authenticates the user using that token. The process flow for the Kerberos authentication is illustrated in Figure 2.11.

If the Web server is a Microsoft Internet Information Server (IIS), the *Integrated Login* setting must be unchecked and the *Anonymous Access setting* must be checked.

Figure 2.11 Process Flow of the Kerberos Authentication

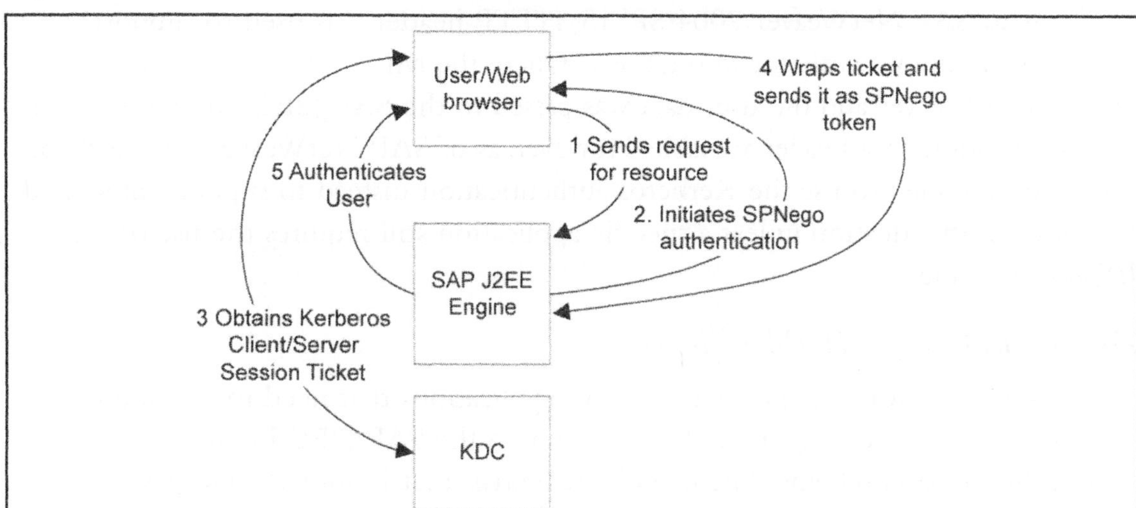

Using Header Variables for SSO

SAP J2EE Engine supports the use of external Web Access Management (WAM) products where users are authenticated using the *HTTP header*. A user only has to authenticate once against the external product and he or she can access subsequent Web AS Java applications with SSO. You may consider this authentication mechanism if you are already using it to protect other resources or if you want to use external authentication methods such as token cards or biometrics.

When the user accesses an application on the SAP J2EE Engine, the WAM product authenticates the user and returns an authenticated user ID to the SAP J2EE Engine as part of the HTTP header. The SAP J2EE Engine then compares this user ID against the UME. If a match is found, the user is authenticated and access is granted to the required application.

To use header variables for authentication, you need to check whether login module *HeaderVariableLoginModule* exists in the active user store and add it to the login module stack. Appropriate security measures need to be put in place when using header variables for authentication to ensure data integrity and privacy protection.

For example, set up a security policy where users can only access the SAP J2EE Engine through an intermediary server (for example, SAP Web Dispatcher) so that direct access to the SAP J2EE system is prevented.

For additional security measures, you should consider using client certificates with SSL so that the SAP J2EE Engine can trust the user information contained in the header variable based on its trust relationship with the intermediary server.

Prior to SAP NetWeaver 2004 SPS15, HTTP header was used to support integrated Windows authentication; this is where the Microsoft IIS was used as an intermediary server and the user data was passed to the SAP J2EE Engine using the *IISproxy* module in a header variable. However, as of SAP NetWeaver 2004 SPS15, it is recommended to use the Kerberos authentication instead to support integrated Windows authentication unless a specific application still requires the use of the *IISproxy* module.

Authenticating RMI-P4 Clients

RMI-P4 clients (for example, external Java applications that need to communicate with SAP Web AS system) are authenticated onto the SAP J2EE Engine using the *basic* authentication scheme. The client's credential (that is, user ID and password) is provided as environment properties in the source code. The naming system of the J2EE Engine verifies the client against the security role settings to determine whether *InitialContext* can be obtained. If required by server-side remote objects (for example, EJBs, Java classes), credentials from the *InitialContext* can be propagated.

Authorization Concept

The authorization concept for SAP J2EE Engine provides access to user using a role-based identity management approach while preventing unauthorized access to ensure protection of important and sensitive data within the SAP security infrastructure. When the user log on to the J2EE Engine, the system authenticates and sets access control by either assigning position-based roles to the user or assigning objects using access control lists. This ensures the user can only execute those roles and objects to which he or she has been granted access.

In order to execute an action in SAP J2EE Engine, the user needs to have authorizations or permissions allocated to his or her user store. These authorizations are combined into a position-based role to represent a logical combination of activities for performing a specific function or task. The administrator then assigns the role directly to the user ID in the user store.

On the other hand, the authorization concept for EP systems is based on permissions, security zones, UME actions, and the *AuthRequirement* property. Authorization is based on the UME access control lists methodology, which maps the authorizations for resources to the users and user groups using Access Control Lists.

User Stores

SAP J2EE Engine stores user management data using two main user store providers: User Management Engine (UME) and Database Management System (DBMS). By default, the J2EE Engine's user management uses DBMS user store where a database is used to store user data. You can activate and switch to UME user store using Visual Administrator.

UME User Store Provider

J2EE Engine's user management can use UME User Store Provider as the active user store. It can be configured to read and write user management data from multiple data sources such as Lightweight Directory Access Protocol (LDAP) directories, databases, and SAP Web AS ABAP systems, as well as flat files, as shown in Figure 2.12. EP systems also use UME as their user stores.

With the possibility to integrate with an existing external data source such as LDAP, this is highly efficient and cost effective for the business as you can leverage your existing system infrastructure from an implementation and administration standpoint. You can also use the UME user store to provide centralized user management for all SAP Web AS Java applications. To configure the UME user store, you can use the Visual Administrator tool.

The UME model is made up of several components:

- *User Management* data source stores the user data (for example, database, LDAP directories, SAP Web AS ABAP systems, and external systems).
- *Persistence Manager* handles all user management requests and controls the data traffic to the data stores.
- *Persistence Adapter* connects the data source to the Persistence Manager.
- *Replication Manager* replicates UME data by generating XML documents and sending them to external systems.
- *Applications* access the UME using user management APIs.

UME provides some preconfigured data source configurations (template XML files) for dealing with user management data corresponding to each data source scenario. When it comes to deciding which data source combination is suitable for your scenario, as part of defining your User Management Strategy, you need to take into account how your system fits into your overall system landscape, where you want to store your user data, and roles, as this has some implications on how you maintain users and roles in your system. To specify the data source configuration file, you can check in the UME property *ume.persistence.data_source_configuration* in the Security Provider of the J2EE Engine. In addition, UME also provides features such as self-registration with approval workflow, notification, and emails.

DBMS User Store Provider

When the J2EE Engine uses DBMS User Store Provider as the active user store, user data is stored in a pre-configured internal database of the J2EE Engine as shown in Figure 2.12. It is managed by the **User Store** service in the Security Provider of the J2EE Engine. You can use Visual Administrator to configure the DBMS user store.

Figure 2.12 UME and DBMS User Stores

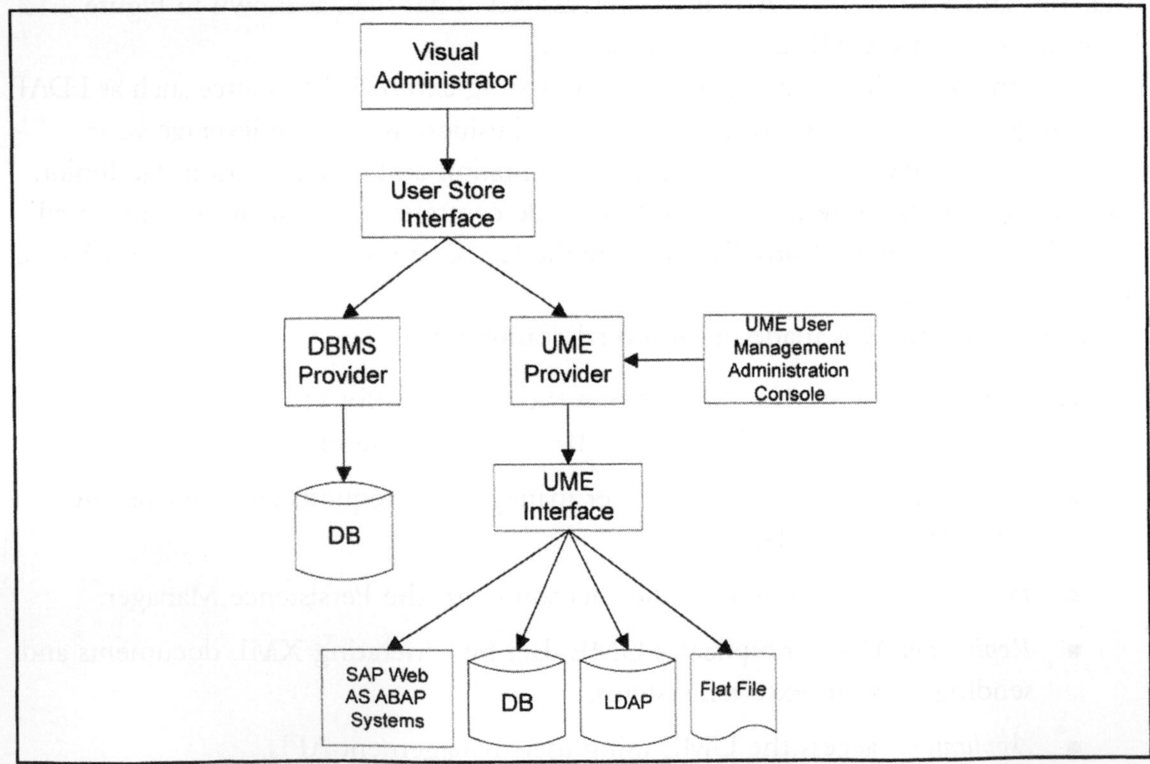

Authorization Checks

Authorization checks on the SAP J2EE Engine can vary in accordance with the authentication approach used for the application and with the application type. It is based on performing all necessary authorization checks, when a user executes an activity on the SAP J2EE Engine, to ensure that the user actually has permission to perform that activity.

J2EE Web applications are authenticated using the Declarative or Programmatic approach so the authorization check happens in the J2EE Engine, whereby you specify which application should check permissions and the corresponding role that is to be checked. While Web Dynpro applications and Portal iViews for Enterprise Portal systems are authenticated using the Programmatic approach, so the authorization checks take place in the application coding rather than the J2EE Engine. For specific resources (for example, documents/folders in a repository or objects in the Portal Content Directory), access control list (ACL) is used for authorization checks.

Roles or Permissions

There are two main types of roles or permissions you can create for access control in the J2EE Engine:

- J2EE security roles are *activity-based* roles that support both the Declarative and Programmatic approaches.
- UME roles (or permissions) are *instance-related* roles that support the Programmatic approach.

From a practicality standpoint, it is important to note that you should not mix the use of J2EE security roles and UME permissions. By implementing the same role or permission approach across your applications, it makes it easier to manage user and role administration. Additionally, you can define *instance-based* ACLs to control access to resources in the SAP J2EE Engine.

With additional access control methods used in the Enterprise Portal system, you can create the following:

- *Portal Permissions*, based on ACLs, define Portal user access rights to portal objects in the Portal Content Directory (PCD), which is the central repository of the Portal content.

- *Security Zones* are permissions for controlling access to Portal components and Portal services.
- *UME Actions* are permissions for controlling access to UME iViews and functions.
- *AuthRequirement* property is an iView property used in EP 5.0 to define which users have access to master iView or Java iView derived from master iView. EP 6.0 supports this property for backward compatibility.

J2EE Security Roles

As mentioned earlier, J2EE security roles are *activity-based* roles, which support both the Declarative and Programmatic approaches. This means you can decide whether to use purely Declarative or also Programmatic role references.

You use the *Declarative* approach when you want to protect access for static information or applications (for example, subsets of applications with different URL paths). The developer specifies the J2EE security role to be checked in the deployment descriptor (an XML file) for the application and no programming is required. The administrator assigns the role (for example, Management Accountant) with activity-based authorizations (for example, releasing accounting block) rather than by instance-based authorizations (for example, company codes), and then maps the security role to corresponding users or user groups. Hence, all users assigned with the Management Accountant role can release accounting block for all company codes.

With the *Programmatic* approach, the developer uses a method to perform an authorization check against individual control elements (for example, an EJB or a Web resource) in the application so that when the user accesses the control element, the application checks whether the user has the necessary role. This is called a "role reference." The role references defined can be consolidated into a position-based J2EE security role, which relates only to the application it was defined in. The J2EE security role is then assigned to the corresponding users or user groups (see Figure 2.13).

There are two types of security roles you can deliver in the SAP J2EE Engine:

- Application-specific J2EE security role with which you can protect application resources (for example, URLs or EJB methods); it is also specific to that particular application.

- Server-specific J2EE security role with which you can protect any resources defined by the relevant service (for example, Keystore views); it can be created by a service or by the administrator.

Figure 2.13 Relationship between Control Elements, Role References, Security Roles, Users, and User Groups for Programmatic Role References

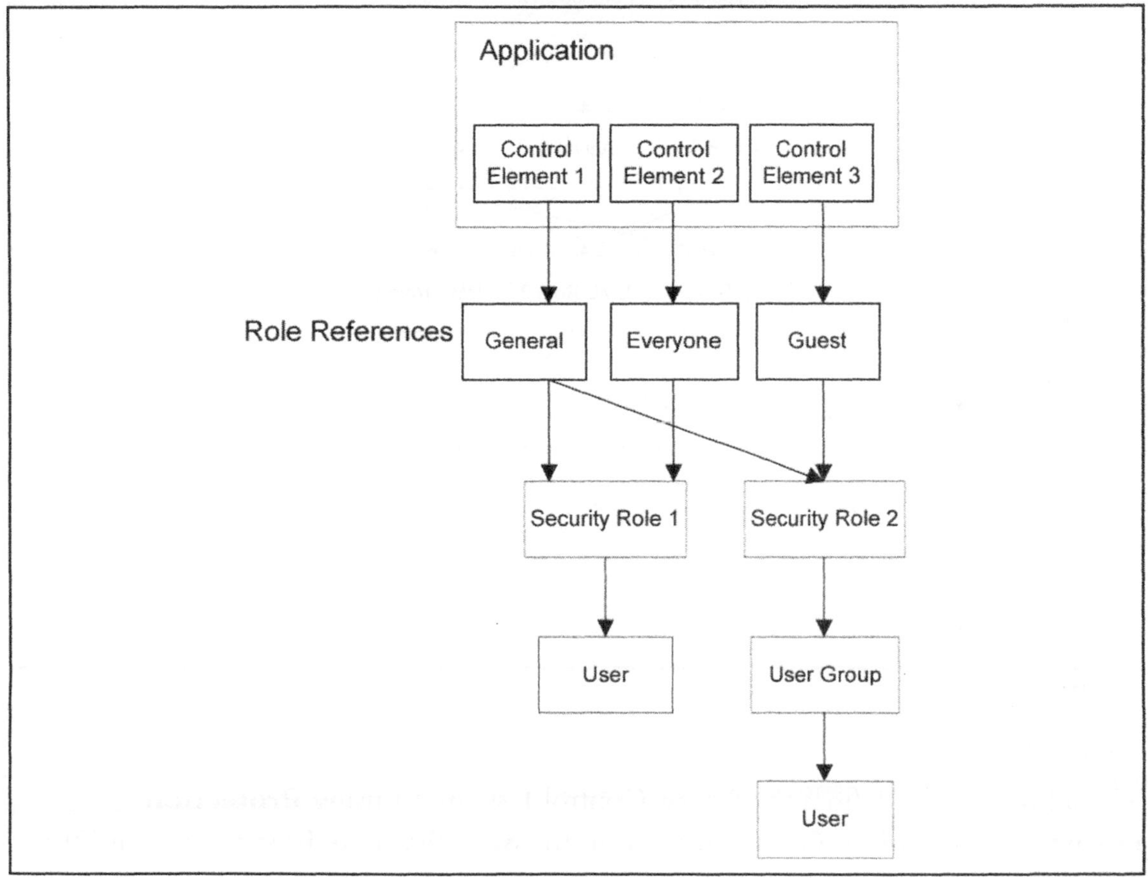

UME Roles (or Permissions)

With this approach, you can define fine-grained permissions and perform more complex and flexible authorization checks. The complexity of these permissions is simplified by assigning the permissions to fewer actions.

The developer defines the permissions or uses predefined permissions in the Java application, and groups the relevant permissions together into an action by defining it in an XML file (*actions.xml*). The administrator then assigns the actions to roles using the UME administration console (permissions are not visible in the administration console) and assign roles to users (see Figure 2.14).

Figure 2.14 Relationship between Permissions, Actions, UME Roles, Users, and User Groups for UME Permissions

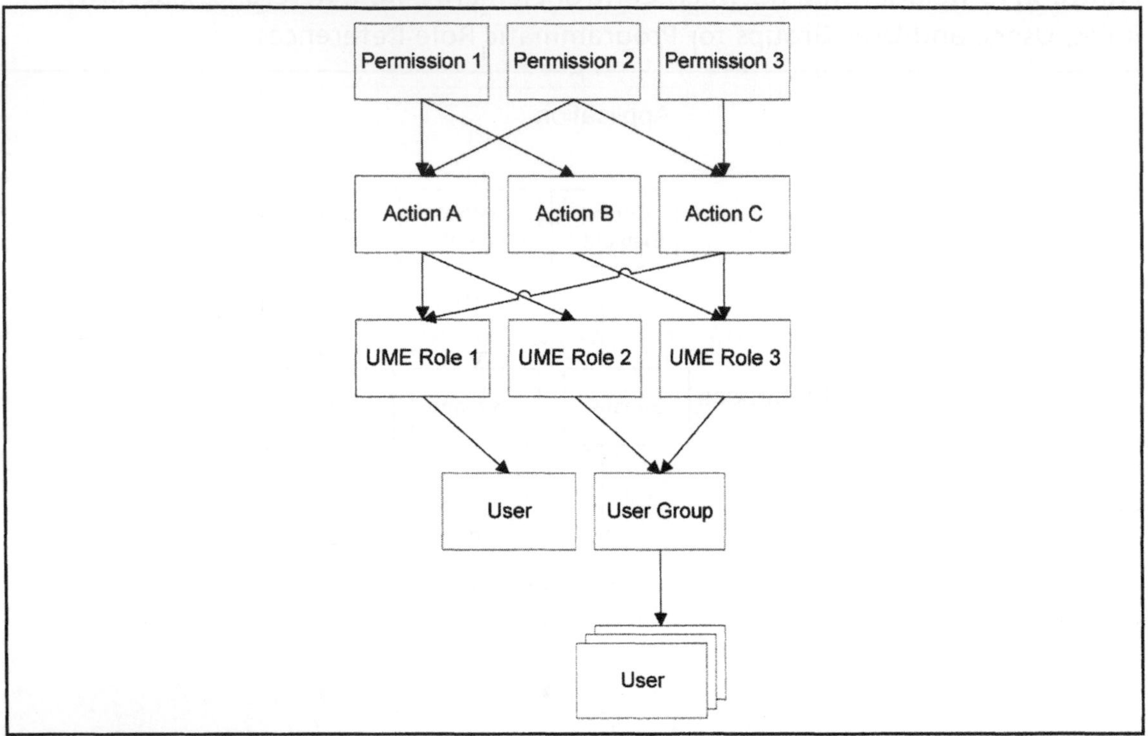

Access Control List

The administrator defines the Access Control List (ACL) using **Protection Domains and Policy Configuration** in the **Security Provider** service on J2EE Engine and assigns the authorizations for accessing resources to the relevant roles. The developer defines the J2EE security role using the corresponding API. The administrator then uses the Security Roles tab page in the Visual Administrator to map users to the role based upon their job functions.

Only users that are mapped to at least one of these roles can access the resource. Otherwise, you can define UME access control lists, which is where the ACL maps the authorizations to users and user groups rather than roles. With this method, however, the access control can only be administered in the application context.

Portal Permissions

Portal Permissions define portal user access rights to portal objects within the PCD and the permissions are based on the ACL. Permissions are set on portal objects such as Portal Catalog folders, iViews, pages, layouts, roles, worksets, packages, and systems. All portal objects can be assigned directly to a portal role. A role is a folder hierarchy consolidating other portal objects. The content of a role is based on the company structure and information requirements of the portal users. The role structure defines the navigation structure of the portal for the end user. Worksets are generic and reuseable structures containing user-specific tasks and activities. Worksets must be assigned to a role and not directly to users. The relationship between roles, worksets, iViews, and pages is illustrated in Figure 2.15.

When a portal user tries to access a portal tool that displays a particular portal object in the PCD, the objects are filtered corresponding to the user's portal permissions. If the user is permitted to access the portal object, the permission level set for the user determines the actions and operations that the user can perform on that object as well as what objects the user can access in the runtime Portal environment. You can use the Permission Editor to assign object permissions.

Use the *less is more approach* when assigning permissions to users, making sure that you provide users with the minimum set of permissions that he or she requires to fulfill his or her tasks.

Figure 2.15 Relationship between iViews, Pages, Worksets, Roles, and Users for Portal Permissions

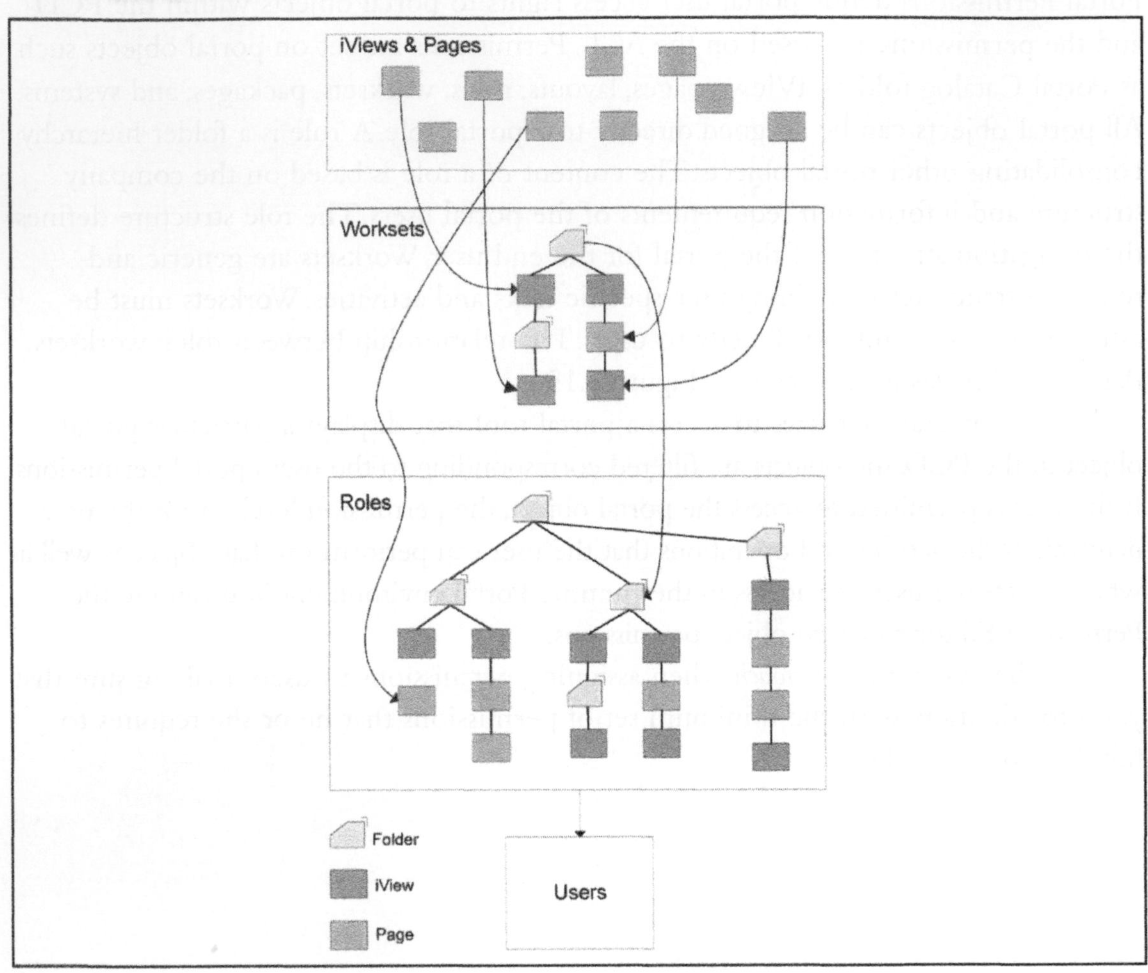

Security Zones

Security Zones control which portal component and portal services users can access using the descriptor file (*portalapp.xml*). A security zone specifies the Vendor ID, security area, and safety level. You can control the access to the portal components and services by assigning portal users permissions to the hierarchical structure of the Vendor ID, security area, and safety levels in the Portal's security zone. You can also control access to the portal component by either a direct URL or through a role-assigned iView, based on the portal component.

Generally, the portal components are accessed via iViews. This is where a user launches an iView at runtime, and the Portal Runtime (PRT) checks if the user has adequate permission to the role object containing the iView. If the user is authorized, he or she can view the iView's content. You have the option to use Security Zone for iViews and activate a second level of security check by setting a Java Virtual Machine parameter (*-Dcom.sap.nw.sz = true*) using the J2EE Config Tool. In some circumstances, the portal components are accessed by a direct URL.

UME Actions

UME action is a collection of Java permissions that define which activities a user can perform, specifically for UME iViews and functions. UME actions can be assigned to UME roles or portal roles, and the roles can be assigned to the user. UME Actions, such as *UME.AclSuperUser* and *UME.Manage_Roles*, have super administrative permissions and both actions should be restricted to administrators only.

Authorization Groups

Users can be grouped together into user groups for ease of user administration. J2EE user groups are created in the Security Provider service **Policy Configurations | Security Roles | User Mappings** tab in the Visual Administrator. UME user groups are created in *Group Management* in the UME administration console.

User Management

User Management is a core function to the business. For many organizations, it is not uncommon for new access request forms to take up to two weeks to fulfill as it involves complex coordination and integration with human resources, waiting for the appropriate business approvals, and the actual provisioning of access. This complicated process can leave new employees unproductive for days or weeks waiting for their access and can become a provisioning problem for the organization.

Effective user management should streamline the process for adjusting access rights when users get promoted or leave the organization. By shortening the time and complexity of user provisioning, it can help reduce the number of help desk calls, increase employee productivity, and frequently is a source of cost savings.

As users have access to more applications and having to remember more access credentials than ever before, organizations have to contend with the increasing workload of managing these access credentials across different environments. A risk is involved with managing multiple identities for users and this demands tighter access control.

Integrating user management can help tackle many user management problems such as data redundancies, complex administration process, and slow provisioning response. In return, offer some relief in the form of higher quality service delivery, lower cost, and increased speed.

For example, if an employee quit, then theoretically all access to systems should be revoked; however, there is an element of risk where an administrator may have missed revoking the user's access to the SAP Enterprise Portal system, in which case the user may still be able to access the system. The simplest way to mitigate this risk is to integrate user management and use a centralized user store that other systems must synchronize with. This way, the user's access is deactivated in one system and triggered in all other necessary systems.

It is very important to implement a proper design early on in the project, as it can make or break any User Management deployments.

Integrating User Management

Integration of User Management is the consolidation of user and authorization data across multiple systems into a centralized user store. All user management data is maintained centrally in one system.

This can not only help to make user administration easier, but also reduce data redundancies and management overhead, increase transparency, and improve security privacy.

When you are dealing with SAP Web AS Java systems, there are two user management options you can use depending on your system landscape:

- Lightweight Directory Access Protocol (LDAP) synchronization integrates user management data of multiple systems (SAP and non-SAP) into one system.
- SAP Web AS ABAP.

Using Lightweight Directory Access Protocol Synchronization

With Lightweight Directory Access Protocol synchronization, you can integrate user management, since several systems (SAP and non-SAP) can be synchronized with the LDAP directory service for user information. The synchronization process enables you to exchange user information to/from the LDAP directory server in your system landscape.

You can use this option for the User Management Engine (UME) of your SAP AS Java system if you want to manage user passwords in the LDAP directory, including reusing Windows authentication to log on to the Portal system.

Alternatively, you can use this configuration to access non-SAP systems that share access to the LDAP directory. The LDAP directory may or may not synchronize with other AS ABAP systems.

Using SAP Web AS ABAP

You can use this option if your AS Java system accesses user data and other services of the AS ABAP system.

Alternatively, if there are multiple ABAP-based systems in your system landscape and CUA is used, you can use either a CUA Child system or the CUA Central system as the data source.

Use the CUA Central system as the data source if all users in the CUA landscape need to access the AS Java (for example, through a Portal). In this configuration, the AS Java can have *read-write* access to the user master data records. This enables the administrator to use the UME to manage user data.

Use a CUA Child system as the data source if only some of the users need to access the AS Java (for example, through usage type Process Integration of SAP NetWeaver Exchange Infrastructure). In this configuration the AS Java should be restricted to *read-only* access for user master records.

User Administration

The two tools you can use for user administration in the SAP J2EE Engine are Visual Administrator and UME administration console. The one to use depends on the user store and data source you implement for user management:

- For UME with ABAP: Use SAP Web AS ABAP transaction SU01 for user management, making sure the user IDs are the same in the UME user store and AS ABAP system.
- For UME with LDAP: Use UME User Management or Visual Administrator.
- For UME with database: Use UME User Management or Visual Administrator.
- For DBMS user store: Use Visual Administrator.

Some user administration functions for the Visual Administrator and UME administration console include the following:

- Create, edit, delete, lock, and search user ID.
- Set, change, and generate password and password rules.

- Assign one or more roles to the user.
- Create, manage, and delete user groups and members.
- Maintain other user settings such as email address and assign public-key certificate, etc.

Role Administration

For *Role Administration* in the SAP J2EE Engine, you can use the Visual Administrator and UME administration console; the one to use depends on the user store and data source you implement for user management:

- For UME with ABAP: Use UME User Management or Visual Administrator.
- For UME with LDAP: Use UME User Management or Visual Administrator.
- For UME with database: Use UME User Management or Visual Administrator.
- For DBMS user store: Use Visual Administrator.

The role administration functions are protected so that only the administrator's role has access to the role administration functions. For the access paths:

- In Visual Administrator, use the Security Provider Service and choose the **Runtime | Policy Configurations | Security Roles** tab.
- In the UME administration console, choose **Role Management**.

Integrating User and Role Administration

In complex system environments with SAP NetWeaver Portal and ABAP-based systems, user and authorization data across multiple systems needs to be consolidated into a centralized user store (that is, Integrating User Management). It can become very complicated and time-consuming to manage creation and modification of roles as well as user assignments. For these reasons, you should select one system as the leading system for managing your roles and user assignments.

If you select AS ABAP system as the leading system then you have to add Portal to the AS ABAP system landscape. This is called the *ABAP-Centered Role Administration* as the roles are maintained in the AS ABAP systems. The established

ABAP authorization concept can form the basis for any new Portal roles created in the AS ABAP systems, which must be manually uploaded back to the Portal system.

On the other hand, if you select Portal system as the leading system then you have to add the AS ABAP systems to an existing Portal system landscape. This is called the *Portal-Centered Role Administration* as the roles are maintained in the Portal system. Existing Portal roles can form the basis for any new ABAP roles, which must be manually redistributed back to the ABAP system.

Additionally, if you want to use transaction **SU01** and other ABAP user management tools for role assignment, then you can assign ABAP roles directly and Portal roles indirectly. This is called *ABAP-Centered Role Assignment*. Since there is no direct relationship between the ABAP roles and Portal roles, your authorization concept must keep track of the Portal role mappings to ABAP roles.

If you want to use Portal user management tools for role assignment, then you can assign Portal roles directly and ABAP roles indirectly. This is called *Portal-Centered Role Assignment*. Any updated role assignments must be redistributed manually to the ABAP systems.

Securing Transport Layer for SAP J2EE Engine

It is important to protect the network infrastructure from a data integrity and privacy protection standpoint as it supports the necessary communication for your business. SAP J2EE Engine uses various protocols to protect the communication with its communication partners. Hence, the mechanism used for the Transport layer security and encryption depends on the protocols used (see Figure 2.16).

- For Internet protocols, such as HTTP, RMI, P4, you can use the SSL mechanism to provide the protection.
- For Directory access protocols, such as LDAP, you can also use SSL.
- For RFC protocol, you can use SNC with the Java Connector.
- For ODBC protocol, the security mechanism depends on the driver.
- For Telnet protocol, the security mechanism is Virtual Private Network.

Figure 2.16 Transport Layer Security for SAP Web AS Java Systems

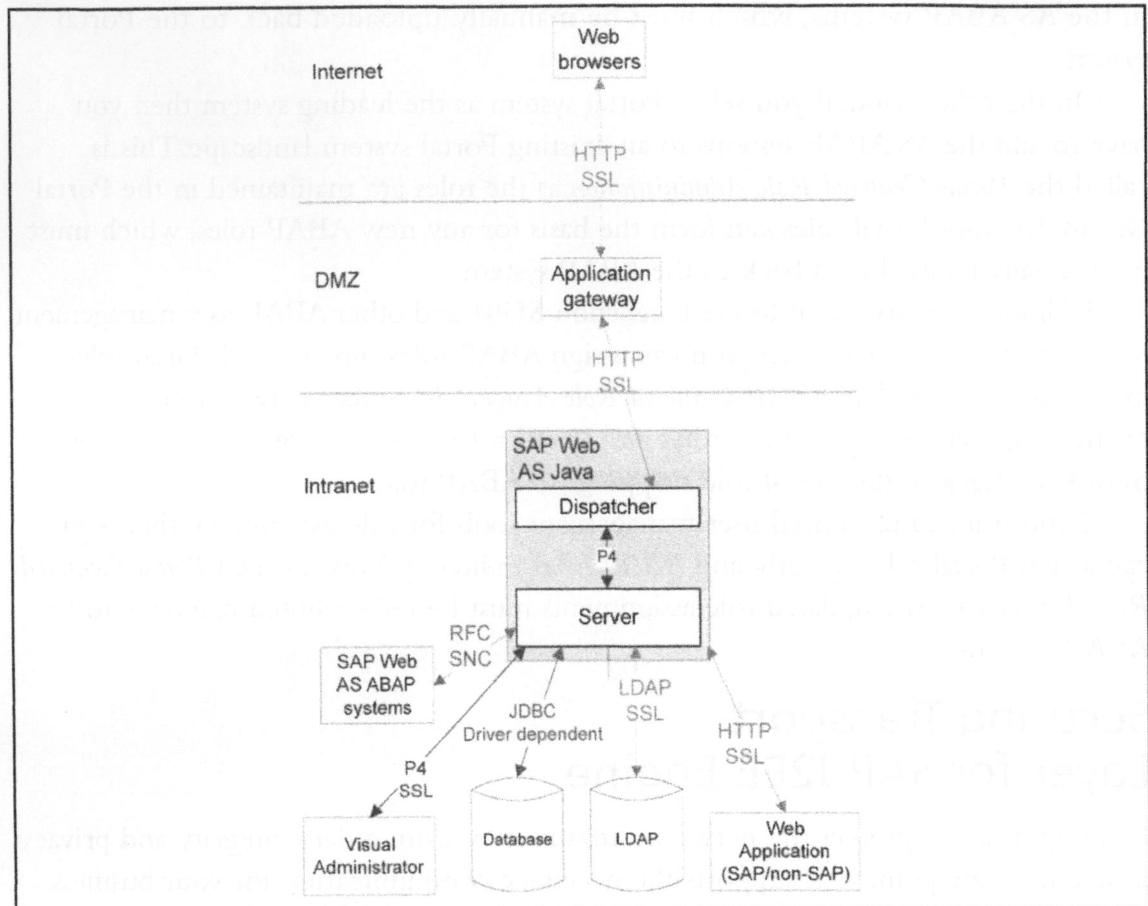

A secured network topology can prevent security threats such as computer viruses, denial-of-service attacks, eavesdropping, and theft of enterprise information. It is highly recommended to use a demilitarized zone (DMZ) to establish network infrastructure. DMZ adds an additional layer of security to an organization's local area network (LAN) because an external attacker only has access to the equipment in the DMZ rather than the entire organizational network.

Some systems (for example, Enterprise Portal) require a medium level of security or higher. To achieve this level of network security, a *multiple network zone* is required (see Figure 2.17). In this network architecture, the backend systems (for example, SAP ABAP-based systems, and corporate directory servers) are placed in the high security area (that is, Intranet). The Portal server, SAP Web AS for Internet services (for example, for Web Dynpro applications, Business Server Pages, Java Server Pages), and other Web services are placed in the inner DMZ. Application gateways and other intermediary devices (for example, SAP Web Dispatcher) are placed in the outer DMZ. For additional security measures, you can protect each zone with additional firewalls.

Figure 2.17 Using Multiple Network Zones

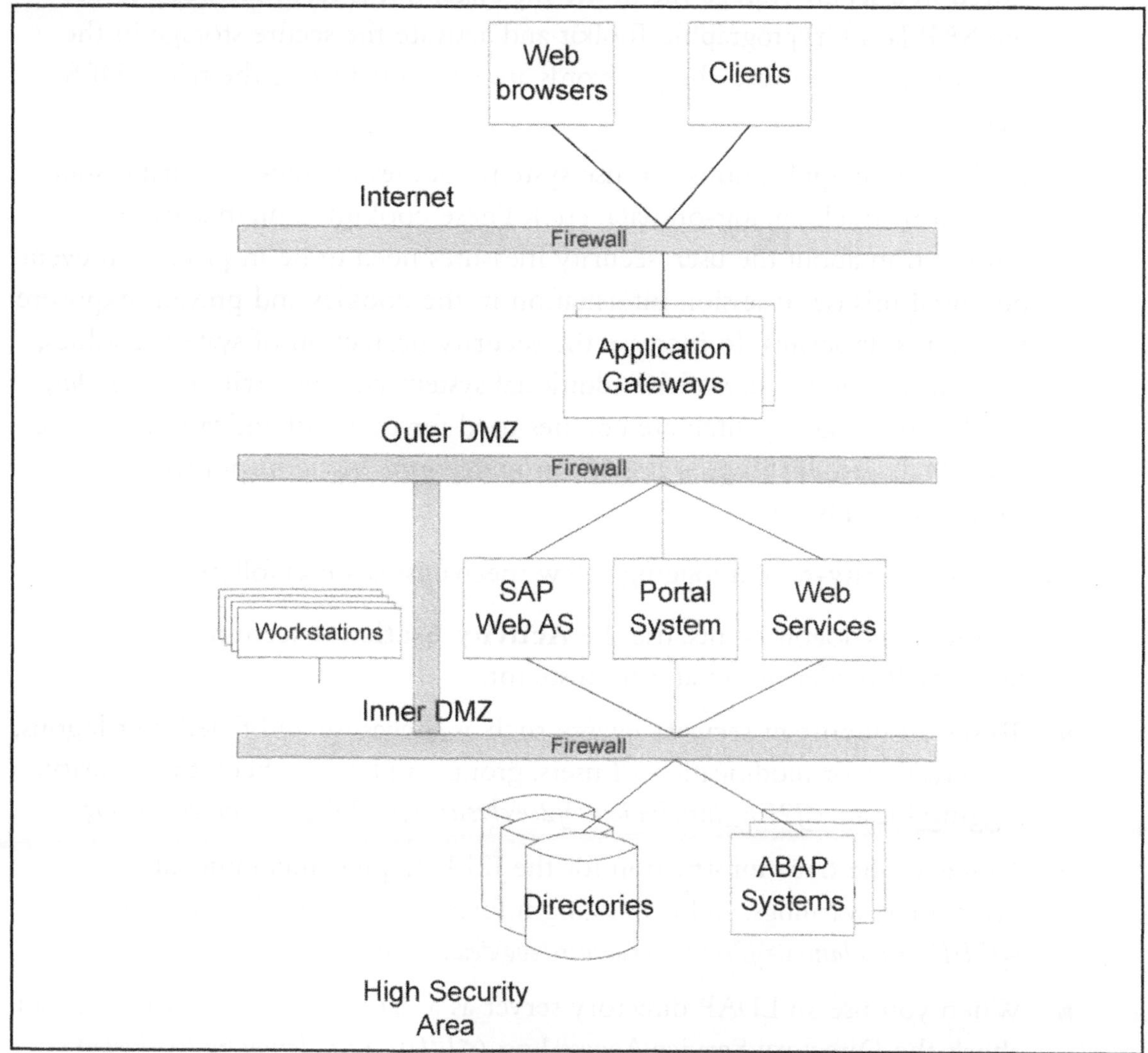

Enforcing Security Policies

It is imperative that you have a framework of security policies under which the maintenance and administration of security is conducted within your SAP environment. A well-defined security policy with a defined set of protocols can support the organization in mitigating any potential security risks and ensures that there is a consistent approach for all relevant parties. Here is a list of suggested security policies:

- For securing administrator passwords store in the file system (for example, for Software Deployment Manager SDM), the user ID and password are stored in a secure storage file in the file system. It is recommended to use the SAP Java Cryptographic Toolkit and activate the secure storage in the file system. In this case, the passwords are encrypted using the triple-DES algorithm.
- J2EE Engine applications can use system cookies to track user data (such as sessions tracking, log-on data, etc.). These cookies contain sensitive information about the user; security measures need to be in place to prevent potential misuse of session information in the cookies and prevent exposure to client side scripts. To increase the security protection of system cookies, you can enable the use of the additional system cookie attribute *HttpOnly*. For log-on tickets (which are cookies used for user authentication), set the User Management Engine (UME) property ume.logon.httponlycookie to the value TRUE.

In terms of security-related logging, a few mechanisms are as follows:

- To see users' logon events, use the **Activity Statistics** section of the Security Provider in Visual Administrator.
- To see all important security events, such as successful and failed user logons, and creation or modification of users, groups, and roles, check the security logging file in *<J2EE_installation>\j2ee\cluster\serverX\log\system\security.log.*
- To see all the trace information for the J2EE Engine, including all the exceptions, warnings, and debugging information, check the trace file in *<J2EE_installation>\j2ee\cluster\server0\log\defaultTrace.trc.*
- When you use an LDAP directory server as a data source for UME, you can check the Directory Service Access Log *(<J2EE_installation>\j2ee\cluster\server<n>\sap.access.audit*) and Directory Service Connection Pool Log *(<J2EE_installation>\j2ee\cluster\server<n>\sapum_cpmon_<hostname>_<port>_<object_ID>.log*) for monitoring and troubleshooting the connections.
- To disable any optional services on SAP J2EE Engine, check SAP Note 781882.

GRC

Governance, Risk, and Compliance (GRC) is a phase commonly used by corporate customers, software vendors, consultants, and analysts. Like many industry terms floating around, GRC can mean different things to different people. Some analysts apply the term GRC as workflow tools to track compliance with the Sarbanes-Oxley law, while others use GRC to refer to products for monitoring and logging of IT system activities. GRC is a complicated concept because it covers a broad scope.

Governance is the process of setting policy for an organization. *Compliance* is the process of adhering to those policies. *Risk Management* is the process of addressing uncertainty and making decisions to balance risk and opportunity based on the organization's mission and tolerance for risk.

Each element of GRC is important and tightly related. Governing, managing risk, and responding to compliance obligations are ongoing and critical organizational tasks. The real value in addressing governance, risk and compliance together is in bringing various disparate functions within an organization to identify business risks, implement appropriate controls to mitigate those risks, and improve the business processes efficiently and effectively.

There are many different approaches for a GRC program within an organization. Most of the time, these can overlap. Some of the more common initiatives include the following:

- Risk Management
- IT Security
- Business Controls and Operations
- Finance and Audit

The determining factor for the approach an organization chooses to take depends on the business driver. For example, the decision may be driven by a combination of regulatory requirements, the desire to gain the competitive edge by providing better privacy protections for customers, the desire to reduce public relations risk, or the need for business controls to be better monitored, controlled, and audited to improve the bottom line.

SAP GRC is an application that provides an integrated approach to identifying efficient and effective controls and compliance for business processes and cross-enterprise systems, reducing the cost of compliance by automating and streamlining controls.

It analyzes the enterprise-wide risk management process in accordance with legal requirements and is recommended by best practice management frameworks. There are three main areas to the SAP GRC solution:

- Access Control
- Process Control
- Risk Management

As organizations need to manage multiple user identities across different systems, it becomes an arduously manual task to find out who has access to what data and to what systems; this can be a risk for the organization as it cannot truly protect enterprise information asset without having clear visibility. SAP Access Control can mitigate this risk, it enables compliant user provisioning to one or more systems to ensure any changes (for example, creation of user accounts, role changes for employee promotions and when employee leaves the organization) that occur in the environment are compliant and controlled automatically by the embedded preventive controls to stop Segregation of Duties (SoD) violations.

This can be particularly useful for organizations where there may be up to10 staff in the whole IT department to support the user provisioning process. In this case, it can commonly take up to 2 weeks to fully provision new users into their systems. SAP Access Control also performs automatic user access reviews. This proactive audit process ensures user access stays compliant all the time. If the SAP Access Control is integrated with SAP Identity Management (IdM), then the solution is not limited only to SAP systems. It can be cross-platform and cross-function, with access control as the integration point for IdM solutions specifically in the risk management, process control, and IT governance areas.

Internal control is quite commonly managed and documented using spreadsheets which can have some limitations. SAP Process Control provides various tracking tools and interactive reports which enable members of internal control, audit, and business process teams to effectively manage compliance activities (for example, monitor assets, assess accounting, and financial controls, promote operational efficiency, and audit accounting and financial data to prevent fraud) in an integrated approach with the SAP ERP systems.

Risk management is an organizational activity that integrates the recognition, assessment, and mitigation of risks as well as developing appropriate strategies to manage it. SAP GRC Risk Management enables an enterprise-wide risk management process (that is, planning, identification and analysis, response and monitoring) where organizations can benefit from a proactive risk management effort and streamlined reporting.

SAP GRC Access Control

SAP GRC Access Control provides a compliance foundation for access controls with intrinsic preventive controls to stop SoD violations and helps companies to comply with regulatory requirements such as Sarbanes-Oxley (SOX).

SAP GRC Access capabilities include:

- *Compliant User Provisioning* (formerly known as Access Enforcer) provides a workflow engine to automatically process user security requests. This means activities such as business approvals for user security requests and user notification of new accounts are driven by workflows. With this capability, you can better track security authorization approvals for user provisioning (for example, new user requests, role changes for employee promotion, terminations) to the environment, enforce SoD policies and ensure that there are no new SoD risks introduced without management approval.
- *Enterprise Role Management* (formerly known as Role Expert) provides a methodology for developing, documenting, and simulating the security roles before they are assigned to users with inherent risks.
- *Risk Analysis and Remediation* (formerly known as Compliance Calibrator) provides real-time compliance monitoring and controls, integrated within the ERP system. It also provides business rules for SoD risks which the management wants to monitor, analyze, and prevent in the future.
- *Superuser Privilege Management* (formerly known as Firefighter) manages the access of superusers to emergency and sensitive transactions through timely notification and tracking facilities. This means if an analyst is assigned superuser access for emergency troubleshooting purposes, all the activities performed with the superuser access are logged.

Security for SAP GRC Access Control is addressed on the presentation, application, and transport layers. All of the security aspects are based on restricting access at each level to authorized users or systems only. This should form part of your overall SAP security strategy.

- The *Presentation* level represents various forms of front-end applications (for example, SAP GUI for Windows) used to access the SAP GRC Access Control. As data is exchanged over exposed networks (for example, Internet), it introduces risks to the security of the communication to the SAP GRC Access Control system. To ensure communication is protected, users must be authenticated successfully before they are allowed into the system; this security mechanism is called user authentication.
- The *Application* level represents the application logic within the SAP GRC Access Control system. Because important and sensitive data can be accessed in the system, some risks are introduced if access control is not properly managed. To prevent unauthorized access, access control is protected based on the authorization concept and user management.
- The *Transport* level supports the necessary communication for the whole system landscape. Data that is exchanged over unsecured network is not protected; it becomes a huge risk to the data integrity, privacy protection, and other security threats. To ensure data is communicated securely, security protocols such as SNC and SSL must be used. SAP GRC Access Control uses various protocols to protect the communication with its communication partners as shown in Figure 2.18.

Security SAP GRC Access Control is based on the SAP NetWeaver. Hence, the security concepts on user authentication, user management, role administration, and role assignments are also the same as the security concepts on the security concepts for SAP NetWeaver.

For specific implementation details and procedures for SAP GRC Access Control, please refer to Chapter 5, "Governance, Risk, and Compliance."

Figure 2.18 Transport Layer Security for SAP GRC Access Control

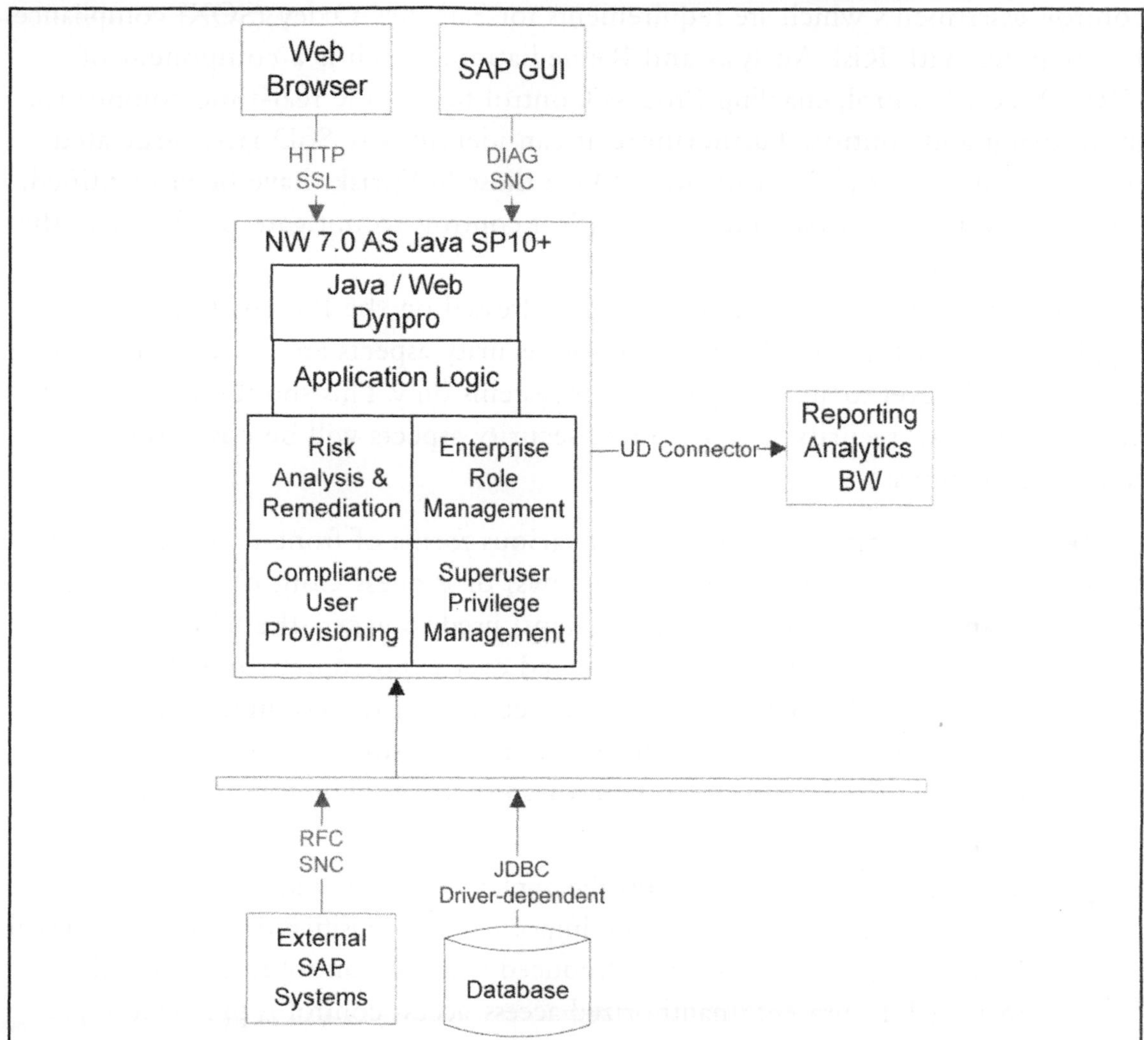

SAP GRC Process Control

SAP GRC Process Control provides various tracking tools and interactive reports which enable members of internal control, audit, and business process teams to effectively manage compliance activities. It enables organizations to document their control environment efficiently, automate test and assessment of controls, track issues to remediation, and certify and report on the state and quality of internal controls.

SAP GRC Process Control can automate time-consuming tasks, such as controls assessments which are requirements for Sarbanes-Oxley (SOX) compliance. It integrates with Risk Analysis and Remediation, which is a component of GRC Access Control, enabling Process Control to provide real-time compliance monitoring and controls. Furthermore, it can identify any SoD risks associated with critical actions and permissions. Once these SoD risks have been identified, you can use Risk Analysis and Remediation controls to mitigate or eliminate the compliance risks.

Security for the SAP GRC Process is addressed on the Presentation, Application, and Transport layers; all of the security aspects are based on restricting access at each level to authorized users or systems only. This should form part of your overall SAP security strategy. Some security aspects will be covered in the following sections:

- The *Presentation* level represents various forms of front-end applications (for example, SAP GUI for Windows) or Process Control clients (for example, NetWeaver Business Client) used to access the SAP GRC Process Control. As data is exchanged over exposed networks (for example, Internet), it introduces risks to the security of the communication to the SAP GRC Process Control system. To ensure communication is protected, users must be authenticated successfully before they are allowed into the system.
- The *Application* level represents the application logic within the SAP GRC Process Control system. Because important and sensitive data can be accessed in the system, some risks are introduced if access control is not properly managed. To prevent unauthorized access, access control is protected based on the Process Control Security Model.
- The *Transport* level supports the necessary communication for the whole system landscape. Data that is exchanged over unsecured network is not protected; it becomes a huge risk to the data integrity, privacy protection, and other security threats. To ensure data is communicated securely, security protocols such as SNC and SSL can be used. SAP GRC Process Control uses various protocols to protect the communication with its communication partners as shown in Figure 2.19.

Figure 2.19 Securing Transport Layer for SAP GRC Process Control

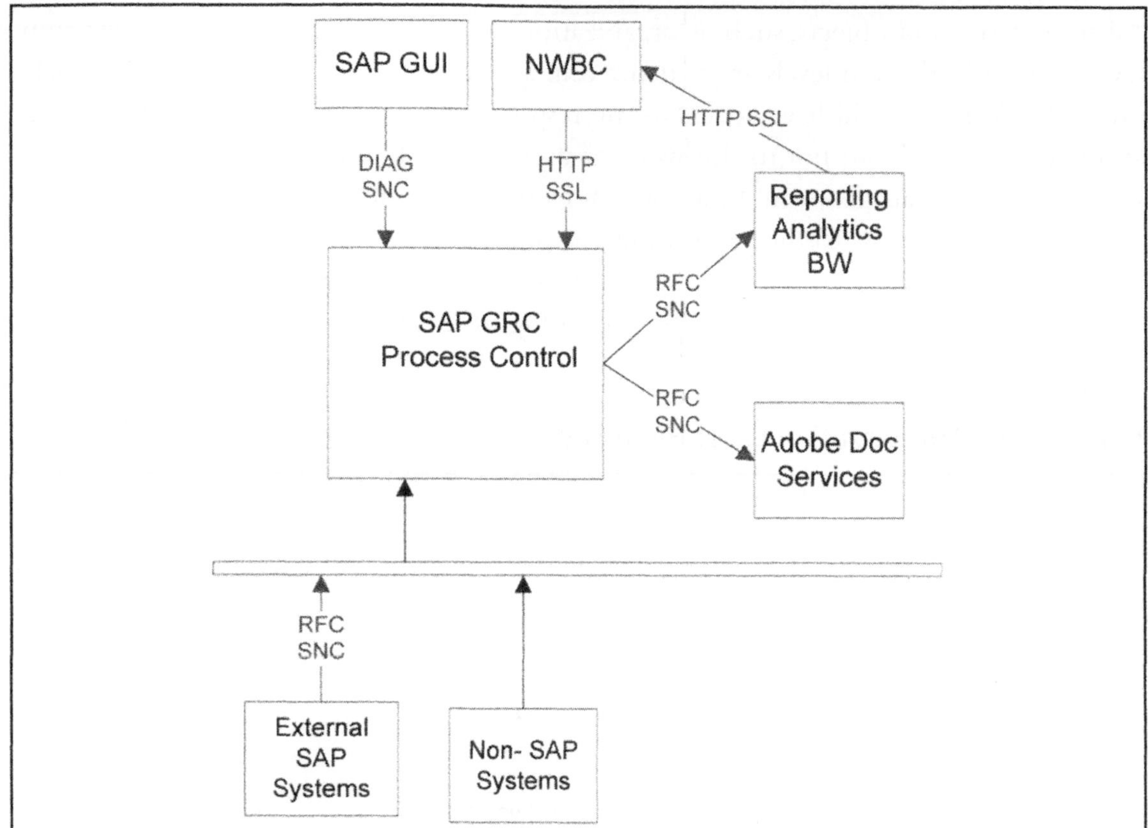

Authorization Concept

The Process Control security model is based on the job roles and organizational hierarchies within an organization. Within the hierarchy, you may have access the work of subordinate colleagues but not the work of senior colleagues. If there are multiple organizations or business units, your access is restricted so that you would only have access to your own organization and not another organization. Implementation of Process Control security requires backend authorizations, master data, and Process Control authorizations.

Process Control authorization is based on job roles and the organizational hierarchy, with the authorization levels structured in a similar way to an organization hierarchy that consists of *roles*, *tasks*, and *objects*. It is the combination of the authorization levels of the roles, tasks, and objects within Process Control that determines a user's access.

Authorization Level

All roles, tasks, and objects, such as organizations and processes, have an authorization level. The authorization levels are structured in a hierarchy similar to an organizational hierarchy. A user would have access to the responsibilities of users with a subordinate authorization level, but not to the work of users with a higher authorization level. For example, a manager would have access to the responsibilities of a supervisor, but would not have access to the responsibilities of a director.

The authorization level hierarchy is in order of highest authorization level (Corporate) to lowest (Control) as shown in Figure 2.20.

Figure 2.20 Authorization Level Hierarchy

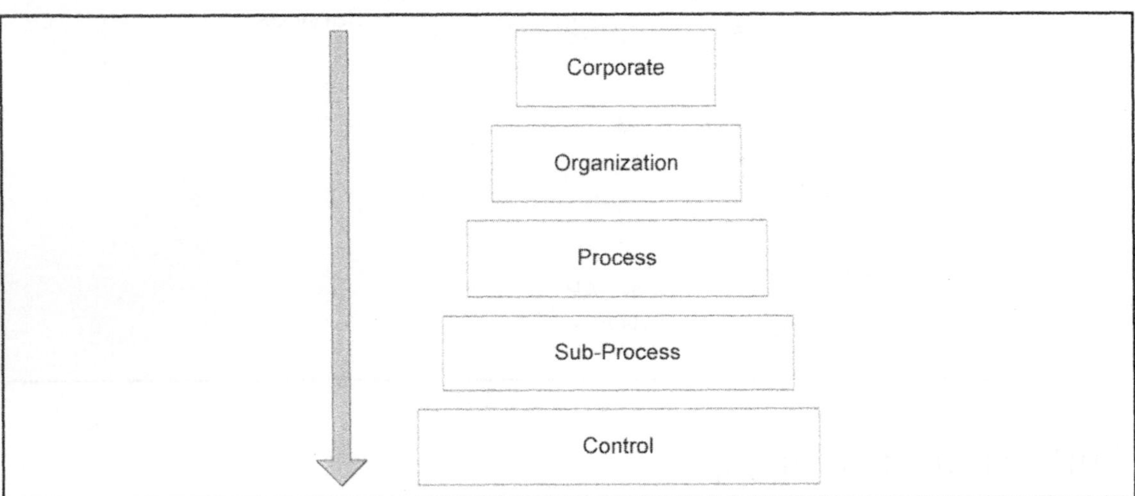

Task

Tasks enable users to perform an action (for example, edit, view, assign, or approve). Process Control tasks are predefined and most can be assigned to one or more roles. You can control what a role can access by assigning specific tasks (for example, perform control design assessment, review manual test of control effectiveness). These tasks enable the workflows within Process Control.

Each task must have the following attributes:

- *Role-Task authorization level compatibility* to ensure the authorization level of a task is at the *same or lower* authorization level than the authorization level of the role to which it is assigned. For example, a task at the Process authorization level may be assigned to a role with an authorization level of Process or Sub-process. This restriction is called a *minimum-role level*.

- *Relationship Type:* In a one-to-one relationship type, only one person receives the task relative to a given object. Process Control provides this function by limiting the assignment of certain tasks to one role within an organization. This relationship is called *role unique*. If the task assignment violates this restriction, an error message displays: *Task is already assigned to role*. Further assignment is not permitted. In a one-to-many relationship type, a task may be assigned to one or more roles.

Roles

Roles are a grouping of tasks which can be assigned to many users. By assigning users with similar responsibilities to the same role, you ensure that they perform the same tasks and have similar authorizations.

When assigning tasks to a role, you must make sure the role authorization level is the *same or greater* than the task authorization level. For example, a role with a Process authorization level may be assigned tasks with an authorization level of Process or lower, but not higher, and be assigned to an object at the same level or lower level.

Objects

Objects are assigned to roles and use the same authorization levels as tasks and roles (that is, corporate, organization, process, sub-process, control) to set up organization and process hierarchies. When assigning a role to an object, the object authorization level must be the *same or higher* than the role authorization level. It is important to note that this object authorization level determines the level of data access within an organization and process hierarchy for SAP Process Control; and it is a different concept than the authorization object for SAP Web AS ABAP systems.

To illustrate this principle, let's use an example to compare two roles with different organizational level as shown in Table 2.2. The Internal Corporate Control Manager is a corporate-level role so it can view all organizations within the corporation, as well as create or modify the organization hierarchy. The Organization Owner is an organization-level role, it can only view the assigned organization hierarchy and it is not allowed to create or modify the organizational hierarchy.

Table 2.2 An Example of Object Authorization

Role	Role Authorization	Task	Task HierarchyObject
Internal CorporateControl Manager	Edit Hierarchy	Corporate Functions	Corporate Data Level access
Organization Owner	Display Hierarchy	Organization Functions	Organization Data Level access

SAP GRC Risk Management

SAP GRC Risk Management manages the enterprise-wide process of risk planning, risk identification and analysis, risk response, and risk monitoring based on legal requirements as well as best practice management framework recommendations.

The process covered by GRC Risk Management includes the following steps:

- *Risk Planning* determines the risk management approach in each business area or project. This includes setting up the risk management organization and defining risk threshold values.
- *Risk Identification and Analysis* identifies risks for further analysis and prioritizes them based on the tolerance for risk with different attributes, such as probability of occurrence and potential loss associated to the risk.
- *Risk Response* is the action needed for responding to a risk. One action may be to actively mitigate the risk to reduce probability of occurrence and/or potential impact.
- *Risk Monitoring* includes regular updates of risk information and reporting to monitor the progress along the risk management process.

With the above processes, you can proactively assess and monitor risks, provide streamline reporting, and set the appropriate responses to mitigate the risks.

SAP GRC Risk Management is an add-on component based on SAP NetWeaver 7.0 SP10. Hence, the security concepts are also based on the same security concepts as AS ABAP and AS Java systems. As GRC Risk Management functionalities are accessed using WebDynpro Java Technology, authentication and authorization concepts are based on the same concepts as SAP Enterprise Portal and SAP Web Application Server.

For specific implementation details and procedures for SAP GRC Risk Management, please refer to Chapter 5, "Governance, Risk, and Compliance."

Backend: UNIX/Oracle

Operating system and database, the backend systems, are mandatory components of an SAP system. SAP system simply will not run without either of those components. Security measures must also take place at the operating system and database levels to ensure integrity and protection of the data. Security attacks, such as viruses, worms, or other malwares, can affect the operating system and database if the systems are not regularly checked for the latest security patches. Any vulnerability in the backend systems should also be addressed; this adds another aspect to the SAP Security concept.

In the next sections, various SAP-specific security concepts for UNIX and Oracle are covered.

Security for UNIX

Many SAP implementations run on UNIX. The UNIX platform is a robust and versatile operating system that allows people to do many different things. If a UNIX system is not properly secured, then it can potentially become a serious risk to the organization, especially when the security is breached. For example, a person who should not have access on the UNIX system accidentally deletes an important database file from the productive live environment resulting in downtime. If this occurs, the production system downtime can cost the business in lost revenue, reduced employee productivity, and even regulatory penalties.

With these serious implications in mind, it is very important to ensure proper security measures are in place on the UNIX systems.

These security measures should include installing the latest security-related patches, protecting operating system files and resources, restricting operating system access, protecting network access, and restricting physical server access.

Installing Latest Security-Related Patches

You can eliminate well-known security-related vulnerabilities (for example, viruses, other malware, or software bugs within the applications) by simply patching your operating systems with the latest operating system vendor software and firmware patches. It is recommended that you keep up-to-date with latest security-related patches that are released by your operating system vendor.

Restricting Operating System Access

Access to the UNIX system should be restricted to administrators only. More specifically, you must protect the administrative user IDs such as root, <sid>adm and ora<dbsid> as shown in Table 2.3 and limit the number of operating system users on the UNIX system.

Table 2.3 UNIX Administrator User ID

User ID	Primary Group	Additional Groups	Comment
root	root	root	Root user
<sapsid> adm	sapsys	oper, dba, sapinst	SAP system administrator
ora<dbsid>	dba	oper, sapinst	Database administrator

Note:<sapsid> is the SAP System ID and <dbsid> is the Oracle Instance ID).

For security monitoring and audit purposes, logging should be activated so that you can track user activities and prevent any potential misuse of access. For further information regarding logging, see the documentation provided by your operating system vendor.

Protecting Operating System Files

In UNIX, there are a large number of files used for administrative purposes. Without getting too elaborate with the technical details, there are two parts to protecting a UNIX file: what is set in the permission structure and what is set for the Set User ID/Set Group ID (SUID/SGID) property. Each file has the SUID/SGID property for setting permissions so that owners with SUID and groups with SGID can access that file. The permission structure provides a specific on-off switch for controlling read (r)/write (w)/execute (x) access to the file for the owner, others in the group, and all other users (or world). Alternatively, the permission can also be represent in binary, in which case -rwxr-x—x can also be represented as 751. The first "-" means that this is a file and not a directory. A program is denoted by a file which can be executed.

When you create a new file, the permissions are determined by User File Creation Mode Mask (UMASK) definitions. An UMASK is a four-digit octal number that specifies the default access rights for newly created files and directories, where the value of the digit indicates which access privileges should be *removed* (that is,. Set 0 to remove none, set 2 to remove write, and set 7 to remove all). For example, you can set the UMASK to 0027 for user ID <sid>adm which is a common setting for SAP systems; the permissions are defaulted to 750 for all new files created by <sid>adm.

Password files should be protected by using a dictionary-attack program. You can also use a shadow password file to allow only the *root* user to access the password information.

To prevent any files or directories from any unauthorized changes, the SAP system is stored in a special directory structure within UNIX as shown in Figure 2.21. The files and directories in this directory structure are protected with defined access authorizations as shown in Table 2.4.

Figure 2.21 SAP System Directory Structure for UNIX

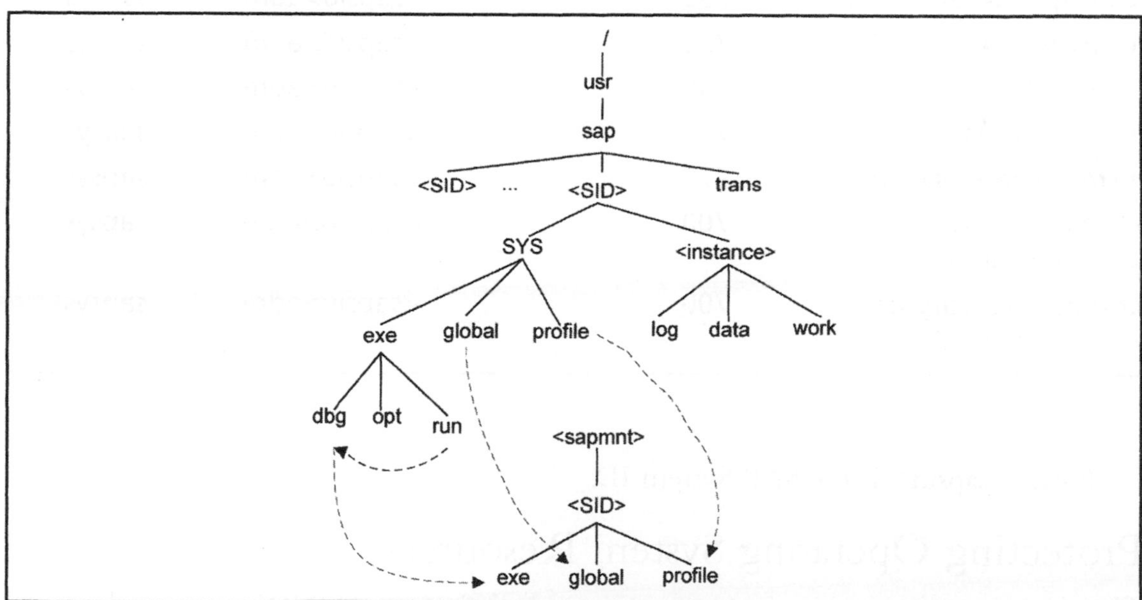

Table 2.4 Permissions for SAP Directories and Files

SAP Directory or Files	Access Privilege in Octal Form	Owner	Group
/sapmnt/<SAPSID>/exe	775	<sapsid>adm	sapsys
/sapmnt/<SAPSID> /exe/saposcol	4755	root	sapsys
/sapmnt/<SAPSID> /global	700	<sapsid>adm	sapsys
/sapmnt/<SAPSID> /profile	755		
/usr/sap/<SAPSID>	751		
/usr/sap/<SAPSID> /<Instance ID>	755		
/usr/sap/<SAPSID> /<Instance ID>/*	750	<sapsid>adm	sapsys
/usr/sap/<SAPSID>/ <Instance ID>/sec	700	<sapsid>adm	sapsys
/usr/sap/<SAPSID>/SYS	755	<sapsid>adm	sapsys
/usr/sap/<SAPSID>/SYS/*	755	<sapsid>adm	sapsys
/usr/sap/trans	755	<sapsid>adm	sapsys
/usr/sap/trans/*	770	<sapsid>adm	sapsys
/usr/sap/trans/.sapconf	775	<sapsid>adm	sapsys
<home directory of <sapsid>adm>	700	<sapsid>adm	sapsys
<home directory of <sapsid>adm>/*	700	<sapsid>adm	sapsys

Note: <sapsid> is the SAP System ID.

Protecting Operating System Resources

There are many operating system resources which run on a UNIX server; only some are actually required to run a SAP system. Some of these operating system resources are network-related as the service allows access to the server and appropriate security measures should be taken when using these services. To prevent network vulnerabilities from denial-of-service attacks, you must disable any unused or unnecessary operating system services (for example, echo, daytime, chargen, time, ftp) by editing in the */etc/inetd.conf* file. And make sure to close both the UDP and TCP ports for each service that is being disabled; disabling only one type of port without the other does not make the operating system more secure.

For any operating system services that you do use, you should protect these services with appropriate permission settings and limit their use to only within a secured local area network (LAN). Use monitoring tools to track user activities and detect any potential attacks on the services. Refer to your operating system vendor for information regarding scripts and directions for hardening of your systems.

Some network and access services which are commonly used in SAP systems include:

- Services *rlogin* and *remsh/rsh* permit remote access to UNIX machines. When a user logs on to the system, the files */etc/host.equiv* and *$HOME/.rhosts* are checked, and the user can log on without a password if either of these files contain the hostname or IP address of the connection originator or a wildcard character (+). You should never allow a non-root user to run commands *rsh* or *rlogin* to root as this can impose a high security risk, especially when an unauthorized user can potentially obtain root administrator access to any systems. Unless you require these services for specific reasons, it is recommended that you deactivate both of these services in the *inetd.conf* file; and delete the file */etc/hosts.equiv* or make sure the file is empty.

- *Sendmail* service is a Mail Transfer Agent (MTA) for UNIX systems. Systems running this service are vulnerable to remote denial-of-service attacks as the system can be used to relay SPAM junk mail. If you need to use the *Sendmail* service, ensure that you are running either the latest version of your vendor's operating system or a version of Sendmail with anti-SPAM relay features.

- The *Network Information System (NIS)* service is used to manage user data and passwords centrally. This service enables any UNIX machine in the LAN to read password files (including shadow password files) by using the *ypcat passwd* command. This can pose a significant security risk particularly if the service is not protected properly and unauthorized users can access user data and passwords.

- Another service that should be used with precaution is the Network File System (NFS), which makes directories available across the network. This service is commonly used in the SAP system landscape to make transport and work directories remotely accessible over the network. You must not export directories with SAP data to arbitrary recipients using NFS to ensure data protection and prevent unauthorized access to the SAP data.

- X-Window service provides a standard toolkit to build graphical user interfaces (GUI) on UNIX systems. You must ensure access to the X-Window service is restricted because misuse of this service can be a security problem. For example, misuse of the *xhost* command can put your display in a WYSIWIS (What You See Is What I See) mode where others can see your display; or misuse of the *xkey* command enables others to snoop on your keystrokes, however this can be prevented by using the *Secure Keyboard* option. This service is only used during the SAP installation process and it should be disabled if not required.

Restricting Physical Server Access

Data centers or other areas where the SAP servers reside are all vulnerable security points with a driving need to control access. Many organizations spends millions of dollars on enterprise information assets housed in these servers, and still some depend on just a locked room to keep them safe. Keeping these high value items in an enclosed space increases the vulnerability to common physical threats such as theft, criminal, or accidental physical damage.

Physical access to the SAP servers should be closely monitored and controlled. Only authorized administrators should have physical access to the server, this can prevent users from being able to misuse system administration functions (for example, changing the boot settings or pressing on the reboot button). For auditing purposes, you should also activate logging to ensure all administration activities are tracked.

Protecting Network Access

Security threats, such as worms and hackers, can intercept network traffic by monitoring traffic transmitted over your network.

You can prevent unauthorized access to your SAP systems at the network level by appropriately placing firewalls and application-level gateways (for example, SAProuter, SAP Web Dispatcher). The protected firewall is placed outside the network and configured to accept only a defined set of services (for example, SAP application, client/server sources, protocols) to pass through different network zones while keeping some other services out.

Securing an Oracle Database

The database instance is a mandatory component for an SAP system. An invaluable enterprise information asset is housed in the database, and it must be properly protected against unauthorized access. Security measures must also take place at the database level to ensure integrity and protection of the data.

Some of these security measures include installing the latest Oracle security patches, protecting standard database users, protecting database files, and protecting the Oracle listener on the database.

Installing the Latest Oracle Security Patches

You can eliminate well-known security-related vulnerabilities (for example, worms, viruses, malwares, or software bugs within the applications) by patching your database with the appropriate Critical Patch Updates (CPUs). It is recommended that you check security alerts regularly and only apply the latest SAP-supported CPUs provided in SAP Service Marketplace, as this ensures that the CPU does not conflict or overwrite any previous CPUs.

Protecting Standard Database Users

To prevent unauthorized access to the Oracle database, access to the Oracle standard database must be restricted to administrator access only. Passwords for these database users must be kept in a secure location.

- SYS – Oracle dictionary owner
- System – Oracle standard DBA user
- OPS$<SAPSID>ADM – SAP User
- OPS$ORA<SID> - SAP User
- SAPR3 – SAP database structure
- SAP<SAPSID> - SAP database structure
- SAP<DBSID>DB – SAP database structure

The SAP ABAP-based system accesses the database using the OPS$ mechanism. This is a double-authentication mechanism where a person needs a key to open the front door and then gets a second key from the cupboard to open a safe. With this mechanism, the database user SAPR3 / SAP<SAPSID> is the person trying to log in to the database as user OPS$<operating_system_user> (the house key). Once logged in successfully, the database user retrieves the password from the *SAPUSER* table (the second key) and uses this password to log on to the database as database user sapr3 / sap<sapsid>. To ensure that this security mechanism is protected, you should change the password regularly for the database user sapr3 / sap<sapsid> using the *BRCONNECT* command and the operating system user <sapsid>adm using the *passwd* command.

It is highly recommended to change all standard passwords for Oracle standard database users to prevent authorized access. Standard database users that are not active should also be locked down. You should also remove any unnecessary authorizations, such as the following:

- The *CREATE DATABASE LINK* authorization should be deactivated for all database users and database roles that do not require this authorization. Users who required the *CREATE DATABASE LINK* authorization and who have received this authorization implicitly via *CONNECT* role up to now, should either be assigned this authorization directly or via their own role.
- Limit users assigned to the *PUBLIC* user group. Users who require one or several of these authorizations and who have been assigned these authorizations via the *PUBLIC* user group up to now should either be assigned this authorization directly or be assigned a role defined for this purpose.

Protecting Database-Related Files

It is important to protect access to all database-related files or directories and prevent any unauthorized changes to these files and directories. Any unauthorized or unexpected changes that may occur can have adverse and serious effects on the database (for example, unauthorized user accidentally deletes a data file; this can cause problems when the database tries to access that data file). The Oracle database is stored in a special directory structure within UNIX and the files and directories in this directory structure are protected with defined access authorizations as shown in Table 2.5.

Table 2.5 Permissions for Oracle Files and Directories in UNIX

Oracle Directoryor File	Access Privilege in Octal Form 4.x	Owner	Group
/oracle/<DBSID>/sapdata*	755	ora<dbsid>	dba
ora<dbsid>	755	ora<dbsid>	dba
/oracle/<DBSID>/sapdata*/*	755	ora<dbsid>	dba
/oracle/<DBSID>/sapdata*/*/*	640	ora<dbsid>	dba
/oracle/<DBSID>/oraarch	755	ora<dbsid>	dba
/oracle/<DBSID>/oraarch/*	640	ora<dbsid>	dba
/oracle/<DBSID>/saparch	755	ora<dbsid>	dba
/oracle/<DBSID>/sapreorg	755	ora<dbsid>	dba
/oracle/<DBSID>/sapbackup	755	ora<dbsid>	dba
/oracle/<DBSID>/dbs	755	ora<dbsid>	dba
/oracle/<DBSID>/sapcheck	755	ora<dbsid>	dba
/oracle/<DBSID>/sapstat	755	ora<dbsid>	dba
/oracle/<DBSID>/saptrace	755	ora<dbsid>	dba
/oracle/<DBSID>/saptrace/*	755	ora<dbsid>	dba
/oracle/<DBSID>/saptrace/*/*	640	ora<dbsid>	dba
/oracle/<DBSID>/origlog*	755	ora<dbsid>	dba
/oracle/<DBSID>/origlog*/*	640	ora<dbsid>	dba
/oracle/<DBSID>/mirrlog*	755	ora<dbsid>	dba
/oracle/<DBSID>/mirrlog*/*	640	ora<dbsid>	dba

Protecting the Oracle Listener

Oracle listeners can be stopped inadvertently by any operating system account, not just the Oracle administrator (that is, ora<dbsid>). Without this service running, users will not be able to connect to the database. This means even SAP system startup will fail because the startup process requires database user sapr3 / sap<sapsid> to connect to the database.

To prevent unauthorized access to the Oracle Listener, it is recommended that Oracle Listener be protected either by listener password or authenticated using the operating system.

Summary

Security for SAP needs to be addressed on the presentation, application, transport, database, and operating system levels. All of the security aspects are based on restricting access at each level to authorized users or systems only. This should form part of your overall security strategy.

We looked into the security concepts and models SAP uses to address some of the security issues faced by many organizations today.

User authentication (for example, user ID and password, client certificates, SAP log-on tickets) ensures that identities of users, programs, or systems are verified before access is permitted. Proper authentication is an essential part of security as there are many security threats such as viruses, worms, and information and identity theft are continuing to rise. Communication and data exchange within the SAP environment should be protected with Secure Network Communication and Secure Sockets Layer for data integrity and privacy protection. Switching logging and tracing tools within the SAP Web AS will enable better monitoring and visibility of any potential issues that may arise.

SAP uses the role-based identity management approach for the authorization concept. With the possibility to integrate user management data (for example, with Central User Administration or Lightweight Directory Access Protocol), user management becomes easier, with faster provisioning and significant cost savings.

You can increase content security with the use of a Virus Scan Interface. Secure Store and Forward mechanism protects data and documents using digital signatures and digital envelopes.

SAP Governance, Risk, and Compliance provides an integrated approach to identifying efficient and effective controls and compliance for business processes and cross-enterprise systems, while reducing the cost of compliance by automating and streamlining controls.

Solutions Fast Track

ABAP

- ☑ Authorization concept is role-based and user management can integrate with CUA or external directories.
- ☑ By integrating user management, you can maintain user data centrally in one system.
- ☑ DIALOG and RFC connections can be protected with Secure Network Connection; HTTP connections can be protected with Secure Sockets Layer.

J2EE

- ☑ Applications on J2EE Engine can use either Declarative authentication or Programmatic authentication.
- ☑ UME user store providers can store user data in multiple data sources (such as LDAP, databases, SAP Web AS ABAP systems, flat files); DBMS user store providers can store user data in a pre-configured internal database of the J2EE Engine.
- ☑ The two main type of roles in the J2EE Engine are the J2EE security role and UME role.

GRC

- ☑ SAP GRC Access Control has workflows for user provisioning and performs automatic user access reviews.
- ☑ SAP GRC Process Control provides tracking tools and reports to manage compliance activities.
- ☑ SAP GRC Risk Management enables proactive risk management and streamlines reporting.

Backend: UNIX/Oracle

- ☑ Keep up-to-date with latest security-related patch levels for known bugs and fixes.
- ☑ Protect all SAP and Oracle files and directories, as well as the operating system resources.
- ☑ Protect the Oracle listener with listener password or authenticate using operating system.

Frequently Asked Questions

Q: What are trusted systems?

A: Trusted systems are two systems with a relationship of trust set up between them. For instance, if you have set up a trusted relationship between system A and system B, then system A trusts system B. This means the user can log onto system A and start a transaction in system B without entering a password (using user ID from system A). In the case where a specific user ID and password is stored in the RFC destination for the trusted system, all RFC connections result in that same user ID connecting.

Q: What is Identity Management?

A: For SAP it means the management of user accounts including role or authorization assignments.

Q: How do you migrate existing users to CUA?

A: You can use the migration tool provided in transaction SCUG to migrate existing local users.

Q: Which system should I use for CUA?

A: It is recommended by SAP to use a standalone ABAP-based system (for example, Solution Manager). From a system maintenance perspective, it is easier to apply patches and perform Basic-only upgrades.

Q: Is it possible to use different authentication mechanisms, such as allowing normal users to use strong authentication such as client certificates, while system administrators use user ID/password?

A: Yes, this is possible by setting profile parameter *snc/accept_insecure_gui = U.*

Q: Single Sign-On suddenly stopped working; what could the reason for this be?

A: It may be due to an expired server certificate on the system that normally issues the SAP Log-on Tickets. Certificates for servers usually last for a year. The error message is triggered when the receiving system checks the certificate. To avoid the certificates from expiring, there's a new report that provides a warning a few months before the expiration on the validity of installed certificates.

Q: How can I integrate the user management of the portal with that of other systems?

A: The portal user management allows you to use a variety of user stores for storing and retrieving user data. It allows you to leverage existing user repositories in your system landscape rather than having to set up a new user repository. For instance, if you are using your portal in a system landscape that includes many non-SAP systems, you can use an LDAP directory and configure the portal to use the LDAP directory as its user store. On the other hand, if you are using your portal in a system landscape that consists of SAP systems only, you can set up Central User Administration (CUA) on one of the ABAP-based systems and configure your portal to use the ABAP user management as its user store.

Q: Is it possible to restrict telnet access for a specific J2EE user?

A: Yes, you can restrict telnet access for a specific J2EE user by using the Security service runtime panel under the Resources tab in Visual Administrator. Go to System | Telnet; from Users on the Server tree, you can either grant or deny access to J2EE users.

Q: Can you integrate SAP GRC Access Control with SAP IdM?

A: Yes, you can now integrate NW IDM 7.0 & GRC 5.3.

Chapter 3

ABAP

Solutions in this chapter:

- Architecture
- Design
- Tools
- Implementation

☑ Summary

☑ Solutions Fast Track

☑ Frequently Asked Questions

Introduction

In the pre-NetWeaver days, there was SAP R/3 and you logged on to the system with the SAP GUI, which created a logon session. Your authorizations were granted by assigning profiles to your user ID, which allowed you to execute transactions and access data in tables based on those authorizations. SAP executed ABAP, which is their own programming language, to perform all the functions that had been delivered in the system and configured in the customer's implementation.

In today's environment, we still have the standard R/3 system executing ABAP programs, but we also have a portal environment that executes Java, a different kind of programming language, which is not SAP-specific. We also have portal roles that are assigned to user IDs in the portal environment that can then access R/3 functionality—in other words, ABAP programs.

This chapter will focus on the R/3 environment that executes the ABAP programs, referred to as the ABAP environment. This ABAP environment is what we have come to know as the SAP R/3 system, but is now only a part of the SAP NetWeaver environment.

This chapter will discuss the architecture, design aspects, tools for the security administrator, and the implementation points for an SAP R/3 ABAP security environment.

Architecture

ABAP architecture for SAP security involves the planning and design of the security environment that will be implemented to give your user community the ability to perform their jobs while keeping corporate resources and data secure.

In this section, we will discuss identity management and the components involved, including user IDs and passwords as well as security roles and authorization concepts.

You should devote some time to the planning and design of your security environment in order to create a good architecture that will provide you with the opportunity to give your company a system that protects its resources and data as well as provides your user community with the ability to perform the business tasks required to fulfill the business objectives.

Identity Management

What in the world is identity management? Well, the short version is that it is a means to manage your user ID information and the security (access rights) assigned to you. This is so that, when you want to access your account, the system you are logging on to can verify you are you and provide your logon session with the access you are entitled to.

If we limit our scope to SAP, which is the purpose of this discussion, we are talking about managing user accounts and the role assignments, which provide the authorizations you are assigned within an SAP system. I highly recommend you visit SAP's Developer Network (SDN) at www.sdn.sap.com/irj/sdn/security where you will find additional information on identity management as it pertains to the SAP security environment.

SAP has a collection of tables that are generally referred to as the user master record. Although many in the SAP world refer to the user master as if it is a single entity, it really isn't a single physical record, but a logical record. As anyone who has an understanding of databases knows, a logical record is created when related data is linked together. For an SAP user master record, the link is usually the user ID. Tables are included with the user ID as a key that contains your name, date, when the ID was created, and contact information like phone, e-mail, and fax number. Additional tables link the assigned roles and the authorizations those roles contain. Everything that is needed to verify that you are you and to assign the proper security once you have passed the authentication steps is included in these linked tables.

However, in SAP your user ID might be replicated multiple times across a landscape because SAP security is client-dependent. You might have the same user ID but different access in different SAP systems, even different SAP clients within the same SAP system.

As your user ID is replicated, errors might be introduced in the spelling of your name or any other information due to the potential to make key entry mistakes. It quickly becomes a management nightmare for the security administrator to keep abreast of everyone's ID. And what happens when someone changes their name due to marriage, divorce, adoption, or other reasons? Or changes jobs (which means a change to the access rights that need to be assigned)?

SAP developed CUA, Central User Administration, to be able to centrally manage and provision user IDs across complex SAP landscapes. Within the central CUA system, your user ID with all the appropriate information is entered one time and distributed across the landscape to the designated systems and clients you have been authorized to access, along with the proper roles that have been approved for your access.

When a change occurs, perhaps your phone number changes, that change can be updated in the central CUA system and synchronized out to all locations, which avoids the previous tedium of logging in to each client, as well as the potential for key entry errors.

CUA has a tool, a transaction called SCUM, which lets you specify which parts of the user master record will be maintained in the CUA central system only, and which parts of the user master record can be maintained in the remote or child system. SCUM also lets you specify parts of the user master record that can be maintained in both the central system and the child system.

But CUA is primarily for keeping SAP systems in sync. What about your corporate identity? CUA has been designed so it can be fed from your Lightweight Directory Access Protocol (LDAP), system which many corporations use for managing network IDs. So when a user ID is created or changed, that information can be mapped into CUA, and CUA can synchronize it across the SAP landscape so everything matches.

CUA

CUA provides a centrally managed environment for creating and maintaining user IDs and access rights. Access rights are provided via the ABAP security role, which is created and maintained with the profile generator (see Figure 3.1).

Figure 3.1 CUA

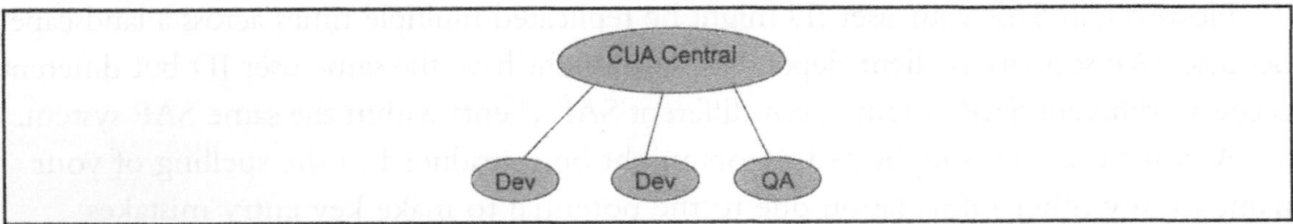

Anyone who has had to log on to numerous clients to add a single ID into a SAP landscape can appreciate the benefits of a centralized system for maintaining IDs in SAP. Even more so, a greater appreciation for a centralized system is gained when a user must be removed or locked out of the SAP environment.

As we have already indicated, user security in SAP is client-dependent, meaning it must be set up and maintained in each client to which a given user is authorized to have access. This can be very time consuming, and prone to error and inconsistencies.

Inconsistencies can arise in the user master record for a person's name, contact information, company address, and all other fields in the user master that specifically pertain to that person.

For example, user ID TRAJones should belong to Robert A. Jones. When we look into the sandbox client we see the user ID TRAJones has Bob Jones on the name fields. Is this the same person, or has the user ID been unwittingly assigned to two people? It is hard to tell simply from the name. While the user ID is unique within a given SAP client, it doesn't have to be unique across the landscape. This can be very problematic especially if Robert A. Jones is a power user with broad access rights, while Bob Jones is a new user with limited access.

If Bob Jones requests his password to be reset in say a development system where Robert A. Jones already has the ID TRAJones, Bob Jones may be given access that he should not have. Not only is it a problem that we now have an unauthorized user in the development client, the real owner of the ID, Robert A. Jones, now cannot use his ID because the password has been reset.

A centralized system for administering user IDs helps eliminate this type of problem by allowing the security administrator to have one place to maintain user IDs. One user master record can be created with all the appropriate personal information maintained one time that reduces the potential for entry errors, and by having one location where all IDs start, it eliminates the potential of using the same ID for multiple persons.

CUA in SAP is basically an ALE (Application Link Enabled) application. ALE allows connectivity between SAP systems and their clients and lets data be exchanged. In the case of security administration, it updates the user master record.

A critical part in the CUA configuration is the logical system name. A logical system name is simply a way to uniquely name clients within a network. It lets an electronic conversation take place within the network without any confusion over who a message is intended for.

For example, if you wanted to have a conversation with Bob, but there were several Bob's in the room, how would you make sure you gain the attention of the correct Bob and that your conversation is received by the Bob you want to talk to?

In SAP, the logical system name refers to a specific client in a specific system or SID. You can see what the logical system name of your client is by using transaction SCC4 (see Figure 3.2).

Figure 3.2 The Logical System Name

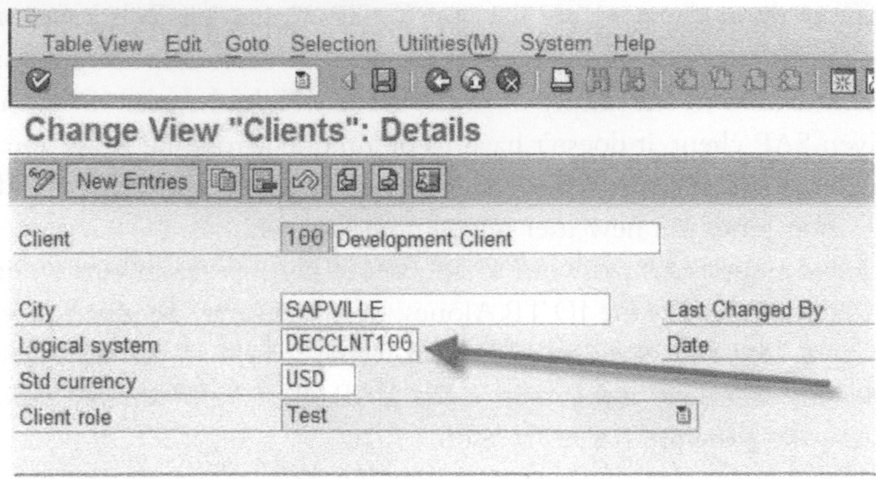

CUA also depends on RFC, remote function calls, to carry on the conversation between systems. The RFC connectivity is accomplished by RFC destinations. RFC destinations provide a technical connection at the network layer so a conversation can be held between two SAP systems. In the case of CUA, the central system and a child system are connected via RFC destinations. The referral to the central system and child system is used throughout the CUA documentation to provide a way of distinguishing a master–slave relationship, although that terminology generates unsettling connotations. The central system (the master) sends updates to the child (the slave). This might not be politically correct terminology, but it helps keep our minds straight as we work in the CUA environment to know where we are logged on to and what function is performed there.

It is important when setting up a CUA environment that you name your RFC destinations with the same name as your client destination logical system name.

For example, if my child system's logical system name was DECCLNT100, then the RFC destination created in the CUA central system must be named DECCLNT100. There is not much room to be creative here because if you do not follow this simple rule, your CUA system will not work.

It is commonly recommended to use the first three characters of the logical system name to indicate the SAP SID, system identifier, name. In DECCLNT100, DEC is the SID name for a development ECC system. The next four characters, CLNT, are a mental reminder that we are working with a client, not the SID. Finally, to help us keep our minds straight about which client we are working with, we fill in the client number as the last three positions. So, DECCLNT100 is client 100 in the development ECC system. Now, whenever we see DECCLNT100, we know exactly what system and client that is.

These two items—the logical system name and the RFC destination name—are key architectural items in a CUA configuration and you should give some thought to the names that will be used in your landscape before starting a CUA implementation project. It is recommended you draw a map showing the CUA central system in the center with the child systems surrounding it. Apply the logical system names to each component so you can have a visual reminder of your plan and be certain you use the right naming conventions when creating the logical system names and RFC destinations.

SAP has provided a configuration transaction that lets you set up many of the configuration aspects of the the CUA environment. This transaction is called SALE.

Partner profiles and ports also come into play, but the logical system name and RFC destination name seem to give new users to CUA the biggest problem.

When you are designing your CUA environment, it is recommended that the CUA central system be placed in a separate client in your Solution Manager system. Be sure to check out the documentation on service.sap.com/security. You will need an OSS marketplace ID, but some good documents out there will help you set up your CUA environment by walking you through each step. Once you are logged in to OSS, navigate to "Security in detail," then "Secure User Access," and then "Identity management." You will find several documents on central user administration.

LDAP (Lightweight Directory Access Protocol)

Directory service provides a central user repository that is stored in a directory for maintaining user data. The directory works much like a corporate address book, storing information such as:

- Personnel data (name, address, phone number, organization, department)
- User data and security information (user accounts, authorizations, public key certificates)
- Information about system resources and system services (system ID, application configuration, printer configuration)

Based on a client-server architecture, directory service enables different applications within the system landscape to access the central user repository over a network or the Internet. As the user data can be administered centrally at one location, it reduces data inconsistencies and redundancies of user information. Moreover, it reduces the total cost of ownership for each application that accesses the user repository.

Many organizations already use Lightweight Directory Access Protocol (LDAP) directory services for managing and organizing information for their corporate resources such as users, computers, and applications. It makes sense to leverage these existing directory services and integrate user management on SAP Web AS systems with these directory services so user master records are maintained in one central system.

For SAP Enterprise Portal, User Management Engine (UME) can use a LDAP directory as its user persistence store. As of SAP Web AS 6.10, ABAP-based systems can also synchronize with a LDAP directory to integrate user data in one central system. In system landscapes where there are many SAP Web AS ABAP systems and CUA is used to integrate SAP user master records, LDAP directory can be the central system for creation of new user data, and this new user information is synchronized and created in the SAP CUA, then the *imported* user information is subsequently distributed to the connected child systems.

In order to integrate the LDAP directory service with the SAP Web AS ABAP system, the LDAP connector is required. The LDAP connector is a software component that controls the information flow between the SAP Web AS ABAP system and the directory service using a standard protocol LDAP over the TCP/IP port 389. It provides this functionality in the form of application program interface (API) or a collection of function modules that provides the mechanisms for connecting, reading, searching, creating, modifying, renaming, and deleting directory entries.

The LDAP connector loads the LDAP library (a program called *ldap_rfc*) at run-time, so from a technical perspective, the LDAP connector is actually program *ldap_rfc* that runs as a registered server program. This LDAP library is delivered as part of the SAP kernel and is also available from SAP Service Marketplace at http://service.sap.com/swdc.

You can set up the LDAP connector as part of the SAP ABAP-based system, in which case the executable is stored in the kernel directory */usr/sap/<SID>/sys/exe/run*. Or alternatively, if the LDAP connector is not available for your operating system, the LDAP connector can run on the directory server as a stand-alone program. The benefit of setting up the LDAP connector as part of the SAP Web AS ABAP system is that it can be monitored and managed using the Computing Center Management System (transaction RZ20).

Configuration of the LDAP connector requires the RFC destination LDAP for establishing the connection between the SAP Web AS ABAP system and the directory server. A logical LDAP server needs to be defined to map to the physical location of the directory service. The communication type used by the LDAP connector to connect and bind the LDAP directory service is maintained and stored in the secure storage. Transaction LDAP is an administration tool for maintaining all of the LDAP Connector settings mentioned earlier.

In order to enable synchronization of user data between the directory service and SAP Web AS ABAP system, SAP data fields must map to the attributes of the directory service using transaction LDAPMAP. If the desired mapping is not a simple 1:1 relationship, then function modules can be used to define a more complicated mapping procedure. For example, use function module *MAP_CONCAT_CHAR* for concatenating *first name* and *last name* fields into a *fullname* field, and use function module *MAP_SPLIT_CHAR* for splitting *telephone number* into two fields *tel_number* and *tel_ext*.

A field can be mapped to one or more attributes. An attribute can be assigned to one or more fields. However, for any fields that do not exist, you must extend the schema in the directory by importing a LDAP Data Interchange Format (LDIF) file. The LDIF file can be generated using the report *RSLDAPSCHMEAEXT*.

For each field-attribute mapping, appropriate mapping indicators and synchronization indicators must be set. A mapping indicator is set indicating whether the mapping is used for import to an SAP database, export to a LDAP directory service, a search filter, a Relative Distinguished Name for creating new directory entries, or required and system entries. A synchronization indicator is set indicating whether field-attribute mapping is imported or exported to determine the direction of the synchronization.

Once mapping is defined, report *RSLDAPSYNC_USER* can be executed or scheduled to synchronize the user data. Transactions LDAPLOG and SLG1 can be used to check for error messages during synchronization.

Standard User ID/Pass

In SAP, identity management is the fancy term for setting up and managing the user ID, password, and access rights. Basically, we need a unique identifier in the SAP system to be sure you are you. You may not see the significance of this, but your user ID is used to not only contain personal information about you in the system but also to assign your access privileges (authorizations).

Your password is used to ensure that the associated user ID is being used by a valid authenticated user. Any action logged in the system is done with the user ID that performed the action.

You need to have a method or procedure that will ensure a unique user ID for every person that is authorized to use the SAP system.

Since many companies already have networks in place, it is a common practice to use the network ID as the SAP user ID. This provides advantages because the active directory is used to first authenticate the user at the network level. SAP has also provided extensions that allow the interaction between the active directory and SAP for single sign on, creating user IDs in the SAP system, and so on.

A user ID that has some built-in structure also allows the administrator to quickly identify the type of user as well. For example, if all contractor IDs started with C, while the ID of all company employees started with E, a user ID report could be used to quickly identify who was an employee and who was not.

In SAP, the user ID field is 12 characters long, so if you are planning to use an external source for unique ID creation, then keep this limitation in mind.

Passwords should be kept private and never shared with anyone. In the world of security identity management, the user ID helps identify who you are, while the password provides proof that you are the owner of that ID. As discussed earlier, logging within the system is done with the user ID, so any actions done in the system are traceable to the owner of that ID. If you share your password, you can be held accountable for how it was used.

A simple search on the Internet will return many recommendations for password rules. The basics are to establish a minimum length, using combinations of characters and numerics. If your system allows you to, and SAP does, also use a combination of upper- and lowercase characters. A password of at least six positions with a combination of characters and numerics should be a good starting point.

Because passwords can become complicated, try to establish a phrase that can be remembered. Think in terms of the vanity license plates where I have seen people get very creative.

For example, 1w2G2sC could represent **I** **w**ant **2** **G**o **2** **s**urf **C**ity. I substituted a numeric one for I and then mixed up the upper/lowercase first character and substituted the number 2 for the word "to."

This type of password uses different combinations while giving me something I can remember, because I never want to write down my password.

Never use your name, first or last as part of your password, nor should you use words that can be looked up in the dictionary since some creative types will try to do brute force password hacks using dictionary words.

Role, Profile, and Authorization Concepts

What is the ABAP authorization concept? In what we refer to as a standard R/3 SAP system, all the code that executes is written in SAP's own programming language called ABAP. In pre-NetWeaver versions, it was a given that the SAP system was an ABAP system, but now we have parts of the SAP environment that are written in Java and are more "web centric," so when we begin talking about SAP security we need to distinguish what part of the SAP system we are discussing because the authorization concept in the standard R/3 system that is primarily written in ABAP is a different model than what we find connected to our Web portals.

SAP's definition of the ABAP authorization concept from http://help.sap.com is as follows:

> The ABAP authorization concept protects transactions, programs, and services in SAP systems from unauthorized access. On the basis of the authorization concept, the administrator assigns authorizations to the users that determine which actions a user can execute in the SAP system, after he or she has logged on to the system and authenticated himself or herself.
>
> To access business objects or execute SAP transactions, a user requires corresponding authorizations, as business objects or transactions are protected by authorization objects. The authorizations represent instances of generic authorization objects and are defined depending on the activity and responsibilities of the employee. The authorizations are combined in an authorization profile that is associated with a role. The user administrators then assign the corresponding roles using the user master record, so that the user can use the appropriate transactions for his or her tasks.

What Is a Role?

A role is created in an R/3 ABAP system using the profile generator to specify the menu of transactions the user is authorized to execute. Each transaction is protected in the ABAP code that executes by one or more authorization objects, which in turn may contain from one to ten authorization fields, representing business data that have been determined in the design of the transaction/program needing to be checked in order to allow access. Many authorization objects contain the authorization field activity to determine what activity the user is allowed to access—for example, display activity or change activity. Sometimes, again based on the design of the program, an authorization object may be used to simply check to see if the user is authorized to access specific business data. The authorization object might have one field that represents the type of data and the authorization value is the data value the user is authorized to access. For example, the Logistics Controlling object *M_BCO_WERK* has one authorization field called WERKS, which represents PLANTS and is intended to provide the capability to limit the access of document evaluations down to the Plant level. Each SAP ABAP program implements an authorization concept using authorization objects to protect functionality and/or data within the SAP system. Authorizations are created to give access based on access rights that a given user is allowed to have by checking the user's authorization values against the rules that have been coded into the ABAP program.

Definition of a Profile

Although we use the profile generator (PFCG) to create a role, as its name implies the PFCG generates a profile. The profile is created from the authorization objects and authorization field values entered into the role. The concept of a profile is a holdover from pre-PFCG days when the security administrator had to manually create the authorizations, but in order to be able to assign those authorizations to a user ID, he/she had to collect them in a profile that could then be assigned to a user ID. The profile is still used as a collection of authorizations, but is now generated by the profile generator tool and associated with the role. When the role is assigned to a user ID, the SAP system looks up the profile and automatically assigns the associated profile.

SAP Authorization Concept

The authorization concept then protects SAP applications and data from unauthorized accessed by combinations of authorizations that are checked in the ABAP program at runtime against the allowed authorizations that have been assigned to the user ID to determine what that user can execute in the SAP system—as well as the data that user can access by means of an authorization check that is part of the coding in the ABAP program. Many authorization objects in an SAP system have been designed to be used by the ABAP program to protect functionality as well as data. It is important to remember that the authorization objects are designed and created as part of the overall program design and are part of the SAP security system called the *authorization concept*.

Single Sign-on and Certificates

In a system landscape with many different types of SAP systems, where more and more users have multiple passwords to access different SAP systems, the requirement to keep track of all these passwords creates predictable problems. The users must enter their SAP user ID and password repeatedly when working through different SAP systems—and it is not an uncommon occurrence for users to call the Helpdesk because he or she forgets or loses passwords. Consequently, users end up logging more Helpdesk calls, administration and support costs grow for the organization as a result, and the productivity of the users and organization suffer.

With Single Sign-on (SSO), users only need to authenticate once and can access subsequent systems (both SAP and non-SAP) without the need to reenter his or her user ID and password. By reusing existing user credentials, the productivity of the users and organization can be increased.

Generally speaking, SSO for SAP Web AS ABAP systems can be implemented in two ways:

- Using SAP logon tickets
- Using client certificates

With *SAP logon tickets*, the user is authenticated using the logon ticket as the authentication token. The user only needs to be authenticated once (for example, using a valid user ID and password) and the system issues a logon ticket to the user. With this logon ticket, the user can access subsequent systems (SAP and non-SAP systems) without the need to reenter his or her user ID and password.

It is recommended that you identify one system in your environment as the ticket-issuing system before you configure other systems to accept tickets from this system.

To configure the SAP Web AS ABAP system to issue logon tickets, you must set the following profile parameters in transaction RZ10:

```
login/create_sso2_ticket = 2
login/accept_sso2_ticket = 1
login/ticket_expiration_time = <required time>
```

The issuing system must be assigned a public and private key pair in the SSO Personal Secure Environment (PSE). It must also be assigned a public-key certificate.

One maintenance task, which is often overlooked, is forgetting when the public key certificate expires, which can impair users' SSO capabilities to the systems since they are not able to receive any logon tickets. Hence, it is important to check and replace the SAP Web AS ABAP system's SSO PSE before the public key certificate expires.

In order for the SAP Web AS ABAP system to accept logon tickets, the accepting system must verify the SAP logon tickets. The first verification check ensures that the login ticket is from a trusted source, the accepting system checks its SSO Access Control List and confirms the issuing system details. The second verification check ensures that the accepting system can verify the issuing server's digital signature. If the certificate is signed by a SAP CA, then the accepting system accepts the logon tickets without further information. Otherwise, if the certificate is self-signed, then the accepting system checks in its certificate list and confirms the issuing server's certificate details.

On all of the accepting systems, you must install the SAP Security Library (or SAP Cryptographic Library). This SAP Security library is available at http://service.sap.com/swdcunder Download | Support Packages and Patches | Entry by Application Group | Additional Components | SAPSECULIB.

The SAP Cryptographic library is available under Download | SAP Cryptographic Software.

In addition, the profile parameter *login/accept_sso2_ticket* must be set to *1* on all accepting systems. Use transaction SS02 (SSO administration tool) to automatically establish the appropriate configuration for the accepting system. For example, it checks whether the profile parameters have been set correctly, shows the accepting systems' SSO Access Control List as well as the certificate list.

However, if the SAP Web AS ABAP system needs to accept SAP logon tickets from a J2EE Engine, then in addition to installing the SAP Security Library and implementing the profile parameter login/accept_sso2_ticket, you must also import the J2EE Engine's public key certificate manually into the Personal Secure Environment (PSE) using transaction STRUST or STRUSTSSO2 (Trust Manager). Also, the J2EE Engine's details must be added to the Access Control List.

Users must have the same user ID across all of the systems and their Web browsers must accept cookies to ensure that credentials stored in the SAP logon ticket can be reused.

Since SAP logon tickets are not safe from replay attacks (especially because cookie mechanisms are based on repeated transmissions), it is important to ensure that SAP logon tickets cannot be intercepted when transmitting using a cookie. It is recommended to use SSL (or HTTPS) and ensure all SAP servers are in one common DNS domain.

For *client certificates*, on the other hand, users must have their X.509 client certificates as part of a Public-Key Infrastructure (PKI). PKI enables users to securely and privately exchange data in a public network through the use of a public and private cryptographic key pair that is obtained through a trusted authority.

Any user who tries to access the SAP Web AS ABAP system must present a valid certificate to the server using the Secure Sockets Layer (SSL) protocol. The server then decrypts the logon request using its private key; only the server can decrypt this logon request. If the authentication is successful and the server can indeed map the user's Distinguished Name in the certificate with a valid SAP user ID on the AS ABAP system, then the user can log on to the system. The authentication takes place in the underlying SSL protocols. Hence, no user ID and password entries are necessary.

To ensure that certificates are issued from a trusted source, it is recommended you use certificates signed by a trusted Certificate Authority (CA) or SAP CA. This means the chosen CA becomes the designated one, and the AS ABAP system (the private key) and user who access the AS ABAP system must possess a valid certificate signed by the chosen CA (the public key). The corresponding user's private key must be stored in a secure location. You can use security measures such as password-protection or smart cards for this.

In order for the SAP Web AS ABAP system to accept certificates, the system must be set up for SSL, and the profile parameter *icm/HTTPS/verify_client* must be set to *1*. The CA root certificate must be imported onto the accepting system's PSE certificate list using transaction STRUST. Additionally, table USREXTID must be maintained with user mapping details.

With the distribution of client certificates, you also have the option to use SAP Trust Center Service (TCS), with which you do not have to manually update table USREXTID. This is where users are automatically assigned with client certificates by calling the certificate request service. The certificate request service is a Business Server Page (BSP) application, which is accessed in transaction SICF under **default_host | sap | bc | bsp | certreq**. With this option, the user accesses the certificate request service when the user is authenticated, the Web browser generates the user's public and private key pair and sends a certificate request to the SAP system, this certificate request is then sent to the SAP TCS. The SAP TCS verifies the request, generates a SAP Passport and allocates it to the user's Web browser. The SAP system automatically maps the SAP Passport or certificate to the user's account, and maintenance of table USREXTID is not necessary. The SAP Passport allows the user to access subsequent SAP systems without reentering user ID and password.

From a security and risk management perspective, it is important to note that there are some situations where a reauthentication may be required for extra protection due to an increased business risk. For example, if users access SAP systems that contain highly sensitive information, then a stronger two-factor authentication mechanism such as smart cards or password tokens may be necessary. Or perhaps an administrator with powerful rights requires a stricter authentication. Also, users with access to certain business-critical SAP transactions should trigger a reauthentication when accessing these transactions to ensure and verify that the person sitting in front of the computer is really the person who originally signed on. This element of control ensures that implementation of SSO does not compromise on security.

Password Rules

In an SAP system, password rules are implemented via system parameters that let you set minimum restrictions on password creation to encourage your users to use strong passwords. Passwords must be at least three characters in length, with a maximum of 40. This is set with parameter login/min_password_lng. Password lengths were a maximum of eight characters up until version 6.40.

Post–version 6.40, you may further define password restrictions to strengthen the password with the following parameters:

login/min_password_letters

login/min_password_digits

login/min_password_specials

login/min_password_lowercase

login/min_password_uppercase

login/min_password_diff

For more information on these parameters, use transaction RZ11.

SAP enforces some additional restrictions on passwords, which are predefined in the system and not changed via parameters. For example, the first character cannot be either the exclamation point (!) or the question mark (?). Also, the first three characters cannot be the same—for instance, AAA. Nor can the password be SAP* or PASS.

You can also populate the table USR40 with a list of impermissible passwords—passwords that are not allowed, such as days of the week, months of the year, and other dictionary words that a hacker might easily guess or use in a program to forcefully attack your system. You can also include patterns—for example, monday*—in the exclude list. A search can be conducted on the Internet to find lists that can be downloaded and inserted into USR40.

A user ID is a fairly public piece of information, but is not valuable without the password. A password that can easily be guessed is like no password at all. In addition, passwords that are complex drive users to record their password somewhere where it can be found, again giving the password no value.

In addition, passwords that never change become more susceptible to being breached the longer they are in use. A password aging policy should be included to require users to change their passwords with some frequency, and passwords that have previously been used should not be reused, or at least not reused within a given time frame. Many systems restrict reusing a password until some number of new passwords are used. For example, in SAP the last five passwords cannot be reused; however, on the sixth password change you can reuse the first password.

The parameter, login/password_expiration_time, can be used to set the expiration time for when a user must change their password. Use transaction RZ11 and review all parameters associated with passwords in SAP by entering login/*password*, and then search to implement a password policy according to your company's requirements.

Strong passwords protect the user ID from misuse. Therefore, you can create a password strategy using the SAP system parameters and load the USR40 table with common passwords that should not be used because they could be easily guessed or "hacked" using a dictionary program.

Using Secure Communication

As there are data transfers between various client and server components of the SAP Web AS ABAP system, appropriate security measures should be in place to protect the integrity and privacy of the data transmitted over the network.

Depending on the type of communication used, the connections can be protected in two ways. Securc Sockets Layer (SSL) is employed to protect Hypertext Transfer Protocol (HTTP), P4, and LDAP connections, while Secure Network Communication (SNC) is used for protecting SAP protocols, such as Dialog and

Remote Function Calls (RFC) connections, between client and server components of the AS ABAP system.

HTTPS

Secure Sockets Layer (SSL) is a cryptographic protocol that provides secure communications over the Internet and prevents others from eavesdropping on the data exchange. SSL can provide data encryption, server-side authentication (the server identifies itself to the client), client-side authentication (the client identifies itself to the server), and also mutual authentication (where the identities of both the client and server are verified). The SSL protocol uses public-key infrastructure to ensure data confidentiality over the network.

You can use SSL to provide secure HTTP, P4, and LDAP connections between client and server components of the SAP Web AS ABAP system. When accessing URLs that require an SSL connection, the prefix https: is used in the URL instead of http:, causing the message to be directed to a secure port instead of the default port 80.

For authentication with SSL, the server must have a public-private key pair and public-key certificate. It must possess one key pair and a certificate to identify itself as the server component, and another key pair and certificate for identifying itself as a client component. These key pairs are certificates that are stored in the server's Personal Security Environment (PSE).

In order to enable SSL on a SAP Web AS ABAP system, the SAP Cryptographic Library toolkit must be implemented. SAP Cryptographic Library supports the use of encrypting functions and digital signatures, the library can be downloaded from the SAP Service Marketplace at http://service.sap.com/swdc under **SAP Cryptographic Software**. You can install the SAP Cryptographic Library on the SAP Web AS ABAP system in the kernel directory */usr/sap/<SID>/sys/exe/run.*

Some SSL profile parameters must be implemented on the SAP Web ABAP system before SSL is enabled. These profile parameters include:

```
sec/libsapsecu = /usr/sap/<SID>/SYS/exe/run/libsapcrypto.so

ssl/ssl_lib = /usr/sap/<SID>/SYS/exe/run/libsapcrypto.so

ssf/ssfapi_lib = /usr/sap/<SID>/SYS/exe/run/libsapcrypto.so

ssf/name = SAPSECULIB

icm/server_port_<xx> = PROT=HTTPS, PORT=<httpsport number>,
TIMEOUT=<timeout in seconds>

icm/HTTPS/verify_client = 1
```

Once the AS ABAP system is restarted and the profile parameters are activated, the HTTPS service should be enabled. This can be verified in transaction SMICM, from Menu Goto | Services. For system landscapes with a large number of SAP WebAS ABAP systems, the LDAP connector can be set up on the CUA Central system so that any imported user data from the directory server can be distributed to the CUA client systems using ALE technology.

SNC

You can use Secure Network Connection (SNC) to provide a secure authentication for protecting communication between various client and server components of the AS ABAP system that use the Dialog and RFC protocols.

SNC basically requires the integration of an external security product with the SAP Web AS ABAP system to provide additional security functions that are not directly available with SAP systems. The external security product must be certified by the SAP Software Partner Program.

SNC can provide various levels of authentication (verification of the identity), integrity protection (detects any changes to the data that may have occurred during the communication), and privacy protection (provides encryption of the message), depending on what the external security product can provide.

For SNC authentication with client components (for example, SAP GUI for Windows), you are required to integrate with an external security product that has been certified for use by SAP.

For authentication between server components (for example, connection between ECC and BW systems), the default security product you can use is called SAP Cryptographic Library. Cryptographic algorithms from the security product ensure the privacy protection of communication by encryption, keeping others from eavesdropping on communications.

Some additional security measures may be necessary for certain security products to ensure that security is not compromised. For example, if the security product uses public-key technology (for instance, client certificates), then you need a public-key infrastructure (PKI). In which case, appropriate security procedures must be put in place for generating and distributing keys and certificates to the users and system components. You must also ensure these private keys are stored in a secure location, whether through the use of crypto boxes or smart cards, and that the public keys are signed by a trusted Certificate Authority.

It is also important to note if SAP Cryptographic library is used, because there may be some limitations to its use since some countries place various restrictions on the use of encryption in software applications.

Design

Security implementation does not just happen. It requires an understanding of the business processes, the risk tolerance of the client company, and any legal requirements that must be adhered to.

In order to implement a security solution, good design is necessary. This chapter will cover strategy considerations, standards, guiding principles, and role development steps, and provides a security matrix template to get you started.

Strategy Considerations

A successful implementation can be better achieved if you spend some time planning and developing a strategy for security implementation. A strategy is nothing more than a plan of action designed to achieve a particular goal—in this case, security implemented that provides all users with all the access needed to achieve their daily tasks but no excessive access that could allow them entry to data or functions they should not have.

Somewhere during my security career I came across the following quote and wrote it down for inspiration, but I don't know who to attribute it to.

Security is not an option. The responsibility of management is to protect and strengthen the assets owned by the business on behalf of the investors. Those assets are constantly at risk due to external and internal attacks.

I often refer to this quote to encourage myself to be diligent in establishing proper security controls and other mechanisms, and to be a responsible member of the organization.

The following 11 items should help you form an effective strategy. They outline what should be expected in an adequate and comprehensive security policy.

Acquire or Develop a Security Policy

A security policy will:

- Provide the basic framework for all security decisions
- Reference any existing guiding principles, policies, or regulations that impact security access

- Specify the scope that will be covered by the policy (who/what is covered)
- Identify the core policy group and scope of authority for resolving any and all security conflicts
- Define data classifications, which should be based on the sensitivity, risk, and importance of the corporation's assets (for example, strategic/proprietary, confidential/restrictive, public)
- Include a statement on sharing user accounts and whether multiple accounts per user are allowed
- Provide guidelines on the violation process—what happens when a security breach is committed
- Identify the following roles and responsibilities:

  Trustees – Reviews/approves access rights

  Sponsors – Reviews/establishes policies governing system access

  Administration – Establishes process and procedures for carrying out and adhering to corporate policies

  Audit services – Participates in establishing solid controls and conducting reviews to ensure compliance

Establish a Core Policy Group

A core policy group will:

- Provide initial guidelines based on established company security policies
- Provide an interpretation of policy as it relates to issues that arise
- Serve as the arbitrator for cross-team security issues and conflicts

Authorization to Corporate Data and Application Functionality Will Be via Role Assignment to User IDs

Roles are designed to support business processes. Base roles are copied and modified to restrict data access. Common functionality will be included in a common role for mass assignment.

Establish a Role Ownership Matrix That Will Maintain Segregation of Duties (SOD)

A role ownership matrix will:

- Review/approve initial development
- Review/approve role assignment to user IDs
- Review/approve ongoing changes to roles

Establish Approval Procedures

Approval procedures are used for issuing user IDs, assigning roles to user IDs, and creating new roles and changing existing roles.

Establish a Role Development Methodology

A role development methodology should be a simple build process that is low maintenance. It should include a minimum number of roles per user ID. It should be positioned for post-implementation changes.

Establish a Testing Methodology

A testing methodology includes a unit test and integration test/negative testing. It is a step toward moving to production sign-off procedures.

Establish a Change Management Procedure for Post-Production Role Changes

A change management procedure for post-production role changes includes justification for the changes (scope), approvals, testing, and sign-off.

Role Documentation Will Use the Security Section of Role Matrix

The format for the role matrix will be transaction/role matrix. Organization levels should be included. Critical/sensitive data should be included.

Establish Security Administration Procedures

Security administration procedures are used for creating user IDs. User IDs are created with templates, and they can be distributed. User IDs should be centralized under CUA. Role assignment changes can be distributed and should be centralized under CUA. Lock/unlock procedures can be distributed. Password resets can be distributed. Role development/maintenance should be centralized.

Custom ABAP Code Will Be Assigned a Transaction Code and Be Secured via One or More Methods as Deemed Appropriate by Local ABAP Security Guidelines

Custom ABAP code should adhere to general policy guidelines. It also should adhere to ABAP security guidelines.

I highly recommend you invite the Audit group to review all procedures prior to implementation. Ideally, invite the audit group to be part of the security development group to ensure adherence during the design and initial build.

Standards

A very helpful area to get established before you get your security implementation started is the area of naming standards.

Naming standards help the security administrator when creating reports, filtering for specific information, and in some cases being able to apply authorizations to the correct group of users while restricting access to others.

The following list of key points described in this section should be used to start your naming standards, and then added to as additional situations arise.

Naming Standards

Naming standards should be established for the following:

- **Roles** (composite, simple, and derived – 30 characters)
- **Table authorization groups** (four characters)
- **Program authorization groups** (eight characters)
- **Spool/Print Authorization Field** (12 characters); BDC session names (12 characters)
- **Batch User IDs**
- **Printer Names** (general and restricted or special use) This applies to all printers regardless of who accesses them. General printers can be used by any user, while restricted or special-use printers must be authorized to be used.
- **Tables** All tables will be assigned under a table authorization group. The default &NC& will not be used.
- **Printers** Printer names must have a consistent format to be able to identify a single printer or group of printers via a naming specification using wild cards—For example, PR_M*, which could represent all printers at the main office.

Roles

In this section, we'll discuss roles. First, we'll explore role names in general. To create a new activity group, perform the following steps:

1. Complete the **Role Name** field.
2. Fill in the **Role Description** field.
3. Select the **Description** tab and enter a brief description outlining the purpose and/or scope of this role.
4. Below the description, create a **Change Log** section with the following column headers: **date**, **initials**, **change description**, and **tracking number**.

To modify a role, perform the following steps:

1. Always add transactions using the Menu tab.
2. Use a single role (non-derived role).

3. Unit test for added Tcode (if any). It should know the Tcode-related objects with proper field values.
4. Use SU24 to update Tcode with related objects.
5. PFCG
6. Document the **Change Log** section on the **Description** tab.
7. Add the transaction (if any) using the Menu.
8. User Expert mode for profile generation and "Read old status and merge with new data" to bring new Tcode-related objects and values.
9. To verify New objects and values and adjust.
10. Complete the change log under the description tab

Role Naming

Now we'll discuss three approaches for role naming: the team, hierarchical, and positional. For the team approach, use the following:

Characters	1–3	Team ID
Character	4	Delimiter: "-" for simple; "+" for composites; "&" for ancillary
Characters	5–30	Unique description of role (no spaces allowed, use _)

For the hierarchical approach, use the following:

Characters	1	Hierarchy level (O-Organization, D-Department, S-Section, R-Role)
Characters	2–4	Hierarchy level code (ACT-Accounting, MKT-Marketing)
Character	5	Delimiter: "-"
Characters	6–30	Unique description of hierarchy level (no spaces allowed, use _)

For the positional approach, use the following:

Characters	1–3	Organization ID (HR, ACCT, CUS)
Character	4	Delimiter: "-"
Characters	5–30	Unique description of the position (should be the job title; no spaces allowed, use _)

All custom code your company creates should follow the SAP authorization concept. We don't want to undermine the delivered security strategy by writing code that provides functions and access to data that does not incorporate a security model. Therefore, you need to include some standards for ABAP/4 code development.

- Determine Security for custom ABAP/4.
- All ABAP/4 custom code will employ a security method.
- Operating system files (datasets) that are accessed by ABAP/4 programs will be protected with SAP authorizations.

Guiding Principles

You should create a document that will let you capture all decisions that guide your security decisions. These guiding principles dovetail with the standards you need to develop what we discussed earlier.

While this document can be as formal as you want it to be, you should be prepared to keep it updated since security tends to evolve as a company becomes more knowledgeable with the technology.

As a suggestion, you might use the following outline or use it as your starting point.

Objective: Here, you need to lay out the objective of this document.

Example: The objective of these guidelines is to provide context for the development of roles and security authorizations within the SAP system. The focus is on those areas that are considered medium to high risk from a business perspective, with the intent of ensuring that business integrity is not compromised or that confidential data is not accessed by nonauthorized persons. In addition, these guidelines are intended to protect the integrity and stability of the SAP system.

You should establish the **scope** this document will cover, and if you are leveraging off an existing corporate policy document, you can include it here.

Example: These guidelines are based on the **xxx Information Systems Security Policy** (reference number if available). They are classified as general guidelines and apply across all functional areas within the SAP system.

Group the guidelines into sections to let you both organize them and better locate them as the need arises. The following are some examples:

- **ABAP programs** No program will be directly executed, if a transaction is not assigned, then a custom transaction should be created and assigned to the program, and the transaction assigned to the respective role.

- **Restrictions by organizational unit** These roles will be restricted by company code xxxx.
- **Restriction by Functional activity** These roles will be restricted by Display or Update activity.
- **Batch Processing** Batch processing will be based on a "batch user." Batch user IDs will be created based on functional requirements—for example, a batch user ID for payroll processing. This approach can also be used in conjunction with centralized scheduling of batch jobs if required, whereby the Batch administrator schedules jobs and sets the job to execute using the authorizations granted to the batch user.
- **BDC Naming conventions** A consistent naming convention will be followed to allow restricting access to the BDC session data. Each group will define their own session names and ensure all BDC jobs conform to that convention. For example, HR BDC sessions will begin with HR_ followed by descriptive terms to identify the functions (for example, upload employees).
- **Table authorization groups** All custom tables will be assigned to a table authorization group. The use of the default authorization group &NC& is prohibited.
- **Spool/Print authorization groups** (12 characters)
- **Program authorization groups**
- **Logical command names**
- **Use of table access transaction codes like SE16, SE17, SM30, SM31**
- **Use of developer authorizations outside of a sandbox/development environment**
- **RFC user names**

This document will continue to change as new areas needing access restrictions are discovered and decisions concerning that access are made.

Without a guideline document to establish existing ground rules and capture new ground rules, you, as the security administrator, will be in a defensive posture, which will make your job even harder.

There are always challenges to restrictions, and as a security administrator, you will be faced with those challenges daily. Restrictions are not intended to prohibit access that is needed to get the business activities done. Restrictions are put in place to protect the corporate investment, and to protect the system integrity and confidentiality of the data the system contains.

Role Development Steps

Role development needs to follow a prescribed process just like any other development effort. Good design cannot be accomplished without good requirements. This holds true whether you are developing programs or security roles. A general rule of thumb is to create security as broadly as necessary to allow individuals to do their job, and thereby support the business, while imposing any restrictions necessary to enforce both legal and company regulations.

It seems like whenever you read about a security breach, an insider is involved. You should be sure the system cannot be compromised from external attacks, but also be aware that insider attacks are more prevalent. The only way to absolutely secure a company's system and the data it contains is to not allow any access, which is, of course, not an acceptable solution. Thus, we must find a balance that allows the users of the system to access both the functions and data they need to help support the company.

It is important to establish a role development methodology, which is basically a template you can use to fill in the blanks, make the process repeatable, and ensure a measure of confidence that when a given role is assigned to a person, it will allow him/her to complete all the steps of his/her job, giving them access to only that data they require.

In order to align the security roles to the business needs, I have come up with a process that begins with the business processes coming out of the blueprint phase. My take on this is that if we build security roles that directly support the business processes being used by the business and for which the SAP system is being configured to support, then we accomplish the previous considerations and are better able to partner with our functional project team members to meet the business needs both from a functionality standpoint as well as a security standpoint.

Every business member has corporate responsibilities to safeguard the assets of their business. It may sound like corporate hype, but if the company can compete or even get an edge in their respective marketplace, then that company can become a better place to work and earn a living in without some of the drastic measures, like wholesale layoffs, to bring the bottom line within whatever goal the executives are trying to reach to satisfy the shareholders.

To begin the role development process, it is important that the functional groups clearly define the business processes that will be implemented.

The next step is for the functional groups to determine segregation of responsibilities and further break up the business processes into logical components that take into account what I call break points. A break point is essentially a point in the business process where we need to stop for a review or a hand-off. An example might be in the purchase order process where a requisition is created and released, but the approval and assignment to a buyer is done by someone else. This is a segregation-of-duties hand-off and these functions should be in separate roles. Another example might be the segregation of creating a vendor account in the system and paying a vendor. If these actions were not segregated, it would be quite easy for an unscrupulous employee to defraud his/her company and redirect monies out of the company and into his/her own account.

Business rules generally dictate these types of segregation of responsibilities, and that is why it is incumbent on the functional side to define these points in the business process so we can build the security to enable the business to assign access in a way that will support the business process and defend it from potential abuse.

Once the functional team has defined the break points and grouped the business process steps into logical groupings based on those segregation-of-duties requirements, the next step is to determine how those steps are completed in an SAP system. SAP implements business functionality by way of transactions. For each business step, there may be one or more SAP transactions that will need to be executed. Someone with both business acumen and SAP knowledge will be needed to complete this mapping of SAP transactions to each business process step. Again, it is important that each grouping be identified as to whether it is intended to be done by the same employee or whether it must be segregated (for example, done by someone else). Each grouping is a candidate for a security role. The actual groupings need to be identified by the functional teams. The goal is to build functional components that can be used wherever this business process is needed. For example, it doesn't make a lot of sense to redesign and build a separate role for every functional group for entering time. The business process will be the same, so why not follow the key considerations of a simple build process—for instance, low maintenance—and build a time entry role that can be used wherever time entry is needed. Keep in mind that a separate role is not needed for each and every business process. If, for example, you have three separate business processes, but in the practical application of the business environment these processes are always executed by the same resource (employee), then these three business processes should be built into the same role. It just doesn't make efficient sense to build separate roles that are then always assigned together. Build one role and make one assignment. Only create separate roles when there is a business need to assign them separately.

Once these groupings are done, it is time to build the actual security role in SAP. These requirements should be provided to the SAP security team, who will use this information as input in their initial build process. What comes next is identifying any business data restrictions that should be incorporated into the security roles. Remember, our goal is to build a reusable component, so if we have a role that supports a given business process, but the business says we need to restrict items based on company code, then we can simply copy the base role and enter the company code values based on the business needs. Our base functionality will be repeated in the copied role, and the data restrictions will enforce the business data requirements. I recommend you fully test the base role for functionality before copying for the data restrictions. This way you don't have to repeat changes in the base role in the copies while testing is still in progress. Make the copies only after you and the business are satisfied that the functionality of the role is right. This saves time and avoids errors.

Let's take a moment now to address the use of derived roles. A derived role and what I called a base role are essentially the same. Each is created to provide the security for specific functionality, and then copies of that base role are created with the same functionality but with different data. For derived roles, the data that is different is organization-level data. This is maintained in the profile generator (PFCG) via the organization level button. When you create or maintain a role that has organizational level data, you click the organizational level button and a screen pops up with the organization-key fields. You enter the prescribed values and the PFCG automatically fills every authorization field in every authorization object that matches the organization level field you just filled in.

This auto-fill feature is time saving. Further more, if the parent role of the derived role is changed—that is, a transaction is added or taken away, you can instruct the profile generator to automatically generate the derived child roles for you. Again, a timesaver.

When you use the base role and copy or clone that role to create another role to have the same functionality but different data, any changes to the base role must be manually made in the copy as well. You may be saying to yourself, well I'll just use the derived role because it is much easier. If you drew that conclusion you would be right, as long as you follow the rules for derived roles. There is a gotcha you need to be careful about when using derived roles, however. When the derived role has data changes that are not organization-level changes, you still must maintain those fields manually. In addition, if you happen to generate the derived role, you will lose all non-organizational level field values because the PFCG will overwrite all fields except organization level fields with the values from the parent.

This is the main purpose of using derived roles. All non-organization level field values should come from the parent. Also, it is good practice to leave all organization-level field values null in the derived role.

Security Matrix

Although it sometimes gets cumbersome, most companies keep track of their role requirements using excel spreadsheets. An example of a matrix layout is shown in Table 3.1. Although I have kept this simple for demonstration purposes, once you start getting 20 to 30 roles or more, a basic spreadsheet gets a bit unwieldy.

Table 3.1 Security Matrix Template

Role Name	Role_A	Role_B	Role_C
Data Requirements:			
Company Codes	1010-2200	All	1000
Doc. Types	A*-F*	All	ZSER
Asset Class	10000-50000	All	20001-30000
Transactions:			
AB03	X	X	X
FB03	X		X
FB01		X	
FB02	X		X
SM37	X	X	X
SP01	X	X	X

In the sample role matrix shown in Table 3.1, you see the role names across the top and then as you look down the left-most column you see a data section with the data values specified for each role. As you move down that left-most column, notice the transactions listed with Xs under the role column, marking where that transaction should be located. This type of role matrix allows the security administrator to cut and paste into the PFCG menu to quickly build the roles' initial menu. The data section is used to fill out the authorization fields with the specified values whenever that field is encountered within the role.

This type of matrix is easy for anyone to review and audit the role values against the role requirements.

In addition to showing the assignment of transactions and data values to the respective roles, I always request that an additional tab in the spreadsheet be filled out for each role. Each role should have a short line of text with the basic functionality of the role. This line of text is placed in the role description field when the role is created and shows up on reports along with the role name. I also request that a fuller narrative of the role's purpose be provided. This is for both the auditors as well as future role approvers. The auditors can verify the link between business functionality and the security role for that functionality, and the role approvers have a reference sheet to match up role assignments to persons doing that work in the business.

Another tab that can and should be included in the role matrix is for composite roles. You can create a row/column matrix showing which simple roles make up a composite role. Composite roles can be made from the simple process roles to form positional roles that conform to HR position descriptions. You should provide the same descriptors for the composite roles as you did for the simple process roles to make the documentation complete.

Tools

No matter what type of work you do, tools help you do that work. Tools will often let you do your work faster and with more accuracy. As a security administrator, there are tools you should be become aware of and familiar with in order to accomplish your daily tasks.

AL08

Transaction AL08 is very useful for monitoring the users that are logged onto a given SAP system. Use it to view all users from all application servers. You will see a summary at the top of the list of total active users, which will be followed by a section for each server configured in the SAP system. The search feature on AL08 lets you search for specific user IDs, which is quite handy when trying to find a specific user ID in order to terminate the session.

BDM2

If you need to troubleshoot IDOC problems while working in a CUA central system, BDM2 is an invaluable tool. When an IDOC is sent from the CUA central system to a child system for processing, the child system receives the IDOC information from the CUA central system, creates a new IDOC and IDOC number, and then uses the new IDOC for processing.

Without a map to know what the new IDOC number is in the child system, it becomes very difficult to trace the progress of the CUA update from the central system to the child system. You would have to use WE05 and do the best you could to match up the IDOCs based on date/time stamps and the data in the IDOC, which is a very tedious and time-consuming process.

BDM2 provides the IDOC tracing from the central CUA system to the child system, which makes life a whole lot easier for the security administrator when troubleshooting a CUA processing problem. Take a look at the figures that follow.

First, we run BDM2 to get the selection screen (see Figure 3.3).

Figure 3.3 BDM2 IDOC Tracing

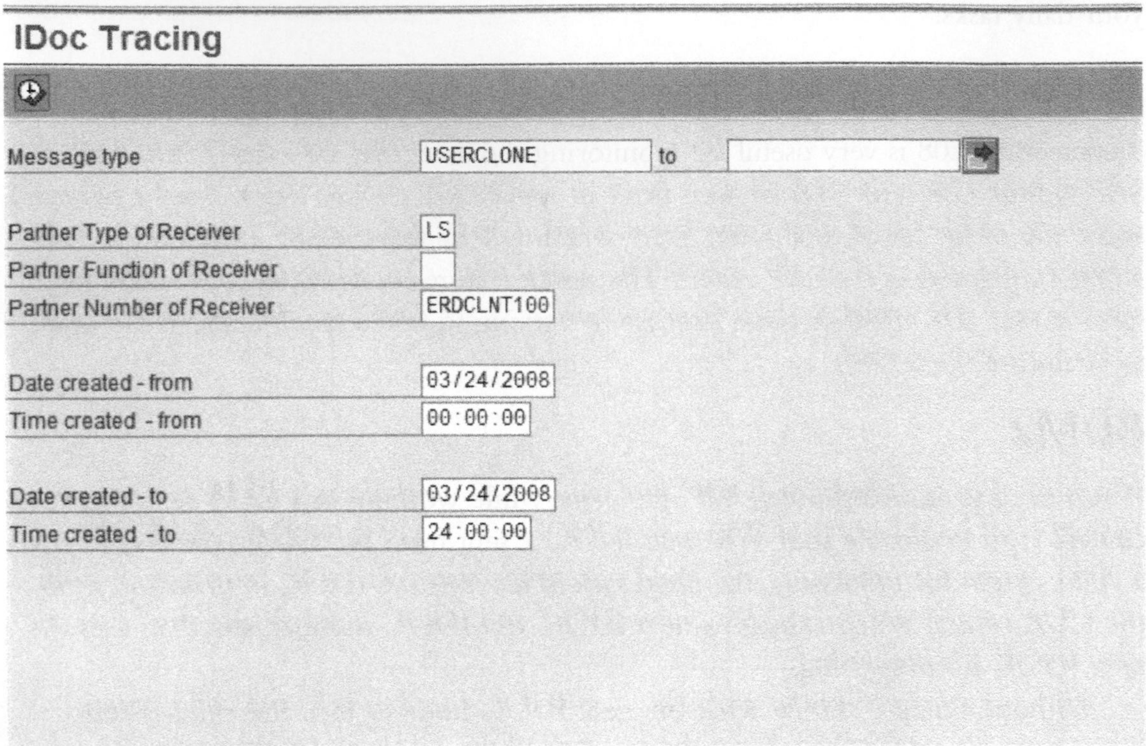

IDoc Tracing

Message type	USERCLONE	to	
Partner Type of Receiver	LS		
Partner Function of Receiver			
Partner Number of Receiver	ERDCLNT100		
Date created - from	03/24/2008		
Time created - from	00:00:00		
Date created - to	03/24/2008		
Time created - to	24:00:00		

Enter the necessary information in the selection fields. CUA uses message type USERCLONE and the partner type is always LS. The partner number of the receiver is the logical system name and, of course, you need to enter selection dates to restrict your search to the data you are most interested in.

Figure 3.4 provides you with a breakdown of the number of IDOCs found based on your selection input—in this case, we have found 38 IDOCs with a status of 53.

Figure 3.4 IDOC Tracing IDOC Summary

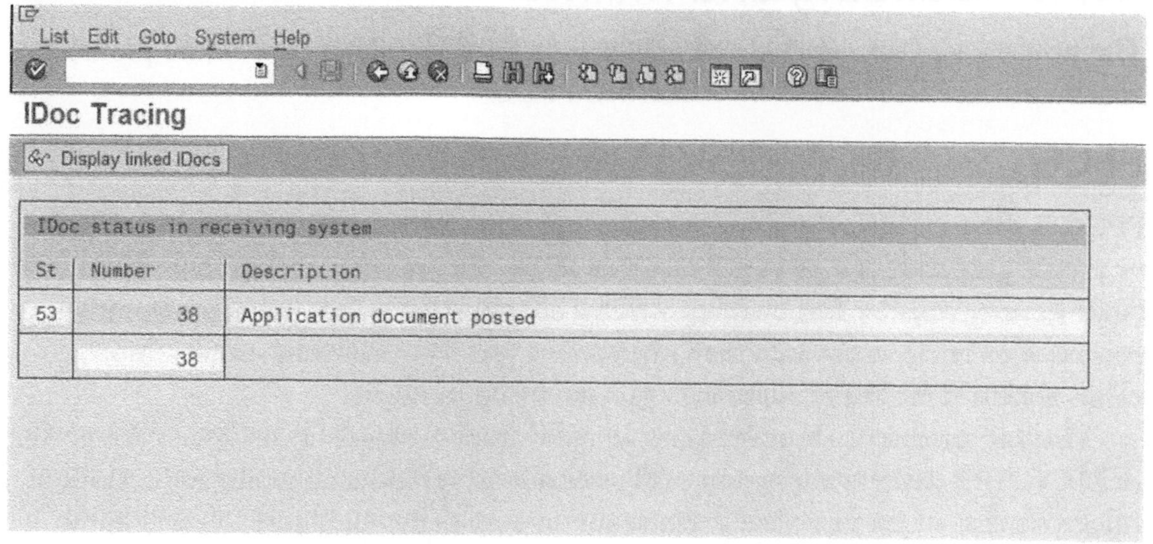

St	Number	Description
53	38	Application document posted
	38	

By doubling-clicking the status line, we get a display that shows us the mapping or trace of the IDOCs we sent from the sender to the receiver. We can then use this to log on to the receiver and continue our analysis without having to search for the right IDOC in the receiver, child system. See Figure 3.5.

Figure 3.5 IDOC Tracing IDOC Detail

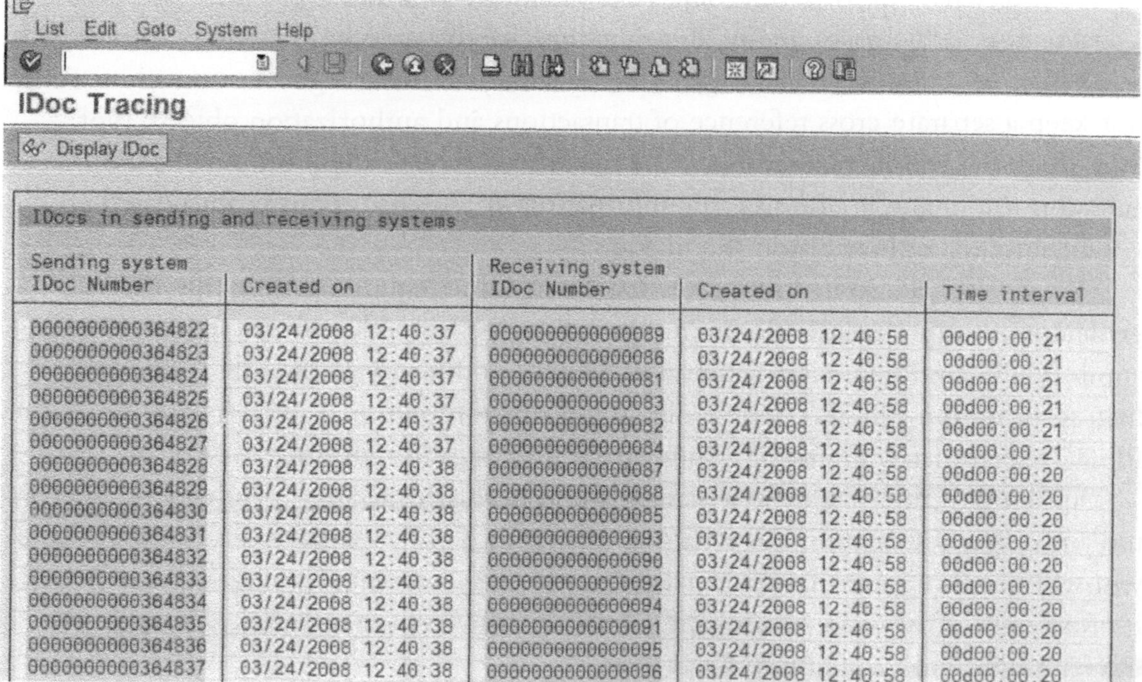

Sending system IDoc Number	Created on	Receiving system IDoc Number	Created on	Time interval
0000000000364822	03/24/2008 12:40:37	0000000000000089	03/24/2008 12:40:58	00d00:00:21
0000000000364823	03/24/2008 12:40:37	0000000000000086	03/24/2008 12:40:58	00d00:00:21
0000000000364824	03/24/2008 12:40:37	0000000000000081	03/24/2008 12:40:58	00d00:00:21
0000000000364825	03/24/2008 12:40:37	0000000000000083	03/24/2008 12:40:58	00d00:00:21
0000000000364826	03/24/2008 12:40:37	0000000000000082	03/24/2008 12:40:58	00d00:00:21
0000000000364827	03/24/2008 12:40:37	0000000000000084	03/24/2008 12:40:58	00d00:00:21
0000000000364828	03/24/2008 12:40:38	0000000000000087	03/24/2008 12:40:58	00d00:00:20
0000000000364829	03/24/2008 12:40:38	0000000000000088	03/24/2008 12:40:58	00d00:00:20
0000000000364830	03/24/2008 12:40:38	0000000000000085	03/24/2008 12:40:58	00d00:00:20
0000000000364831	03/24/2008 12:40:38	0000000000000093	03/24/2008 12:40:58	00d00:00:20
0000000000364832	03/24/2008 12:40:38	0000000000000090	03/24/2008 12:40:58	00d00:00:20
0000000000364833	03/24/2008 12:40:38	0000000000000092	03/24/2008 12:40:58	00d00:00:20
0000000000364834	03/24/2008 12:40:38	0000000000000094	03/24/2008 12:40:58	00d00:00:20
0000000000364835	03/24/2008 12:40:38	0000000000000091	03/24/2008 12:40:58	00d00:00:20
0000000000364836	03/24/2008 12:40:38	0000000000000095	03/24/2008 12:40:58	00d00:00:20
0000000000364837	03/24/2008 12:40:38	0000000000000096	03/24/2008 12:40:58	00d00:00:20

Roles – Building and Maintenance

The primary tool for creating and maintaining security roles in SAP is the profile generator which is accessed via transaction PFCG.

PFCG

PFCG is the transaction you use to create and maintain security roles in SAP. PFCG, or profile generator, is a powerful tool that allows the security administrator to quickly build security roles by first building a menu of transactions that instruct the profile generator to bring in authorization objects that you then maintain authorization values for based on the requirements you are trying to meet.

That last statement about bringing in authorization objects is the key to the power of PFCG. SAP delivers the system with associations of transactions and authorization objects so that when you place a transaction in a role's menu, the PFCG will know what objects to include in the authorization section of the role. Many security administrators new to SAP often don't know or understand this relationship. Further, many don't know they can make adjustments to these relationships by using another transaction called SU24, as well as add relationships for custom transactions.

While this discussion is focused on PFCG, it is hard to discuss PFCG without mentioning SU24. SU24 is the configuration transaction for PFCG. Using SU24, you can control what authorization objects are included in a role every time you place a transaction in the role's menu. This function aids the role build process because you don't have to rediscover what objects are necessary to make a given transaction work, nor keep a separate cross reference of transactions and authorization objects. Not only does the profile generator add the necessary objects whenever a transaction is added to the menu, it also uses the information in SU24 to remove objects when a transaction is removed from the menu.

You should take some time to review the documentation on using the profile generator at http://Help.SAP.com. You can also select the Help menu option once you are in PFCG and then select application help to go directly to the role maintenance help section from PFCG. There is also an information button, **Ctrl + F3**, on the main PFCG screen that will provide a summary of the steps for creating a role.

Speaking of the main PFCG screen, you should already have a role name ready to use and a brief description of what that role is for before starting a role build because you will need to enter that information in the role name and role description fields. For example, if we were creating an FI role for the Accounts Payable Manager, the screen might look something like Figure 3.6.

Figure 3.6 PFCG

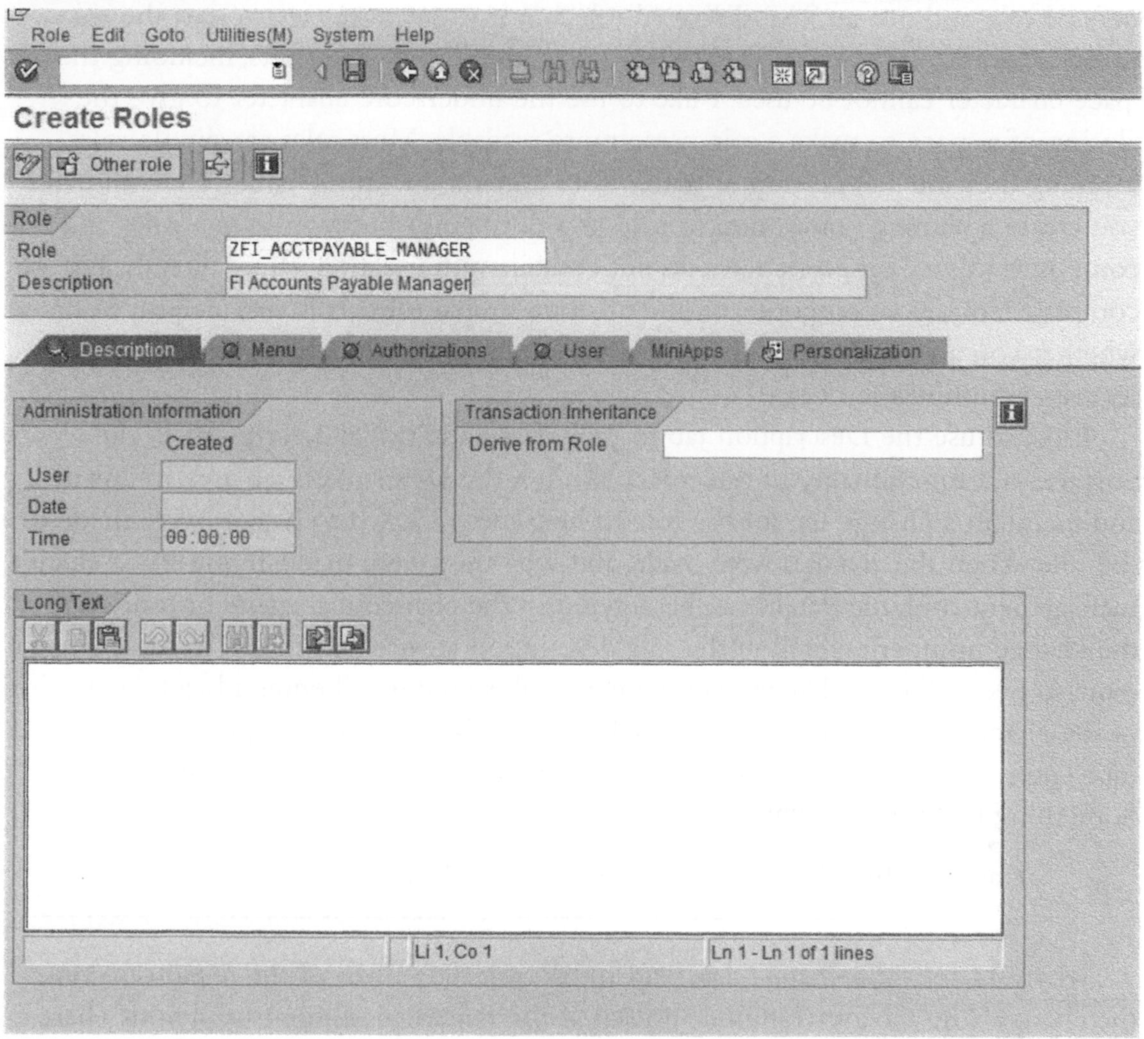

Note that I have started the role name with a "Z" followed by "FI" to denote this is an FI role. Having a group indicator like "FI" as part of the naming convention lets me group all FI roles for inventory purposes, for reporting purposes, mass transports, and distributed security purposes. If you wanted to limit access to just the FI roles, you could use the naming convention to accomplish it via security authorizations.

Use your naming conventions to create a role name. Although I started this role name with a "Z", the only restriction SAP puts on the naming convention you use is that you should not start your role names with "SAP" because this is SAP's name space and you could risk having your role's data overwritten by SAP during upgrades.

Using a "Z" to start the role name only reenforces recognition that this is a user-defined role and not an SAP-delivered role, but it is not necessary to start the role name with a "Z". Other restrictions are that some special characters, including the space character cannot be used. I like to use the underscore character to give the illusion of a space to make a role name more readable. Most roles are simple roles, meaning they are a collection of transactions and authorization values. I recommend you create a naming convention to help you distinguish between simple roles and composite roles. Composite roles do not contain authorization values directly, but are comprised, or are a composite, of one or more simple roles. It is very helpful to know whether you are working with a simple or a composite role when performing your security administration tasks.

I like to use the Description tab to provide an additional description of the purpose and functionality of this role. I also use the Description tab area to create and maintain a change log for the role to help me track what changes were made to the role, when the changes were made, and why they were made. If you use a change management tool, the details can be entered in the change management tool and the change number entered in the role description area to track back to the change request. Even when a change management tool is used, I still enter a brief description of the change so I don't have to go back to the original change request unless I need more detail. I try to keep the change log in the description area of the role simple. Something like the following:

```
Date    Initials    Change Number       Description
-----   -------     ----------------    ------------------------------
```

where Date is the change date, and Initials are the initials of the person making the change. The Change Number, if used, is the reference number from your change management system, while the Description is a brief narrative of what changed (for example, *Added transaction xxxx*). This change log in the role itself has saved me countless hours of investigations and analysis time when a change I thought had gone to production didn't make it and we were still getting complaints about the role not working. By looking at the change log in production, I can quickly see if the change is there. Sometimes there is a delay in the transports, and sometimes a transport gets overwritten. A change log in the role itself helps me do some quick analysis and often clues me in on which direction to take next.

Once you have entered the role name and description, you should press the save button. You will also be asked if you want to save when you select the Authorizations tab, if you haven't already save it. You should get in the habit of saving a role often. Just like when working on any other document, saving often might just save you hours of work if you encounter a system error and lose what you were working on. Having selected the Authorization tab, you will now be ready to maintain the authorization values. When you first create a role, the PFCG will look at the SU24 configuration and pull in all the objects associated with the transactions you entered on the role's menu. Subsequent editing of the role will require you to decide how you will enter the maintenance mode. Selecting the Change Authorization Data button will simply put you into change mode where you can update the authorization fields as needed. However, if you have maintained new values in SU24, you will want PFCG to update the role with those new values, so you will want to select "Expert Mode." Selecting expert mode will present you with the options on entering change mode.

The first option will delete all the authorizations and start over. This is not usually selected unless you have a real mess with the role's authorizations and need to start over and bring in a fresh copy of the objects based on the transactions.

The second option is to edit the old status, which is the same as simply entering change mode, the first button.

The third option under expert mode is what you will normally use, which is to read the old status and merge the new data. The new data is any SU24 changes. This feature of PFCG is something you must keep aware of because not only can SU24 be used to add objects to transactions, it can also be used to remove objects. If you are not aware of the changes going on with SU24, you could very likely disable a role that was working.

Let's look at an example. We have a role that has transaction FI03, which is a display transaction for FI. It comes delivered in SU24 with object *F_BNKA_MAN* turned on, meaning every time we enter FI03 in a role's menu, PFCG will also bring in authorization object *F_BNKA_MAN*. This is good because the programs that run for FI03 perform an authorization check against this object and we need this object in the role to allow someone to use FI03. If for some reason another security administrator deactivates *F_BNKA_MAN* in SU24 for FI03 and we use expert mode to read the old status and merge the new data, the PFCG will look at the authorization objects configured for FI03, see that *F_BNKA_MAN* is no longer associated, and remove it from the role. If we were maintaining the role to simply add a new transaction, the effect of the change in SU24 would essentially "break" the role for FI03.

A rule of thumb I tell my clients when using SU24 is that you should always check what the impact will be, especially if you are removing an object from a transaction.

You can use the "where used" section in the reporting transaction SUIM to determine where a given transaction is used. You should get into the habit of verifying the impact to other roles whenever you are making changes in SU24 in order to minimize the unexpected changes that can be introduced. Authorizations that are inadvertently taken away are hard to diagnose and can cause your user community to become distrustful of the system, not to mention cause damage to your own credibility. I suggest you take a look at OSS note 113290, which discusses how the merge process of authorization data works in the PFCG.

I have found that clients usually have their ABAP programmers create the custom objects as part of their programming tasks. I do highly recommend to my clients that the ABAP programmers should inform and work with security in creating these custom objects.

Security-Related Parameters Setup

Parameters in SAP control various functions and system configurations for how the SAP application starts up, allocates resources etc. In addition, security related parameters determine restrictions for the security environment. For example, password lengths and logon time outs are just a couple of examples. RZ10 and RZ11 provide the tools to establish the parameters and set the values for the SAP application.

RZ10

RZ10 is a BASIS tool to perform profile maintenance. Now, these profiles are not authorization profiles but profiles that contain parameters that determine how the SAP system and application servers are configured. For the security administrator, TU02 is a better tool for reviewing the settings of the system parameters in my opinion.

RZ11

RZ11 provides the documentation for system parameters. Unfortunately, a complete documentation set for all parameters is not supplied by SAP.

To use RZ11, execute the transaction. You should be presented with a simple screen, like that in Figure 3.7, with a single field where you can enter in the parameter name, and then click the display button and see both the documentation about this parameter as well as the default setting and current setting.

Figure 3.7 RZ11

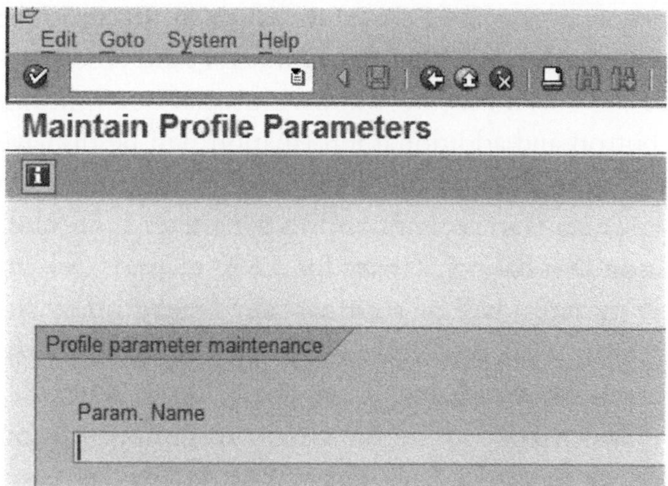

For example, we may be interested in what the parameter rdisp/gui_auto_logout is. Enter this into the **Param. Name** field and click the **Display** button. You should see a screen like that in Figure 3.8.

Figure 3.8 RZ11 Parameter Attributes

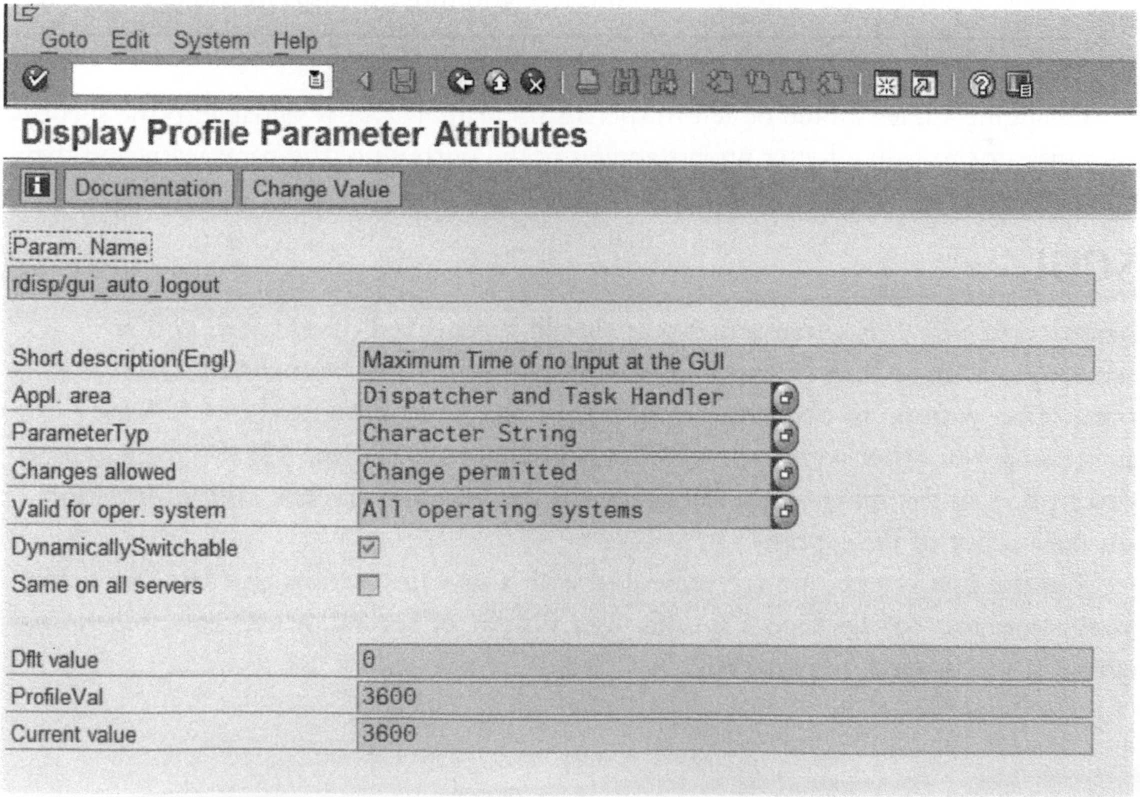

Goto Edit System Help

Display Profile Parameter Attributes

Documentation Change Value

Param. Name

rdisp/gui_auto_logout

Short description(Engl)	Maximum Time of no Input at the GUI
Appl. area	Dispatcher and Task Handler
ParameterTyp	Character String
Changes allowed	Change permitted
Valid for oper. system	All operating systems
DynamicallySwitchable	☑
Same on all servers	☐
Dflt value	0
ProfileVal	3600
Current value	3600

In addition to a short description for this parameter, please note the fields at the bottom of the display that give the Dflt value, which in this example tells us that the default value is zero. Also note that the ProfileVal field is set to 3600 and the current value is also 3600. You may be wondering what 3600 means. Well, click the **Documentation** button and additional information will be displayed. In addition to more clarification on this parameter, if you scroll down to the **Unit** section you will find that the value set is in seconds, so this parameter is currently set for 3,600 seconds. A user session that has no activity for 3,600 seconds (for the mathematically challenged, that's 60 minutes) will be automatically logged off by the system.

Other information that is useful from RZ11 can be obtained by observing the check box for DynamicallySwitchable. If this check box is selected, it means this parameter value can be changed while the system is running—in other words, a value change does not require a stop/start of SAP to activate a new value.

NOTE

The dynamic change to the parameter is lost at the next system restart. If you want to set the parameter permanently, you must set this in the profile file.

Changing values should be left to the BASIS team. RZ11 is valuable to the security administrator to gain a better understanding of the purpose of the parameters and their current values.

SCUL

Transaction SCUL is a transaction that should be checked often when you are working within a CUA (Central User Administration) environment. SCUL is the transaction you use to check the records that have been submitted to CUA for processing—in other words, the CUA log. Please see OSS note 632486 for a general description of the functions, information on the selection screens, and information on the output of the report.

On the first screen, you are presented with a selection screen that lets you tailor your log report to check on a specific user, system, or several other fields, depending on what you want to report on.

In addition, there is a selection area where you can specify certain types of log records called statuses and certain status records. In CUA, when you save a user master record in SU01, three status records are created. One to update the user master information related to the logon, the address, and the default tabs. A second status record is created for role changes, and a third record is created for changes on the Profile tab. See Figure 3.9.

Figure 3.9 SCUL

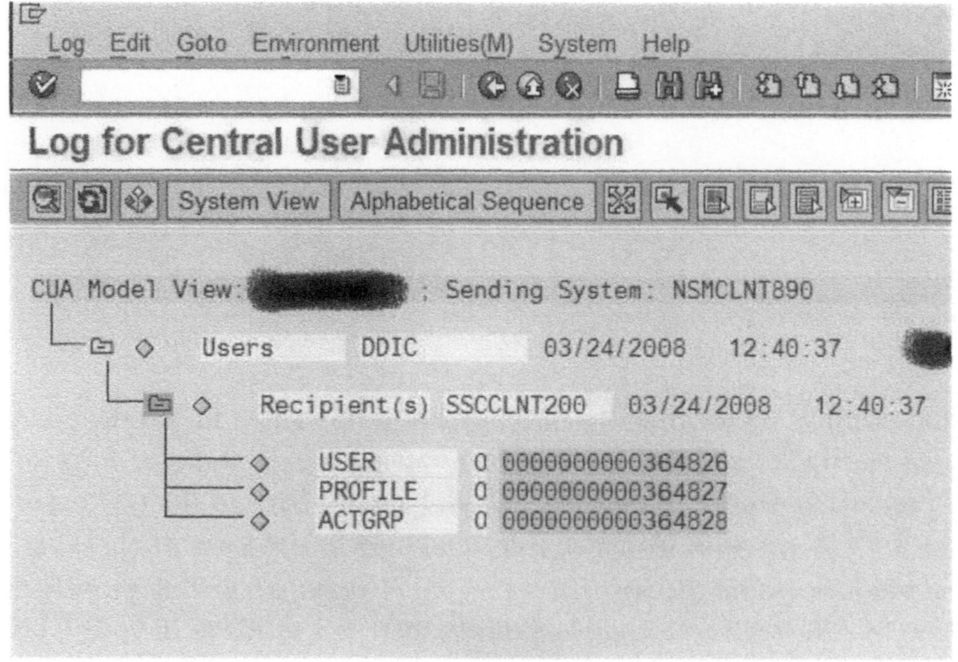

Notice the number to the right of the USER, PROFILE, and ACTGRP entries. These numbers are the IDOC (intermediate document) number, which is a format SAP uses for electronic document exchange between systems. If we double-click one of these numbers, we are taken to the IDOC status screen (shown in Figure 3.10), where we can check the status of the IDOC processing.

Figure 3.10 IDOC Status

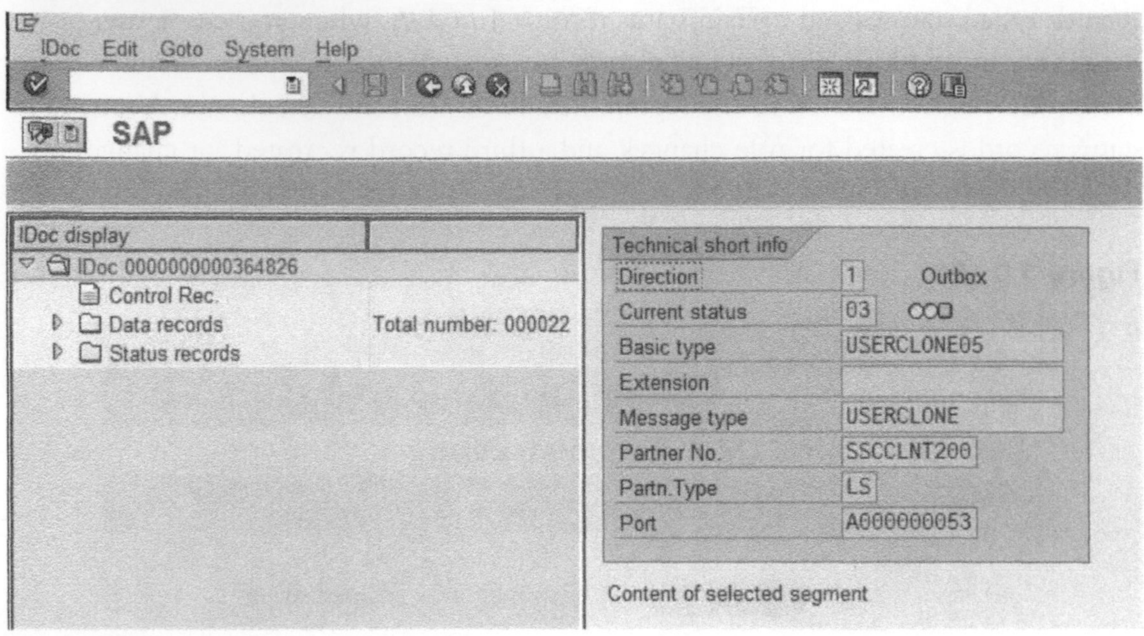

In this example, we see that the current status is 03, which means the CUA system has created the IDOC and sent it on to the receiving system and is waiting on the receiving system to process the IDOC and send a status back to the CUA system.

When a CUA system is involved, you should get in the habit of checking the CUA log often to ensure the user master record changes are getting processed. Records in SCUL that never complete means there is a problem in your CUA system and you need to get it resolved quickly because CUA IDOC records that are not processed when received will sit in a queue until someone takes some action to resolve the hold up. Sometimes the problem is just that too many IDOCs were received for the receiving system to process due to resource availability and all that is needed is to restart the process. Unprocessed IDOCs for CUA mean that the changes you have been submitting are not getting completed in the receiving system. If you follow up with another change to the same user master record without resolving the earlier change, then you risk having the latest change overwritten by the change that is still pending.

I see many clients who get frustrated with CUA because of this very situation. They see it as unreliable and more trouble than it is worth. CUA is not without its problems, but with a little care and feeding and making sure all records are processed when submitted, it becomes a very useful tool.

SE93

While this transaction is actually a developer's transaction, the security administrator can use it to determine the program, screen, and whether there is a minimum authorization object required to run the transaction. I use it mostly to determine if the transaction is a parameter transaction. A parameter transaction is a transaction that runs another transaction, with parameters that control how that transaction should run. In other words, screen input is supplied by the parameter values given.

Execute SE93 and you are presented with an input screen to enter the transaction you want to review. For example, transaction SCC4 is used to display/maintain clients within a SAP system. SCC4 is actually a parameter transaction that executes SM30 with parameters to view table T000. Go ahead and try it. Enter **SE93**, then in the **Transaction Code** field, enter **SCC4**, and press the **Display** button. A screen should appear with information about SCC4. You should see a field that gives the transaction text, and below that should be the default values for the transaction to be called for SCC4. Notice that transaction SM30 is used. If you scroll down to the bottom of the SE93 display, you should see that a viewname of T000 is to be used in "Show" mode. If this parameter transaction was to be used to initially update the table, instead of "Show" you would have seen "Update."

With the information we see using SE93 for SCC4 and knowing that SM30 is protected by the authorization object *S_TABU_DIS*, we know that for the value "Show" we would need to set the following: activity = 03. We would then need to look up the table authorization group assigned to T000 to complete the authorization values and allow a role to be able to run SCC4 and display the client table.

Now use SE93 to look at transaction SM01. SM01 is used to lock transactions in a system to prohibit anyone from executing the locked transaction. SM01 is an administration type of transaction and therefore should not be given to users who are not system administrators. SM01 has an authorization object assigned to it with an authorization value. Anyone who tries to execute SM01 must have this authorization in order to run this transaction. This is an early authorization check that takes place immediately after the system checks whether the user is authorized to run the transaction. In other words, the SAP system checks this authorization before it lets the user execute the code attached to the transaction.

Look at SM01 in SE93. You should see the transaction text, the program and initial screen that will be executed, and also a field for authorization of the object. Next to this field is a button labeled Values. Press the Values button and you should see both the authorization fields and values needed. Some ABAP programmers do not enter any values here, and when a user runs the transaction, SAP will first check that the user is authorized to execute the transaction by looking for S_TCODE in the user's authorizations with the value equal to the transaction value. Next comes the check to determine if an authorization object is assigned and if values are assigned. If no values are assigned, then SAP checks to see if the user has the object in his/her user master record, and if yes, allow the transaction to execute the code assigned.

I believe every SAP security administrator should be familiar with SE93 because there is valuable information that can be obtained about the authorizations that may be needed for certain transactions. Not all transactions will have an object attached to it for this early check, but as we perform our security administration activities, the more we understand how SAP works, the better we are able to do our jobs.

SM04

SM04 gives you a listing of the users logged on, and if you are an administrator, you can terminate a user session. Terminating a user session is handy when a user session has been hung up and other settings in the system do not allow more than one logon session.

If you find yourself needing to terminate a user session, execute SM04, double-click the user ID, and a pop-up screen showing an overview of the sessions this user has active will display (see Figure 3.11).

Figure 3.11 SM04

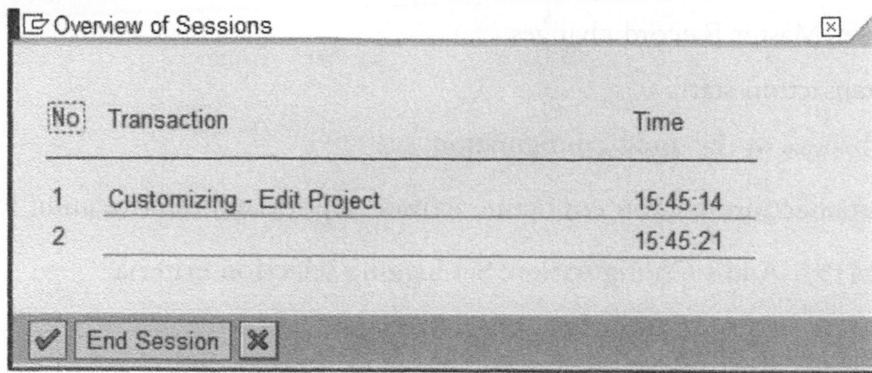

Sometimes a user will have multiple internal sessions running for the same logon session. To terminate a session, select the session from the overview and click the **End Session** button. The caution here is that if a user was in the middle of some activity, all data will be lost.

A problem with SM04 that many administrators do not realize is that SM04 only shows the users that are logged on to the same application server that the administrator is logged on to. This can be misleading when multiple application servers have been configured and activated because you may mistakenly think there are much fewer active users in the system than there really are. To see all users on all servers, use AL08.

Security Auditing

SAP provides the Audit Information System (AIS) that allows you to create a monitoring profile to log those items you select and can latter create a report of those items to be able to monitor your system.

SM19 and SM20

The Audit Information System (AIS) provides a means of logging additional activities in the Security Audit Log that are not captured in the System Log. AIS is a tool designed to take a more detailed look at specific activities occurring in the SAP R/3 System, such as:

- Dialog log-on attempts
- RFC log-on attempts

- RFC calls to function modules
- User Master Record changes
- Transaction starts
- Changes to the audit configuration

Three transactions let you configure, activate, report, and remove audit log entries:

- SM19 – Audit Configuration: Set logging selection criteria
- SM20 – System Audit Log: Local Analysis
- SM18 – Purge old Audit Files

SM18 is primarily a BASIS responsibility for maintaining the file system, so we will skip over this transaction and look more closely at SM19 and SM20.

AIS lets you specify the information you want to audit (capture in the audit log) with transaction SM19. The R/3 AIS then keeps a record (log) of all activities that correspond to your selection criteria. You will be able to specify via SM20 all logged entries, or you can specify a subset of the log entries to report. It is important to note that only the selections configured via SM19 can be reported with SM20.

To configure AIS to start collecting log entries, use transaction SM19

A screen will appear displaying two tabs (shown in Figure 3.12): a Static Configuration tab and a Dynamic Configuration tab. The only real difference is that the top frame of the screen on the Static Configuration tab has a field for you to enter the name you want to save your settings in (called the active profile). The Dynamic Configuration tab has a list of active servers to distribute your setting to. We will see a sample of that screen in a few minutes.

Figure 3.12 SM19

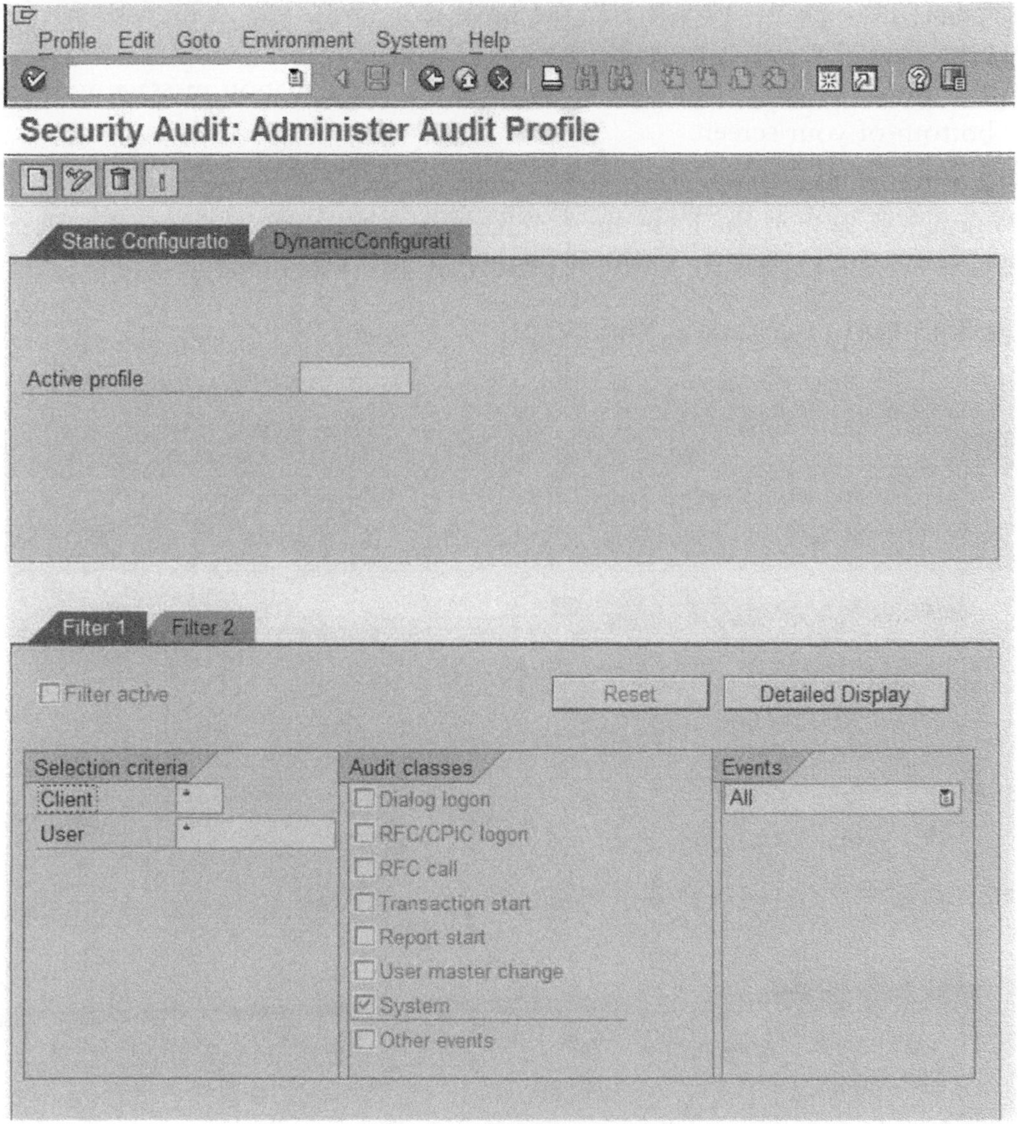

When using the Static Configuration tab, select **Create**, and then enter a name for the profile. The profile name is a name you pick and will be saved in the database. I usually select a name that somehow denotes what I am logging—for example, RFC_TRK for tracking RFC access. You only have eight characters, so a little creativity is needed.

Once you have entered the profile name, you can set up the filter. We will cover setting up the filter when we discuss the Dynamic Configuration tab because it is the same for either static or dynamic configurations.

On the Static Configuration tab, once the filter settings are complete, you save the settings in the profile by selecting the **Save** icon at the top of the screen.

A prompt will appear asking if you want to distribute this to all servers, which of course you do. After selecting yes to distribute, a confirmation message will appear at the bottom of your screen.

This filter should be reactivated when the SAP server is brought up.

So now let's look at the Dynamic Configuration tab and check out the filter settings. Select the **Dynamic Configuration** tab (see Figure 3.13).

Figure 3.13 SM19 Dynamic Configuration

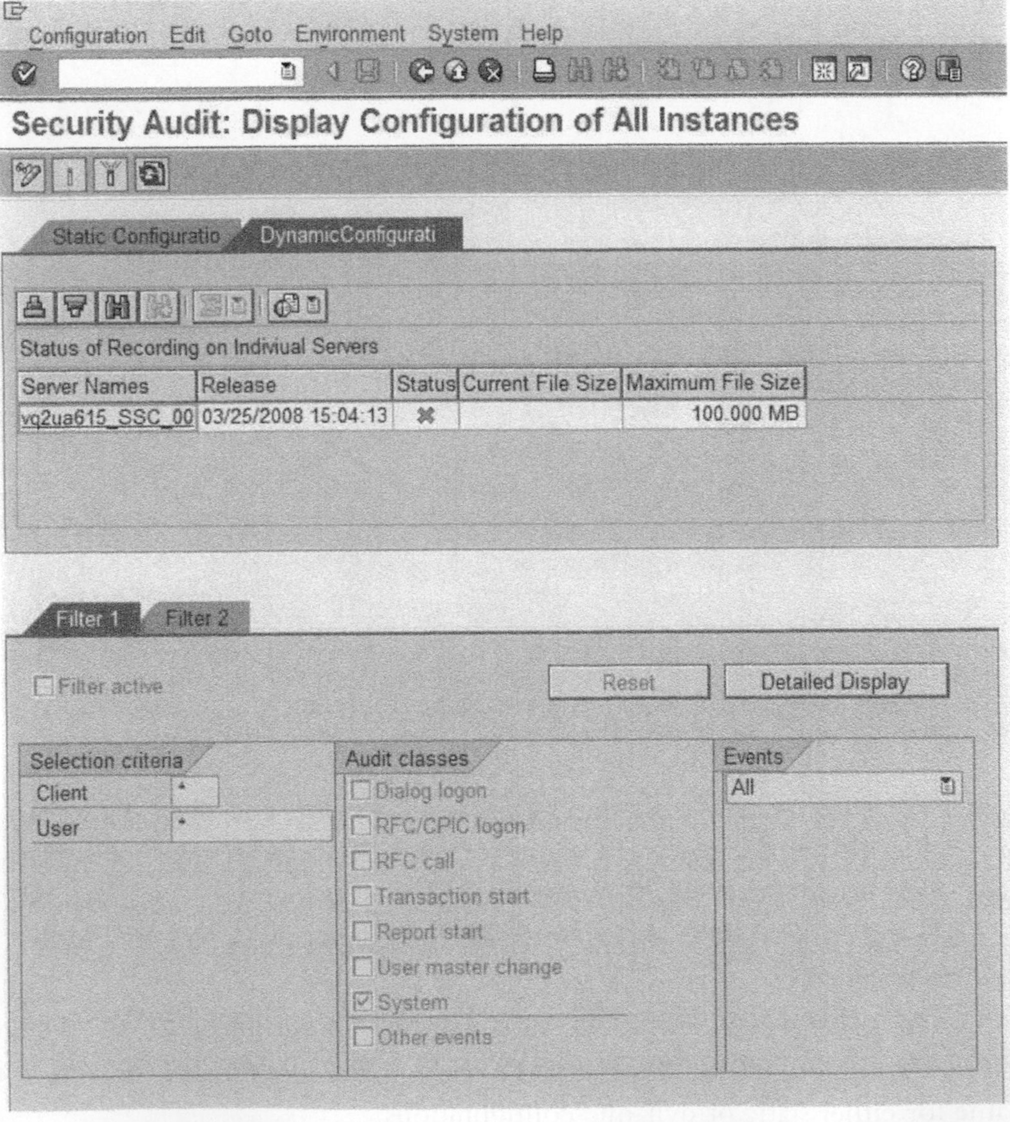

Notice in the top section of Figure 3.12 that instead of a profile name there is a listing of active servers. This example only has one active server.

We need to activate a filter to set it up. Click the **Display/Change** button (pencil icon) and then choose the **Filter Active** check box. Each filter represents a configuration record for specifying unique audit selection criteria for logging events.

The Filter Active check box indicates whether a specific configuration is actively logging the respective selections.

Audit Classes are the items you select to log. For more information on Audit Classes, click the **Detail Configuration** button.

Enter the client you want to log (the user). (I usually leave this with the asterisk, unless I have been asked to set up logging for a specific user.) Then, select the audit classes you want to log.

Note: For the Clnt and User fields, you cannot specify a generic selection—for example, BOB*.

Once your selections are made, you are ready to activate this filter and begin logging.

Click the **Activate** icon. A confirmation prompt will notify you that the configuration has changed and ask if you want to distribute the change to all servers. Again, of course you do.

The server status will change to indicate that the AIS configuration changes are now active on the server and you should get a confirmation message at the bottom of the screen. See Figure 3.14.

Figure 3.14 SM19 Save Configuration

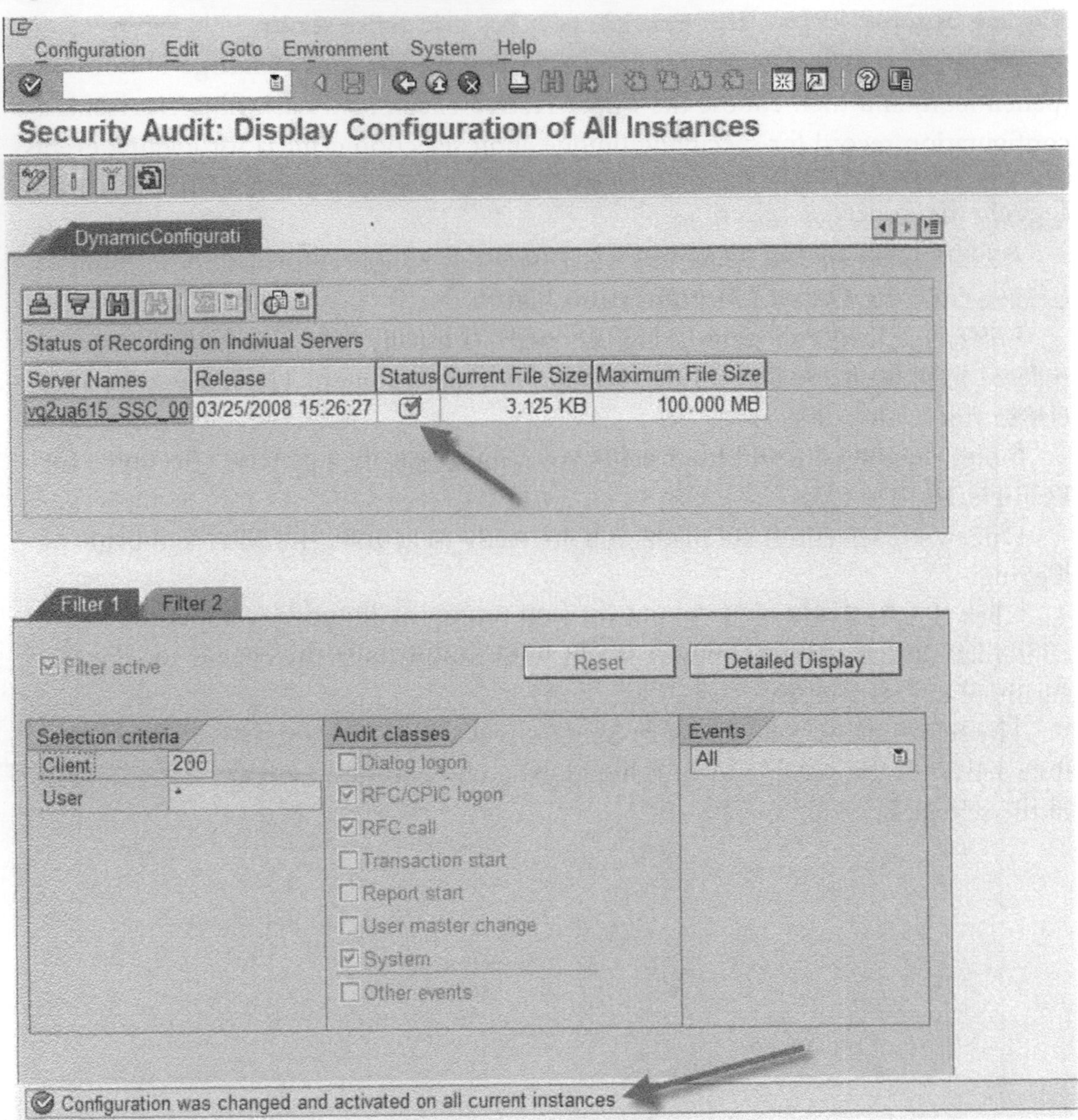

You are now logging the activities you selected. To create a report, we use SM20. SM20 lets you display specific activities from the audit log file for a given time frame (see Figure 3.15).

Figure 3.15 SM20

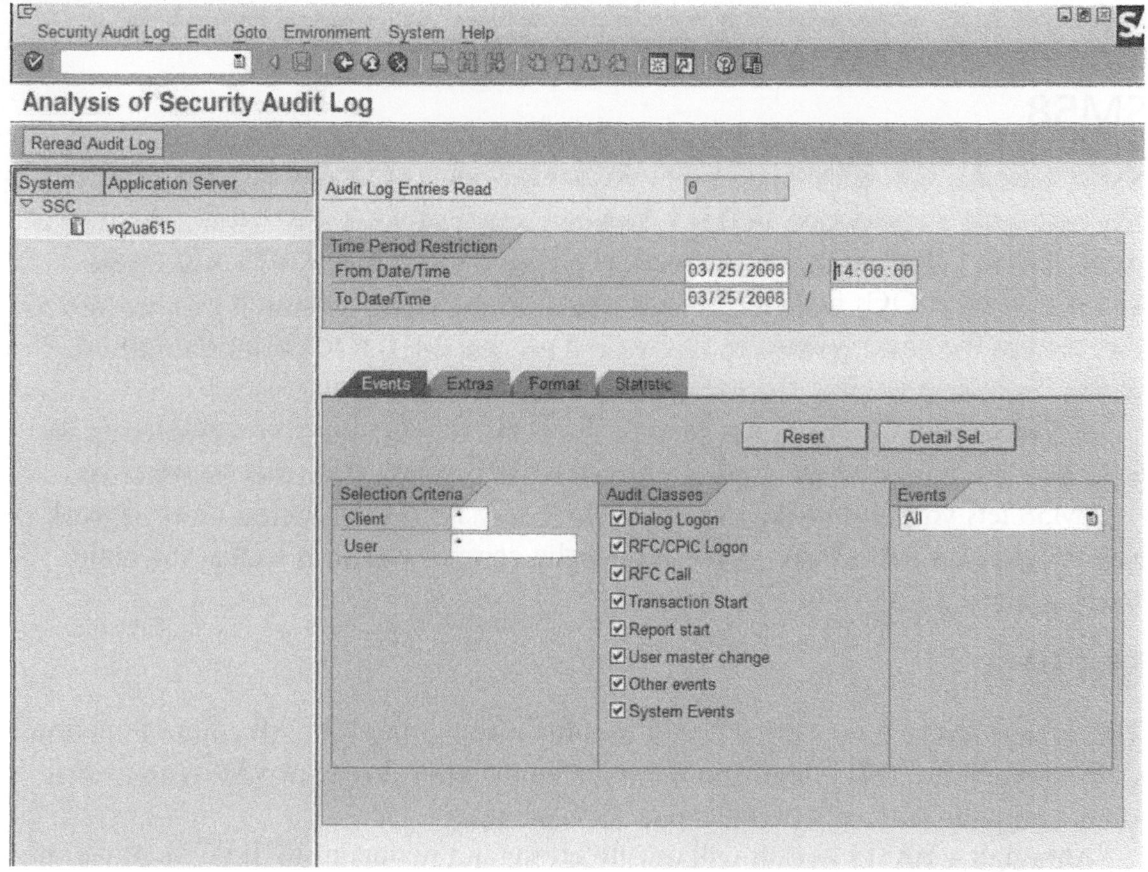

- **Time Period Restriction** This section lets you specify a start/stop date/time for extracting messages from the audit log. In addition, you can enter a specific user ID and/or transaction to report.
- **Audit classes** This lets you specify only the types of events to report on. The selections must have been previously configured to collect the events via SM19.
- **Events:** This lets you specify the level of events to report on. The selections must have been previously configured to collect the corresponding level of events via SM19.

Once your selections have been made, click the **Reread Audit Log** button to start the report. Remember, if you haven't set AIS to log a specific Audit Class with SM19, you will not get any records in your SM20 report.

RFC (Remote Function Call)

```
Remote function calls provide communication between SAP systems as well as
communication from external systems.
```

SM58

SM58 provides you with access to the Asynchronous RFC Error Log. An RFC is like executing a transaction in that it kicks off a unit of work. Sometimes the unit of work doesn't complete and leaves work pending. CUA executes RFCs to create and distribute IDOCs from the central system to the child systems. RFCs are also executed in the child systems to receive and process the IDOCs from the central system, including sending the status back to the central system.

If resource availability issues prevent the RFC transaction from completing its task, then there may be incomplete units of work pending that must be restarted.

SM58 lets you review the logs and, if necessary, restart the logical units of work. You should routinely check SM58 in both the central system, as well as the child systems, when a CUA system is active.

SM59

Transaction SM59 is actually a BASIS tool for maintaining RFC (Remote Function Call) destinations. RFC destinations are the connections between SAP systems that allow communications between clients and systems.

Although a BASIS person will usually set up and maintain the RFC destinations, the security administrator will often be requested to provide user IDs and passwords that will be set up in the RFC destination and used to log on remotely and execute remote function calls. You should create a secure area where you can keep track of these user IDs and passwords because the correct combination of user ID and password must be set in the RFC destination as well as the remote system. Many times I have had to synchronize these IDs and passwords because someone decided to change one but forgot to change the other. It is particularly problematic when the same user ID is used for more than one system. I've seen connections from BI (Business Intelligence) systems and clients used to maintain master data use the same user ID in production, and if the password is changed—say, in production—then you must change it in both remote systems as well as on the RFC destinations.

It is important that the authorizations assigned to this user ID be only broad enough to accomplish the tasks for which this RFC is required. In addition, the user type should be set up as a system user so dialog sessions cannot be initiated.

The response I usually get when I make this recommendation is that because it is a system user it poses no security threat; however, that could not be further from the truth. Don't ever let anyone talk you into assigning SAP_ALL to a background user that is assigned to an RFC destination because, after all, it is a background user. The whole point of assigning a user ID to the RFC destination is to allow automatic logon and execution of RFCs. If SAP_ALL or other broad access is assigned, then this system user could be used as a backdoor into your system with full access privileges.

Here is an example of what I found at one client's location. RFC connections were set up between DEV and QAC. The user was a dialog user with SAP_ALL. Similar connections were set up between QAC and PRD. I pointed out the security risk, but the client didn't think it posed a concern so I demonstrated how I could remote log on from DEV to QAC and then repeated that process to remote log on to PRD. When I performed a status, my user ID showed that I was the remote user in PRD with SAP_ALL privileges and every transaction I executed was logged not as me, but as the remote user.

You must be just as diligent at creating roles with proper access for system users as you are with dialog users because someone with a little knowledge about the SAP communication subsystem could breach what might otherwise be a good security implementation.

Now, you may be astute enough to be saying, "Well, if they had only made the RFC users as type system and not dialog that would solve the problem." Not so. It would only alter the problem. Someone knowledgeable enough to understand the RFC communications could still execute RFCs from one system to a remote system. All that would be needed would be the RFC destination name and access to execute remote function calls, which is usually available in back-end systems. In my previous example, I could have executed an RFC to create a user on the remote end and then assigned SAP_ALL to that user. Once that is done, I could log on as that user and repeat the process to the next destination—in this case, PRD.

It would take some knowledgeable tracking through the system logs to become aware of this breach and then track it back to the source. By the time you become aware of the breach and track it back to the source, though, the damage is already done and the perpetrator is probably already gone.

One more caution about RFCs… External access is done by third-party companies making use of SAP's robust RFC communication system to provide services that SAP doesn't. This benefit could come at a cost if the third-party software stores the logon information in a script that is easily read—and believe me, this happens all too often.

Rule of thumb: Only provide the access needed to get the job done. Don't let someone talk you into assigning SAP_ALL or some other broad access because they don't want to provide you with the requirements and do the steps necessary to test the role. A role for an RFC user should adhere to the same development steps as any other role you build. The only difference is that instead of transaction codes built on a menu, you will be working more at the object level to identify the RFCs and then the functional authorization objects that are checked. This does take time, but if it prevents a system breach, it is time well spent. Make use of the system trace, ST01, to determine what authorizations are being checked, and use this information to build the roles needed for RFC users.

Security Trace

The security trace is a primary tool for the SAP security administrator. However, you must remember it is only a tool and to get the most benefit from a tool you must use the tool properly.

ST01

ST01 is one of the primary tools in the SAP security administrator's tool bag. ST01 gives us a peek inside the running ABAP program to reveal the SAP authorization concept in action by capturing the ABAP code executing the authority check against specific authorization objects. Although the security administrator uses ST01 for analyzing the authorizations needed for a given transaction, ST01 is not just for authorization traces. You can trace other actions within a running ABAP program and ST01 is a useful tool for the ABAP programmer as well. It is important to note that ST01 is a single-threaded process per application server. You must start the ST01 trace on the same application server as the user ID that you want to trace is logged on to. Furthermore, if someone has already activated ST01, you cannot change the trace parameters without affecting the other trace. This is what is meant by being single-threaded. Only one activation per server can be done at a time.

If you don't know by now, the SAP authorization concept is implemented in SAP within the APAP code that executes behind every transaction code. The ABAP code looks at the authorization values that have been set for an individual by way of the role(s) that have been assigned to the user master record and compares those values to the values the program designer expects to validate, whether the user is authorized to run this program, or this particular function of the program, as well as whether the user is authorized to access the specific data being requested.

Let's pause for a moment to look inside an ABAP program at the authorization check because we really need to understand this to be able to properly analyze the results from an ST01 trace.

What happens when a user executes a transaction? The first authorization check that occurs is a check that is done by the code at the kernel level. The kernel level is the SAP code running at the operating system level. We have no control over this since SAP has built this check into the lowest level of the SAP system.

The next check is also at the transaction level, but is what I call a "sanity check" for lack of a better term. The programmers can tie authorization objects to the transaction to perform an early check to see if the user has the basic authorization to execute this transaction. Usually this is the authorization object that is used in the program with specific values, but at this earlier check point SAP simply verifies that the user can continue past the transaction onto the actual code behind the transaction. You can verify whether a transaction has an object attached by using transaction SE93.

What follows next? SAP now checks the ABAP code to determine if the program is secured with a program authorization group. This program authorization group can be assigned by the ABAP programmer, but is not used that frequently. If the user has passed the preceding checks, the ABAP programmer may have coded specific authorization checks in the program's code to check specific values. For example, if our user is trying to execute transaction SM31, the SAP system will first check against the object *S_TCODE* to verify that the user is authorized to execute this transaction. The other checks just described will also take place, but I want to describe the authority check that will be done in the code. From experience I know that the object the code will check against will be *S_TABU_DIS*. This object is used to verify whether the user is authorized to access a group of tables and what type of access: display only or display and change.

The authorization object *S_TABU_DIS* has two authorization fields: the activity authorization field and the authorization group field. When the program is trying to determine whether the user is authorized, the program reads the user master record of the user ID that is executing the program and brings in all instances of the object *S_TABU_DIS*. An instance is simply a copy of the authorization in the role(s) assigned to the user ID that is active and has values assigned to the authorization fields. So let's say the user ID has role(s) assigned that include the following instances of the authorization object *S_TABU_DIS*.

Instance 1:
Activity = 03
Authorization group = FC

Instance 2:
Activity = 02, 03
Authorization group = FA
Instance 3:
Activity = 03
Authorization group = SA

In our example, the table in question belongs to table authorization group SA. The user is trying to read values from the table. The program will perform an authorization check against each instance, and each authorization field in each instance, until the program finds a match to the values it is looking for or runs out of instances to check. Let's pretend we're computers and perform the authorization check.

First, we get the values from the first instance. Remember the program is trying to validate whether the user is authorized to read values from the table so the authorization values the program is using to check with are activity = 03 and authorization group = SA.

The program compares the activity from instance 1, which is equal to 03, to the value the program is expecting, which is 03, and compares the authorization field value FC with the value it is looking for, which is SA. We see that while the activity field values match, the authorization group field does not, so this authorization check fails. This is called "and" logic because both fields—activity "and" authorization—group must match; otherwise, the check fails. The program then loads the values from the second instance and checks again. The check against the second instance finds a match with the activity field, but the authorization group still doesn't match. The program now loads the third instance and finds that both the activity field and the authorization group field matches, so the authorization check passes and the code to load the values from the table is executed, letting the user see the results on his/her screen.

If the third instance had activity = 03 and authorization group = MM instead of SA, when the authorization check was performed and a match was not found, and there were no more authorization instances to check, the code would have branched to display the "You are not authorized" message and then terminated without displaying any records from the table.

The preceding discussion on how the authorization check is done is important because every time the program performs an authorization check (compares the values expected to the values assigned to the user master record), ST01 traces those checks when turned on and captures the values being checked, reporting whether the authorization check was successful or not.

The following is an excerpt from a trace on transaction CJ01:

```
Client:      210        User:  TST_User      Transaction
Trans ID:    430AD13255F400310000000080A3B83E
Work process     3 PID         0              Date:    08/23/2005
Start:       15:06:28:490,458     Finish:     15:06:28:574,396
First Block of Dialog Step                     Last Block in Dialog Step
Block Version:        490                      No. of records:    2
File Version:         1
15:06:28:490  AUTH      - - -            S_TCODE    RC=0     TCD=CJ01;
15:06:28:518  AUTH      - - -            C_PROJ_TCD RC=0
       PSARG=0101;TRTYP=H;
Client:          210     User:  TST_User      Transaction   CJ01
Trans ID:    430A733455F2002D0000000080A3B83E
Work process  3 PID            0              Date:      08/23/2005
Start:       15:06:53:227,241     Finish:    15:06:53:449,326
First Block of Dialog Step                     Last Block in Dialog Step
Block Version:        688                      No. of records:    3
File Version:         1
15:06:53:227  AUTH      - - -            C_PROJ_KOK RC=0
       KOKRS=UK00;PS_ACTVT=01;
15:06:53:238  AUTH      - - -            C_PROJ_PRC RC=0   PRCTR=' ' SAPREPU;
                                         PS_ACTVT=01;
15:06:53:247  AUTH       - - -           C_PROJ_VNR RC=0
       PS_VERNR=00000000;PS_ACTVT=01;
```

We see in the top most block information identification of the client where the trace was done, the user ID, date, time, and other information about the work process that really doesn't provide much value to our analysis. Following the informational block is the trace results. Please note the lines that are time stamped with the column value "AUTH". These are the results that were captured by the trace when an authorization check was performed. First, we see the authorization check against the authorization object *S_TCODE*, which checks whether the user was authorized to execute the transaction. The RC = 0 means that the Return code of the authorization check was zero, which means it passed the authorization check and so the user is authorized to execute the transaction. TCD = CJ01 on the same line is reporting the transaction code that was checked.

The next line we see is for authorization object *C_PROJ_TCD*. If a program authorization group had been checked, we would have seen the object *S_PROGRAM*, but since *S_PROGRAM* is not checked here it tells me that the program attached to transaction CJ01 is not assigned to a program authorization group. RC = 0 (again, return code = 0) and the values being checked were for authorization fields PSARG, with the value of 0101 and the authorization field TRTYPE with a value of H. This tells me that the user, TST_User, has authorizations for transaction CJ01, along with the authorization object, *C_PROJ_TCD*, and the authorization values in the authorization fields that were checked. A return code of anything other than zero means the authorization check failed.

Now, just because an authorization check fails doesn't necessarily mean you need to rush out and update the user master record. Maybe it failed because it was supposed to fail. You have to remember when using ST01 trace that this is a tool, and you as the security administrator must use some judgment as you analyze the ST01 trace results. Remember, these authorization checks are how the programmer is trying to determine what the code should do. An authorization check pass means the code branches one way, while an authorization check failure usually means it branches to an exit, giving the user an authorization failure message before exiting.

There are times when the program simply bypasses certain functionalities and keeps on running. An example I often use with my clients is background processing. When a user submits a job for background processing, the SAP code needs to determine if the user has background administrator authorization rights. If the user has background administrator rights, then certain functions are allowed that aren't allowed for non-background administrators. When running a ST01 trace on these functions, you will often see a check against the object *S_BTCH_ADM* looking for the value "Y" in the authorization field to determine if the user has background administrator authorizations. If this authorization is found, then other checks to determine what functions in the background the user is authorized for do not need to be checked. However, if the *S_BTCH_ADM* authorization check fails, then the program will branch and check object *S_BTCH_JOB* to determine what functions the user is authorized for in background processing.

I have users bring an SU53 report to me all the time demanding I update their authorizations with *S_BTCH_ADM* because that is what the report shows, but it only shows what failed and not necessarily what was needed. Usually what is needed is an authorization from *S_BTCH_JOB*. This is what I mean about using judgment as you analyze the ST01 trace. ST01 is a tool, and like all tools it is useful when used correctly.

So you may be saying to yourself how do we use ST01? It is not that complicated to turn ST01 on, run the transaction you want to trace, and then turn off

ST01 and perform the analysis. When you execute ST01, you are presented with a selection screen that has several options you can turn on for tracing. We are only interested in tracing the authority checks, so select the authorization check box. Please refer to the online help of your system to find out how to set up a filter for tracing only a single user ID. Once you have selected the authorization check box, click the button to turn the trace on. Now have your user run the transaction and perform any and all functions they would execute under normal business processing. Once they have completed their processing, click the button to turn off the trace. I usually click the trace off button twice to be sure the trace results have been flushed to the trace file so I can review the results. That's all there is to it. The real magic comes in the analysis, and your judgment in determining which objects and authorization values are needed to allow this transaction to be used. Remember, our goal as security administrators is to provide all the authorization a user needs to perform his/her job, but no more than that. If we get too liberal with the authorizations, we run the risk of allowing abuse. If you have a question about whether a specific object is needed, skip it and run your test again. If the test works without the object, that becomes your proof positive that the check was being done but not necessarily required.

SU01

SU01 is the primary transaction code in a security administrator's tool box. It is used to create, maintain, and remove user IDs within a given SAP client. When you run SU01, you are presented with several tabs, each representing a different area of the user master record.

The Address tab has sections to let you record personal information about the user. In fact, there is a section called person, which has one required field for the person's last name, with all the other fields being optional. A generally accepted practiced is to enter both the person's first and last name, along with those fields that let you enter titles and location information. However, location information generally becomes outdated as people change jobs and offices, which simply becomes an administrative burden to keep this information in sync.

There is also a section for communication information such as phone number, fax, and e-mail. These fields are often part of the user master information that is stored since this type of data is usually fairly static.

The next tab is the Logon tab. This tab holds data about your logon account. The user type is usually Dialog, which lets you log on to the client with a dialog session, meaning you can interact with the SAP system with screens that accept your commands and provide communication directly to your screen. In other words, this is an interactive session. Other user types are System, which is used for non-Dialog users for background (batch) processing. For more information about other user types, please see the SAP help section. You can get more information by running SU01, selecting the **Logon Data** tab, placing your cursor in the **User Type** field and pressing **F1**.

The password field is mandatory. There is a wizard button that will let you generate a password that will initially be saved in the screen field as text, which you can copy and later paste into a notification e-mail to the person that belongs to that ID. There is also a Deactivate button that can be used to deactivate the password prompt.

A deactivated password is used in situations like single sign-on where the user ID is authenticated externally and then SAP accepts the credentials. A user ID with a deactivated password cannot use the SAP GUI to log on. It is recommended that for your support staff, BASIS, and security administration, you do not deactivate their passwords even when using single sign-on. Logon via a single-sign-on method will still work and you retain the ability as a backup measure of allowing your support staff to log on to resolve issues if the SSO connection is down.

Other useful fields on the Logon tab are the user group, which can be used in reporting to filter users that belong to a specific user group. This field is also used in the authorization concept when setting up distributed SU01 administration. User groups are created with transaction SUGR.

The validity period on the Logon tab establishes when a user ID becomes active and when that user ID expires. This feature is very helpful with new hires because the user ID can be set up in advanced but not active until the designated date, and also used for terminations to deactivate the user ID automatically on a prescribed end date.

There is an Other Data section that can be used for accounting information, but I haven't seen these fields used very often.

The SNC tab is only used when you are using Secure Network Communications. For more information on SNC, please see the SNC user manual in the SAP Service Marketplace (http://service.sap.com/security) under Security in Detail | Secure System Management. Also, please refer to SAP Note 66687: Use of Network Security Products.

We now come to the Defaults tab. This tab lets you set up defaults for your session. The most generally used fields are the decimal notation format, as well as the date and time formats.

Under the Spool Control section you can set the default printer to use. Different opinions exist about whether to set the Output to immediately flag or not. When this flag is set, any output is immediately sent to be printed. In my experience, this should not be set because if a user sends a huge report to the spooler and only wants to view the output for selected pages, they inadvertently add additional network traffic, clog the printer queue, and waste valuable paper.

Thus, you should not set this to print immediately but instead train your users to set this at print time via the output properties.

The Parameters tab is user-driven. If your company has standard parameters for users, then you can add them here; otherwise, this tab can be updated by the user though the menu: System | User Profile | Own Data.

The Roles tab is a critical tab since this is where you establish the authorization right for this user. You enter role names here and can establish validity periods. Note, in order for the validity periods to actually take effect, you need to schedule the background job PFCG_TIME_DEPENDENCY. SAP's help documentation recommends scheduling this background job daily, but I have found that a more frequent period produces better results because this functionality performs a user master comparison that syncs the user ID with the authorizations defined in the role. The frequency really depends on the amount of change in your systems with users being added and deleted, and how much change occurs with role assignments. I suggest you schedule the job to run every couple of hours and review the job log to determine how long it takes to execute. You adjust this frequency as needed, hourly, quarterly, and so on.

The Profile tab will get populated from the profiles generated from the roles. Direct assignment of profiles to the user master record is not advised. There are always exceptions, but as a rule of thumb, authorizations should be assigned from roles that have been designed to provide specific access. Never assign a generated profile to a user master record.

The Groups tab is a fairly recent extension on the user master record and is used for grouping users primarily for reporting purposes. There is no authorization check against this field.

I have never needed to maintain the Personalization tab, so I am going to provide a direct quote from SAP's help document.

On the *Personalization* tab page, you can make person-related settings using personalization objects. You can call this tab page both in role maintenance and in user maintenance.

Finally, we come to the License Data tab. Here, you specify the user type from the pull-down menu.

For more information about user types, see the SAP Service Marketplace under the path http://service.sap.com/licenseauditing| System Measurement Named User | User Classification.

Once all appropriate data fields on the associated tabs have been completed, click the Save button to save the data and create the user master record.

SU02

SU02 was used before the introduction of the profile generator to manually create profiles that would ultimately be assigned to user IDs.

This transaction, while still active in the SAP system, is essentially obsolete. In fact, when you execute SU02, a message is displayed to that fact. See Figure 3.16.

Figure 3.16 SU02

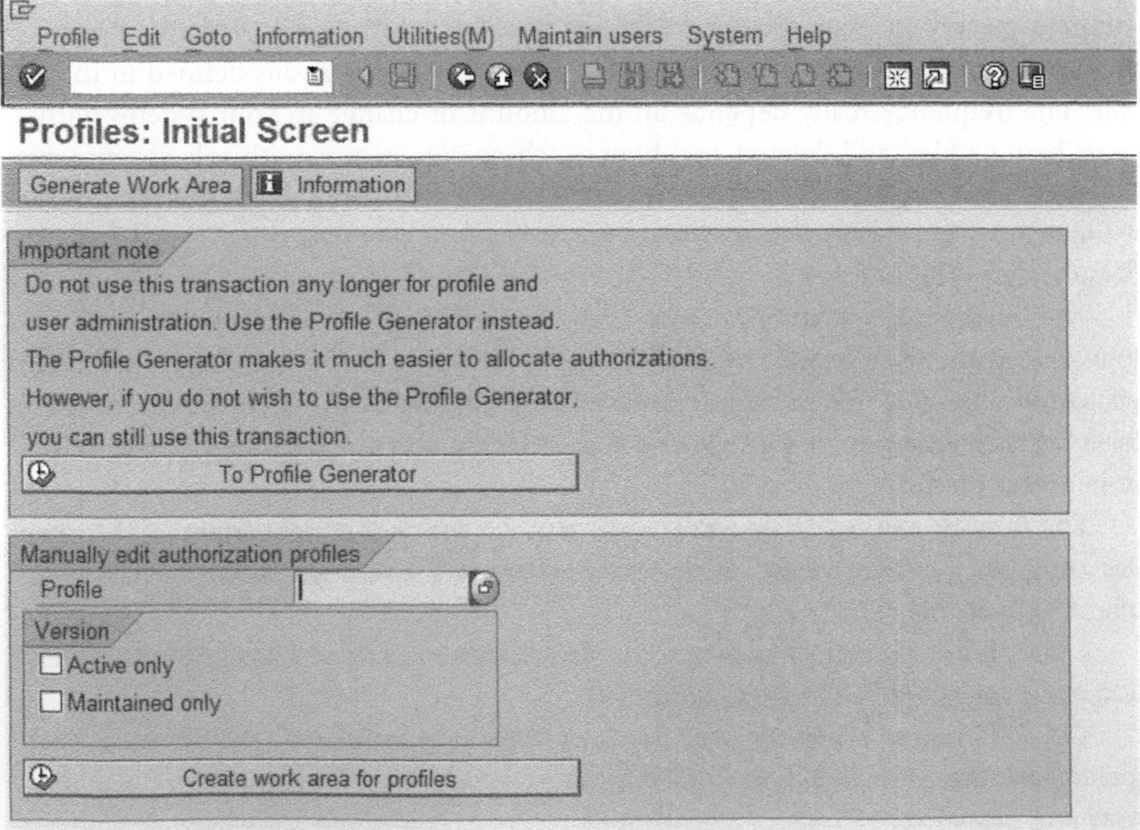

I encourage you to use the profile generator instead of manually maintaining profiles since the profile generator is much easier to use and is recommended by SAP for authorization administration.

SU03

SU03, like SU02, was used before the introduction of the profile generator to manually create/maintain authorizations that were then entered into profiles that would ultimately be assigned to user IDs.

This transaction, while still active in the SAP system, is essentially obsolete. When you execute SU03, you do not get an obsolete message like you do with SU02, but you should use the profile generator to maintain authorizations since the profile generator is much easier to use and is recommended by SAP.

SU24

This transaction is used to configure the profile generator so the PFCG knows what objects should be brought into a role when transactions are added to the role menu. We discussed SU24 when we covered the transaction PFCG because these two transactions go hand in hand.

To reiterate from that discussion, SU24 lets you control what authorization objects are included in a role every time you place a transaction in the role's menu. This function aids the role build process because you don't have to rediscover what objects are necessary to make a given transaction work, nor keep a separate cross-reference of transactions and authorization objects. Not only does the profile generator add the necessary objects whenever a transaction is added to the menu, it also uses the information in SU24 to remove objects when a transaction is removed from the menu.

My recommendation for using SU24 is that you include every object discovered from your traces and SU53 that are checked for any given transaction. However, you should only include authorization values in SU24 when you are certain those values are static. When I say static I mean the values for the authorization field will never change no matter what role it is placed in. An example would be a display transaction that has an activity field. This is a designed transaction for displaying and should not be used for any other activity. In this case, the activity field in SU24 can and should be entered with the display values. By adding the values in SU24, these values are automatically added to the role when the transaction is added to the role's menu. This means one less decision you need to make on authorization values and keeps consistency across your roles for this transaction use. If you have an authorization field where the value could be different depending on what role it is used in, you should leave that authorization field open in SU24 and maintain the value in the role.

Another thing to remember when making SU24 changes is the impact on existing roles. Because SU24 modifies the authorization objects and authorization values associated with transactions, any changes you make could impact roles that have the transaction in its menu.

I highly recommend when using SU24 that you always check what the impact will be, especially if you are removing an object from a transaction. You can use the "where used" section in the reporting transaction SUIM to determine where a given transaction is used. You should get into the habit of verifying the impact to other roles whenever you are making changes in SU24 in order to minimize the unexpected changes that can be introduced. There is plenty of change that goes on in a production system with roles being assigned or removed, and roles being changed driven by business requirements, that you don't need the additional headache of changes taking place that you are not aware of because of an update made in SU24 and then inadvertently changed in a role that was under normal maintenance.

In addition to making a decision on whether you add authorization values to the authorization fields in the objects added in SU24 for a given transaction, you also need to set the object to be recognized by the profile generator so the PFCG will bring in the objects you want it to bring in. In the newer SAP versions (like ECC 6.0), there is a proposal field you need to set to the value *Yes*. In older versions, there is a check indicator field that you need to set to *Check/Maintain* in order for PFCG to recognize the object as being needed for the specific transaction.

SU53

SU53 is a transaction that every SAP user needs to know how to run. While it is not complicated to enter SU53 in the command box, it is important to understand the usage of SU53.

I see a lot of false SU53 reports because it is not run at the point of error. SU53 is what I call an immediate-point-in-time error report. Meaning it provides us with an error report for a specific point in time but loses its value as soon as the user performs any other activity in SAP.

I employ the illustration of a memory location to explain the use of SU53. In SAP, a single memory location is used by SAP to record the information about what authorization check failed. Every time an authorization check is done in SAP, this same memory location is overwritten. If a user encounters an authorization error and then performs other transactions before creating the SU53 error report, the error information is lost.

I usually recommend that users create a second session, then go back to their original session and try the transaction again to reproduce the authorization error. Immediately, when the authorization error message is received, the user should switch to the second session and run SU53 from there. This usually gives accurate error reports and does not jeopardize the information in the memory location.

It is also important that the user open the pull-downs to reveal the whole error message, including the objects and values that were being checked.

The SU53 report has two important sections (see Figure 3.17). The first section—Authorization Check Failed—is critical for the security administrator because this section lists the authorization object and the values being checked that failed.

Figure 3.17 SU53

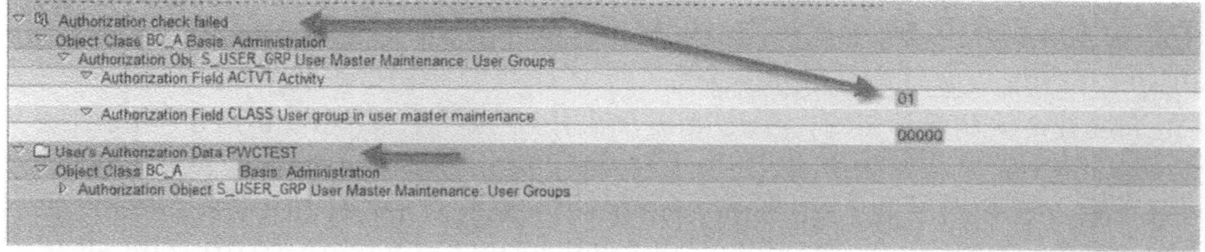

The second section—User's Authorization Data—lists the authorization values for the object that failed and the values the user currently has. Sometimes the object in question has not been entered in the user master record because it does not exist in any assigned roles.

All users should be instructed about creating a SU53 report and forwarding this report along with their error submission. The security administrator will need to know whether it is approved to make the necessary changes indicated in the SU53, and to which role. Included in the error submission should be the transaction that the user was executing at the time of the authorization error in case SU24 needs to be updated.

An SU53 submission should kick off a review/approval process rather than just be submitted to the security group. Each company is very likely to have a different procedure in place. Unless the security administrator has the authority to approve or reject the access, the first stop for the SU53 report should not be the security administrator's desk. Two questions must be answered before the error can or should be handled by a security administrator. First, should the user in question have this access? Or asked another way: Is the access that is producing the authorization error within the scope of the user's responsibilities? If the answer is yes, this access should be allowed for the user. The next question should then be: Does this user have the correct role(s) assigned? Many times there is an omission in role assignments and so a simple role addition is all that is required.

If the user should be authorized and he/she has the correct role(s) assigned, then the request should be forwarded to the security group for analysis and role updating. Remember though, the security administrator needs to know which role should be updated, and all change management processes should be followed to ensure the change is approved, documented, tested, and put into production according to standard procedures.

SUGR

Transaction SUGR lets you create those user groups that can be used in the user master on the Logon And Groups tab.

This transaction is pretty straightforward. Run SUGR, enter a user group name in the entry field, and then click the **Create** button. Now enter some descriptive text. The text field is not mandatory, but good practices dictate that you should indicate the purpose for this group. For example, user group SECADM is for all security administrators.

It is also possible to assign user IDs to this group at this point instead of via SU01.

Sometimes Security needs to do mass updates on users regularly. If you can create a User Group for those users, it will certainly make the mass update easier through SU10. For CUA master, all user groups must be defined in related child systems as well.

SUIM

Transaction SUIM is a collection of reports you can use to query the SAP system to create custom reports about the user information system.

When entering SUIM, you are presented with nine categories, as Figure 3.18 shows.

Figure 3.18 SUIM

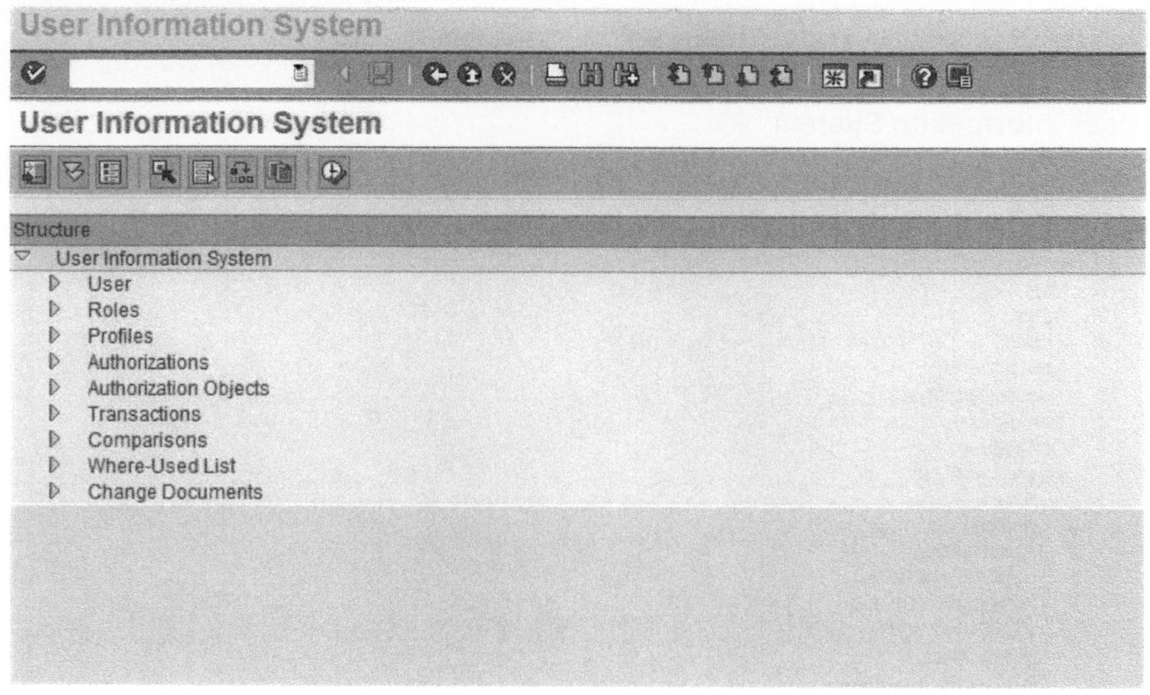

As you can see, reports that are specific to users, roles, profiles, authorization objects, and so on can be created. The sections I use most often are the "Where-used" and "Change Documents" reports. Selecting these, you can see the further divisions for selection, as shown in Figure 3.19.

Figure 3.19 SUIM Report Groupings

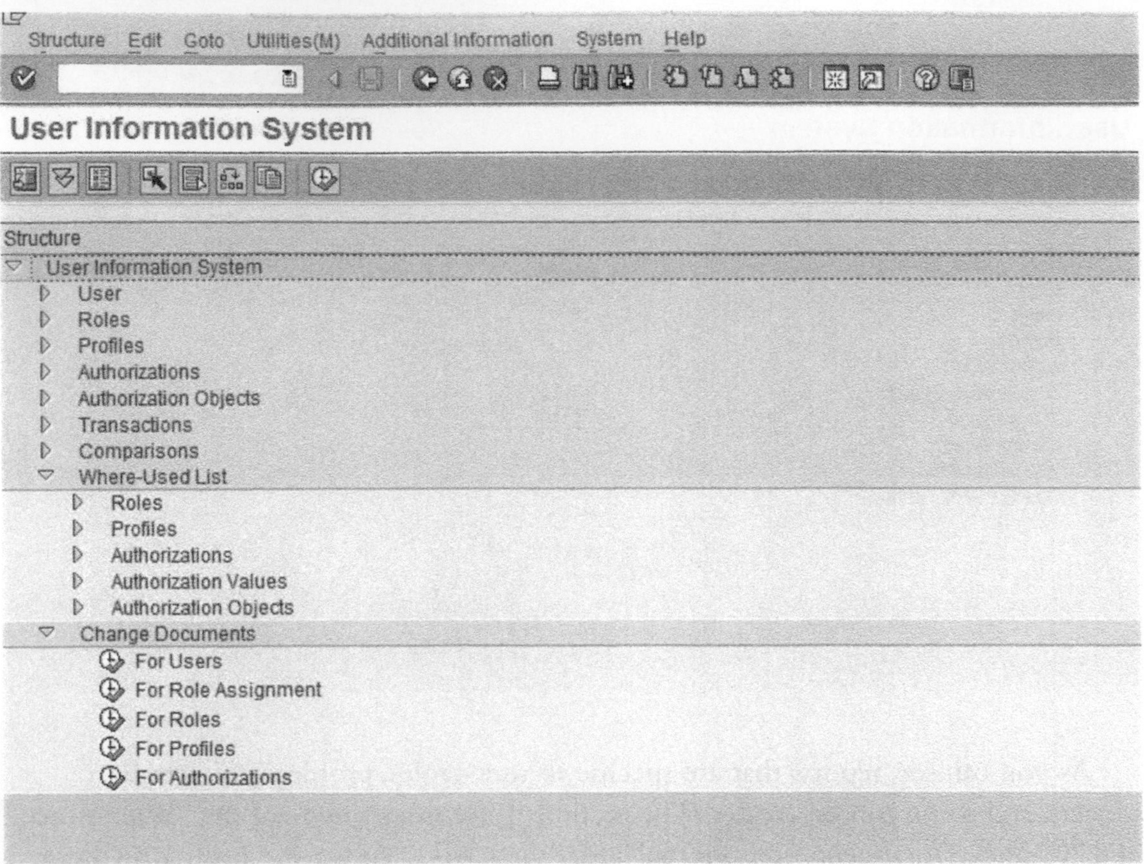

The Where-used reports let you determine users of specific roles, or where specific authorization values are used. I alluded to using SUIM to determine the impact that changes made in SU24 made on roles. SUIM is the tool to determine where a given transaction is being used, as well as specific authorizations, so you can see the impact and take the necessary steps to avoid wreaking havoc across your security model.

The Change Documents section is very helpful when tracking down changes to roles, roles assignments, and changes to authorizations.

These reports are simple selection screens that you complete with query values and date ranges to create the report you need. These reports can be printed to the SAP print queue or your default network printer. The reports can be downloaded to your local hard drive, and because of the Microsoft integration, they can be exported to Excel.

SUIM is an excellent tool for investigations, analysis, and audit reporting. SUIM can be used by you, the security administrator, as well as auditors, managers who approve access, and anyone else who needs user information reports.

TU02

I promised earlier that I would come back to TU02, so here we are. TU02 lets you look up any parameter that is active in the SAP system. While RZ10 is used by the BASIS administrators to configure the system, some parameters are activated with default values even though they were not specified in RZ10.

Execute TU02 and if your system has multiple application servers, you will be presented with a list of servers. Select the server you want to review and double-click it. A screen report will be presented with all active parameters for that application server. You can now scroll down the list and review the parameter values and modification date. You can also use the find function to search for a parameter. For example, one parameter I usually check when I start on a project is the parameter that needs to be set if you want to record changes to tables that have been set up to capture the data changes made to it. If you want more information on table logging, you should perform a search on SAP Market Place, OSS notes for Table Logging. Two OSS notes worth looking at are OSS # 1916 and 112388.

Use the search function to find the parameter rec/client. This parameter is turned off when delivered by SAP, but you can turn it on if you find you want to track changes. I usually recommend this parameter be turned on because the client table, T000, is set up to log data changes, which is usually an audit point to track who modifies the client settings.

As a security administrator, I find transaction TU02 to be a valuable tool for reviewing the parameters that are active in the system and the values that have been assigned. I usually keep a list of security parameters I am specifically interested in and check them with TU02 regularly to determine if they are active, the values assigned, and whether any changes have been made. You can use the Excel features to capture the parameters in TU02 and keep a history that can be reviewed over time for changes.

WE05

WE05 is used to search and display IDOCs in a given system. We enter in the selection screen the parameters we need, like date/time ranges or the IDOC number if we know it, and for CUA IDOCs we might want to restrict our selection to just the message types processed by CUA, so we enter **USERCLONE*** in the selection field **Basic Type** and press the **Execute** button.

The resulting screen should be a listing of IDOCs that match our selections. If we double-click one of the IDOCs, we should find ourselves looking at the IDOC display screen, which is the same we would see by double-clicking the IDOC from the CUA log screen from transaction SCUL.

Tools make the job easier. If you were not already aware of the tools discussed earlier, you should make a point of knowing and understanding how these tools should be used to help you in your security administration responsibilities.

Implementation

Now that we have discussed the architecture and design of an ABAP security environment and covered some of the tools the security administrator needs, it is time to implement. The following section covers some items that may come up at implementation time.

Identity Management

Identity management is all about user ids and access rights. A central identity management system provides consistency across all your systems, SAP as well as non-SAP systems. SAP has provided the central user administration system with and interface to the LDAP directory to assist you in managing user ids and access rights in the SAP system and allows you to externally connect to a centralized system via the LDAP directory.

Setup of CUA

We've already discussed the value of using CUA (Central User Administration) in a SAP landscape to make life a little easier on the security administrator and the key configuration points. Here, I want to review the basic steps required to set up CUA. You can find some good reference material in the way of cookbooks on SAPNet, or follow this link to the Public accessible SAP online help where the following steps were acquired:

http://help.sap.com/saphelp_nw70/helpdata/en/42/ea3014b2201bdae10000000a11466f/frameset.htm

1. Specify logical systems.
2. Assign logical systems to clients.

3. Define authorization roles for system users (see OSS note 492589 to get you started with SAP-delivered roles designed for CUA).
4. Determine existing RFC destinations and system users.
5. Create system users with roles.
6. Create an RFC destination for the target system.
7. Create the Central User Administration.
8. Set up field distribution parameters.
9. Synchronize and distribute company addresses.
10. Synchronize user groups.
11. Transfer users from new systems.
12. Display and process distribution logs.

Setup of LDAP Con

This section provides an overview of the required steps involved for setting up the LDAP connection.

1. Install the LDAP library. As mentioned earlier, the LDAP connector actually calls the program *ldap_rfc* at runtime, and so program *ldap_rfc* runs as a registered server program. This LDAP library is delivered as part of the SAP Kernel and is also available from the SAP Service Marketplace at *http://service.sap.com/swdc*. You can install the LDAP library in the kernel directory */usr/sap/<SID>/sys/exe/run*.
2. Create RFC destination to program *ldap_rfc*. Go to transaction SM59 and create an RFC destination of connection type *T* with activation type *Registered server program* to program *ldap_rfc* for establishing the connection between the SAP ABAP-based system and the directory server.
3. Create a new LDAP connector. Go to transaction LDAP, click the **Connector** button and create a new LDAP connector that uses the RFC destination maintained in the previous step.
4. Create a new logical LDAP server. In transaction LDAP, click the **Server** button. Create a new Server and maintain the connection details to the physical location of the directory service.
5. Maintain the LDAP system user. In transaction LDAP, click the **System User** button. Create a new LDAP System User to maintain the logon details

for the communication user used by the LDAP connector to connect to the LDAP directory server. This binding information (the user ID and password) is stored in the secure storage.

6. Check whether the LDAP connector is operable. The connection between the SAP Web AS ABAP system and the directory server can be checked in transaction LDAP.
7. Mapping of SAP data fields to directory attributes. In order to enable synchronization of user data between the directory service and SAP ABAP-based system, SAP data fields must map to the attributes of the directory service using transaction LDAPMAP. A field can be mapped to one or more attributes. An attribute can be assigned to one or more fields. If the desired mapping is not a simple 1:1 relationship, then function modules can be used to define a more complicated mapping procedure. For example, use function module *MAP_CONCAT_CHAR* for concatenating *first name* and *last name* fields into a *fullname* field, and use function module *MAP_SPLIT_CHAR* for splitting *telephone number* into two fields: *tel_number* and *tel_ext*.
8. Extending directory schema. For any fields that do not exist in the directory, you must extend the schema in the directory by importing a LDAP Data Interchange Format (LDIF) file. The LDIF file can be generated running the report *RSLDAPSCHMEAEXT* on the SAP Web AS ABAP system.
9. Setting mapping indicators. For each field-attribute mapping, an appropriate mapping indicator needs to be set. A mapping indicator determines whether the mapping is used for import to a SAP database, export to an LDAP directory service, a search filter, a Relative Distinguished Name for creating new directory entries, and required and system entries.
10. Setting synchronization indicators. Additionally, synchronization indicators are set to indicate whether field-attribute mapping is imported or exported to determine the direction of the synchronization.
11. Synchronizing user data. Report *RSLDAPSYNC_USER* can be executed or scheduled to synchronize the user data. Transactions LDAPLOG and SLG1 can be used to check for error messages during synchronization.
12. Configuring alerts for LDAP connector. The LDAP connector can be monitored and managed using the Computing Center Management System

(transaction RZ20). Some common exceptions that may occur during implementation of LDAP connector:

NO_AUTHORIZ The ABAP authorization check failed. The authorization object checked is *S_LDAP* with the LDAP server used.

CONFIG_ERROR Error in the configuration in the SAP system (for example, a nonexistent LDAP server ID was specified).

LDAP_FAILURE If the export parameter *LDAPRC* is not reset, this exception is triggered when the directory sends an error code.

CONN_OUTDATE The LDAP connection was terminated because it was inactive too long.

NOT_ALIVE The connection between the application server and the LDAP Connector has been terminated.

SAP Generic Users

In general, two classes of generic IDs exist: SAP-developed and Customer-developed. These are not generic IDs, they are standard user IDs delivered by SAP, and are referred to as such by SAP.

The following users (SAP-developed generic IDs)—SAP*, DDIC, SAPCPIC, EARLYWATCH—are delivered with the SAP system and are well documented, including the default passwords used.

Because these IDs and default passwords are well known, as the security administrator you should ensure that these standard users are protected by changing the passwords immediately. SAP* is a special case because it does not need a user master record, but you should still create a user master record and change the password. When a new client is created, the coding in the SAP system automatically defaults the password for SAP* to "PASS" and assumes SAP_ALL–like authorizations until a user master record is created and appropriate authorizations are assigned. Some best practices recommend that SAP* be locked, but I believe that if you neutralized the authorizations by creating a user master record for SAP* with no role or profile assigned, and then change the password, you have adequately protected your system from improper use by this user. Locking the ID doesn't hurt, but for all intents and purposes it doesn't really add much more protection.

User DDIC is used by the SAP system for ABAP dictionary activities and should never be locked. To safeguard against unauthorized use, you should change the password for DDIC.

SAPCPIC and EARLYWATCH are also users with special purposes in SAP and should also have their passwords changed as soon as possible.

You can run report RSUSR003, which will give a report on these standard users and indicate whether the passwords are still the default passwords or have been changed for each client within the current SAP system.

Single Sign-on and Certificates

When implementing Single Sign-on (SSO) across a large system landscape, where many different types of systems and many different authentication methods are available, it is quite a complicated process of evaluating which authentication methods are both easy to implement and work best for your system landscape. This is the reason why using one authentication method for all systems is the easiest way to ensure SSO is consistently implemented. The authentication method recommended for this is SAP logon ticket.

As mentioned earlier with SAP logon tickets, the user is authenticated using the logon ticket as the authentication token. The user only needs to be authenticated once (for example, using a valid user ID and password), and the system will issue a logon ticket to the user. With this logon ticket, the user can access subsequent systems (both SAP and non-SAP systems) without the need to reenter his or her user ID and password.

It is recommended that you identify one system in your environment as the ticket-issuing system before configuring other systems to accept tickets from this system. Users must have the same user ID across all of the systems, and their Web browsers must accept cookies to ensure that credentials stored in the SAP logon ticket can be reused.

For configuration of the SAP Web AS ABAP system that issues logon tickets, you must first set the following profile parameters in transaction RZ10:

login/create_sso2_ticket = 2

login/accept_sso2_ticket = 1

login/ticket_expiration_time = <required time>

Then, use transaction STRUST to assign a public and private key pair, as well as the public-key certificate in the issuing system's SSO Personal Secure Environment (PSE).

For configuration of all accepting systems, you need to install the SAP Security Library (or SAP Cryptographic Library). This SAP Security library is available at http://service.sap.com/swdcsunder Download | Support Packages And Patches | Entry By Application Group | Additional Components | SAPSECULIB.

Or for additional encryption capabilities, you can use the SAP Cryptographic library which is available under Download | SAP Cryptographic Software.

On all of the accepting systems, you must set the profile parameter *login/accept_sso2_ticket* to 1. Then, use transaction SS02 (SSO administration tool) to establish appropriate configurations for the accepting system. This transaction checks whether the profile parameters have been set correctly, and shows the accepting systems' SSO Access Control List, as well as the certificate list.

For SAP Web AS ABAP systems that need to accept SAP logon tickets from a J2EE Engine, not only do you have to install the SAP Security Library and implement the profile parameter *login/accept_sso2_ticket*, you must also import the issuing J2EE Engine's public-key certificate manually into the Personal Secure Environment (PSE) using transaction STRUST or STRUSTSSO2 (Trust Manager), and you must add the J2EE Engine's details to the accepting system's Access Control List.

In terms of implementing client certificates, the SAP Web AS ABAP systems must be first set up to support Secure Sockets Layer (SSL) communication. The required steps for doing this will be described in a later section in this chapter titled "Implementing Secure Communication."

On all SAP Web AS ABAP systems that accept certificates, the profile parameter *icm/HTTPS/verify_client* must be set to 1 and the Internet Communication Manager (ICM) must be restarted to activate the profile parameter.

Next, use transaction STRUST or STRUSTSSO2 (Trust Manager) to import the CA root certificate into the accepting systems' PSE certificate list and maintain table USREXTID to update user mapping of user IDs to the appropriate certificates.

If you require the SAP Web AS ABAP system to automatically distribute client certificates, you can implement SAP TCS, by performing the following additional steps:

1. Set profile parameters login/certificate_request_subject to *CN=&UNAME, OU=&WPOU, O=mySAP.com User, C=DE* and login/certificate_request_ca_url to *https://tcs.mysap.com/invoke/tc/usercert*.
2. Prepare the accepting system's PSE to use for signing the certificate requests. You can either use an existing PSE entry or create a new entry in table SSFAPPLIC with the values:

Field	Value
APPLIC	CERTRQ
B_TOOLKIT	X
B_FORMAT	X
B_PAB	X
B_PROFID	X
B_PROFILE	X
B_DISTRIB	X

3. Create a Secure Store and Forward (SSF) application using transaction SSFA by adding a new entry with values:

Field	Value
SSF Application	CERTRQ
Security Product	SAPSECULIB
SSF Format	International Standard PKCS#7
Private Address Book	<PSE filename>.pse
SSF Profile Name	<PSE filename>.pse
Distribute PSE	Activate

4. Create a PSE using transaction STRUST (Trust Manager).
5. Register the system on the SAP TCS at *http://service.sap.com/TCS* under **SAP Trust Center Services in Detail | SAP Passports** in your SAP solution. Generate a certificate request for the accepting system's PSE from step 2 using transaction STRUST. Send a customer message to SAP with the content of the certificate request to obtain the accepting system's signed public-key certificate. Once you have obtained the public-key certificate, you can import this certificate into the PSE.
6. Create a new role containing authorization object *S_USERCERT* (activity 49) and assign this role to users who need to use the certificate request service.

Password Rules

Most security professionals agree that a strong password is essential to protecting your ID from being compromised. But what constitutes a strong password? The following notes are a compilation from across the Internet.

The SANS institute, which is generally regarded as a good source for security information, training, and preparation for security certification describes poor or weak passwords as having the following characteristics:

- A password with less than 15 characters
- A password that can be found in a dictionary
- A password that is used in common language, such as:
  - A pet's name
  - The name of someone you know, whether real or make believe
  - Recognized terms from, say, an industry or a profession
  - Any personal information such as dates, ages, phone numbers
  - Word or number patterns such as 123456789, abcdef
  - Any of the preceding simply spelled backward
  - Any of the preceding simply prefaced or suffixed with a number like bob1, 12lake

The SANS institute also provides a list of characteristics they consider make for a strong password.

- Passwords that contain both upper- and lowercase characters
- Passwords that contain digits and punctuations
- Passwords that are 15 characters or longer and are alphanumeric
- Passwords that are not based on any personal information

In addition, the SANS institute recommends that passwords for user IDs be changed every four months and never longer than six months. They further recommend that system-level passwords be changed at least quarterly. In SAP, the system level ids would be SAP*, DDIC as well as administrators like BASIS and security adminstrators or any power user with broad authorizations.

It should be obvious, but as long as we are covering password policy: Passwords should never be written down where they can be discovered, nor should they ever be shared with anyone. So you might be saying, "Wow, a 15-character alphanumeric password that I can't write down nor share with someone to help me remember it…? What am I to do?"

While SANS recommends a password length of 15 or more characters, what I have seen in practice is seven or greater characters. In earlier SAP systems, the password length was fixed at a maximum of eight characters. The justification for a longer password is that it makes it harder for a password cracker to crack it.

A practice that seems to incorporate the preceding recommendation, but that still provides you with a way to remember that long password, is to create a pass-phrase you will remember. With a pass-phrase, you can substitute numbers for characters. If you have ever seen those vanity plates many people have on their cars, that's a good example of substitution.

For example, I start with the following: thisisanexampleofapassphrase. Now I perform some substitutions in order to be within the recommended guidelines, and the results are:

Thi$i$anExample0faPassPhrase

I've capitalized some of the characters, substituted dollar signs for the character *S* on the first two instances and substituted the number *0* for the letter *O*. This is something I can fairly easily commit to memory, and so will adhere to the preceding recommendations.

In the newer versions of SAP, the BASIS team can set system parameters to help enforce a password policy, and as the security administrator you can maintain table USR40 in SAP, which is a list of passwords that are not allowed. The following OSS notes: 2467, 379081, 450452, and 862989 should provide you with a good start on setting up the parameters, while using USR40 in SAP will help enforce your password policy.

If you need a template to start compiling a password policy, see www.sans.org/resources/policies/Password_Policy.pdf, which is available by SANS for your use. The SANS password policy is not geared toward SAP, but the recommendations can be adopted for use in a SAP environment.

Authorization Objects

Every authorization object needs to be documented to provide the security administrator information on the purpose and use of the object. Unfortunately, even SAP does not provide documentation for every authorization object, which makes understanding the authorization concept for that object very difficult.

You should try to establish some object documentation standards that your developers can follow when you find you need to have custom authorization objects created. Yes, there are times when you will need to create a custom object that will be incorporated in custom ABAP code, which makes for a perfect time to capture the necessary documentation on why this object was needed and how to use it.

Transaction SU21 can be used to create the authorization object as well as the documentation. While we are on the subject of custom objects, I usually try to group the custom objects in a "Z" object class. You can create custom objects in any of the SAP object classes, and some companies like to keep the functional area association by assigning the new custom object in the same class. If we have a custom object for Finance, then the object will probably be created in the "FI" object class. I like to create a custom object class and locate all my custom objects separately from the SAP objects. You can create your own ZFI object class for all Finance custom objects or just create a single custom object class for all custom objects. Usually you don't have that many, so I find that a single custom object class works just fine. The important point is to be consistent.

Custom authorization object documentation should include the following three sections: Definition, Defined Fields, and a procedure area that I will expand on in the following sections using the documentation from authorization object *S_TABU_DIS*.

The following sections are the minimal documentation requirements.

Definition

The definition establishes the purpose and/or use for the object.

Defined Fields

The defined fields should be listed with the valid values to be used.

Procedure

The procedure section helps explain how this object is to be used. Examples with field values and explanations should be provided.

Definition

This definition provides authorizations for displaying or maintaining tables. The object only controls access using the standard table maintenance tool (transaction SM31), enhanced table maintenance (SM30), or the Data Browser, including access in Customizing.

Defined Fields

The object contains the following fields:

Authorization group for DD objects: Authorization for tables by authorization class according to table TDDAT.

Enter the name of the allowed classes. Table classes are defined in table TDDAT.

Activity: Allowed operations.

Possible values:

- **02** Create, change or delete table entries
- **03** Display table entries only

Procedure

Field	Values
Authorization Group	ZZZZ
Activity	03

With this authorization, the user can display records in any table in the ZZZZ authorization group.

Field	Values
Authorization Group	YYYY
Activity	02, 03

With this authorization, the user can display and update records in any table in the YYYY authorization group.

Documentation, whether for a program or an authorization object, captures the purpose and use of the item so you have a future reference whenever needed. The persons who specified the requirements for the custom object, as well as the persons who created the object, might not be around in the future to ask, so by including the documentation with the object you have a ready reference when you need it.

Authorization Groups

Authorization groups are used in SAP where it is more advantageous to provide access based on groups rather than by specific function. To pass the authorization check, the user must have authorization to the combination of both the activity and the authorization group. Master data records often have an authorization group field, as do posting periods in FI. You will also run into authorization groups when working with asset classes, business partners and a great many other areas within SAP. Many times the authorization check doesn't even take place until and authorization group is assigned—for example, on master data records. When a master data record is accessed, the authority check is skipped if the authorization group field is blank. I have provided additional detail on three common authorization groups you almost always run into: table, programs, and spool output.

Tables

Authorization groups for tables are a way to ease the authorization concept for the many tables in SAP. It quickly becomes unmanageable to establish an authorization for every table in the SAP system because of the sheer numbers involved. In an ECC 6.0 system, there are over 300,000 tables and each new SAP release seems to increase that number. For example, in a 3.1G R/3 system, there were just over 36,000 tables. Even 36,000 tables present an unmanageable number to create discrete authorizations.

Because of this numbers game, SAP has implemented an authorization group concept to make granting table access a little easier. By grouping similar tables into table authorization groups, a single authorization can provide access to a great many tables. However, the catch is that the tables should have something in common because once the access is granted to the group, all tables in that group will be subjected to the same authorization. For example, HR master data is generally grouped using the PA authorization group. The authority check is performed against the authorization object *S_TABU_DIS* and you can set the Activity field for change or display and the Authorization Group field to the table authorization group value.

You can see which tables are in a given group by querying table TDDAT with transaction SE16. For example, to see the HR tables in authorization group PA, enter PA in the Authorization Group field, CCLAS, and execute. You can also see what authorization group is assigned to a table by entering the table name in the Table Name field and executing.

Your next question might be, "How do I assign authorization groups to tables?" I'm glad you asked, because to assign a table to an authorization group is as easy as executing transaction SM30. In the Table/View field, enter the maintenance view name **V_DDAT_54** and press the **Maintain** button. A pop-up warning that the table is cross-client will appear. Just click the green arrow to continue. Now click the **New Entries** button, enter the table name and authorization group, and save. This should prompt for a transport number to let you transport this change across your landscape.

Table authorization group names are limited to four characters, so you will have to be a bit creative, and you won't be able to give it a readable meaningful name.

Programs

Authorization groups for programs subject the access of programs to an authority check. You assign an authorization group to programs in the attributes section under SE38. An alternate method is to use program RSCSAUTH to assign the program authorization group to a program. You should refer to OSS notes 694148 and 338177 on using RSCSAUTH.

However, before you assign an authorization group to a program, you must create it. Creating a program authorization group is done by simply placing an entry in table TPGP, which can be done using transaction SE16. For more information on creating program authorization groups, see OSS note number 127591.

But why would you use a program authorization group? When a program does not have an internal authorization check, the program authorization group can be used to determine whether the user is authorized to execute that program. The authorization object *S_PROGRAM* is checked with the action field value of SUBMIT, and the authorization group set to the value assigned to the program.

S_PROGRAM is also checked when a user is trying to create or maintain variants for a given program. In the case of variants, the action field in *S_PROGRAM* is checked for VARIANT, and the authorization group is checked for the authorization group value assigned to the program.

One other use of program authorization groups is to restrict the execution of programs in the background. When a program authorization group has been assigned to a program and a user attempts to schedule that program for background processing via transaction SM36, an authorization check is triggered in SAP against *S_PROGRAM*. In this case, the action field is checked for the value BTCSUBMIT, and the authorization group field checks for the value assigned to the program. I want to underline an important point about the background execution of programs because I have run into developers and other consultants that didn't understand this next point. When a program is executed in the background, the transaction code that might be assigned to that program does not get checked; therefore, the program authorization group or an authority check coded in the program is the only protection you have for that program.

I use program authorization groups when a program has single functionality—that is, when it has only one purpose and I want to be able to control who can run it.

A simple yes or no is all that is needed to verify that someone is authorized to execute a given program, and a program authorization group provides that simple check. I also use program authorization groups when I am expecting a group of similar programs to be created that will be run by the same group of users. For example, a set of reports that access the same data. The different reports provide different summation levels or different formatting. All the reports might not be designed at implementation, but it is expected that more will be created over a period of time. I can create a program authorization group that the developers will assign, add the authorization to the appropriate role, and whenever a new report is created using that program authorization group the users are automatically authorized and we do not have to go through change management to add the new report, especially when that new report is just a revision, with no new functionality running against the same data source and intended for the same user group.

Of course, this method can be abused, so it is important that code development review security requirements and determine whether each new program meets the requirements that would allow the "grouping" of new code into the same group of programs that are using the program authorization group. The new code needs to have similar functionality or access similar data. If the programmers begin dumping all their new code into the same program authorization group, you will no longer be able to control who can execute the program, which defeats the authorization concept and your company's security strategy.

Spool

Spool authorization groups are used on the output attributes to enable the sharing of spool output in SAP. You can see this field in transaction SP01. Select your spool output, and then click the little Hat symbol or use the menu selection **GOTO | Request Attributes (F8)**. Look on the tab titled **Spool Attributes** and find the **Authorization** field. See Figure 3.20.

Figure 3.20 Spool Authorization Group

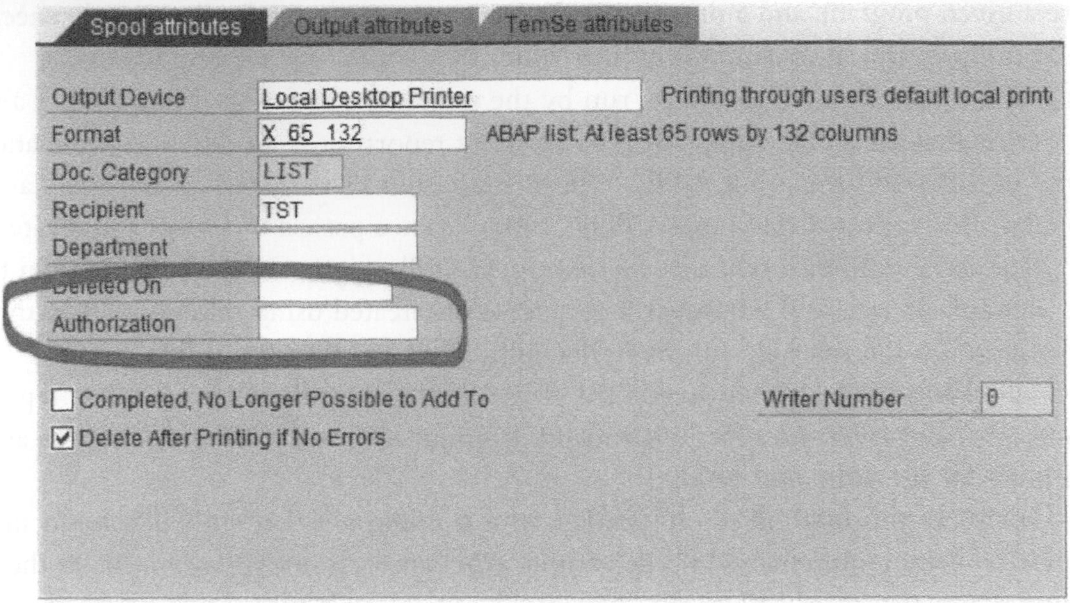

This field can be set after the output has been created and is being held in the spool queue, but not if it has been printed. You can also set this field at the time you are creating the spool by selecting print properties. Then, click the down arrow next to the box labeled **Spool Request**. Double-click the field **Authorization**. An entry box should open to let you enter the spool authorization group, save it, and then allow your output to be sent to the spool. You should also set your output to spool only if it is set to print immediately.

Once a spool authorization group is set, all users who have been given this authorization will be able to access it.

The authorizations are created using two authorization objects: *S_ADMI_FCD* and *S_SPO_ACT*.

The first step is to provide the selected roles that are to be granted spool queue access authorization using authorization object *S_ADMI_FCD*. The authorization value SP01 will limit access to the logged-on client.

NOTE

These users will now be able to *view*, *print*, *download*, or *delete* ANY output from ANY user while that output exists on the spool queue, depending on the actions set up in the following steps.

The next step is to create a naming convention that can be used within the groups when sharing spool output.

TIP

The naming convention can use any characters and ranges from 1 to 12 characters in length. A hierarchy can be devised to allow different levels of access.

Here is an example: For Support Center…

Support1 – Only level 1 support persons could view these reports.

Support2 – Only level 2 support persons could view these reports.

Support3 – Only level 3 support persons could view these reports.

Support* – This would provide authorization to all support levels.

Now we need to create authorizations into the respective roles based on the naming convention defined in the previous step with authorization object *S_SPO_ACT*.

NOTE

These authorizations for the specified spool authorizations *are not dynamic*. They are set into the authorizations for the specified role and the person who has been assigned that role will be limited to his/her reports on the spool output, and those defined with the naming convention, or reports with no authorization specified.

To be able to see other spool output, create an authorization with *S_SPO_ACT* and the action field set equal to "BASE", with the appropriate authorization group value. This is just the starting point to see items on the spool queue.

You now add to the authorization based on what you want the user to be able to do. The value "DISP" lets the contents of the spool item be displayed, which is what most users are after. You can also control whether they have printing rights or if they can delete the spool. Also, you can grant the authorization to allow the changing of attributes, the authorization field, or the owner. Check the available activities in the authorization object *S_SPO_ACT* to determine what other access you want to provide.

The final step is for the user who creates the spool output to be shared to specify the corresponding naming convention in the Authorization field of the print attributes. ABAP/4 programs can set this with the *NEW-PAGE* command.

NOTE

Exact naming must be used—meaning that if my report is intended to be shared with Support1 persons, using Suport1 in the Authorization field will not work.

The security administrator needs to be aware of authorization group usage in SAP and be prepared to deal with them. Oftentimes, a trace will help you determine the authorization object being checked, but be aware that the authorization check is sometimes skipped if the authorization group field is left blank. It sometimes throws people a curve when a security role stops working because someone decided to place a value in an authorization group field that had not previously been used.

I have had production roles fail when someone updated a master data record by entering a value in the Authorization Group field without verifying the outcome back in development. They were trying to protect specific data and the steps were correct, we just needed to get out in front of the change with role updates before the data was secured to allow the authorized persons access. By adding the authorization group value before the roles were updated resulted in the person making the update not being able to access the record once the Save button was pressed.

File System

One of the powerful features incorporated in the SAP system is that the ABAP code can interact with the underlying operating system. ABAP code can read and write from/to files sitting in the file system at the operating system level and can execute operating system commands. While this is a powerful feature, it is also a dangerous feature because the actions taken are done using the system privileges of the system user that started the SAP application, which usually has broad access rights at the operating system level.

This section will discuss how to set up your security to provide controlled access to the operating system from the SAP application.

Securing the Operating System from the SAP Application with *S_DATASET* and *S_PATH*

First let's talk about reading and writing data from/to files on the operating system level or file system. This function is fundamental when converting an existing system to SAP. Interface files are often generated from the old system and read into SAP to aid in the migration. Sometimes, old systems continue to survive a conversion to SAP because there might be unique features or functions that the existing system provides that perhaps SAP doesn't, and possible interface files from SAP need to be sent to the old system in order to keep it updated. So we have legitimate reasons to provide access from the SAP application to read external files and write data to external files.

To protect this interface function, SAP utilizes its authorization check using the authorization object *S_DATASET*. The authorization check against *S_DATASET* is what is called an automatic check. As of version 3.0E, SAP has incorporated an automatic check at the kernel level, which is the program that is run at the operating system level for all dataset activities. *S_DATASET* has three authorization fields: an activity field, which lets you specify read, write, and delete activity restrictions; a filename field that lets you specify the file name, including the directory path; and a program field, which lets you restrict based on the program name that is trying to invoke the dataset access.

The file name field is restrictive because it is limited to 60 characters, and when you start qualifying that name with a complex directory path, you tend to use up those 60 characters quickly. Normally, this field is not used but is filled with an asterisk.

The activity field should always be used to specify the activity desired. Do not asterisk this field because you should not be giving write privileges when all that is needed is to be able to read.

The other authorization field is the program field. I believe it is a best practice to use this field to limit which program can access the operating system. It is additional work to determine the program name that is trying to open a dataset set, but it is a more secure method than allowing any program a user runs to have the privileges specified in *S_DATASET*. *S_DATASET* only protects the access to the file or dataset set and unless you restrict based on program, any program could open a dataset with the *S_DATASET* authorization.

Okay, so *S_DATASET* protects access requests to datasets or files, but you may be wondering how to protect a specific path or directory. For example, let's assume we are asked to protect the files that are being used to interface with SAP. SAP provides another authorization object, *S_PATH*, which lets you specify a restriction on the activity, read, or change, and the fully qualified directory, or path, that you want to protect. *S_PATH* is also an automatic authorization check done at the kernel level, but SAP delivers this check deactivated.

To activate the *S_PATH* authority check, you need to perform a little configuration. Two tables must be updated in order to activate the *S_PATH* authority check. First, you need to create an entry in the table SPTHB for an authorization group that will represent the path you want to secure. You only have four characters to work with, so a little creativity will be required. For our interface example, the requirements are to secure this interface directory. I will choose the authorization group ZINT. There is no SAP namespace to be concerned about here. I simply choose to use the "Z" as the first character.

Using transaction SM31 option MAINTAIN for the view V_SPT, you will create the authorization group.

1. You will receive a message that the table is cross-client. Just select the green check mark or press **Enter** to continue. You should see the following screen, as shown in Figure 3.21. There may be entries already in this table depending on previous administrative activity.

Figure 3.21 V_SPT

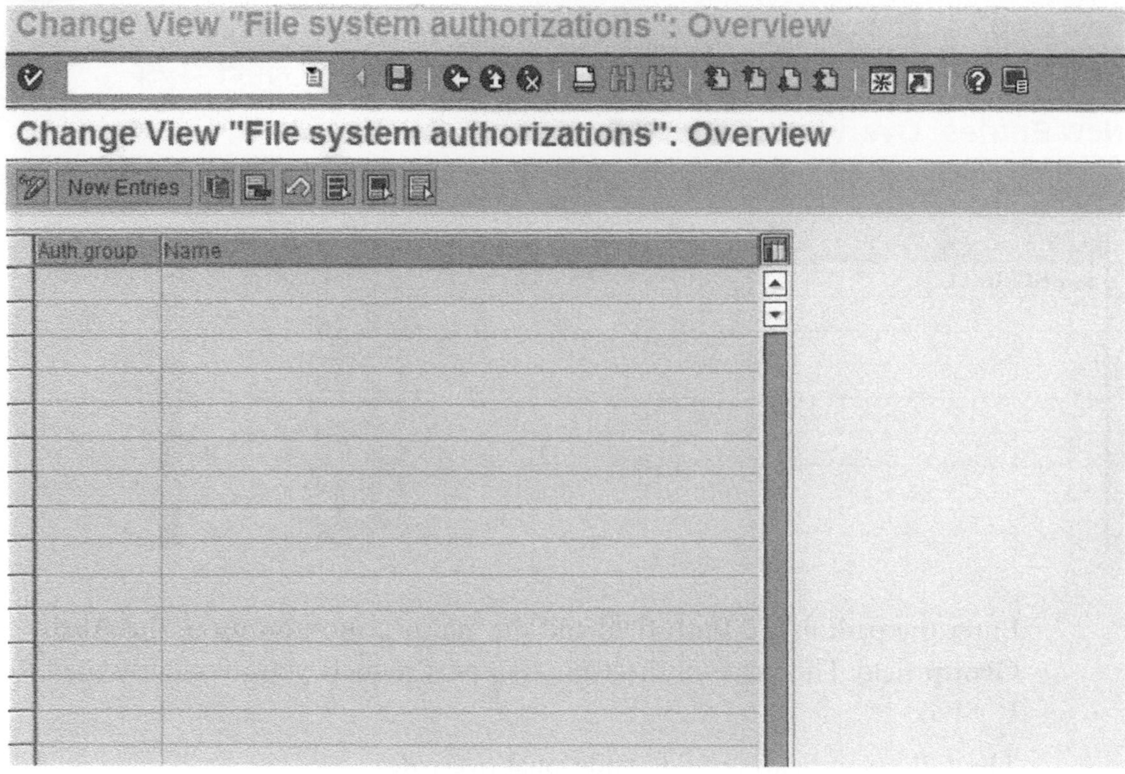

2. Select the **New Entries** option.
3. Enter the authorization group, as well as a short description in the **Name** field, and then save, which will prompt you for a transport request to save your changes.
4. Return to the SM31 initial screen.
5. Again using the transaction SM31 option MAINTAIN, only now for table SPTH, you will create the operating system path and associate it to your new authorization group. You will again receive a message that the table is cross-client. Just press the check mark or **Enter** to continue.
6. A screen will appear that may or may not have entries already, depending on previous activity on your system. Select **New Entries** to specify the operating system path and the new authorization group. This field is case sensitive, so you must match the path exactly as it is at the operating system level (see Figure 3.22).

Figure 3.22 V_SPT entry

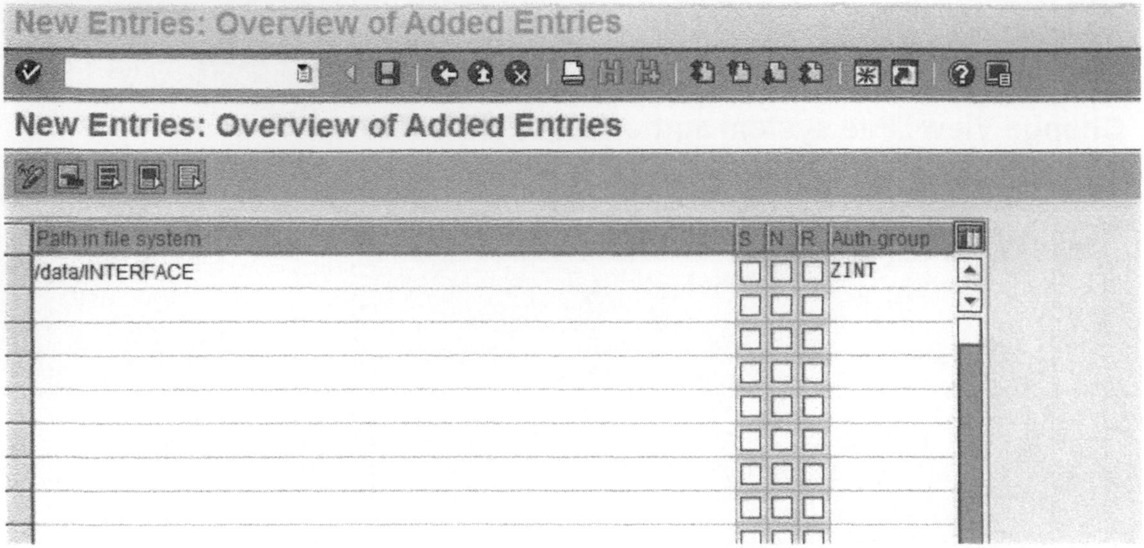

Path in file system	S	N	R	Auth.group
/data/INTERFACE	☐	☐	☐	ZINT

7. Enter the path in the **Path** field and the authorization group in the **Auth. Group** field. Then save to the same transport request you previously used for V_SPT.

   The following fields provide additional overrides.

   S = X if backup is required, or _ if not required.

   N = No read flag—This overrides the activity code in the authorization. X = override, No read allowed.

   R = Read only flag—This overrides the activity code in the authorization. X = override, No write allowed.

8. Return to the SM31 initial screen.

You are now finished. A word of caution, once SPTH is populated, the authority check for *S_PATH* is automatic for the path you just protected. No other directory is affected unless you assign an authorization group to it.

You should plan on having the necessary roles updated and in place before you turn on the PATH authorization check.

BDC Sessions

Batch Data Control (BDC) or batch input is used to upload mass data into the SAP system. Batch input has been used to transfer data from non-SAP systems to SAP as part of the migration process. It is also used when legacy systems survive and are used to feed the SAP system. A batch input session duplicates the screens and data input process that a human user would perform by logging in to the SAP system and running the corresponding transaction to enter and save the data. The batch input sessions automates this process so mass data records can be input into the SAP system without the time it takes for a human to enter all that data.

From a security perspective, if sensitive data is being entered, we need to protect the data based on our company policies for data protection. BDC sessions duplicate the screens that would be used in entering each data record. Therefore, if the BDC session is not protected, then someone only needs to view the session to be able to drill down into the screens to access the data.

BDC sessions are protected by authorization object *S_BDC_MONI* with an activities field to limit what can be done and a session name field to limit what BDC session can be accessed.

It is important that BDC sessions are properly named when they are created because they cannot be renamed once they have been submitted to SAP. You need to establish a naming convention for each group that will be using BDC sessions and implement restrictions using the naming conventions with authorization object *S_BDC_MONI.*

Securing the Operating System from the SAP Application with Logical Commands

Logical commands are used when a user needs to execute an operating system command from the SAP application. Logical commands, or external commands, are set up by the BASIS team using transaction SM69, but are executed by users with transaction SM49.

Any command or script that can be executed at the operating system level can be set up to be executed by a logical command, so this is a very powerful feature in SAP that needs to be managed carefully so only those commands that have been determined to be allowed by non-BASIS users can be executed by those users.

Logical or external commands are protected by the authorization object *S_LOG_COM.* The key authorization field in *S_LOG_COM* is the name field. You need to have a naming standard to be able to effectively grant access to specific commands while restricting access to other commands. The other two authorization fields let you restrict based on application server and operating system type; however, the name field is the primary field we should be concerned with.

In my experience, it is the power users in the functional groups that often get access to logical commands, so a naming convention that incorporates the group name is usually suitable. For example, the HR group may need to be able to transfer files into the SAP environment. This is accomplished by first moving the file to an HR directory and then executing a SAP program to read that file into the SAP application. An external command—say, *ZHRCopyIN*—to perform the appropriate copy into the HR directory can be set up by the BASIS team. The authorization using *S_LOG_COM* can be set up to allow this specific command or any external command that begins with ZHR*. The power of the naming convention lets you establish an authorization that can cover any command set up for HR so that future needs do not require a role update.

The use of logical commands is an acceptable method to provide operating system level access without giving out an operating system level user ID. Be sure to establish and stick with your naming conventions for logical commands and you will be able to provide your user community with operating system level access in a controlled acceptable manner.

Single Sign-on with SAPGUI

To implement Single Sign-on (SSO) with SAPGUI, you have the option of using Kerberos security protocol. Most UNIX vendors ship their own version of Kerberos 5; however, you must check with your OS vendor for support and additional installation documentation, as well as ensure that the version they provide is interoperable with the SAP BC-SNC certifiable interface to GSS-API v2 mechanisms and Microsoft's Kerberos. A SAP test tool, gsstest, can be used to test the interoperability and functions of the third-party gss-api library.

This *Kerberos-based* authentication method is only available with SAPGUI installed on the Windows 2000 platform. With this authentication, you can leverage your existing Windows infrastructure (that is, Windows user ID and passwords, Active Directory server) and enable a SSO solution where users can use their current user context on the desktop (in other words, the Windows domain user) to authenticate to SAP applications without entering their SAP user ID and password. You can also implement Kerberos-based SSO with a PKI-based security library (for example, SAP Cryptographic library) that you may already use for your SAP systems and enable encryption on the data exchange between the SAP Frontend and SAP Web AS ABAP system.

To implement SSO with SAPGUI, you must perform a number of steps:

1. Install the Kerberos library file on the SAP Web AS ABAP system. Use the appropriate Kerberos library file provided by your OS vendor and ensure that the version is interoperable with the SAP BC-SNC certifiable interface to GSS-API v2 mechanisms and Microsoft's Kerberos.
2. Prepare the central instance of all SAP Web AS ABAP systems. Implement the following instance profile parameters on the central instance of all SAP Web AS ABAP systems:

   ```
   snc/enable = 1
   snc/gssapi_lib = <location of the Kerberos library file>
   snc/identity/as = p:<SAP_Service_User>@<DOMAIN_NAME>
   snc/data_protection/min = 2
   snc/data_protection/max = 3
   snc/data_protection/use = 3
   snc/accept_insecure_cpic = 0
   snc/accept_insecure_rfc = 0
   snc/accept_insecure_r3int_rfc = 1
   snc/permit_insecure_start = 1
   snc/r3int_rfc_secure = 0
   snc/r3int_rfc_qop = 3
   snc/accept_insecure_gui = 1 (this will let you map users later)
   snc/force_login_screen = 0
   ```

3. Configure SAPGUI Frontend to enable SSO. Download the program **SAPSSO.MSI** from the sapserv<x> under directory **general/R3Server/binaries/NT/W2K**. This program must be rolled out to all users with SAPGUI Frontend to enable SSO support for Windows 2000.
4. Activate SSO for the SAP Logon window on each SAPGUI Frontend. Select an entry in the SAP Logon window and choose **Properties | Advanced**.

   . Choose **Enable Secure Network Connections**. In the **SNC Name** field, enter **p:<SAP_Service_User>@<DOMAIN_NAME>**. Save the settings. The SAP Logon window will display an icon with a key beside the system entry to indicate that SSO is active for the system.

5. Map SAP users to Windows users. Go to transaction SU01 and select the **SNC** tab. In the **SNC Name** field, enter the corresponding Windows user ID to the SAP user ID using the format **p:<WINDOWS_USERID>@<DOMAIN_**

NAME>. Alternatively, as the user's SNC name is stored in the table USRACL, you can maintain this field by updating table USRACL. You can also schedule the report *RSUSR300* to fill this table automatically on a regular basis.

6. Set profile parameter *snc/accept_insecure_gui = 0* (to reject unprotected logons).

Implementing Secure Communications

We'll now discuss various methods of securing your communications.

HTTPS

In order to protect communications sent over HTTP and enable HTTPS, SAP Web AS ABAP systems must be set up to support SSL. You must perform the following steps to enable SSL on the SAP Web AS ABAP system:

1. *Install the SAP Cryptographic library.*
2. *Implement profile parameters for SSL and restart the ICM to activate the parameters:*

   ssl/ssl_lib = /usr/sap/<>/SYS/exe/run/libsapcrypto.so

   sec/libsapsecu = /usr/sap/<>/SYS/exe/run/libsapcrypto.so

   ssf/ssfapi_lib = /usr/sap/<>/SYS/exe/run/libsapcrypto.so

   ssf/name = SAPSECULIB

   icm/server_port_<xx> = PROT=HTTPS, PORT=<secure port number>, TIMEOUT=<timeout in seconds>

   icm/HTTPS/verify_client = 1
3. *Create and maintain the SSL server PSEs:*

   Use transaction STRUST to create your PSE entries, you can either use a single systemwide SSL server PSE for all servers or use server-specific SSL server PSEs for individual application servers. For a systemwide SSL server PSE, you need to generate a single certificate request. For server-specific SSL server PSEs, you must generate a certificate request for each application server.
4. *Send certificate requests to CA:*

   For each certificate request, you must send it to a CA or SAP CA to obtain a signed public-key certificate for the server.

5. *Import the public-key certificate from CA:*
   Once the CA sends you the client certificate request response containing the signed public-key certificate, you must import this certificate to the corresponding PSE. For systemwide SSL server PSE, you only need to import the certificate to one of the application servers. Additionally, you must maintain the SSL server PSE's certificate list and import the CA root certificate.
6. *Create the SSL client PSE:*
   For the SAP Web AS ABAP system to communicate with other Web servers over HTTPS, the system must have the SSL client PSE. Use transaction STRUST to create your PSE entries, you can use a single systemwide SSL server PSE for all servers and specify the CN part of the Distinguished Name set as *system ID.* Similar to an SSL server PSE, you also need to send the certificate request to CA to obtain a signed public-key certificate, import this certificate to the SSL client PSE, and maintain the SSL client PSE's certificate list.

   In order for the SAP Web AS ABAP system to use *anonymous identity* to communicate with other Web servers over HTTPS, PSE entry is created with the CN part of the Distinguished Name set as *anonymous.* You must then import CA root certificates for the Web servers that the SAP Web AS ABAP system accesses using anonymous SSL client PSE.

   For a SAP Web AS ABAP system to use *individual identity* to communicate with other Web servers over HTTPS, you must define these individual identities in the SSL client PSE. For each individual identity, you must create an entry in table STRUSTSSL and create the appropriate SSL client PSE entry.
7. *Specify the SSL client PSE for the connection:*
   When defining the HTTP destinations for a SAP Web AS ABAP system in transaction SM59, you can specify whether SSL is used, and specifically which SSL client PSE to use for protecting the connection. This enables the use of an HTTPS connection for the RFC destinations.

   You can test the SSL connection and ensure the HTTPS port is opened by using transaction SMICM, from Menu **Goto | Services**. For testing connections where a SAP Web AS ABAP system is the server component, you can start a test BSP application using HTTPS connection with the appropriate secure port number. For testing connections where SAP Web AS

ABAP system is the client component, you can test an HTTP connection in transaction SM59.

SNC

You can use Secure Network Connection (SNC) to provide a secure authentication for protecting the communication between various client and server components of the AS ABAP system that use the Dialog and RFC protocols.

SNC requires the integration of an external security product with the SAP Web AS ABAP system to provide additional security functions that are not directly available with SAP systems. The external security product must be certified by the SAP Software Partner Program.

To implement SNC on a SAP Web AS ABAP system, you must ensure the external security product is installed on each system, check the installation documentation provided by the external security product vendor for any additional procedures. It is recommended that SNC configuration be performed consistently across all AS ABAP systems. However, depending on the complexity of the system environment, you may want to implement SNC in phases, in which case it is possible to adjust the profile parameters on the AS ABAP system accordingly to allow both protected and nonprotected connections.

The following profile parameters are SNC-related and can be implemented on a SAP Web AS ABAP system:

snc/enable = 1 (activates SNC)

snc/gssapi_lib = <location of the GSS-API v2 shared library>

snc/identity/as = <SNC name of the AS ABAP system>

snc/data_protection/max = 3 (maximum level of data protection, where 3 means privacy)

snc/data_protection/min = 2 (minimum level of data protection, where 2 means integrity)

snc/data_protection/use = 3 (default level of data protection, where 3 means privacy)

snc/r3int_rfc_secure = 0 (internal RFC connection is not protected with SNC as time critical performance is required for RFC connection, the communication is protected by the network infrastructure instead)

snc/accept_insecure_cpic = 0 (rejects unprotected connections) snc/accept_insecure_gui = 0 (rejects unprotected connections)

snc/accept_insecure_r3int_rfc = 1 (accepts unprotected internal RFC connections)

snc/accept_insecure_rfc = 0 (rejects unprotected incoming RFC connections)

snc/permit_insecure_start = 1 (programs can start without SNC)

snc/force_login_screen = 0 (logon screen is displayed only when necessary)

Some additional customizing activities are required for maintaining SNC configuration on the SAP Web AS ABAP system, such as maintaining Access Control Lists for users and systems, maintaining output devices, specifying SNC information for RFC and CPIC destinations, and checking canonical SNC names for external security systems.

Once SNC is enabled, the users can log on to the SAP Web AS ABAP system over the SNC layer. As such, the user master records must also be maintained with SNC information. For Dialog users, the SNC information is maintained in transaction SU01. You can maintain the SNC name field in the SNC tab. Alternatively, you can update the SNC names directly in table USRACL. For non-Dialog users, you can update SNC information directly in table USRACLEXT.

Certificates

The implementation process for client certificates has been mentioned already. The following is an overview of the steps involved:

1. Configure the SAP Web AS ABAP system to support SSL.
2. Set the profile parameter *icm/HTTPS/verify_client* to 1 and restart the ICM to activate the parameter.
3. Maintain the AS ABAP system's SSL server PSE using transaction STRUST.
4. Update table USREXTID with user mapping of SAP user IDs to the corresponding certificates.

Setting Up the PFCG_TIME_DEPENDENCY Job

The PFCG_TIME_DEPENDENCY job executes a program that evaluates the validity dates on the role assignments and adds or removes the associated profile(s).

This program should be scheduled in every SAP client where user authorizations are managed via role assignments.

Contrary to what many think, a role is nothing more than a template for authorizations. It is used by the profile generator to make managing and grouping of authorizations easier. Authorizations are indirectly assigned to a user ID via the role; however, no authorization actually resides in a role. All authorizations are in the associated profile(s).

When you create a role with the profile generator, you determine what authorizations will be in that role and the values that will be assigned. To activate a role, you must click the generate button, which generates one or more profiles, depending on the number of authorizations. Authorizations, in reality, are generated in the profile, and until that profile is assigned to a user ID, no access is allowed.

You assign a role via SU01 and when you save the user, the mechanics behind SU01 locate the associated profile and attach it along with the authorizations to the user ID. One of the benefits of role administration is that you can set the validity dates on the role to become active at a future date or deactivated at a future date. However, while the role may be controlled by the validity dates, the profile is not. This is where the PFCG_TIME_DEPENDENCY program comes into play.

When PFCG_TIME_DEPENDENCY executes, it looks at the validity dates and updates the profile assignments. It is recommended that PFCG_TIME_DEPENDENCY be executed at least once per day, preferably shortly after midnight so new roles are activated/deactivated on the day they should be. I would suggest scheduling PFCG_TIME_DEPENDENCY to run once an hour. This assures that user master records are properly synced to the roles and profiles as assignments are changed. More frequent execution can be done, but you should periodically review the job logs to see if the job is completing before the next scheduled execution. Adjust the frequency as needed.

For more information about PFCG_TIME_DEPENDENCY, look at the documentation for program rhautupd_new. PFCG_TIME_DEPENDENCY actually calls rhautupd_new.

Access to TEMSE – Temporary Sequential

This is a temporary area in SAP that holds data that many in security administration overlook. It holds the raw data from spool output, job logs, batch input logs, audit logs, and other data that is not stored in the SAP system permanently. So why should we be concerned about a temporary storage location? We need to be aware of this area of SAP because it can contain sensitive data that needs to be protected.

For example, your HR department performs a payroll run that produces a payroll report detailing the wages, Social Security numbers, taxes, and so on of the employees in the company. That information is protected on the spooler and printed to a secure printer, but that data is also temporarily stored in the TEMSE area as a raw data file. It might not look as pretty as the formatted report, but the data is what needs to be protected, not the fancy formatting.

Data on TEMSE is stored based on object types. For example, spool output is stored with object names beginning with SPOOL and includes the spool number. If the HR payroll reports had been created with spool number 15618, I could find the TEMSE entry by looking for SPOOL*15618. The raw data would then be available for me to access, download, or print as an ASCII data file.

Direct access of the TEMSE area is protected by authorization object *S_TMS_ACT*. While you can specify the object name—for example, SPOOL* or JOB*—to restrict the type of TEMSE data, I find that the action and owner authorization fields provide sufficient protection. With the owner field, you can restrict the access to only those TEMSE objects that the user "owns"—meaning those he/she created—and using the action field further restricts what can be done, such as create, read, delete, and so on. The HR application makes use of the TEMSE area and you will find you need to grant authorizations using the *S_TMS_ACT* authorization object. Be sure to restrict the owner field to either the values "OWN" or "GRP" and get the object name pattern from either the ST01 trace or the SU53 authorization error check report to limit the access provided to the TEMSE area.

System Locks (SM12)

System locks in SAP should only be administered by someone who understands how to manage the locks and the implications of deleting locks. The implications can mean that data corruption can occur if the locks are deleted before the system has a chance to apply all the updates that were pending in connection to the locks.

Generally, I believe access to administer system locks should be left to the BASIS team, but I always get requests to have access granted to SM12. Fortunately, the SAP authorization concept allows us to restrict access to this sensitive system area. The authorization object that protects manual access to system locks is *S_ENQUE*. You can use *S_ENQUE* to provide display-only access with the authorization value DPFU, and if you are forced to grant additional access, you can at least restrict the damage that might be done to the user's own locks by specifying the values DPFU and DLOU. It would allow the user to display all locks in the client and delete his/her own locks.

Production Support

Now that you have implemented your new SAP security environment, you might be thinking you can relax. Wrong. From here out, you need to keep an eye on things to be sure your environment runs smoothly and hopefully does not get breached. This section deals with some items that that fall under the scope of production support—that period of time that starts as soon as your first production user begins using the system and ends when you retire the system. How do you keep an eye on a system like this? You do it by monitoring with a series of reports. In the following paragraphs I will share with you some routines you can adapt in order to keep on top of your security environment.

CUA Monitoring/Troubleshooting

Let's start with CUA because if you are using central user administration, you must make sure it is functioning properly at all times to get the best benefit from it.

Once you have your CUA system up and running, you might think there is nothing more to it than maintaining the user masters and so everyone lives happily ever after. Well, technology is great when it works, but a real headache when it doesn't. CUA is not without its warts.

There are several good notes in OSS you should review for basic troubleshooting, as well as background jobs you can set up to help resolve issues where IDOCs don't get processed. However, when all else fails, you need to understand a few tools to help you diagnose and resolve your unprocessed IDOCs, because if left unresolved, records will not get updated properly and users will have the wrong security. CUA does not self-heal. You must monitor it and resolve problems as soon as possible to keep it working smoothly. I had one client that really did not understand how to diagnose why the IDOC records he was sending would never get processed and kept reprocessing the same change. Then, he would find changes occurring that were not requested. What was really happening was old IDOCs had been left unprocessed and in his effort to resolve the problems, he was triggering old unprocessed change requests, which were processed out of sync. He had a real mess on his hands and he was getting very frustrated. Once we got the system cleaned, put in a few background jobs to help his system maintain itself, and I showed him a few basic tools to diagnose and resolve problems, his system settled down and it became a valuable tool for security administration, as it is supposed to be.

First, it is important to keep your systems up-to-date with support packs, especially your CUA central system. I know the security administrator does not usually apply support packs, but if you have any input in deciding whether to apply the latest support pack or not, use your influence to encourage the application. You will have less trouble if your CUA central system and your child systems are current with the available support packs.

Next, frequently check the CUA log to make sure records are being processed. I will check the log after I save the user master record unless I am processing several at one time. If I am processing several user master record changes simultaneously, I will check the log after I complete the group and refresh the screen periodically until all updates have completed or until enough time has passed that it should have processed. If an update doesn't process, I begin my investigation into why it didn't.

CUA's log can be checked by executing the transaction SCUL. I usually have this transaction on my favorites in the CUA central system. Take note of the initial SCUL screen and verify that there are no unprocessed tRFCs (transactional RFCs). In Figure 3.23, the log screen shows 124 errors. Click the button to review the errors and determine why they occurred. An error message should display that will guide you to your next step to resolve these until you have zero errors. Afterward, refresh your SCUL screen to see if your unconfirmed records have completed.

Figure 3.23 SCUL tRFC Errors

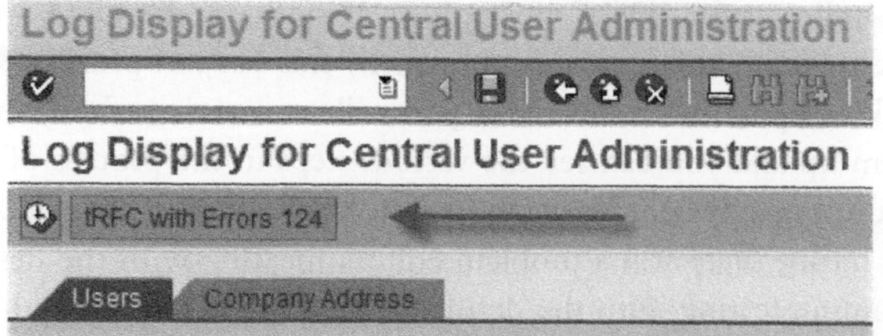

In SCUL, you can select either a system view or a user view. When I am processing several user master updates at a time, I usually select the system view, which displays all the systems where an IDOC has been generated for the user IDs I just updated. I use the user view when processing a batch of user IDs because I am interested in seeing the user list shrink as the records are processed. If I get down to a few IDs remaining in my display, I might switch to the system view to see if there is a common system that might not be processing and I can focus my attention on that system. There may be a common problem that will resolve all the pending changes.

If I find that some of the IDOCs are not processing, one of the first steps I take is to select an unprocessed ID and drill down until I see the three IDOC records for the user ID. Three IDOC records are always generated for a change to the user master record. The USER IDOC which handles changes to the user master record for all information except role and profile assignments. The PROFILE IDOC obviously processes the profile changes and the ACTGRP IDOC, which carries the changes for role assignments.

Once I can see these three records, I can also see the IDOC number generated in the CUA central system as well as the status. IDOCs that have been successfully processed will be green. Warnings will be yellow; errors, red and grey, will indicate that CUA doesn't know what happened. The greens are obviously not a concern. The yellows and reds will usually have an error message tagged to them describing what went wrong, letting you resolve that issue and redistribute the IDOC so it will process.

The greys are unconfirmed and are the IDOCs we need to investigate. The first step I usually take is to double-click the IDOC number of the grey unconfirmed record. This shows the status screen for the IDOC in question and gives us a display—a folder-like icon with the data records, and a folder with the status records. It also gives us a technical short info. box on the right side, which shows—among other items—the current status, which is what I am looking for. A green indicator with status 03 means the IDOC was passed from the CUA application to the system port, which usually indicates the IDOC was sent successfully by the CUA system, and that I need to look at the destination to find out why this has not processed.

If you click to open the status folder, you will see a series of status records. These are read bottom up and you can see the various steps in the process of generating the IDOC and ultimately sending it on its way. Sometimes the top-most status is 02, which usually means there was a problem communicating with the destination. A problem communicating with the destination could be almost anything from a busy network to the destination being down. Check to make sure the destination is up. You can simply try logging on via the SAPGui. If there doesn't seem to be a problem with the up status of the destination, check the RFC connection. You may need your BASIS group to do this for you, depending on how responsibilities have been segregated. Problems with the RFC connection can usually be tracked back to a password change on the RFC user ID in the destination system not matching the password entered on the RFC destination (SM59).

Once you have verified that communication with the destination is not a problem, try to redistribute the IDOC from SCUL. This should allow the IDOC to process properly unless something else is going on.

If the status was 03, meaning it left the CUA central system okay, we have to trace it to the destination. We use transaction BDM2 for this. Record the IDOC number from the SCUL report and run BDM2. I like to create a second session for BDM2 so I can keep SCUL open and refer back to it.

In BDM2, enter **USERCLONE** in the **Message Type** field. The partner type should default to LS. Don't change this. Enter the required field Partner Number of Receiver the logical system name of the child system. Remember, this should match the RFC destination name. If we were looking at an ECC system, the logical system name might be DECCLNT300. Match up the date created with the date on the SCUL report for the IDOC we are tracing and press the **Execute** button. We are expecting to see a single line report for status 53, the number of IDOCs processed with the description field giving the message "Application document posted." This is an indicator that the IDOC was sent to the destination, processed, and status 53 was returned to CUA. This is the normal roundtrip of an IDOC.

What we often see is another line with status 64, meaning the destination received our IDOC but has not processed it yet and we need to find out why. Double-click the line that has status 64 and find our IDOC number from the SCUL report in the column for Sending System. Once this is found, locate the IDOC number that was created in the destination. We will need that number to log in to the destination and investigate why it wasn't processed.

Now armed with the IDOC number created in the destination child system from our BDM2 report, log on to the child system and execute transaction WE05. WE05 lets us enter in date and time criteria for when the IDOC was created. If we are tracking down a current IDOC, then the default date and time fields will be filled with today's date, and the time range will include all day. You can restrict the time range, but we already have the IDOC number, so why don't we just come down to the IDOC number field and enter the IDOC number here and execute this transaction. The screen that appears should be the IDOC status screen, just like the one we see when we double-click the IDOC number from transaction SCUL.

We need to check the technical short info. box to see what the current status is. Status 53 means the child system has processed this IDOC. Recheck in CUA central transaction SCUL because the child system may have completed the processing while we were tracking it down.

If the status is 64, then the IDOC is ready to be processed by the application, but for some reason hasn't. The reason IDOCs get stuck in status 64 is often due to resources, specifically work processes that weren't available when the IDOC arrived. To trigger this IDOC to complete its processing, we can run the program RBDAPP01, enter our IDOC number, and execute, and the IDOC will complete the processing that should have been done automatically.

Resource availability is one of the primary reasons IDOCs fail to process. SAP does not requeue the IDOCs for automatic reprocessing, but jobs are available that can be scheduled to do this for you. You should definitely get a copy of OSS note 333441, which provides tips for CUA problem analysis. OSS note 557610 details the setup of a background job to execute RBDAPP01 and to avoid potential locks when mass records are being processed. OSS note 399271 gives pointers for optimizing CUA performance. If you are the curious type, you might want to get a copy of OSS note 161347, which lists the tables CUA uses.

The central user administration tool can be a very useful tool for centrally managing user IDs and role assignments if it is set up properly and maintained. It can also be one of the biggest headaches you will ever encounter if you don't pay attention and quickly resolve problems that arise. One thing to keep in mind: CUA is an ALE application. You troubleshoot, diagnose, and resolve problems using ALE tools and techniques. The more you understand about how an ALE application works, the better you will be able to maintain your CUA environment.

RFC Access

RFC access is when someone initiates a session that does not come via the SAPGUI, but instead by way of using remote function calls to log on and execute SAP programs. RFC access can sometimes be a bit anonymous when system or special user IDs are involved. We are talking about IDs that have been set up for special connectivity into the SAP system. Perhaps your company has purchased a third-party application that is being used in the SAP environment to supplement functionality. The concern would be that the user ID and password has not been compromised and is being used by an unauthorized person to gain access to the SAP system. If an external system is accessing your SAP system via RFC, you want to be sure they are taking precautions to protect the user ID and password. I have seen applications that executed via a script that had the user ID and password embedded in the script, and the script was just an ASCII text file. This makes the user ID password available to anyone who can open that script file.

Another use of special IDs is for setting up connectivity between SAP systems—for example, setting up access between a BI system and an R/3 system to allow the extract of data for population of data in your BI system. This isn't a lesson in hacking, but these IDs can be used for unauthorized access by someone familiar with RFC communication.

First and foremost, you should have already taken measures to ensure that the authorizations attached to these IDs are not any broader than necessary. We have covered this earlier in the chapter about providing only the authorizations necessary to allow a user to perform his/her tasks in SAP and no more.

Now we get to the monitoring part of this discussion. To monitor RFC access into your system, you can use the AIS system. Hopefully, you remember the discussion in the tools section for SM19 and SM20. If not, go back to that section and review the setup and reporting features. I used an example for setting up an RFC filter that you can use to monitor RFC access into your SAP system.

Once AIS is configured to log the RFC access, you should review the reports frequently. I would suggest daily, but at least weekly.

Daily Tasks

I suggest you perform the following every day, possibly in the morning and then in the afternoon to monitor your system.

SM04 – User Overview

Administrators should consider doing spot checks throughout the day to monitor users and their activities. Are all users using the defined logon groups? Are users logging on using multiple machines? You can check the terminal the user ID is coming from and if the same user ID is logged on from multiple terminals, then that ID is probably being shared. Are there any unrecognizable user IDs (IDs not following the naming convention, and so on)?

AL08 – Users Logged On

Remember, AL08 is an alternate for SM04 and lets you review logged-on users across multiple servers if your system is configured with multiple servers. Again, we are looking for the same things as with SM04, suspicious IDs, or IDs being shared.

SM21 – The System Log

Review all failed logon attempts, ID locks due to failed logon attempts, and errors that result in program dumps. Also check for the message "Failed to activate authorization check for user *xxxx*" where *xxxx* is a user ID. This message indicates that a background job is running for user *xxxx* but user *xxxx* is not active.

SM19 – AIS Configuration

Verify that your AIS configuration is active. You may be wondering why this is a daily task. Sometimes AIS does not reactivate after the system has been cycled, so if you are using AIS for monitoring, you better make sure it is configured correctly and is active.

RZ20 – CCMS Monitoring

If CCMS monitoring is used, review and acknowledge all alerts in the Security Node.

SUIM – User Information

Run reports for Change Documents for Users. Check for administrative locks being set/reset and by whom. Check for repeated password resets. This may indicate a hacking attempt or a user who needs training.

ST22 – ABAP Dump Analysis

Review all dump logs for potential security issues. Common errors you might see here are authorization check errors for *S_DATASET* and *S_RFC*. The RFC errors could be hacking attempts or just a new feature in a custom ABAP program that the developer's put into production without involving security to ensure the proper roles were updated.

SA38 – Run Report RSUSR006

RSUSR006 is a nice little report to check for users who are locked out due to invalid logons. It also provides a password status.

Weekly Tasks

The following tasks can be done on a weekly basis.

SE16 – Table Browser

- Review AGR_DEFINE for new roles, who created it and when.
- Review AGR_TCODES for critical/restricted transaction assignments in the roles.
- Review AGR_1251 for critical/restricted authorization assignments in the roles.
- Review USR02 for new users and who created them.
- Review USR02 for users not assigned to a user group if you use user groups.
- Review USR02 for users that have not logged on for a specified period. These users may be candidates for removal.
- Review AGR_USERS for invalid role assignments to user IDs.
- Use a spreadsheet to format this information (see the following):

Table Name	Purposes
AGR_DEFINE	Composite role vs. single role; role description; creation info
AGR_1251	
AGR_1252	
USR02	
USER_ADDR	

SCC4 – Client Administration

Verify client lock settings.

SCU3 – Table History

Check for Table T000 to review client lock changes and who is making the changes. The server profile parameter rec/client must be set before the table change history is captured.

PFCG – Role Maintenance

Go to **Utilities | Overview Status**. Review the resulting list for any red or yellow lights. Take any necessary corrective action.

Monthly Tasks

The following tasks can be done on a monthly basis.

TU02 – Parameter Changes

Review security parameters for changes.

SUIM – User Information

For users with SAP_ALL assigned, open the **Where Used** section, and then go to **Profiles | In Users**. Enter the SAP_ALL profile name in the Screen field and execute.

Transaction S_BCE_68002111 or Execute Program RSUSR008_009_NEW

This report uses SAP-delivered criteria to create a report where critical authorizations are used. It can be used as is or modified in development and transported forward.

Run Report RSUSR003

Report RSUSR003 lets you check the passwords of users SAP* and DDIC in All Clients. Be sure to uncheck the check box for displaying profile parameters.

Production support is more than just fixing things that break. It is also about supporting the environment to keep it pristine, or at least keeping it from degrading over time. You have devoted much effort to getting your SAP system up and securely running, now you need to monitor it to keep it that way.

Summary

A secure SAP environment starts with a solid architectural approach which takes into account corporate asset protection, business processes, legal restrictions and separation of duties requirements. Identity management and a strong password policy will shore up your defenses from outside attacks

When designing your SAP security environment, take into account the risk tolerance of your company as well as common business policies that are either formally or informally practiced. For example, a private company may be more restrictive of financial data access than a public company that reports financial data on a regular basis. Base your design on a security policy that inclues provisions for the standards you will follow which will drive the many decisions that will arise as you go through implementation.

Know the tools that are available in your SAP system to assist you in reporting, developing, maintaining and monitoring your environment. The security administer's day is filled with many requests and challenges to the policy decisions and can become overwhelming. By knowing and using the available tools to quickly carry out your responsibilities to dispatch some of those demands will allow you to direct your attention to other more important matters.

Implementation puts all the plans into play, but if you have taken the time to put together a good design and are knowledgeable in the use of the available tools, you will have fewer issues that surprise you.

Solutions Fast Track

Architecture

☑ Architecting a secure environment provides a game plan for developing and implementing security to protect corporate assets.

☑ Identity management provides your game plan with a method for keeping user information, identity and access rights, in synchronization across multiple systems.

☑ SAP's authorizaiton concept allows you to assign access rights via the security roles assigned to the user id.

☑ Strong passwords should be encouraged and enforced by system parameter settings.

Design

☑ Design your game plan based on business processes, risk tolerance and any legal requirements that govern your industry.

☑ Develop a security policy as part of your strategy to provide guidedance for decisions.

☑ Consider the standards you will follow for the many components from role naming to printer names to BDC sessions names to aid you in your security development.

☑ Follow a role development process for consistency and the abilitiy to maintain segregation of duties.

Tools

☑ Use the appropriate tools to set up your security environment.

☑ Learn and use the available tools to help you monitor your system.

☑ Use SAP's tools to maintain your system.

Implementation

☑ Implementation puts your game plan into action. CUA with the LDAP connection can help with identity management.

☑ Make sure you update the passwords for SAP's delivered user ids.

☑ Protect the file system from access from the SAP application layer.

Frequently Asked Questions

Q: How can I protect access to a custom table via SM30?

A: Use table authorization groups.

Q: How can I protect data in a BDS session?

A: Establish a naimg convention for BDC sessions and use S_BDC_MONI to restrict access to specific BDC sessions.

Q: How can I protect data at the operating system level?

A: SAP automatically invokes an authorization check for all open, read, update and delete dataset operations against authorization object S_DATASET.

Q: How can I determine who is logged on and what application server they are logged onto?

A: Use transaction AL08.

Q: How can I tell if CUA has processed my user id update?

A: Use transaction SCUL to check the CUA log.

Q: How can I monitor my system for RFC access?

A: Use AIS by setting up a filer for RFC Log on attempts using SM19 and generate a report using SM20.

Chapter 4

J2EE

Solutions in this chapter:

- Users Maintenance
- Single Sign-on
- Changing Passwords
- Setting Up SSL

☑ Summary

☑ Solutions Fast Track

☑ Frequently Asked Questions

Introduction

SAP's Web Application Server (WEB AS) comes in two base flavors, ABAP and J2EE (The Java 2 Platform, Enterprise Edition). Both have distinct and unique characteristics. In this chapter, we will focus on the WEB AS J2EE framework and its particular security concerns.

Before we dive in to the details of J2EE, I wanted to make one point regarding the J2EE Engine itself. In comparison to the robust and mature ABAP engine, in my opinion, the J2EE engine is in its infancy. In fact version 7.0 is really only the second major release of the platform. With that said, fixes introduced with the patches sets called *Support Stacks* are often dramatic changes. It is always good to check the release notes of your current patch release. Test before doing something in production. Something that worked in a previous patch level may work differently after applying a patch. Hopefully this will reduce the number of unpleasant productive surprises.

The J2EE architecture is significantly different than its ABAP counterpart; it is no surprise that the security design and implementation are also very different. Users in the J2EE Engine are based on a user management engine, UME. The UME is the source from which the J2EE Engine accepts and validates logons. The UME can point to sources such as itself or external locations such as the ABAP user management engine.

Users Maintenance

Let's begin the topic of J2EE security with user maintenance by highlighting some special users. All system and service users are important but without a functioning administrator account, the J2EE Engine just will not run. The default administrator account is *Administrator* for a single stack J2EE implementation. In a dual-stack J2EE installation, the administrator account is *J2EE_ADMIN*. In a dual-stack implementation, another important user is the interface user *SAPJSP*. This user connects J2EE and the ABAP engine.

Let's explore how to manage the users in the J2EE Engine. The way we manage users really depends on where the user store is located. J2EE uses the idea of a UME (User Management Engine). We'll talk in more detail about the UME in the next sections. For now, we'll refer to the UME as being located within itself. In UME talk this is defined as *database*, located within itself.

The tool for administering users is the *Visual Administrator* and the identity management user interface via the Web browser (*UME Console*). We'll start with the *Visual Administrator* user interface then discuss the UME console.

In the UNIX environment, you need to properly set up your X session to view the graphical user interface (GUI) interface. In the following example, I have an X server running on my local machine and open a shell session to the J2EE server using a terminal emulator. See Figure 4.1 where I export the DISPLAY variable to the X server address and test my setup by running the program *xclock*. If I am successful, I should get a small GUI clock. I entered these steps for one reason: most security administrators that I've worked with usually have had little reason or need to log on to a UNIX shell. To a UNIX or Basis administrator this is probably basic, but hopefully this helps those of you who are casual UNIX users.

Figure 4.1 Exporting DISPLAY Variable in C Shell and Testing It via Xclock

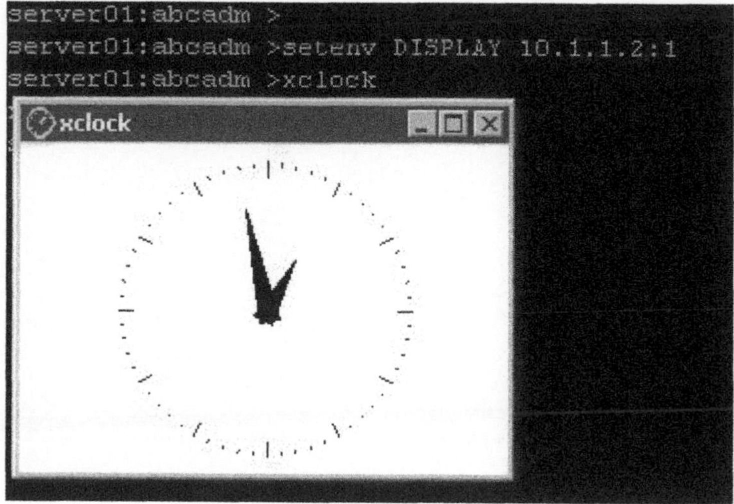

Alternatively, you can open an X session directly using the X emulator interface in commercial packages like Reflections X or Hummingbird. This allows for GUI access without having to explicitly set any environmental variables. I typically avoid this technique since the interface is slow and finicky.

Let's get back to user administration using the *Visual Administrator*. We will focus our attention on J2EE-specific users in the local UME. Navigate to /usr/sap/<SID>/JC##/j2ee/admin and run the script **go**. Start the *Visual Administrator* then select **Default** and enter the password for the *Administrator* user. Drill down the tree (cluster tab) Server > Services > Security Provider. Select the **User management** tab. From here we can perform user maintenance operations. See Figure 4.2 for an overview of the user maintenance interface.

Figure 4.2 Security Provider Service, User Maintenance Interface

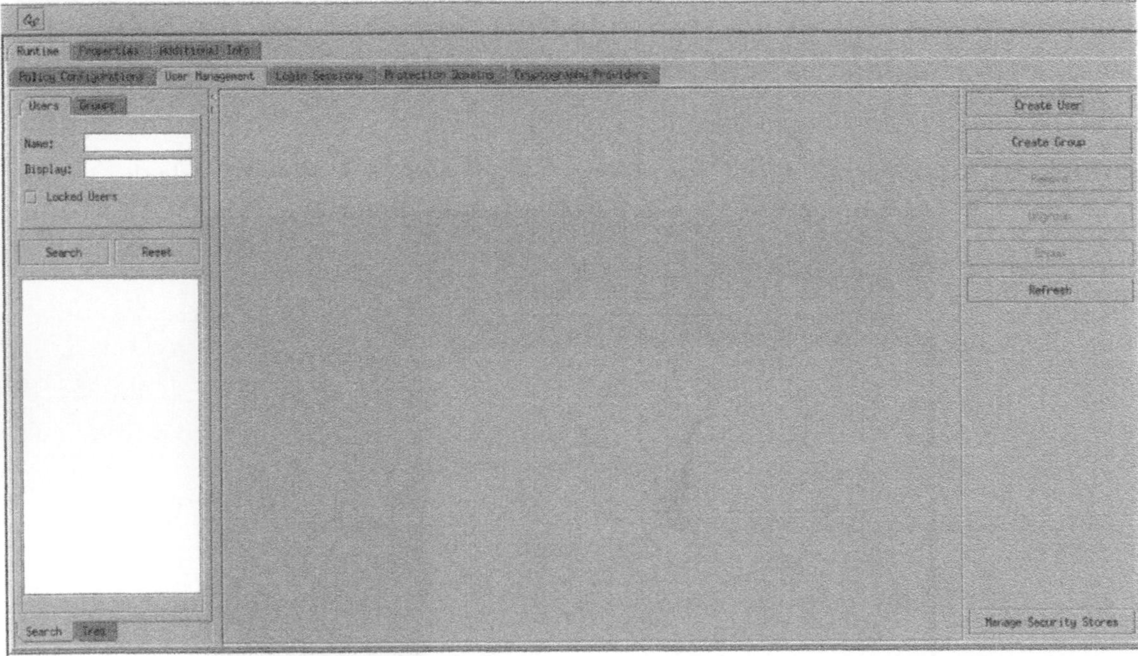

Create a new user by selecting the **Create User** icon on the right side and entering the username and password. The password can be system generated; select the check box **Random Password**. If there are any groups that you need to assign enter or search for them via the pane on the left. Some groups that are system assigned at runtime are *Authenticated*, *Anonymous*, and *Everyone* groups. You also have the option of associating a user with a X.509 certificate. See Figure 4.3 for the create user interface.

Figure 4.3 Create User Interface

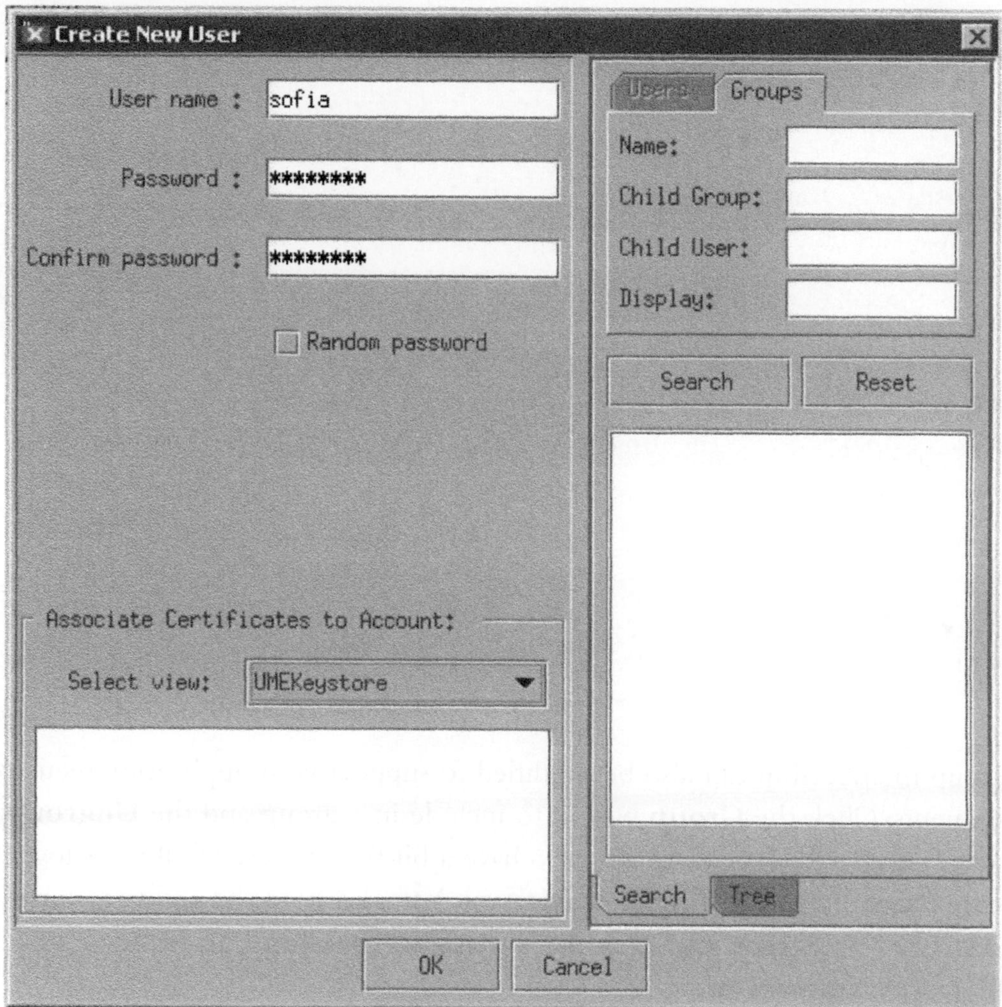

The user account interface shows information such as user creation date and time, last modification time, validity, lock state, groups membership, password change time, and any associated X.509 certificates. See Figure 4.4.

Figure 4.4 User Information

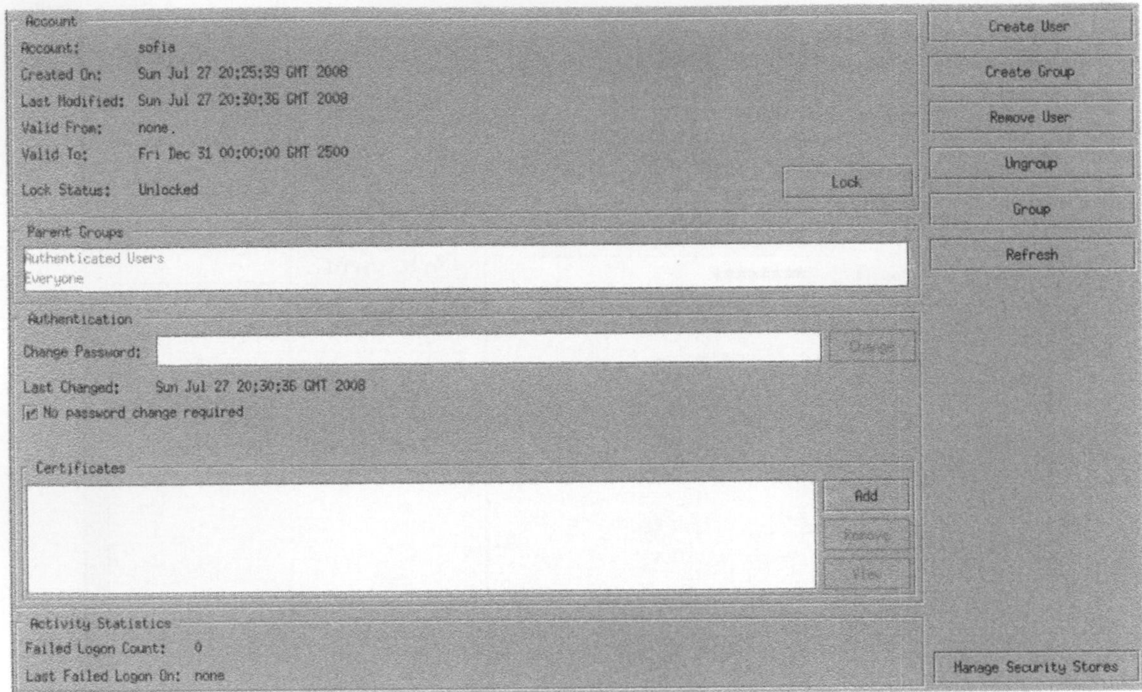

Group membership can also be modified to support your application security requirements. Click the **Group** button to include in a group and the **Ungroup** button to remove from a group.You also have a bird's eye view of all users logged into the system. Select the **Login Session** tab.You also have the ability to terminate sessions. Select the session and click the **Terminate Session** button. See Figure 4.5 for the **Login Sessions** tab.

Figure 4.5 Active Sessions

Runtime | Properties | Additional Info

Policy Configurations | User Management | Login Sessions | Protection Domains | Cryptography Providers

*	Principal	Creation Timestamp	Expires At
1	Guest	Sun Jul 27 20:39:51 GMT 2008	Tue Jul 29 00:26:31 GMT 2008
2	Guest	Sun Jul 27 20:39:41 GMT 2008	Tue Jul 29 00:26:21 GMT 2008
3	Guest	Sun Jul 27 20:39:31 GMT 2008	Tue Jul 29 00:26:11 GMT 2008
4	Guest	Sun Jul 27 20:39:20 GMT 2008	Tue Jul 29 00:26:00 GMT 2008
5	Guest	Sun Jul 27 20:39:10 GMT 2008	Tue Jul 29 00:25:50 GMT 2008
6	Guest	Sun Jul 27 20:39:00 GMT 2008	Tue Jul 29 00:25:40 GMT 2008
7	Guest	Sun Jul 27 20:38:50 GMT 2008	Tue Jul 29 00:25:30 GMT 2008
8	Guest	Sun Jul 27 20:38:40 GMT 2008	Tue Jul 29 00:25:20 GMT 2008
9	Guest	Sun Jul 27 20:38:30 GMT 2008	Tue Jul 29 00:25:10 GMT 2008
10	Guest	Sun Jul 27 20:38:20 GMT 2008	Tue Jul 29 00:25:00 GMT 2008
11	Guest	Sun Jul 27 20:38:10 GMT 2008	Tue Jul 29 00:24:50 GMT 2008
12	Guest	Sun Jul 27 20:38:00 GMT 2008	Tue Jul 29 00:24:40 GMT 2008
13	Guest	Sun Jul 27 20:37:50 GMT 2008	Tue Jul 29 00:24:30 GMT 2008
14	Guest	Sun Jul 27 20:37:40 GMT 2008	Tue Jul 29 00:24:20 GMT 2008
15	Administrator	Sun Jul 27 06:40:26 GMT 2008	Mon Jul 28 10:27:06 GMT 2008
16	Guest	Sun Jul 27 06:25:22 GMT 2008	Mon Jul 28 10:12:02 GMT 2008
17	Guest	Sun Jul 27 06:25:12 GMT 2008	Mon Jul 28 10:11:52 GMT 2008
18	Guest	Sun Jul 27 06:25:02 GMT 2008	Mon Jul 28 10:11:42 GMT 2008
19	Guest	Sun Jul 27 06:24:52 GMT 2008	Mon Jul 28 10:11:32 GMT 2008
20	Guest	Sun Jul 27 06:24:42 GMT 2008	Mon Jul 28 10:11:22 GMT 2008
21	Guest	Sun Jul 27 06:24:32 GMT 2008	Mon Jul 28 10:11:12 GMT 2008
22	Guest	Sun Jul 27 06:24:22 GMT 2008	Mon Jul 28 10:11:02 GMT 2008
23	Guest	Sun Jul 27 06:24:12 GMT 2008	Mon Jul 28 10:10:52 GMT 2008
24	Guest	Sun Jul 27 06:24:02 GMT 2008	Mon Jul 28 10:10:42 GMT 2008
25	Guest	Sun Jul 27 06:23:52 GMT 2008	Mon Jul 28 10:10:32 GMT 2008
26	Guest	Sun Jul 27 06:23:42 GMT 2008	Mon Jul 28 10:10:22 GMT 2008
27	Guest	Sun Jul 27 06:23:32 GMT 2008	Mon Jul 28 10:10:12 GMT 2008
28	Guest	Sun Jul 27 06:23:22 GMT 2008	Mon Jul 28 10:10:02 GMT 2008
29	Guest	Sun Jul 27 06:23:12 GMT 2008	Mon Jul 28 10:09:52 GMT 2008
30	Guest	Sun Jul 27 06:23:02 GMT 2008	Mon Jul 28 10:09:42 GMT 2008

Terminate Session

Creating users via the UME Console is performed via the UME Console, which is accessed via a Web browser interface. Access the URL via the alias /useradmin off the main address for the J2EE server. If your server name is server01, with instance number 00, accessed via Hypertext Transport Protocol Secure (HTTPS), the URL is https://server01:50001/useradmin.

The UME Console is an intuitive interface allowing the administrator to maintain users, groups, roles, and replication. We'll step through the process of creating a user using the UME Console. The first step is to navigate with your browser to the UME Console URL. User can be created via a creation, copy, or import process. We'll choose **Create** for the example. See Figure 4.6 for the UME Console initial screen.

Figure 4.6 UME Console

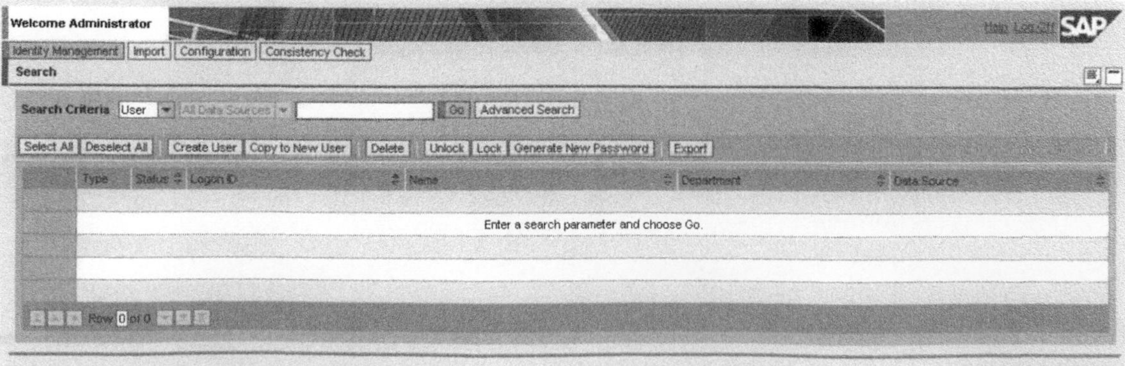

Choose the **Create User** icon and enter user general data (see Figure 4.7).

Figure 4.7 User General data

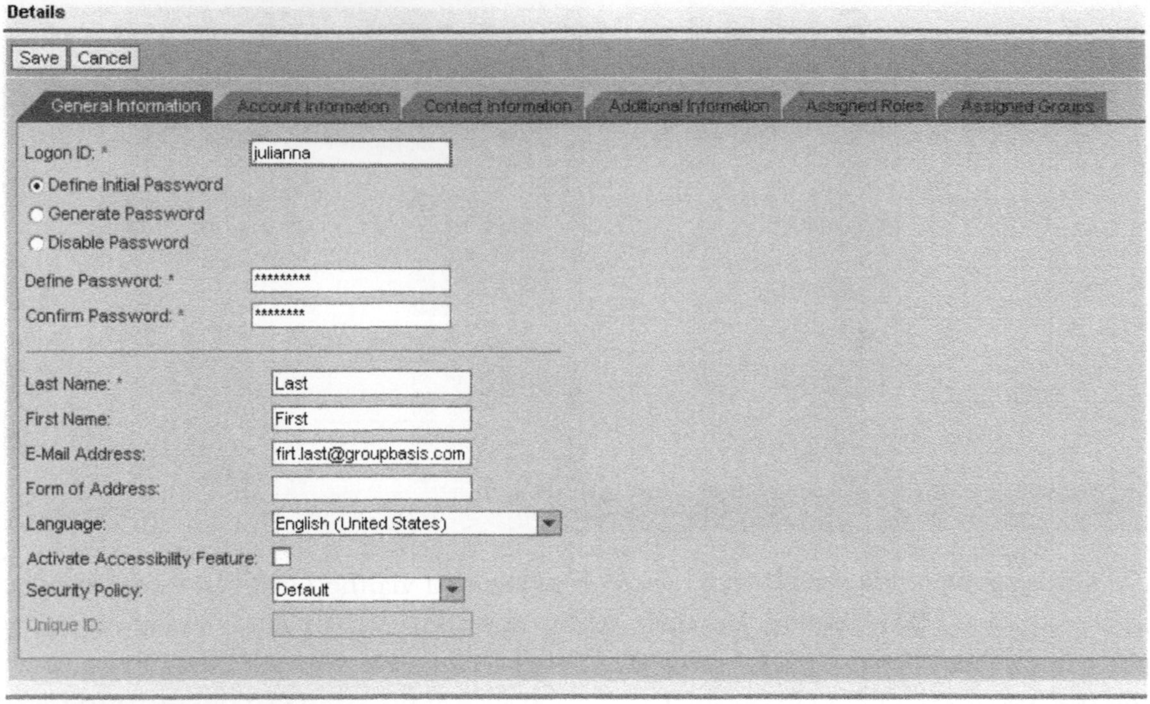

Details

Save	Cancel

General Information | Account Information | Contact Information | Additional Information | Assigned Roles | Assigned Groups

Logon ID: *	julianna
⦿ Define Initial Password	
○ Generate Password	
○ Disable Password	
Define Password: *	*********
Confirm Password: *	********
Last Name: *	Last
First Name:	First
E-Mail Address:	firt.last@groupbasis.com
Form of Address:	
Language:	English (United States)
Activate Accessibility Feature:	☐
Security Policy:	Default
Unique ID:	

See Figures 4.8, 4.9, and 4.10 for tabs **Account Information**, **Contact Information**, and **Additional Information**.

Figure 4.8 Account Information

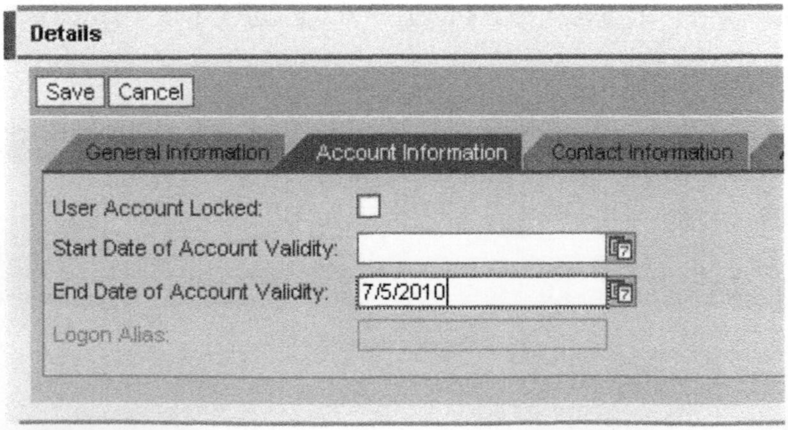

Details

Save	Cancel

General Information | Account Information | Contact Information

User Account Locked:	☐
Start Date of Account Validity:	
End Date of Account Validity:	7/5/2010
Logon Alias:	

Figure 4.9 Contact Information

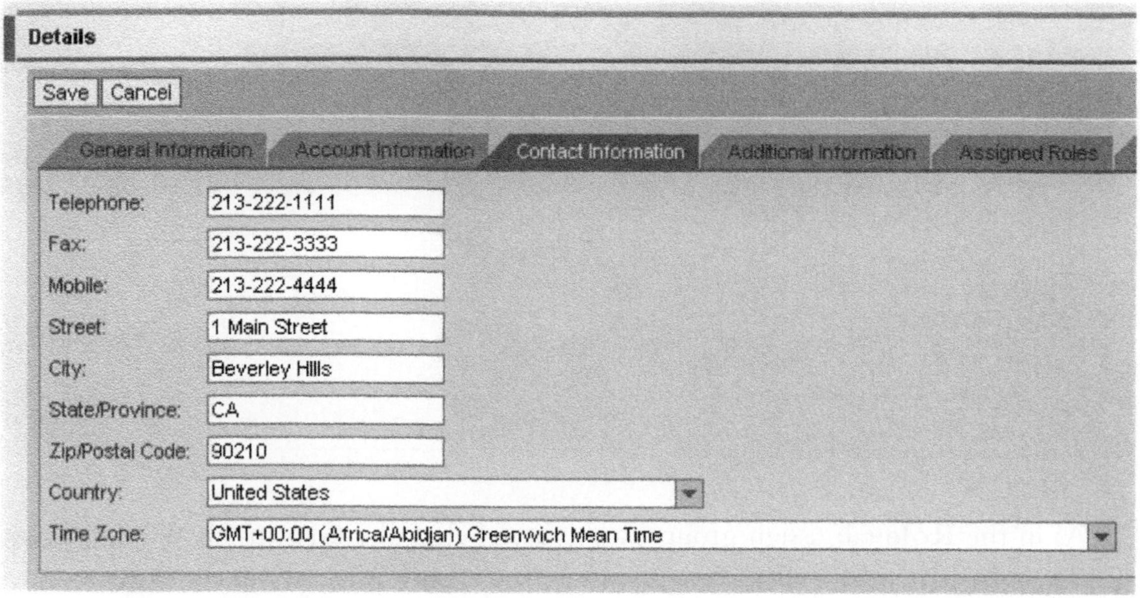

Figure 4.10 Additional Information

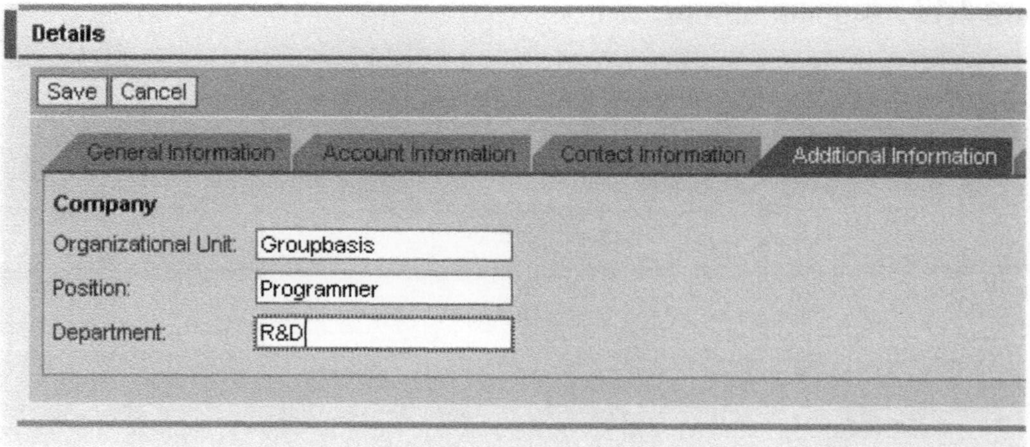

Assign roles using the **Role** tab. Select the role based on your selection criteria. User JULIANNA will be assigned to the Administrator role. See Figure 4.11. Press the **Add** icon on the left lower left pane to assign the selected role to the user.

Figure 4.11 Assigning Roles

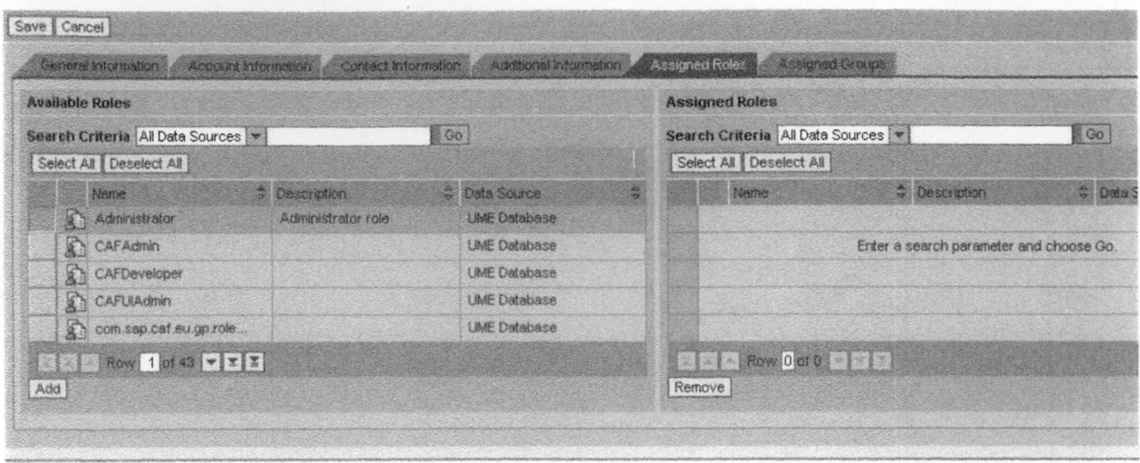

As in the **Role** tab, assign groups to the user. Select the **Group** tab. We will make JULIANNA part of the *Administrators* group. See Figure 4.12. Select the **Add** icon to assign the group.

Figure 4.12 Assigning Groups

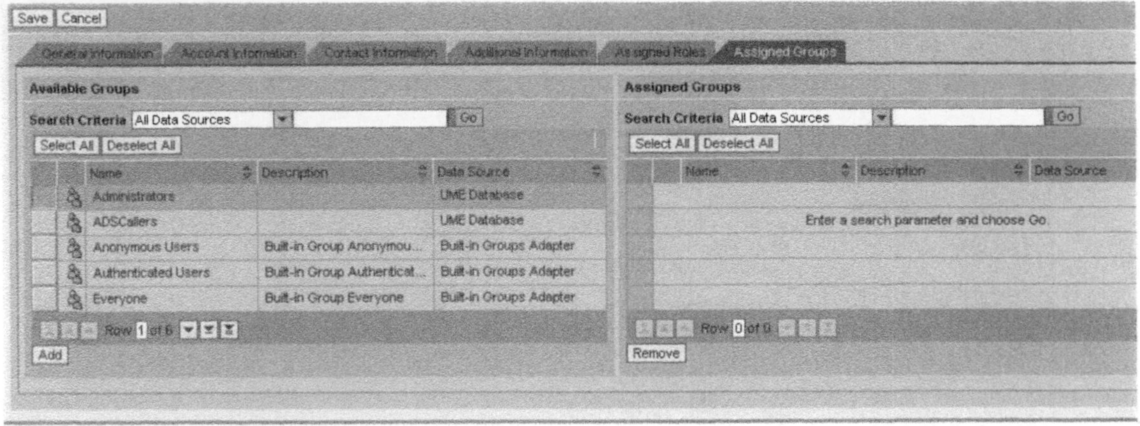

Before closing your session make sure to save your work.

The UME Console also gives you the ability to lock and unlock users. Select the users to be unlocked or locked and select the associated icon (Figure 4.13).

The UME Console has a create feature called export and import. Aside from the actual password, you can export all users, group, and role information. This is a convenient way to back up your data. To step through an export and import process, first select the object to export. In our example, I chose the user that we just created, then selected the **Export** icon (see Figure 4.13).

Figure 4.13 Exporting Users

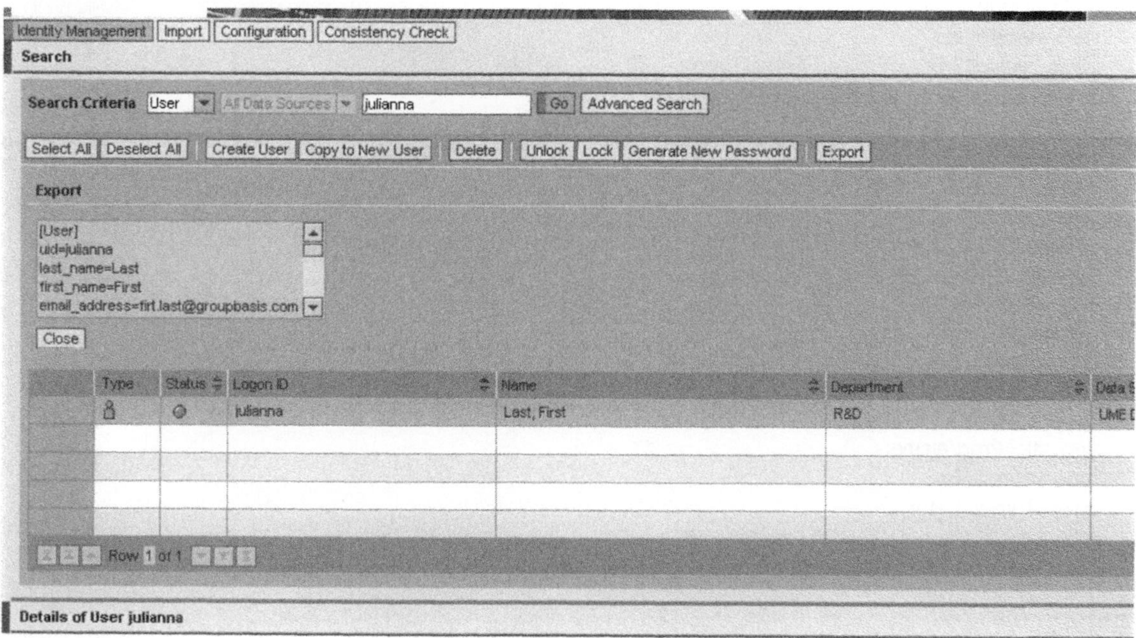

The end result is a flat file format of the data; copy and paste that data to an archive file. To validate that the import process works, let's delete the user. Select the user and press the delete icon. You will be prompted to fill in the reason for deletion. This is default functionality and is intended to help record keeping. After the user is deleted, we will import the user JULIANNA back into the system. Select the **Import** icon and enter either the actual file where the export data is saved or paste the results in the open text box. See Figure 4.14. Select **Overwrite Existing Data**.

Figure 4.14 Importing Users

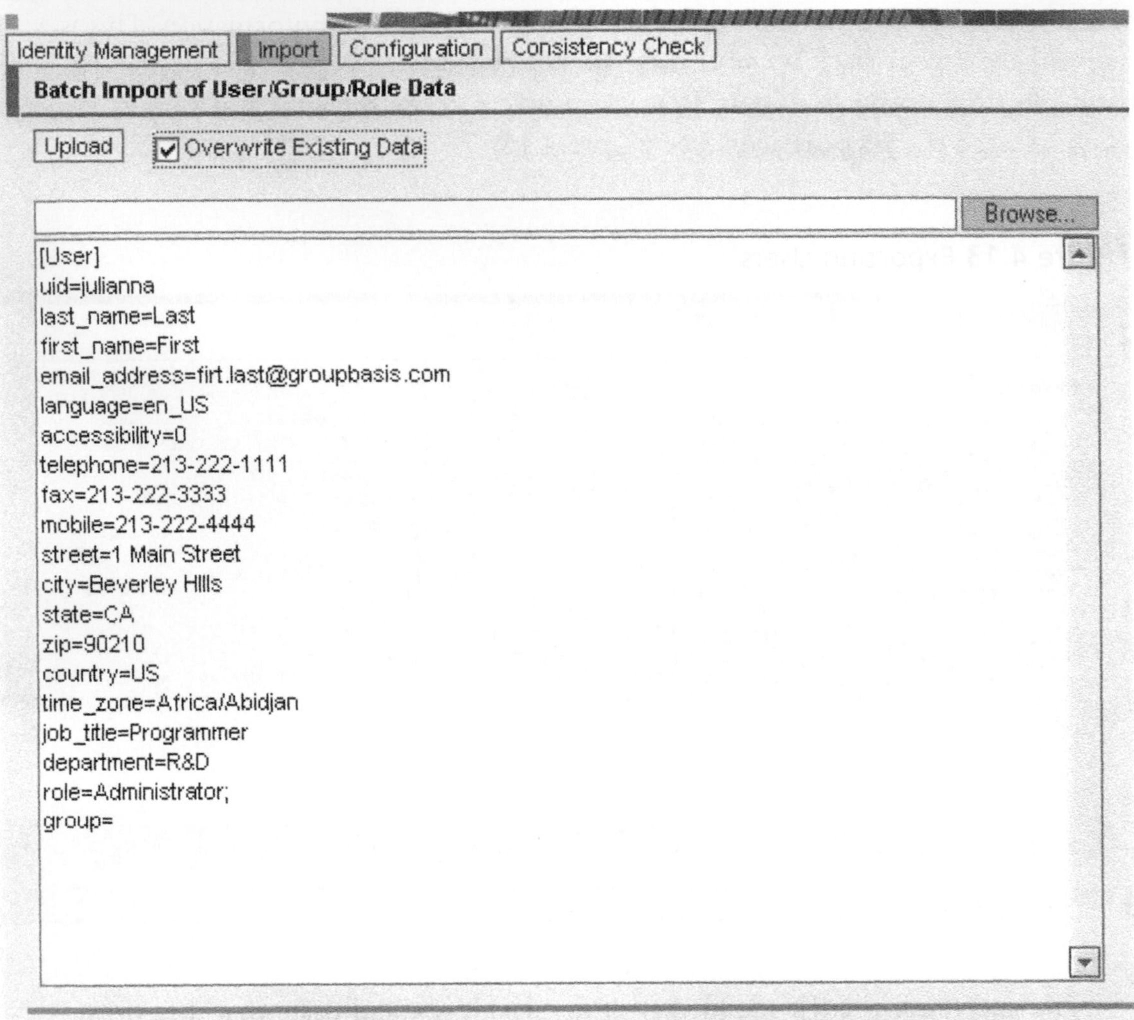

Select the **Upload** icon when you are ready. More than one user can be imported. This utility helps to standardize the user creation process.

J2EE Authorization

The architecture of J2EE security roles are split between J2EE security roles and UME roles. J2EE security roles are standard J2EE security while UME roles are an SAP derivation of the J2EE security concept. When administering J2EE security roles use the *Visual Administrator*, and when maintaining the UME roles use the

Web browser *User Administration Console*. Both J2EE security and UME roles are based on application-specific resource security.

Let's use an example for a J2EE security role (see Figure 4.15). In this example the J2EE security role, $SAP_J2EE_Engine_Upload, is mapped to role references which in turn is assigned to a group, administrators.

Figure 4.15 J2EE Security Role

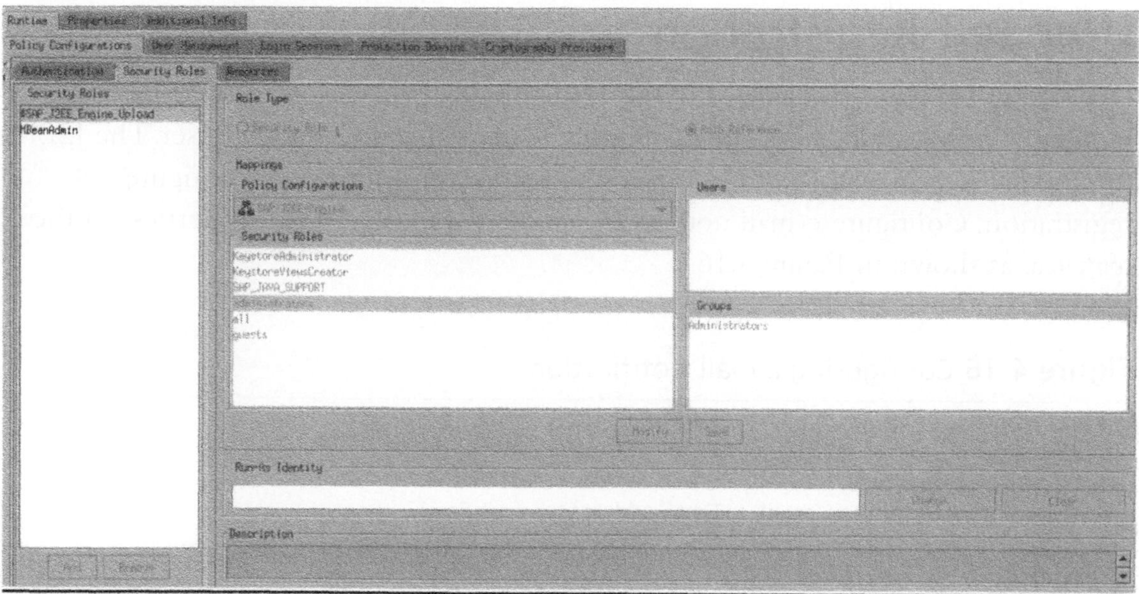

UME roles are administered via the UME Console. UME roles will be your primary method of assigning and maintaining security in the SAP J2EE Engine. As such, security for SAP Web Dynpro applications can be maintained only via UME security roles. UME roles are based on object permissions that are grouped into actions (sets of Java permissions), which in turn are assigned to a role. These roles are then assigned to users and/or groups.

The User Management Engine

The *User Management Engine (UME)* is the centralized user management resource for the J2EE Engine. The default user store for the J2EE Engine, UME, is the data source housed locally in the J2EE database. The UME has the capability of accessing multiple data source such as local databases, Directory Services, and SAP ABAP systems. The configuration is based on the Extensible Markup Language (XML) configuration that defines the UME. Once the UME changes from database to another source, SAP insists that it is not changed again. There are particular and specific restrictions regarding changing the data source; refer to "OSS Note 718383 NetWeaver: Supported UME Data Sources and Change Options." As a rule of thumb, changing from database to another UME is permissible. Refer to the OSS Note for the most current specifications.

User Self-Registration

Depending on your deployment of the J2EE Engine, you may want users to self-register. If permissible, this shifts the burden of user access to the end user. The J2EE Engine has a facility for this. First enable e-mail notifications then configure self registration. Configure e-mail notification by updating the UME properties via the *configtool* as shown in Figure 4.16.

Figure 4.16 Configuring E-mail Notification

ume.notification.mail host	SMTP Mail host
ume.notification.admin_email	Email address for admin
ume.notificatation.system_email	Email address for system
ume.notification.workflow_email	Email address for workflow
Ume.logon.selfreg	Enable self registration link (true/false)
ume.admin.self.privacystatement.link	Privacy link
ume.admin.self.generate_password	Auto password generation (true/false)
ume.admin.self.addressactive	Contact information
set ume.admin.self.addattrs	Enter custom information
ume.admin.selfreg_company	Register a company (true/false)
ume.Selfregister_User	Assigned to a Role

The last step is to create a role and assign the action **Selfregister_User**. See Figure 4.17 for a view of the role called *selfregister*. Without this role, the self registration process will not materialize. The self-registering user will be stopped with an authorization error.

Figure 4.17 Enabling Self-Registration

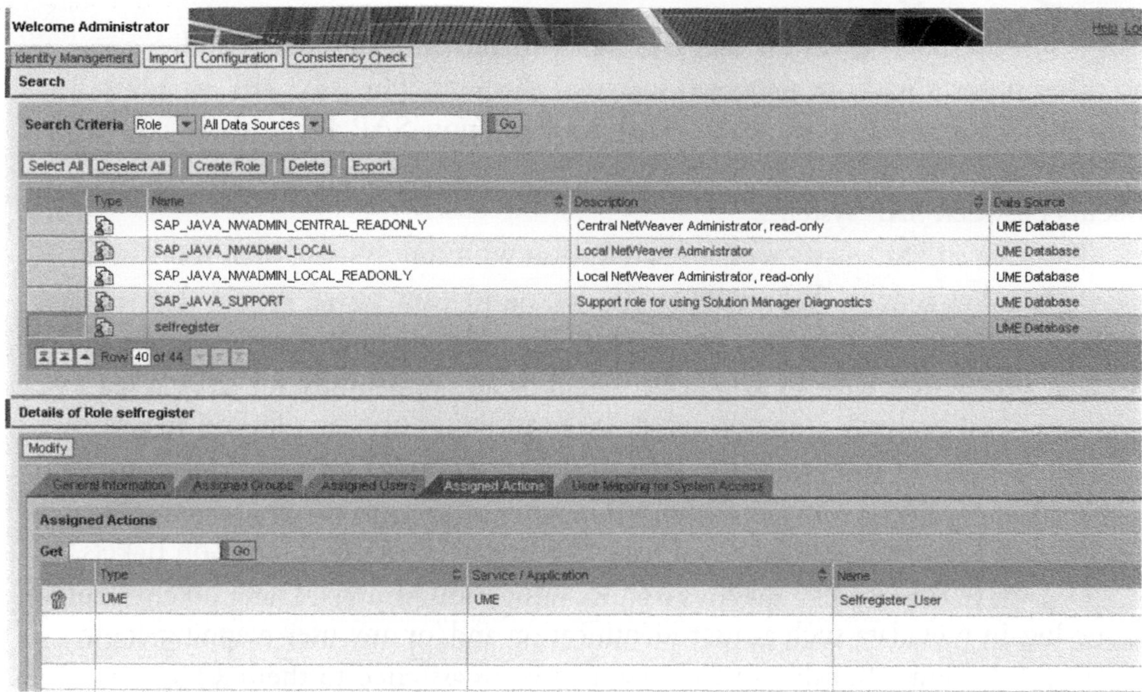

Now when we get to a log-on screen we see the **Register Now** option above the user ID and password fields. See Figure 4.18.

Figure 4.18 Self-Registration Enabled

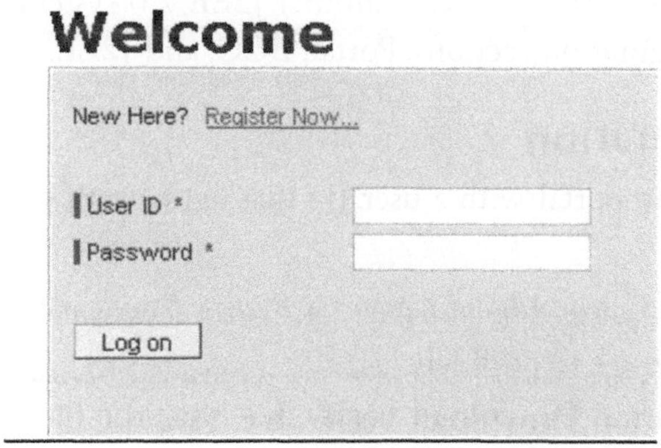

Single Sign-on

Single sign-on (SSO) gives the user the ability to authenticate once then log on to other systems without repeated credential checking. The issue can get a little complicated when we start dealing with SAP and non-SAP applications. For these discussions, I'll focus only on SAP systems. In SAP landscapes, most interfacing occurs between SAP systems.

The idea of SSO starts with authentication with one system, then transparent access to other systems. For example, you log on to your portal system that is based on the J2EE Engine. From the portal, you have links to other systems like ECC and BI. The interaction with ECC and BI would be an opportunity for SSO. What I've just described is a very common setup. SSO can be set up using log-on tickets and actual user ID and passwords. Log-on tickets are based on a trust relationship between applications whereas the user ID and password are merely a forwarding mechanism for basic authentication data. The preferred method is log-on tickets.

Log-on tickets are like tokens given to authenticated users. These tokens contain some log-in metadata such as user identification and/or any user mapping, login system, and validity but do not have any passwords assigned to them. One system is usually the ticket-issuing system (preferably the *SAP Portal*) and all others are accepters of that ticket. When the user authenticates to the *SAP Portal*, the user gets a log-on ticket stored in a nonpersistent cookie resident in the Web browser. Some rules apply to SSO. The username must be the same in all systems. If they are different, you'll need to map user names to enable SSO.

The following example will step you through the configuration of a ticket issuing Portal 7.0 with a ECC 6.0 system and another J2EE 7.0 system. The discussion is split into three configuration sections: Portal, ECC, and J2EE.

Portal Configuration

1. Log on to the portal with a user ID that exists with the same name in the ECC.
2. Navigate to *System Administration* → *System Configuration* → *Keystore Administration* → *Content* tab.
3. Select the button **Download verify.der**. Save the file in a zip format. Extract the file in the zip archive in preparation for importation to the ECC system.
4. Export the *SAPLogonTicketKeypair-cert* using the *Visual Administrator* in X.509 format. The file will be used during Step 1 of *J2EE Configuration*.

ECC Configuration

1. Implement two instance parameters, then allow ticket acceptance.

   login/create_sso2_ticket = 2

   login/accept_sso2_ticket = 1

   Suggest to add login/password_change_for_SSO and specify the meaning of different values. Most companies do not want User to sign on again or even to know their passwords for SAP GUI after they log in through Portal.
2. Restart the ECC instance.
3. Navigate to transaction STRUSTSSO2 and upload the certificate saved in Step 3 in *Portal Configuration* as a binary file.
4. Select Add certificate to PSE and Add to ACL buttons.

J2EE Configuration for SID=DP1 (J2EE Engine)

1. Import the certificate from the ticket-issuing system, Portal. Export in Step 4 of *Portal Configuration*, using the *Visual Administrator* in the *Key Storage* service. Select **Open** *Cluster → Server → Services → Key Storage.* Select the **Runtime** tab then the **TicketKeystore** view, → *Load the certificate.*
2. Select *Cluster → Server → Services → Security Provider → Runtime → User Management*, click the **Change** icon then select **Manage Security Store** icon. Underneath Options, put the following entries, and save your changes when complete:
   - trustedsys1 DP1, 000 (J2EE Engines do not have clients, enter 000)
   - trustediss1 CN=DP1
   - trusteddn1 CN=DP1
   - ume.configuration.active true
3. Update the security provider log-in policies. Using the *Visual Administrator*, Select *Cluster → Server → Services →Security Provider → Runtime → Policy Configurations*, select **ticket** and the **Authentication** tab. Ensure the appropriate log-in modules are available (see Figure 4.19).

Figure 4.19 Log-in Modules

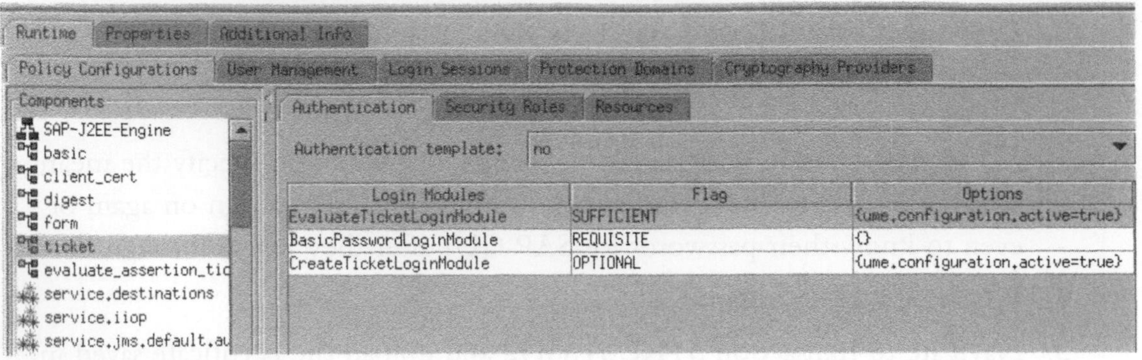

Portal Test

1. Create a connection to the SAP system and client. Use the logical system name for the client. Configure the ITS connection parameters with fully qualified host names. See Figure 4.20. Assign the same logical system name as an alias to the system.

Figure 4.20 ITS Configuration on Systems Configuration in Portal

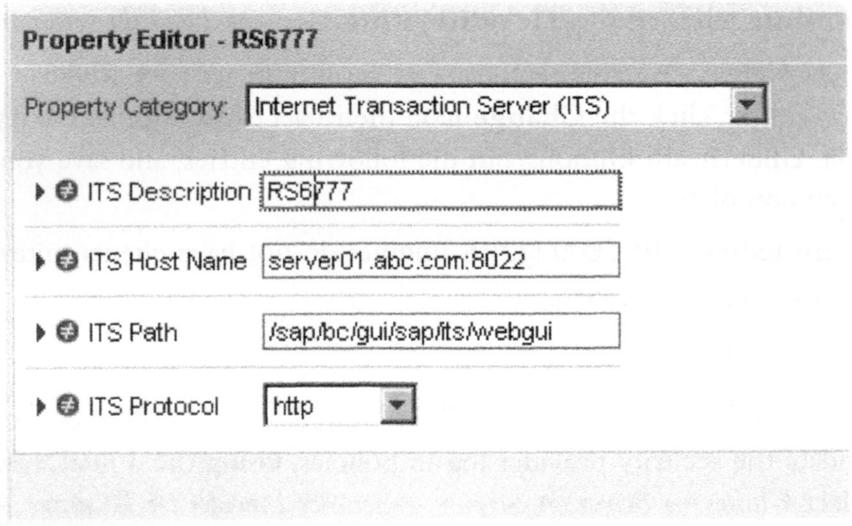

2. For testing purposes create an SAP transaction-based *iview*.
3. Assign transaction code SM04 to the *iview* (transaction can be any valid transaction in ECC).

4. Select **Preview** and you should see the ECC transaction (see Figure 4.21).
5. Now create a URL *iview* as a related link to the J2EE. A preview should allow you to log on seamlessly to the J2EE Engine from the portal using the configured SSO.

Figure 4.21 SSO from Portal to ECC ABAP

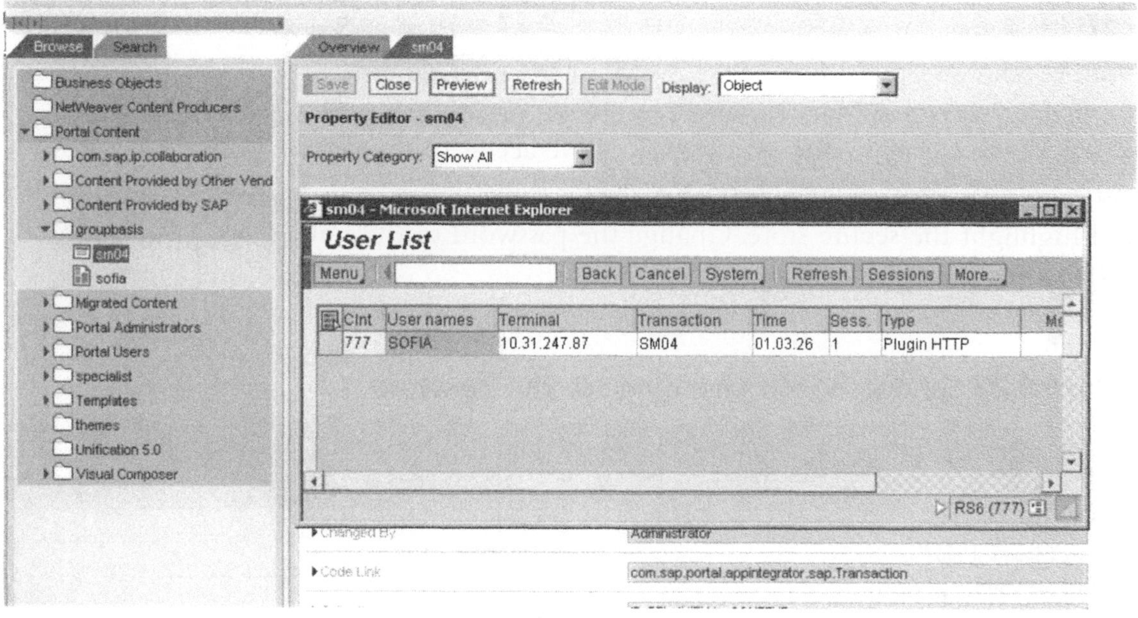

Changing Passwords

If done incorrectly, changing passwords can cause your system to become unavailable. Unfortunately, I've run into this situation quite often. This happens most frequently when untrained administrators haphazardly change these passwords without following the proper steps. Pay particular attention when changing the passwords to the administrator account, communication users, and database schema users. Let's run through the steps for changing the passwords for each of these users.

Before changing the passwords choose one that is consistent with any password rules. When you change the administrator's password, it is best to have all instances stopped. You will avoid unnecessary problems and headaches if you follow this rule. The process of changing the administrator's password means updating the secure store on the file system. Start the *configtool* utility. On UNIX platforms, you will need an X session to start the GUI interface.

Navigate to the central instance and start the *configtool*. The *configtool* can start and run even when the instances are down, though the database needs to be running. Change to the *configtool* directory, /usr/sap/<SID>/JC[XX]/j2ee/configtool (<SID> represents the system name, [XX] is the instance number for the central instance). Start the *configtool* by running the script *configtool.sh*.

Click and select the **secure store** icon. The icon is identified by a picture of a safe. To change the administrator's password highlight the field **admin/password/<SID>.** Enter the new password and click **Add** then then **Save**. The new password will become effective on the next restart of the J2EE Engine.

If the database schema password in the secure store and the database schema password are not the same, you will not have access to the secure store. This leads to our next task, changing the database schema password. As before, start the *configtool* and highlight the secure store. Change the password to the field called **jdbc/pool/<SID>/Password** (see Figure 4.22).

Figure 4.22 Configtool and Changing Schema Password

Secure Store Data

Key	Value
admin/host/AB1	server01
admin/password/AB1	**********
admin/port/AB1	50004
admin/user/AB1	Administrator
jdbc/pool/AB1/ClassName	oracle.jdbc.OracleDriver
jdbc/pool/AB1/Password	**********
jdbc/pool/AB1/Url	jdbc:oracle:thin:@server01:1521:AB1
jdbc/pool/AB1/User	SAPAB1DB

Synchronize the password saved in the *secure store* in the database. In this example, we are using an Oracle 10g database. See Figure 4.23 for changing the password in Oracle for user SAPAB1DB to a new password of *ranger*.

Figure 4.23 Synchronizing the Database in the Database

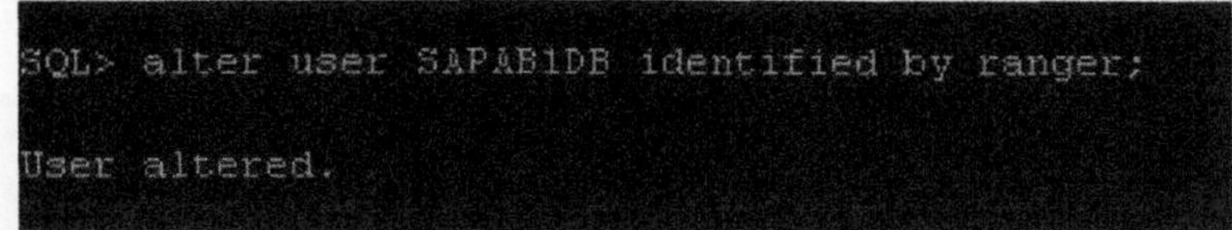

SQL> alter user SAPAB1DB identified by ranger;
User altered.

If UME is connected to ABAP as in a PI implementation, then the procedures to change passwords are different. For the Administrator account, change passwords in the ABAP UME client. If the communication user password is to be changed, change it in ABAP, then also via the *configtool* in the service *com.sap.security.core.ume* located under the tree structure *cluster-data>Global Server* configuration. See Figure 4.24.

Figure 4.24 Changing Passwords for the Communication User SAPJSP

If there are password issues, you will see error messages in the developer work trace files and also in the default trace file. The developer trace files for J2EE processes, like the ABAP counterpart, are located in the work directory underneath the instance directory. For example, if your have a Central instance install of J2EE instance 00, the work directory is /usr/sap/<SID>/JC00/work. The developer trace file is found in the log directory under each server node directory. For example, the default trace file for server0 in the previous example is located in /usr/sap/<SID>/JC00/j2ee/cluster/server0/log. See Figure 4.25, which shows an error relating to the database schema password found in the bootstrap log in the work directory.

Figure 4.25 Error in Password for Database Schema

```
Caused by: java.sql.SQLException: ORA-01017: invalid username/password; logon de
nied

        at oracle.jdbc.dbaccess.DBError.throwSqlException(DBError.java:134)
        at oracle.jdbc.ttc7.TTIoer.processError(TTIoer.java:289)
        at oracle.jdbc.ttc7.O3log.receive2nd(O3log.java:510)
        at oracle.jdbc.ttc7.TTC7Protocol.logon(TTC7Protocol.java:279)
        at oracle.jdbc.driver.OracleConnection.<init>(OracleConnection.java:371)
        at oracle.jdbc.driver.OracleDriver.getConnectionInstance(OracleDriver.ja
va:551)
        at oracle.jdbc.driver.OracleDriver.connect(OracleDriver.java:351)
        at com.sap.sql.jdbc.NativeConnectionFactory.createNativeConnection(Nativ
eConnectionFactory.java:219)
```

Emergency User

When the administrator account becomes disabled or no one can log on because of lost passwords, there is a specific process to remedy that situation. The solution is to activate the user SAP* to perform emergency tasks. When user SAP* is activated, the J2EE system is in single-user mode, and only SAP* can log on. Here is an overview of the steps needed to activate SAP*.

1. Enable SAP* account settings
2. Restart J2EE
3. Log on as SAP* and correct the user issue
4. Disable SAP* account
5. Restart J2EE

In order to enable the SAP* account, start the *configtool* as <sid>adm and edit the UME properties. Enable your UNIX shell for X display; see Figure 4.1 for an example. Navigate to the directory /usr/sap/<SID>/JC<##>/j2ee/configtool and start the *configtool* by issuing the command *./configtool*.

Open the configuration tree and follow it to the UME configuration parameters via Global server configuration>services>com.sap.security.core.ume.service. Make the change to two parameters:

ume.superadmin.activated = true

ume.superadmin.password = set_a_password

Set a value for the parameter *ume.superadmin.password*.

After the new values are implemented, restart the J2EE Engine. Once the parameters are set and the engine is restarted you will be able to logon to the system and make any necessary emergency changes. Often security administrators do not stop and start the J2EE Engine; that task is usually left to the Basis administrators. Nonetheless, I'll cover it briefly. The following steps outline the procedure to stop and start the J2EE Engine.

1. Log on as <sid>adm to all application servers.
2. Execute command *stopsap r3*.
3. Log on as <sid>adm to the Central Services host and execute command *stopsap SCS<##>*.
4. Start the J2EE Engine. Start the SCS first then all application instances.

Password Rules

There are many configurable password rules in the J2EE Engine. There are numerous rules that can be implemented for passwords such as length, expiration, and complexity. Table 4.1 shows a list of commonly configured password rule parameters.

Table 4.1 Password Parameters

UME Password Parameter	Parameter Explanation
ume.logon.security_policy.password_alpha_numeric_required	The parameter designates the minimum number of characters (alpha and numeric) for a password. The default value is 1.
ume.logon.security_policy.password_expire_days	This parameter designates the number of days before which a password must be changed. The default value is 90 days.
ume.logon.security_policy.password_min_length	This parameter designates the minimum length of the password. The default value is 5 characters.
ume.logon.security_policy.password_mix_case_required	This parameter designates the minimum number of upper and lower case letters in passwords.
ume.logon.security_policy.password_special_char_required	This parameter designates the minimum number of special characters in passwords.
ume.logon.security_policy.userid_digits	This parameter designates the parameter designates the minimum number of digits in user logon ID.
ume.logon.security_policy.userid_special_char_required	This parameter designates the minimum number of special characters in user logon ID.

The changes are implemented via the parameter settings in the global configuration service for com.sap.security.core.ume.service. Change the values in the com.sap.security.core.ume.service similar to the process when activating user SAP* via the *configtool.* A restart of the J2EE Engine enables all changes after the changes are saved. Figure 4.26 shows an example for setting the parameter ume.logon.security_policy.password_min_length, for minimum password length of 15 characters.

Figure 4.26 Setting Password Parameters

Key	Custom value	Default value
ume.logon.httponlycookie		TRUE
ume.logon.locale		FALSE
ume.logon.logon_help		TRUE
ume.logon.r3master.adapterid		master
ume.logon.security.enforce_secure_cookie		FALSE
ume.logon.security.local_redirect_only		TRUE
ume.logon.security.relax_domain.level		1
ume.logon.security_policy.auto_unlock_time		60
ume.logon.security_policy.cert_logon_required		FALSE
ume.logon.security_policy.lock_after_invalid_attempts		6
ume.logon.security_policy.log_client_hostaddress		TRUE
ume.logon.security_policy.log_client_hostname		FALSE
ume.logon.security_policy.oldpass_in_newpass_allowed	FALSE	TRUE
ume.logon.security_policy.password_alpha_numeric_required	1	0
ume.logon.security_policy.password_change_allowed		TRUE
ume.logon.security_policy.password_change_required		TRUE
ume.logon.security_policy.password_expire_days	1	99999
ume.logon.security_policy.password_history		0
ume.logon.security_policy.password_last_change_date_default		12/31/9999
ume.logon.security_policy.password_max_length	12	14
ume.logon.security_policy.password_min_length	0	0
ume.logon.security_policy.password_mix_case_required	1	0
ume.logon.security_policy.password_special_char_required	1	0
ume.logon.security_policy.userid_digits		0
ume.logon.security_policy.userid_in_password_allowed	FALSE	TRUE
ume.logon.security_policy.userid_lowercase		0
ume.logon.security_policy.userid_special_char_required		0
ume.logon.security_policy.useridmaxlength		20
ume.logon.security_policy.useridminlength		5

Setting Up SSL

Secure Sockets Layer (SSL) is a quasi-standard protocol and used with Web AS for securing application protocols like HTTP, P4, and LDAP. Establishing a secure connection to the J2EE Engine is an important step towards hardening your J2EE WEB AS implementation. The default communication protocol between the server and client is via HTTP. Implementing HTTPS prevents snooping from unauthorized persons. The default protocol used to communicate between the server and client is HTTP. The secure form of this protocol is HTTPS. Here are the steps to enable SSL in your J2EE Engine:

1. Install the SAP Java Cryptographic Toolkit.
2. Create server keys.

3. Obtain a certificate from a CA.
4. Assign the key pair for SSL use.
5. Implement client certificates.

Installing the SAP Java Cryptographic Toolkit

The installation of the Java Cryptographic Toolkit can be accomplished during the installation phase of the J2EE instance. See Figure 4.27 for the options displayed during the installation of a J2EE Engine based on WEB AS 6.40. WEB AS 7.0 J2EE Engines do not offer this option during installation.

Figure 4.27 Options to Install Cryptographic Toolkit Version WEB AS 6.40

Java System > SAP Java Cryptographic Toolkit
Choose the strength of the SAP Java cryptographic level
SAP Java Cryptographic Toolkit
Cryptography Level
Weak
Strong
SAP Java Library Archive
/CRYPTO/jdk1.4x/tc_sec_java_crypto_signed_fs_lib.sda
Browse...
JCE Unlimited Strength Jurisdiction Policy Archive
sis/install/640_J2EE_SR1/CRYPTO/jce_policy-1_4_2.zip
Browse...
Secure Store Files
Encrypt Secure Store
Key Phrase
Confirm
Additional Information
The SAP Java Cryptographic Toolkit is an optional part of the Java system. You need it to enable SSL and HTTPS connections and to encrypt the secure store in the file system.
We strongly recommend that you use Strong for the Cryptography Level of productive systems. For test or development systems you may also use Weak encryption. That would result in a Base64 encoded passwort encryption only.

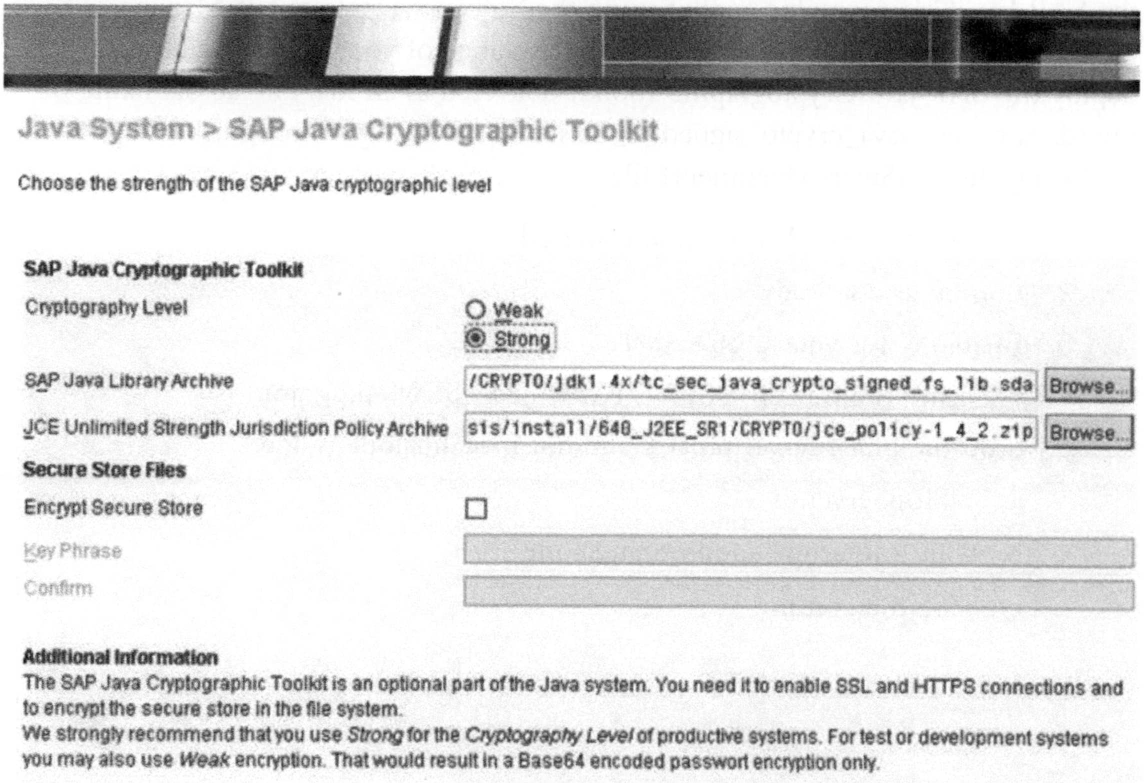

Table 4.2 lists the downloads for the cryptographic toolkit.

Table 4.2 Downloads for the Cryptographic Toolkit

Name	URL
SUN JCE (Java Cryptographic Extension) archive	http://java.sun.com/j2se/1.4.2/download.html > Other downloads
SAP Java Cryptographic Toolkit	http://service.sap.com/swdc > Download > SAP Cryptographic Software > SAP JAVA CryptoToolkit (J2EE Engine as of Release 6.30)

Manual installation of these files is performed in two separate steps. First, deploy the SAP Java Cryptographic Toolkit using the Software Deployment Manager (SDM). The SDM is located on the Central Instance of your J2EE instance. You will deploy the SAP Java Cryptographic Toolkit delivered as an sda. The actual name of the sda is tc_sec_java_crypto_signed_fs_lib.sda. We'll now go through the steps for deploying the sd (Smart Document) file.

1. Ensure that the J2EE Engine is started.
2. Log on as <sid>adm.
3. Enable X for your UNIX shell.
4. Navigate to /usr/sap/<SID>/JC##/j2ee/SDM/program.
5. Stop the SDM server process and put in standalone mode.
    a. ./StopServer.sh
    b. sdm.sh jstartup "mode=standalone"
    c. ./StartServer.sh

6. Start SDM GUI and deploy software.
   a. ./RemoteGui.sh
   b. Click the icon and enter the password for SDM in the password field. Leave the field "User Description" blank, see Figure 4.28. If you forgot the password to SDM reset the password using the commands as the <sid>adm: ./StopServer.sh, ./sdm.sh jstartup mode=standalone, ./sdm.sh changepassword sdmhome=/usr/sap/<SID>/JC##/SDM/program newpassword= sdm, ./sdm.sh jstartup mode=integrated, and ./StartServer.sh.

Figure 4.28 Logging into SDM

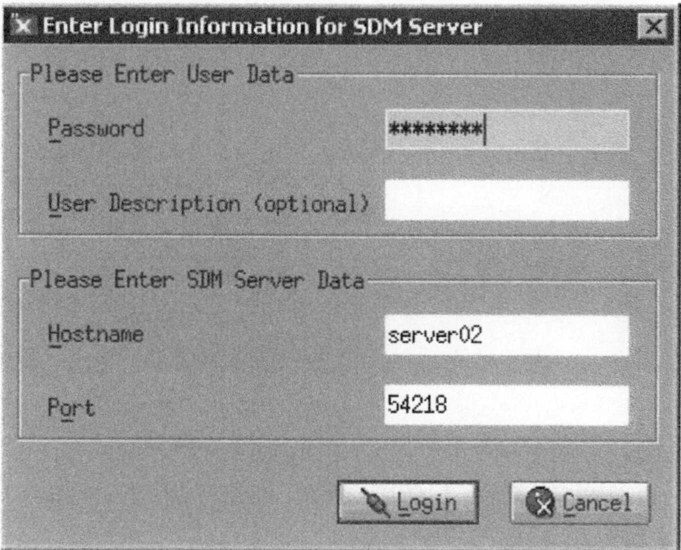

   c. Go to the **Deployment** tab and click the clipboard icon.
   d. Select the tc_sec_java_crypto_signed_fs_lib.sda file to deploy, See Figure 4.29.

Figure 4.29 Deploying an SDA via SDM

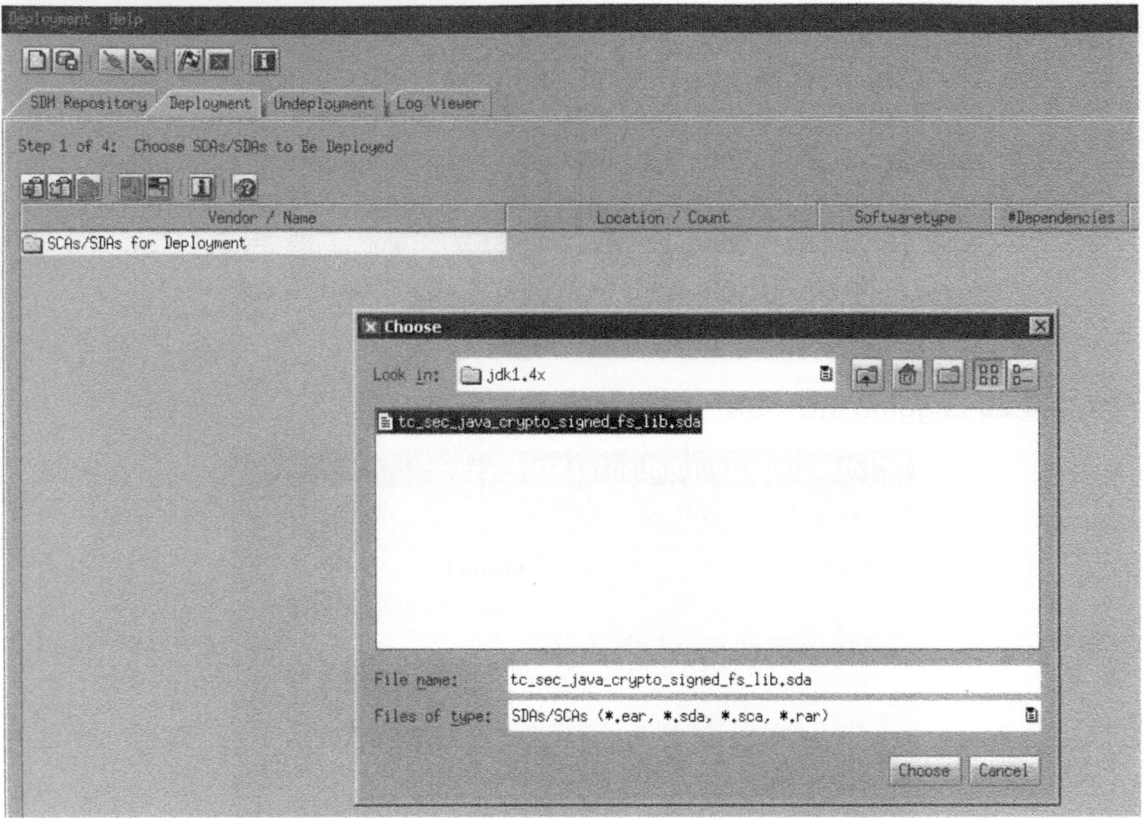

   e. Select **Next** a couple of times and then **Start**.
   f. When complete, click **Confirm** to complete the action.
7. Exit and start SDM server in integrated mode.
   a. sdm.sh jstartup "mode=integrated"
   b. ./StartServer.sh

The second step is to implement the JAVA security archive into the JAVA directory. Copy the archive jce_policy-1_4_2.zip into $JAVA_HOME/jre/lib/security, where $JAVA_HOME is the root directory of the JAVA installation. Set the permissions to UNIX bit notation 644.

On WEB AS versions lower than 7.0 you may need to enable the *SSL Provider* service to start *Always* on J2EE startup. On version 7.0 that is flagged as startup *Always*. You can always check the startup characteristics by navigating through the

Visual Administrator to the *SSL Provider* service. Select the **Cluster** tab then drill down the tree to Server>Services>SSL Provider. Select the "Additional Info" tab. The startup mode should be *Always* (see Figure 4.30).

Figure 4.30 SSL Provider Service Startup Setting

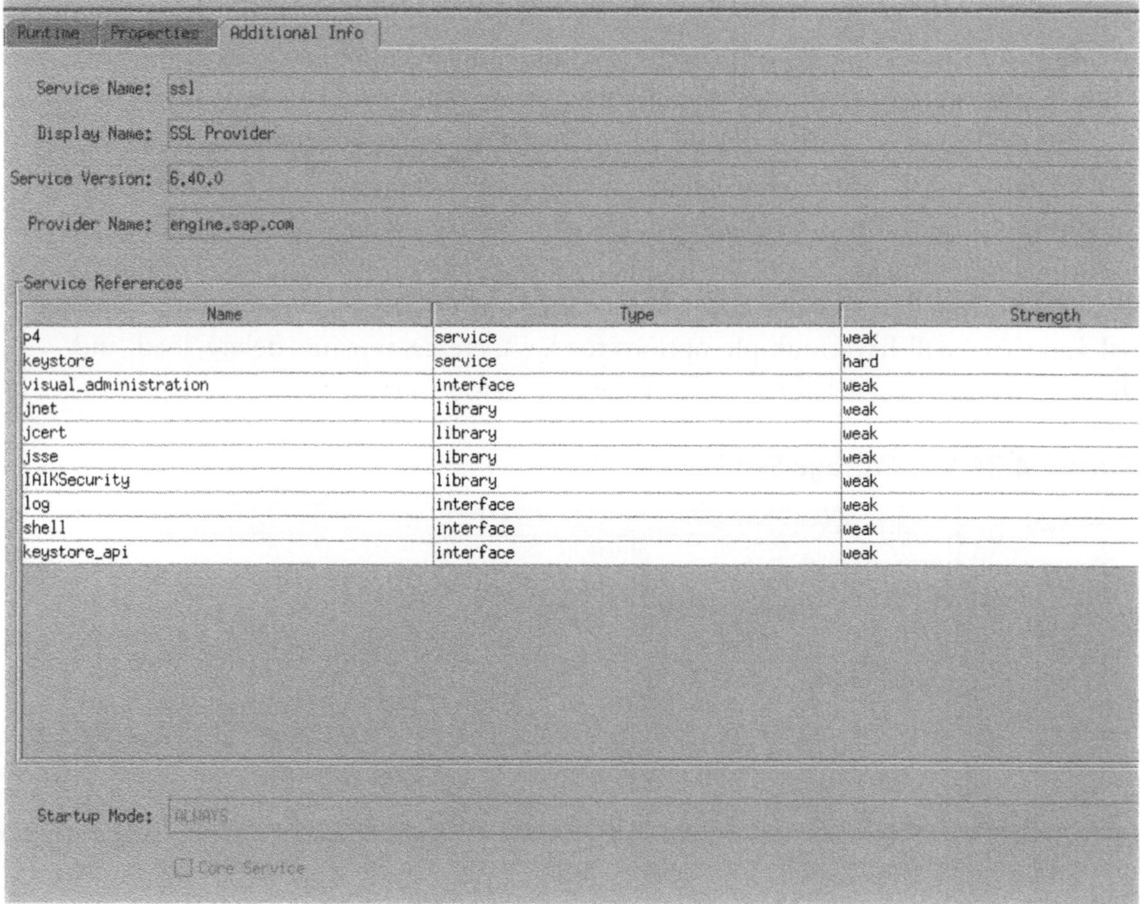

Creating Server Keys

SSL, or secure sockets layer, is a cryptographic protocol originally developed by the Internet pioneer Netscape. The implementation of SSL is based on keys, private and public, to encrypt and decrypt data. Without going into too much detail, the public key is used to encrypt data to the recipient and the private key is used to decrypt the message. The theory behind the implementation of SSL is that only the private key can decrypt the message encrypted with its pair, the public key. In order to share public keys securely, both parties need to trust the public key that the other provides.

This is where the Certificate of Authority (CA) comes into action. If both parties trust the CA then the CA can certify public keys. In our example we have two sisters, Julianna and Sofia, who are on opposite sides of the country. They both need to communicate securely, and fortunately for them, they both trust their mom who acts as the trusted CA. Their mom issues both girls a pair of keys, public and private. When Sofia writes a secret note to her sister Julianna, she requests Julianna's public key from mom and encrypts the secret with Julianna's public key. When Julianna receives the secret note from Sofia, she uses her private key to decrypt the message.

The J2EE comes with a default pair of keys. You can generate a new pair or use the default keys. It is best to generate your key pairs. We use the *Visual Administrator* to administer keys for the J2EE Engine. Make sure to set your X environment then start the *Visual Administrator* by running /usr/sap/<SID>/JC##/j2ee/admin/go. Navigate to the *Key Storage* service under the server process then select the **service_ssl** view. You will have multiple options for keys: create, rename, delete, load, and export. See Figure 4.31 for a view of the *Key Storage* service.

Figure 4.31 Key Storage Service

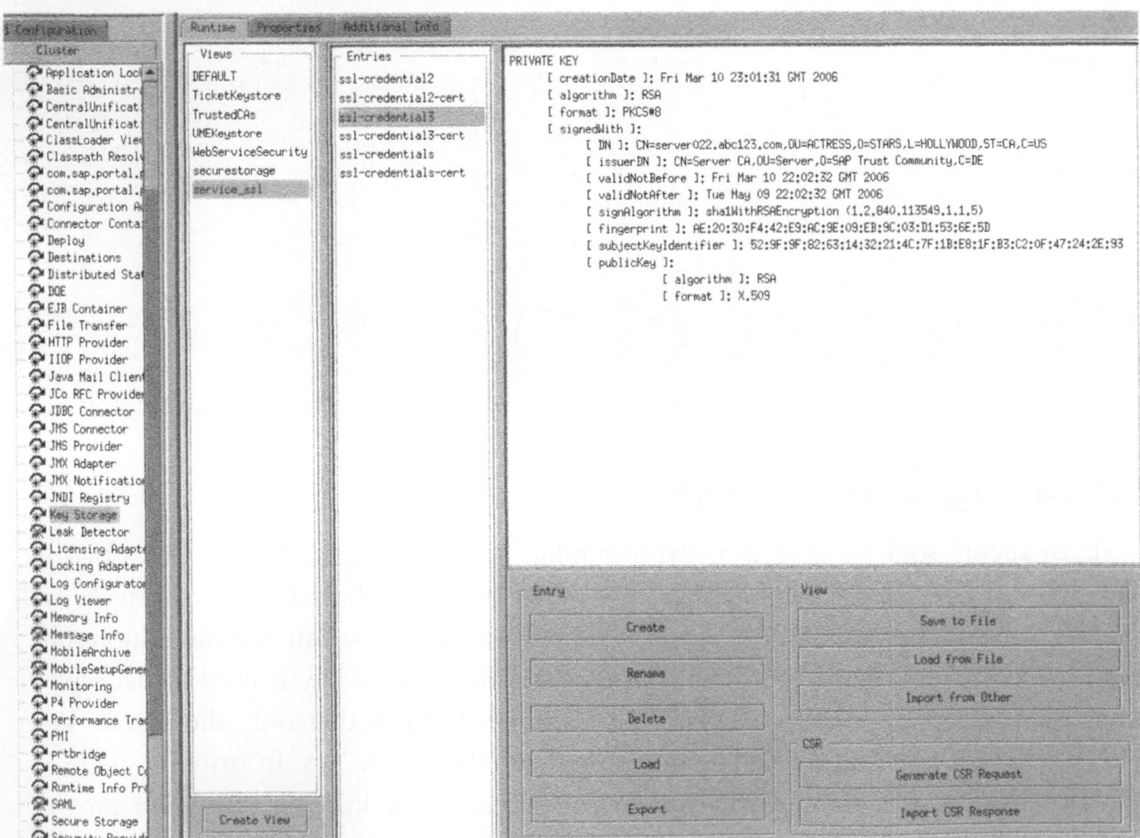

In this example, we will generate a new key pair. Select the **Create** button which is located on the lower right-hand side of the windows pane (refer to Figure 4.31). After selecting **Create** you will be asked to input some data to complete your request. See Figure 4.32 for the data input dialog box. See Table 4.3 for an explanation of the input fields.

Figure 4.32 Key and Certificate Generation

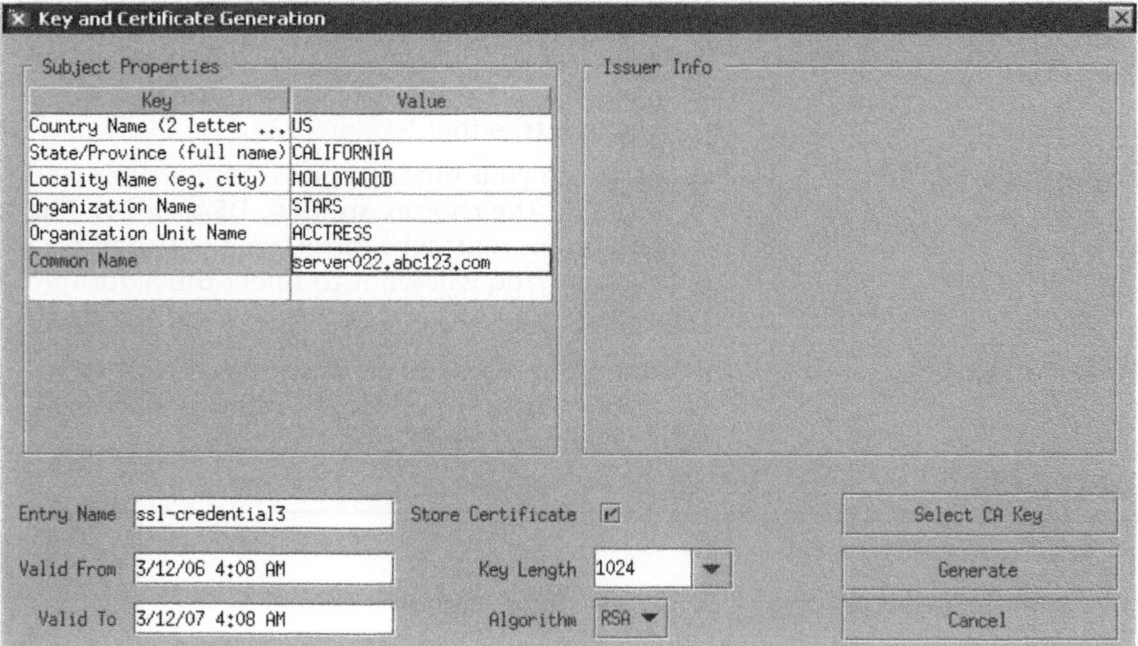

Table 4.3 Key Input Explanation

Key Input	Explanation
Country Name	The 2-letter country abbreviation for your country address. US would be adequate for the United States.
State/Province	The name of your state or province (spelled out).
Locality Name	The name of your city.
Organization Name	The name of your organization. Avoid using special characters.
Organization Unit Name	The subdivision of your organization. Avoid using special characters.

Continued

Table 4.3 Continued. Key Input Explanation

Key Input	Explanation
Common Name	The fully qualified name of your server. Use the format host+domain name.
Entry Name	The name that you will use to associate the key.
Valid From and To	Dates are the validity of this certificate. Use the format yy-mm-dd hh:mm.
Key Length (and Algorithm)	Depends on your organization's requirements as well as your CA. The key length specifies the length in bits, either 512 or 1024.
Algorithm	Depends on your organizations standards as well as your CA. The choices are RSA, DSA, or DH. The three options represent different algorithms for encryption. You will want to select the algorithm that meets your organization's securiyt standards.
Store Certificate	An option to store the certificate in the server (or not). It is best to select this item. Unnecessary keys can always be deleted.
Select CA Key	An option for selecting the CA key.

Finish the key creation process by selecting **Generate**.

Generating Signed Certificates

Now that you have a key, you will need to have it signed by a CA, meaning the CA verifies that your key is who it says it is. In essence the CA vouches for the key's identity. Generate a Certificate Signing Request (CSR) and send it to your CA for approval. To generate the CSR, first select the key pair that you just created then generate the CSR by selecting the **Generate CSR Request** button. See Figure 4.33.

Figure 4.33 CSR Request

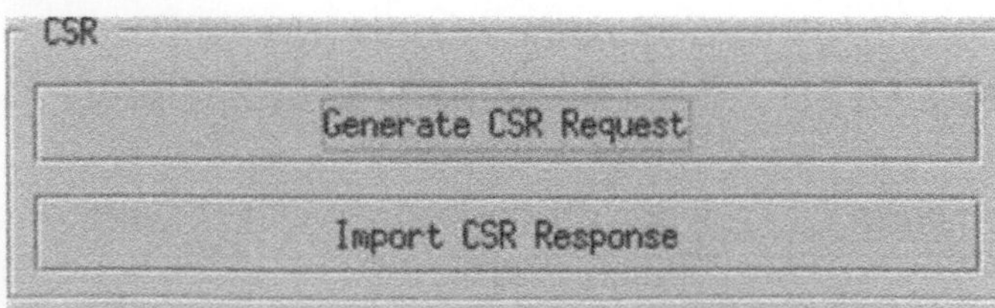

The **Generate CSR Request** button will prompt you to save the output as a file. Save the request on the server. In my example, I saved it in /tmp/myserver.csr. Send the CSR to your CA. Most CAs process your requests online via the vendor's Web site. For our example, I used the SAP Trust Center at http://service.sap.com/tcs as our CA. The SAP trust center processes requests almost immediately. I copied and pasted the CSR into their Web form and instantly received my signed test certificate. Figure 4.34 shows the copy and paste of the CSR into the Web form.

Figure 4.34 Requesting Test Certificates from SAP Trust

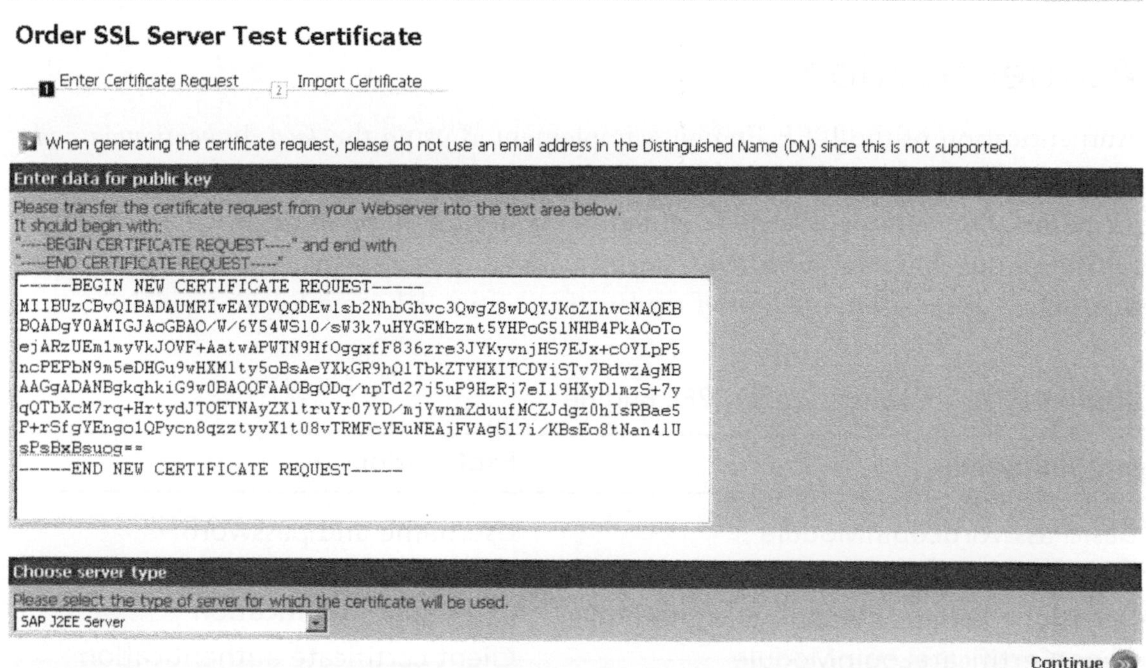

Once you complete the registration process, a CSR response is generated. Copy and paste the CSR response into a file on the server and import that file into the J2EE Engine. Within *Visual Administrator*, navigate back to the *Key Storage* service. This time select the button **Import CSR Response** (refer to Figure 4.33). Select the file that contains the test certificate issued by SAP Trust. Now the J2EE Engine has a signed certificate by our CA, SAP Trust.

The last step is to set the generated and signed key as the actual identity of the J2EE server process. Start the *Visual Administrator* and navigate to the **Cluster** tab Server > SSL provider > Dispatcher. Select the **Server Identity** tab. Here we will make the *ssl-credential3* key our server's identity. Click the **Add** button and select **ssl-credential3**. See Figure 4.35.

Figure 4.35 Server Identity

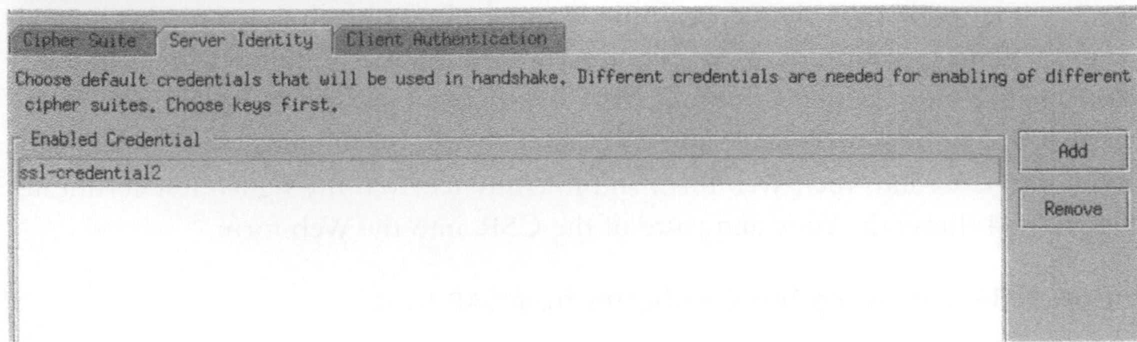

Authentication

Authentication of the J2EE Engine is implemented using the *Java Authentication and Authorization Service (JAAS)* interface standard. The J2EE Engine comes standard with a handful of log-in modules that define the method of authentication. The default log-in module is *BasicPasswordLoginModule,* also known as *username and password.* See Table 4.4 for a list and a brief explanation of the delivered log-in modules.

Table 4.4 Log-in Modules for J2EE Engine

Log-in Module	Explanation
BasicPasswordLoginModule	Username and password authentication
CallerImpersonationMappingLoginModule	External authentication
ClientCertificateLoginModule	Client certificate authentication
ConfiguredIdentityMappingLoginModule	External authentication using 1 mapped identity
CreateTicketLoginModule	Creates SAP Logon ticket
CredentialsMappingLoginModule	Mapped external authentication
CSILoginModule	Authentication using IIOP service
DigestLoginModule	Encoded username and password authentication
EvaluateAssertionTicketLoginModule	Verifies SAP login ticket
EvaluateTicketLoginModule	Evaluates SAP login ticket
HeaderVariableLoginModule	Header variable authentication

Continued

Table 4.4 Continued. Log-in Modules for J2EE Engine

Log-in Module	Explanation
MappingModule	Mapped user authentication
PrincipalMappingLoginModule	Mapped external authentication
SAMLLoginModule	SAML Browser/Artifact authentication
SecuritySessionLoginModule	Log-in ticket-based authentication using download.ear
SPNegoLoginModule	SPNEGO authentication method

Depending on your requirements, you can implement different log-in modules with different flags and options. Use the *Visual Administrator* to view and change the log-in module settings. Flags can have one of four values; see Table 4.5 for a list and explanation.

Table 4.5 Log-in Module Flags

FLAG	Explanation
OPTIONAL	Not required to succeed, other configured login modules are tested if successful or not
REQUIRED	Is required to succeed, other configured login modules are tested if successful or not
REQUISITE	Is required to succeed, other configured login modules are tested if successful
SUFFICIENT	Not required to succeed, other configured login modules are not tested if successful, however if not successful other login modules are tested

Use the *Visual Administrator* to navigate to **Cluster** tab Server > Security Provider. Be cautious; there are no **Save** and **Undo** buttons here. For example, our only requirement here is to be challenged with a valid certificate, so no changes are necessary in the log-in stack. See Figure 4.36 for the configuration interface in the *Visual Administrator.*

Figure 4.36 Log-in Module Configuration Options

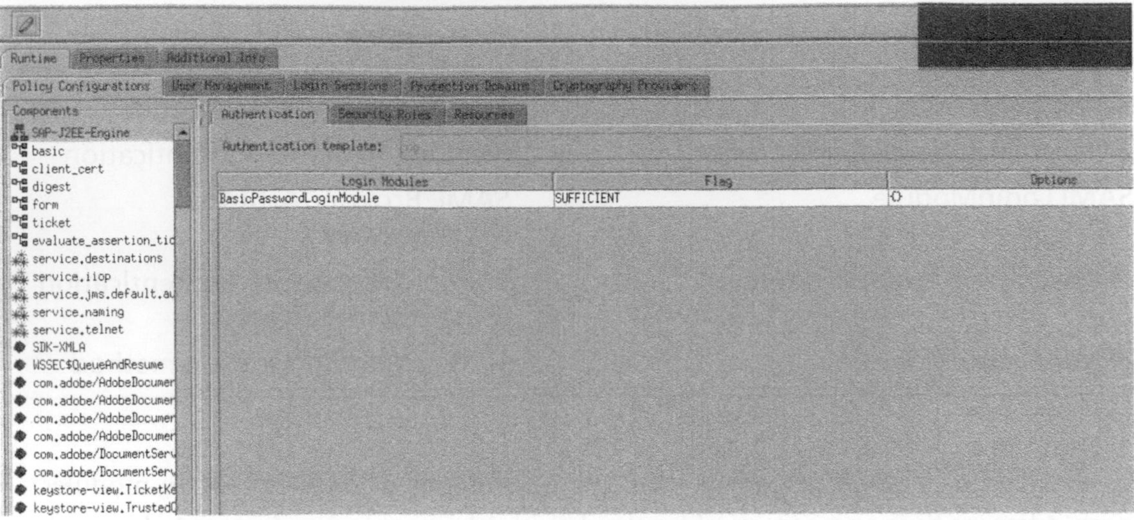

You can also *Create* and *Configure* a log-in module; this log-in module allows you to perform authentication in a different way than with the J2EE Engine.

Implementing Client Certificates

Authenticating via client certificates is another way to log on to the J2EE Engine. The J2EE Engine uses the *ClientCertificateLoginModule* log-in module to handle this requirement. A prerequisite for certificate-based authentication is the implementation of SSL on the server. Authentication using client certificates involves officially registering the requestor, client (Web browser). Now both parties, client and server, are officially registered; electronic dialog is now quite secure. Some organizations require client certificates. This prohibits anyone without a valid and recognizable client certificate from accessing and communicating with the server.

In this example, we will continue using the SAP Trust center as our CA. The SAP Trust center issues *Passports* for single sign-on for their support portal. These *Passports* are really client certificates issued by the SAP Trust CA. I have incorporated this into our example scenario. You will need a valid OSS user ID to obtain a valid SAP Passport. Navigate to the SAP Trust portal via URL http://service.sap.com/tcs and apply for, then install, the Passport in your local browser.

At this point we have all the pieces of the puzzle ready to enable client authentication to the server using certificates. The last step is to configure the J2EE Engine to accept client certificates. This will allow the user to obtain authentication without a username and password.

Log on to the *Visual Administrator* and ensure that the SAP Trust CA is trusted. Navigate to Server > Services > Key Storage. Click the **Runtime** tab and select the **Trusted CA** option. Import the root certificate for your CA. In our example, SAP Trust is our CA (see Figure 4.37).

Figure 4.37 Trusted CA

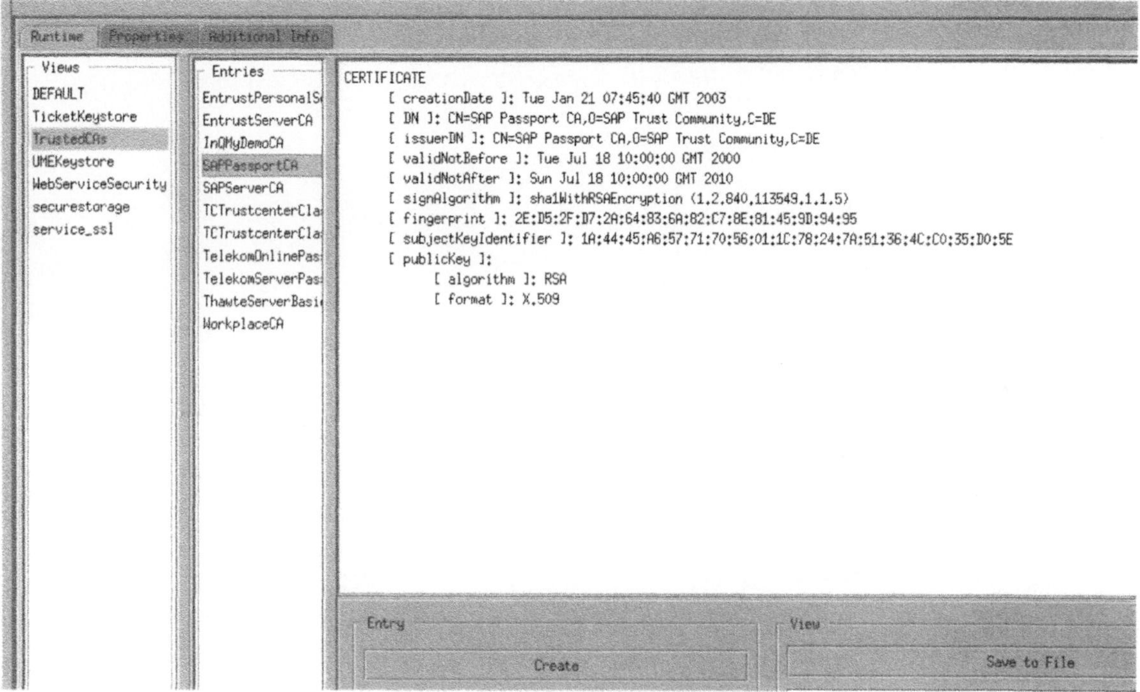

Next, navigate via the *Visual Administrator* to **Server > Services> ssl** to provide and update the configuration to request for client certificates (see Figure 4.38).

Figure 4.38 Requiring Client Certificates

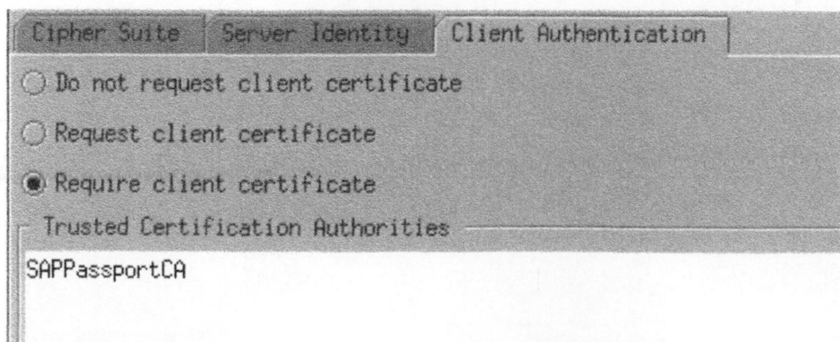

This makes certificates mandatory. Make sure to add SAP Trust as the trusted CA. The user interface labels the SAP Trust CA as *SAPPassportCA*. Finally, perform a test connection via HTTPS using the Web browser that has the SAP Trust client certificate implemented. The default J2EE port for SSL is 5XX01, where XX is the system number. If the server name is server01 and system number is 00, the SSL address is https://server001:50001. You can also see and change these ports in the SSL provider in the runtime tab.

Summary

In this chapter we covered various J2EE security concepts to include user maintenance, single sign-on, passwords, and communicating in SSL. J2EE is the new kid on the block and differs from its ABAP counterpart. The J2EE Engine is highly configurable, enabling the administrator to have a tight grip on the security of the server.

Solutions Fast Track

Users Maintenance

- ☑ Users accounts are maintained using the UME Console or User Management Web interface.
- ☑ Users accounts can be exported using the UME Console.
- ☑ Users accounts can be grouped by groups.

Single Sign-on (SSO)

- ☑ SSO allows the user to jump to different systems without password challenges.
- ☑ SSO implementation allows the exchange of certificates between systems.

Changing Passwords

- ☑ System users have special procedures for password changes.
- ☑ Password rules can be enforced and enabled on the J2EE server.

Setting Up SSL

- ☑ The J2EE server can communicate over the secure SSL protocol.
- ☑ SSL communication can be established with other SAP systems.

Frequently Asked Questions

Q: How do I change the Administrator's password?

A: Change the password in the UME.

Q: How do I export J2EE users?

A: Utilize the export/import feature in the UME Console.

Q: What are keys?

A: Each entity (server, user, etc) is assigned a pair of keys: private and public. The public key is used to identify users and the private key is used for decryption.

Q: What kind of rules can I set for passwords?

A: You can restrict by length, number of special characters, and number of numeric values.

Chapter 5

GRC

Solutions in this chapter:

- Architecture
- Design Considerations
- SAP Tools

☑ Summary

☑ Solutions Fast Track

☑ Frequently Asked Questions

Introduction

As mentioned in the introductory chapter, a comprehensive risk program is critical to project success from a cost, schedule and delivery perspective. This chapter is aimed at describing the components of SAP's Governance, Risk, and Compliance (GRC) offering in depth analysis and helping the user prepare to implement a comprehensive GRC strategy leveraging SAP's tools where appropriate. SAP appears ready to create a paradigm shift with GRC with the operative principle being prevention.

The business world focus on regulatory compliance has created a mandate. Information Technology (IT) must enable organizational improvement in GRC. Solutions must establish risk management and oversight of IT-related processes and controls. This discipline, commonly known as IT governance, is the process of establishing visible, positive oversight of the IT practices, assets, and resources to demonstrate that risks are managed and corporate objectives are supported and achieved, ensuring the proper use of IT resources. The role of a chief financial officer (CFO) is changing dramatically as is a shift in budgetary commitment required in this area.[1] Holly Roland of SAP writes that the new CFO has four main facets in their responsibilities; her treatise is that it is more than just balancing the books. She believes that the CFO is shaping strategic decisions including compliance and decision support as well as transaction and financial processing. Compliance itself takes up more and more prominent a role in the CFO organization as well as in IT. In fact, Gartner reported in 2007 that 8.3 percent of the IT spending is on compliance.[2] This implies that a renewed partnership between CFO and CIO organizations is needed and tools from IT are required to enable the requirements established by these strategic roles.

In considering the IT tools related to GRC, as this book depicts, it is important to keep a focus on the purpose, strategy, and alignment process for implementation. Today's toolset is not the end-all for GRC. It is important to recognize the role of the tools in the overall strategy. Clearly, the integrated software suite is coming a long way in helping corporations effectively manage their risks. But the fact is they are a complement to the process and not the driver. With any implementation, this must be kept in mind. There must still be management tools and processes that accommodate the automated programs available.

As Gartner's Caldwell states, "The entrance of ERP companies indicates that the GRC market is real, and for companies that put an emphasis on operations risk management, adopting a single technology platform can be extremely useful."[2] So, settling on the platform through SAP is a step in the right direction.

Eliminating redundant efforts with systems in different departments is always worthwhile. But, a company must bear in mind the process analysis and strategy that needs to encapsulate the IT enabling system. As SAP brings more robust products to the market in answering customer requirements, further enablement will occur.

As Figure 5.1 indicates, the prior model is an endless loop of problem identification and remediation. There is little or no proactive problem prevention. Reports are nonexistent and further enabled in this very closed self-defeating loop.

Figure 5.1 Endless Discovery Repair Cycle

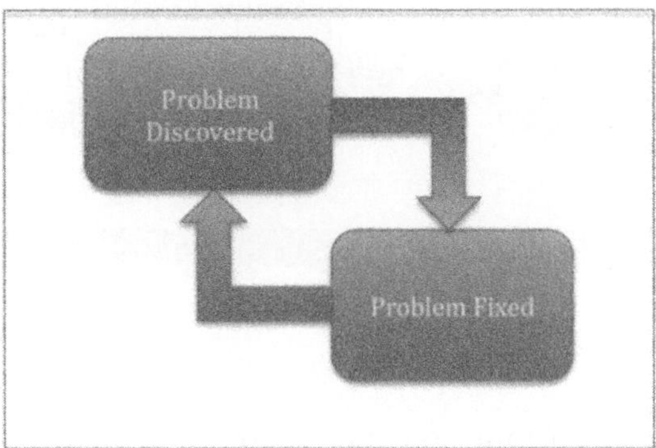

In prevention you must be able to understand the impact if you add a particular transaction. Up front during design is the best place to make these determinations. The key challenges in security are:

- Communication gap among role owners, security administrators, access approvers, and auditors (the stakeholders)
- Audit compliance that is cost effective and efficient
- Endless cycle of role maintenance
- No integration of tools to enforce best practices
- Automating labor-intensive security and control functions
- Seeing security as an afterthought rather then up front in Design
- Compliance (Sarbanes-Oxley, etc.)

The later a problem is found the costlier it becomes. As Figure 5.2 shows in a typical waterfall process without up front planning, problems are not discovered until after production release. This contributes to more risk and higher costs because of how late in the process issues are uncovered. There can also be added risks related to design decisions, that had all issues been considered up front may allowed for alternate implementation strategies or better mitigations. As a result the waterfall nature of the process does not reflect an overall strategic view of the implications of the designed role. Hence the problem is found too late into the process and the rework cycle begins anew; even worse, the rework cycle may begin again annually as new or related issues are uncovered.

Figure 5.2 Typical Waterfall Approach to Security Role Definition

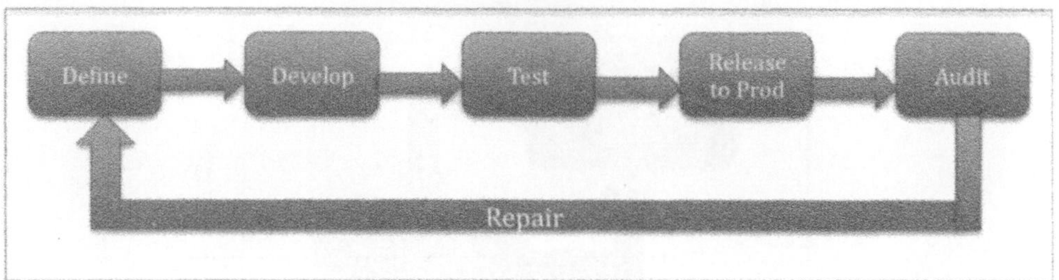

Today most Segregation of Duty (SOD) issues are identified after migration to production when the user is performing the role. This typically occurs during an audit. If the identification of issues can be made during definition, the problem cycle is changed.

The ideal solution would offer:

- Automated SOD analysis
- Support for all security stakeholders
- What-if scenario modeling including real user data embedded in the scenarios
- Legal compliance
- Nonintrusive approach
- Affordability and cost effectiveness

AMR Research announced that companies will spend more than $32 billion on governance, risk management, and compliance (GRC) in 2008, an increase of 7.4 percent over 2007.[3] Spending on Sarbanes-Oxley (SOX) compliance is expected to grow only 2 percent to $6.2B. For the first time since AMR Research began conducting this study in 2003, executives have shifted their GRC budget focus to operational and enterprise risk management-making SOX and other regulatory compliance programs a necessary "to-do," but not a top-of-mind initiative. Thirty-one percent of companies reported that better managing and mitigating risk in the business is the most influential issue driving their GRC investment in 2008. "In this economic climate, companies can no longer focus solely on reactive spending to meet each new regulation," explains John Hagerty, vice president and research fellow at AMR Research. "As executives are becoming aware of how different business and IT risks affect their bottom line, their spending focus is shifting toward approaching risk strategically, not just tactically."[3]

For the last few years, GRC services numbers have been decreasing as companies streamline compliance activities, but as risk rises in importance, companies report they want and need guidance on how to frame the risk discussion in a business context. Thus, GRC initiatives remain an intensely human effort. Two-thirds of budgets (approximately $21.5B) are earmarked for people-related expenses (services plus head count) in 2008. Four hundred and twenty-four IT and line-of-business leaders across all industry sectors in the United States, Germany, and Japan were surveyed for AMR Research's "Governance, Risk Management, and Compliance Report, 2008-2009."

Architecture

SAP GRC addresses some of the key capability requirements on the minds of CIOs and CFOs in the world today. The GRC toolset is brought to market in five components as follows:

- GRC-SCC Virsa Compliance Calibrator

  It supports real-time compliance. It stops security and controls violations before they occur.

- GRC-SAE Virsa Access Enforcer

  It is a workflow-driven tool. It allows users to request extra access and routes the request to an appropriate approver. The user account is automatically updated once the workflow has been approved.

- GRC-SRE Virsa Role Expert

  It is a Web-based tool. It automates the creation and management of role definitions.

- GRC-SFF Virsa Firefighter for SAP

  It enables superusers to perform emergency activities outside of their normal roles. It does so within a controlled, fully auditable environment.
- GRC-SPC GRC Process Control for SAP
- It streamlines and automates the control processes to reduce the cost of compliance.

In the following sections, we will describe the key features, functions, and configurations for each of the SAP tools. Remember, however, that without an overarching strategy for your GRC program, the tools will not solve your challenges. Programs must have perspective on the challenges they are resolving and the strategy being used to solve them. Baseline architecture is needed to ensure minimal wasted, redundant efforts on the tools and projects. As Figure 5.3 shows, the new model for risk management is a far different loop.

Figure 5.3 Revised Risk Management Loop

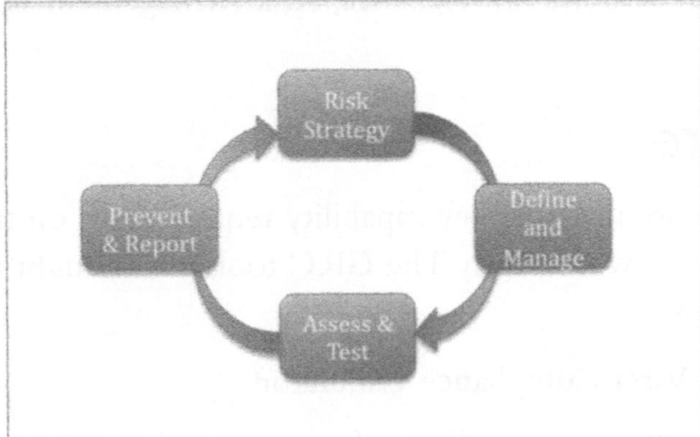

The prior cycle from Figure 5.1 in the Introduction in this chapter was a never-ending costly system lacking strategy. This revised loop offers a feedback mechanism for continuous management oversight and improvement as the risk strategy is maintained. The tools from SAP are aimed at enabling this new strategy for a complete architectural vision. Figure 5.4, places the tools from SAP in the context of this new model.

Figure 5.4 SAP Tools Overlaid on Strategy for GRC

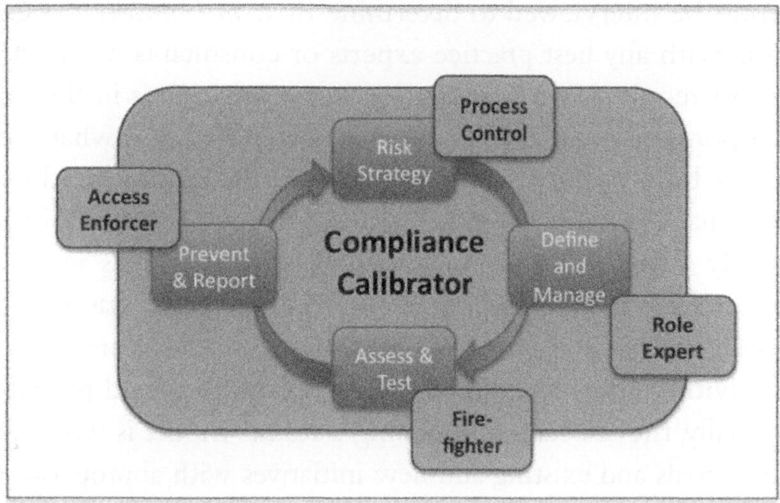

In order to develop a proper GRC Architecture one must define the goals and scope of the project. Building on the model described in Figure 5.5 should prove useful. By considering a merger of the results and planning sections, one builds to the overall methodology stage. This stage is tailored to the needs and processes of the company and IT. Each phase of architecture definition delivers requirements to the next phase to yield the overall architecture. Depending on the size of the effort and resources involved, the phases can be broken into parallel efforts.

Figure 5.5 Development Model for Architecture

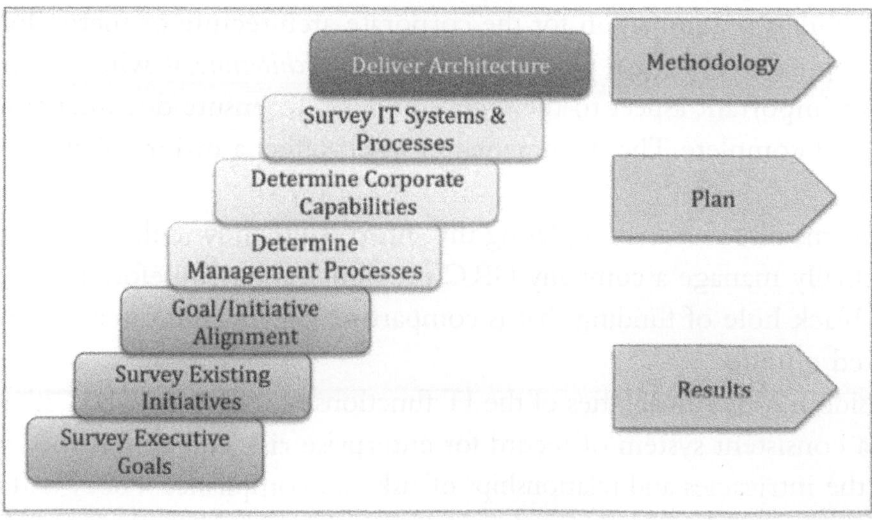

Results definition includes analysis of outputs expected for the overall GRC program. Management must be interviewed to determine their hot buttons for GRC. This includes working with any best practice experts or consultants involved in the project. The report required here is a detailed listing of what is in the minds and hearts of the corporation regarding how they define GRC and what they each believe are the key business drivers motivating them. In addition to the interviewing and analysis of management requirements comes an understanding of what the company is already doing. This must be a comprehensive analysis across every branch of the organization. Each division, department, and so on, usually has some independent activity addressing GRC in their own way and these interviews are aimed at bringing out all of the activities and projects to eliminate redundancy and prioritize resources appropriately. Finally, the last stage in building a results model is working across the company to align goals and existing and new initiatives with appropriate prioritization. This *goal/initiative alignment* is the key output and scope for building the results plan to be fed into the delivery architecture.

Once the scope is fully understood and prioritized from the *results definition phase* of architecture design, one must begin to plan for the GRC program. Determination of existing management capabilities, be they systematic or embedded, is the first key to delivering a plan. Determination of IT systems, processes, and drivers is also a major part of this planning. This *planning phase* includes workflow definition and building of the continuous improvement process for GRC architecture. Marrying management processes and system/corporate capabilities will build a variety of workflows and outputs. These, of course, are to be aligned with results expectations in order to provide the foundation for the corporate architecture or methodology to the GRC approach. This final phase, called *delivery architecture*, is where it all comes together. An important aspect to the entire model is to ensure documentation is consistent and complete. The documentation itself offers a major enhancement to compliance.

What teams discover in completing this effort is just how enlightening it is to be able to formally manage a company GRC program. As stated before this is no longer an ad hoc black hole of funding that is compartmentalized and often mismatched to the expected outputs.

In considering the capabilities of the IT functions as related to GRC, it's important to ensure a consistent system of record for enterprise risk and compliance while managing the intricacies and relationships of risk and compliance. Policy and procedure documentation must be indexed and cataloged as a part of the integration. This is a major step forward for most companies and the state of art in the Enterprise Portal world is at hand to enable this integration and reduce costs independent of the tool a company may use to enable this capability.

Working through the architecture definition, the importance of executive sponsorship and team makeup becomes clear. The team must be cross-functional and aid in breaking down the various islands of GRC. It is no longer appropriate to consider issues by risk managers separately. An integrated architecture breaks down the walls among the different organizations involved in risk and compliance and enables proper workflow communication and prioritization of resources and initiatives, as mentioned above. Once the silos are reduced and the key requirements are understood, an organization can begin to realize the benefits of an integrated foundation from which to manage cross-organizationally. It is believed that organizations with mature processes and GRC architectures will better anticipate and adapt in an unpredictable ever-changing marketplace. It is important as a part of the corporate change management/communications plan that employees understand the program is not about compliance, audit, and regulatory specifications, but rather a mindset to manage and minimize challenges in the work place that bar productivity and reduce effectiveness. Wherever possible, metrics should be developed and inserted in the process, then published and celebrated to further enforce the change in culture.

Design Considerations

So far we have a new model for considering, up front in a program or business strategy, the risks associated with the endeavor and a method of architecting the GRC process to enable a new corporate culture. The decision at this point is to determine the model, the tools, the stakeholders, and the project participants. A key in this work is communications at all levels of the enterprise. This is a major initiative and requires proper attention and involvement.

The team must gather the participants and begin an education process once it understands its stakeholders. Most organizations have a process for communicating key endeavors and this program needs to take advantage of that process. All levels of the organization need to buy in to why and how a GRC program is being managed and addressed. Naturally, vehicles will differ depending on the audience. Once the C-level executives agree on the program and communications the process can start quickly. A risk culture does not happen overnight, but with proper coaching and patience it will take hold. Along with the communications campaign, feedback is essential. Feedback from various constituents will drive the risk analysis details and begin to bring out corporate risks that need to be understood, measured, and mitigated, where appropriate. As the risk culture takes hold program-by-program and project-by-project, the design team can begin to build a model for what is and is not enabled with technology. The technology tools as mentioned before are merely enablers.

As the numbers show, SOX type efforts are not growing as quickly as overall risk identification projects. This means that the IT systems for managing compliance are coming to bear on the challenge, but other challenges are taking a higher priority in the overall organization's strategy. For example, in the Superior Marble Company, let's say a new competitor is coming into the market and margins are decreasing at the same time due to increased costs on manufacturing and transportation eating into the margins. The various management teams must come to grips with the variety of risks associated with these pressures. What are the risks of increased production costs? What are the mitigations? How does the new competition play into this? Is a merger worth investigating? Are certain lines more or less profitable? What is known about the competition and how might they increase or decrease these risks? What are the time horizons for the decisions, the mitigations, and so on? These must be some of the questions and concerns unspoken on the minds of the business leaders at Superior Marble. Now, where is SOX compliance involved? SOX compliance is usually not involved. It is certainly a priority, but not a high priority in light of a business down turn. So, how do you design your risk program? The program must manage your compliance initiatives as well as collect and manage the other more significant risks that must be understood and mitigated. These are all parts of the design process. Figure 5.6 is a diagram showing various parts of the GRC design process.

Figure 5.6 Design Brings It All Together

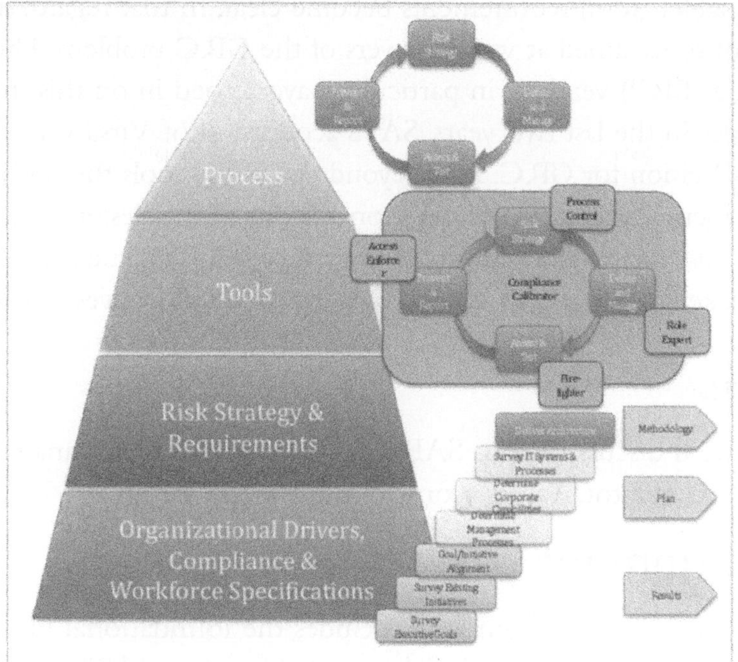

Building off of the architecture model from Figure 5.5, the design brings it all together as shown in Figure 5.6. The basic components from the marrying of organizational requirements and the drivers that feed the GRC program are the foundation to the pyramid for designing the process for the organization. The next level is the risk strategy defined as a part of the organization's priorities and resource specifications. This phase is fed by the initial foundation stage which comes below it. That is, the organizational drivers, compliance and workforce specification phase. The tools are the IT enablers layered on the overall process for GRC. Thus, we can see how design is an amalgamation of the various components into a detailed plan for delivering the GRC architecture.

A major effort in any initiative is monitoring and measurement. This leads to appropriate reporting which translates to documentation drivers and requirements. It is important to build a documentation portfolio that includes standard operating procedures (SOPs), risk requirements, compliance requirements, systematic requirements, and documentation specifications for monitoring, corrective actions, mitigations, and overall analysis. This clearly indicates a mandate for a cockpit type approach to the data. Workflows become important in developing this in order to serve the right stakeholders at the right time with information they find relevant. It is in determining these kinds of details that IT enabler (tool) requirements become clear. In that regard, the market has a large breadth of tools aimed at various layers of the GRC problem. The enterprise resource planning (ERP) vendors, in particular, have zeroed in on this market and made tremendous strides in the last two years. SAP's acquisition of Virsa was a major step in enabling the SAP vision for GRC. But, beyond the GRC tools themselves, a library for workflows and documentation is crucial. Coming out of the design stage, implementing a risk strategy needs to have the right tools to be successful. The next chapter focuses on tools that can make the program a success in light of the objectives put forth.

SAP Tools

In this section, we'll discuss various SAP tools, such as the risk management toolset, the Compliance Calibrator, Access Control, and Process Control.

Risk Management

The risk management toolset from SAP includes the foundational products known as *Compliance Calibrator*, *Role Expert*, *Firefighter*, and *Access Control*. These tools comprise the basic solution set from SAP enabling an end-to-end solution in GRC. Another consideration is documentation. This SAP offers the *Enterprise Portal*. There are four key components to the GRC model. These are detection, mitigation, reporting, and prevention. SAP's product set aligns handily with these.

Risk detection includes the *Access Control* module. With *Access Control*, SAP has extended the risk management toolset to include *Access Enforcer*. It is aimed at prevention and reporting in the overall model. The objective is to identify and prevent access and authorization risks in cross-enterprise IT systems to prevent fraud and reduce the cost of continuous compliance and control. The applications for access and authorization control enable efficient mitigation by automating workflows and enabling collaboration among groups of users. The reporting is robust and comprehensive with role-based dashboards; stakeholders need to actively monitor performance and take actions as needed. Finally, the prevention tools show how once mitigated, risks are prevented from entering production. This includes empowering stakeholders to perform real-time checks for risks, automate administrative tasks, and allow continuous proactive processing for risk analysis.

Figure 5.7 depicts the overall architecture for SAP's GRC toolset. At the foundation lies the *Compliance Calibrator*. This is the tool that enables the enterprise. With the SAP *GRC Risk Management Suite*, you can proactively implement collaborative processes throughout the enterprise. This framework, then, enables the balancing of new business challenges and opportunities in light of compliance and operating risks.

The application provides for best practices in enterprise risk identification, collaborative risk analysis, risk-response management, and continuous risk monitoring and reporting. This allows you to proactively anticipate and respond to changing business circumstances. Interacting with the *Compliance Calibrator* are three tools which work operate interdependently. These are *Firefighter*, *Role Expert*, and *Access Enforcer*. User provisioning is provided through Virsa *Access Enforcer*. *Role Management* is provided by Virsa *Role Expert* and *Superuser Privilege Management* comes from Virsa *Firefighter*. At the top of the pyramid is the *Process Control* tool, which allows automation and process workflow management for streamlining business challenges and eliminating redundancy and manual efforts as well as offering measures to ensure a satisfactory return on investment.

Figure 5.7 SAP GRC Tools

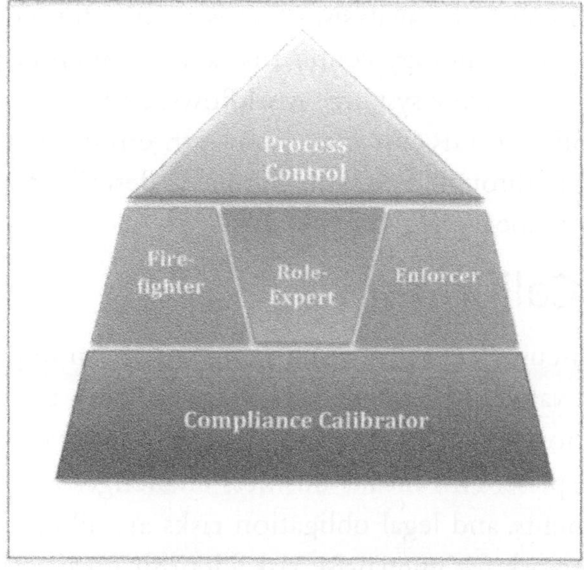

Enterprise Portal

While Enterprise Portal is not a direct GRC product, it is an enabler for all of the new dimension products from SAP. It is also important to recognize that SAP's

Enterprise Portal is only one example of a portal that can be implemented to work with the GRC product set. In fact, many companies run a gambit of portals and it's rare that a single portal standard has yet to emerge. While a small digression, it pays to discuss this in the context of a security book. Often there is no single "Best" when it comes to technology decisions. There is a premise, however, that suggests that having multiple products that serve a similar, if not the same, purpose is redundant. The portal market is a great example of this. Even the portal players themselves offer coexistence rather than be singled out for elimination. I maintain that it is possible for an organization to settle on a single portal technology and accomplish its program and corporate goals and not suffer from a host of integration challenges and potentially redundant efforts. It can also be an operational nightmare to maintain multiple software tools when only one homogenous tool is needed. Clearly, each portal has its strengths and weaknesses. But, in the face of integration challenges, it may be best to determine a single or perhaps even a two-fisted approach to the portal challenge. Choose a default and then justify expansion when necessary. In cases where expansion is justified, determine how far and at what cost it is really necessary. One may find the baseline still works after the analysis. What is clear is the need for a portal. The beauty of having a technology center that acts as an entry point to company policy, key documentations, key systems, workflows, and so on, is a major strategic advantage. When applied to GRC it makes sense to ensure that all of the data is organized and available through a cockpit model as described in the Design Considerations section above.

Compliance Calibrator

As we have already discussed, effective risk management can improve decision making and create significant value throughout the enterprise. With the SAP GRC Risk Management application suite, a firm can implement proactive, collaborative processes throughout the enterprise. This means business challenges an organization faces, compliance requirements, and legal obligation risks are all effectively managed in a best-practice framework for enterprise risk identification, risk analysis, risk mitigation, risk-response management, and continuous risk monitoring and reporting as described in the architectural requirements for a proper risk-driven culture. Hence an organization has the tools needed to proactively manage the business.

With *Compliance Calibrator* as the foundation, there is a value proposition. The issue includes protecting existing value by following the process of identification, analysis, mitigation, reporting, and notification for monitoring and measuring in key risk areas. The additional value comes in creating new methods for addressing corporate risk at the strategic level. Changes in market conditions, for example, must be balanced in terms of risk avoidance against risk response to the new condition. The new value creation includes assessment to capture, track, and address risk and loss events that may otherwise be missed or ignored.

Finally, *Compliance Calibrator* is the means for taking action regardless of system. Managing risk scorecards, key indicators, and hotlists are all automatically factored and monitored in the suite. Further, automatic identification of risks based on specified thresholds, policies, and metrics is available in the suite. In order to best understand the tools and process, some examples are provided. Table 5.1 shows a mapping of TCodes to categories. This is just a sample and not a comprehensive list. A category assessment matrix can then be provided as illustrated in Figure 5.8. Figure 5.8 shows potential segregation of duties conflict areas from the categories.

Table 5.1 TCode Categorization

Categories	Grp #	Transaction Code	Transaction Name
Accounts Payable	1	F-41	Enter Vendor Credit Memo
		F-42	Enter Transfer Posting
		F-43	Enter Vendor Invoice
		F110	Parameters for Automatic Payment
		MR02	Process Blocked Invoices
		MR11	Maintain GR/IR Clearing Account
		F-44	Clear Vendor
Vendor Master Maintenance FI	2	FK01	Create Vendor (Accounting)
		FK02	Change Vendor (Accounting)

Continued

Table 5.1 Continued. TCode Categorization

Categories	Grp #	Transaction Code	Transaction Name
		MK01	Create Vendor (Purchasing)
		MK02	Change Vendor (Purchasing)
		XK01	Create Vendor (Centrally)
		XK02	Change Vendor (Centrally)
Bank Reconciliation	3	FB05	Post with Clearing
		F-04	Post with Clearing
Accounts Receivable (AR)	4	F-26	Incoming Payment Fast Entry
		F-28	Post Incoming Payments
		F-29	Post Customer Down Payment
		F-34	Post Collection
Material Master Maintenance	5	MM01	Create Material – General
		MM02	Change Material
Requisitioning	6	ME51	Create Purchase Requisition
		ME52	Change Purchase Requisition
		ME54	Release Purchase Requisition
		ME55	Collective Release of Purchase Reqs.
Purchasing	7	ME21	Create Purchase Order
		ME22	Change Purchase Order
		ME31K	Create Contract

Continued

Table 5.1 Continued. TCode Categorization

Categories	Grp #	Transaction Code	Transaction Name
		MB01	Post Goods Receipt for PO
		MB0A	Post Goods Receipt for PO
		ML81	Maintain Service Entry Sheet
Physical Inventory	8	MI07	Process List of Differences
		MI08	Create List of Differences with Doc.
Sales	9	VA31	Create Scheduling Agreement
		VA32	Change Scheduling Agreement
		VA41	Create Contract
		V.25	Release Customer Expected Price
		VA44	Actual Overhead: Sales Order
		VF02	Change Billing Document
		V.23	Release Orders for Billing
		V-43	Change Material Price
		VK11	Create Condition
		VBO1	Create Rebate Agreement
		VBO2	Change Rebate Agreement
Customer Master Maintenance	10	FD01	Create Customer (Accounting)
		FD02	Change Customer (Accounting)

Continued

Table 5.1 Continued. TCode Categorization

Categories	Grp #	Transaction Code	Transaction Name
		V-03	Create Ordering Party (Sales)
		V-04	Create Invoice Recipient (Sales)
		V-05	Create Payer (Sales)
Maintain Security	11	SU01	Maintain Users
		SU02	Maintain Authorization Profiles
		SU03	Maintain Authorizations
		SU10	Mass Changes to User Master
		SU12	Mass Changes to User Master Records
		SM01	Lock Transactions
		PFCG	Activity Group Maintenance
		SM59	RFC Destinations (Display/Maintain)
		SM19	Basis Audit Configuration
		SM20	System Audit Log

Figure 5.8 Segregation of Duties Sample Category Mapping

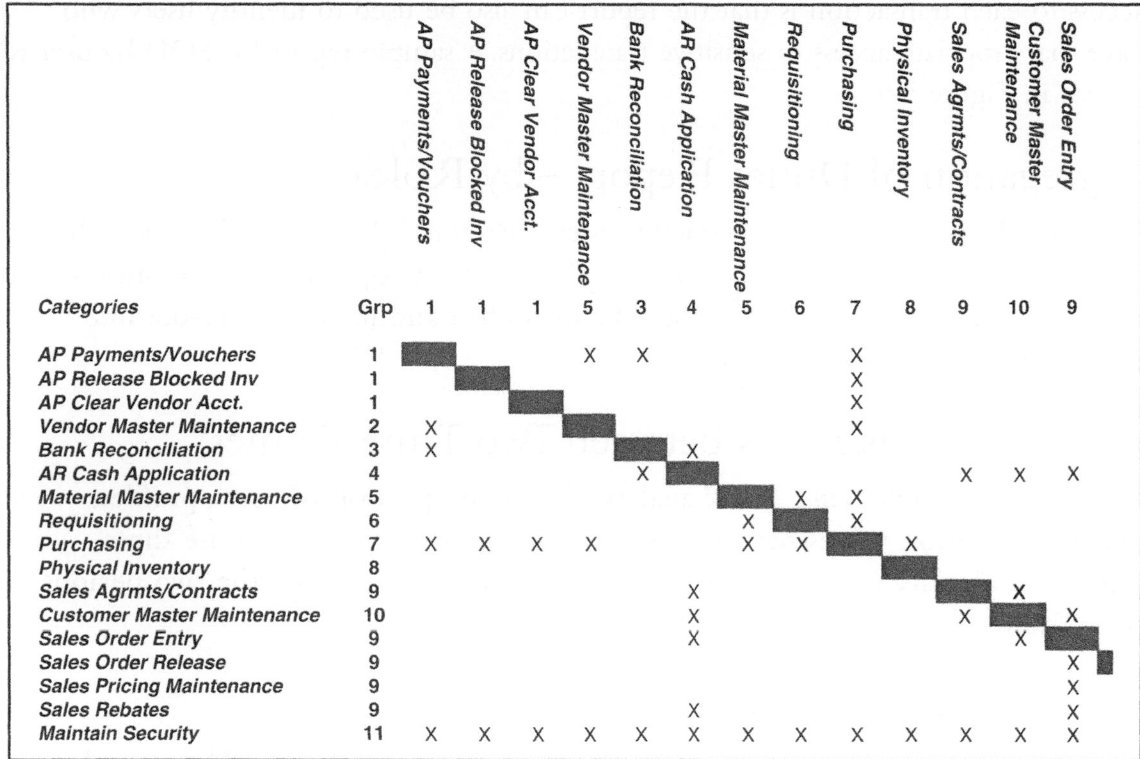

Categories	Grp	AP Payments/Vouchers	AP Release Blocked Inv	AP Clear Vendor Acct.	Vendor Master Maintenance	Bank Reconciliation	AR Cash Application	Material Master Maintenance	Requisitioning	Purchasing	Physical Inventory	Sales Agrmts/Contracts	Customer Master Maintenance	Sales Order Entry
		1	1	1	5	3	4	5	6	7	8	9	10	9
AP Payments/Vouchers	1				X	X				X				
AP Release Blocked Inv	1									X				
AP Clear Vendor Acct.	1									X				
Vendor Master Maintenance	2	X								X				
Bank Reconciliation	3	X					X							
AR Cash Application	4					X						X	X	X
Material Master Maintenance	5								X	X				
Requisitioning	6							X		X				
Purchasing	7	X	X	X	X			X	X		X			
Physical Inventory	8													
Sales Agrmts/Contracts	9						X						X	
Customer Master Maintenance	10						X					X		X
Sales Order Entry	9						X						X	
Sales Order Release	9													X
Sales Pricing Maintenance	9													X
Sales Rebates	9						X							X
Maintain Security	11	X	X	X	X	X	X	X	X	X	X	X	X	X

These types of analysis are generated, in part, automatically by the tools. However, it is important to determine the applicability for the business being analyzed and to add or delete TCodes for the categories as needed. The objective here is to describe the methodology and process. Once the potential SODs are determined, one can assess the impact and determine how to prioritize mitigations. The reporting process aligns with the categorizations as it relates to these items.

Reporting requirements at a minimum should include the following types for a comprehensive report and monitoring strategy. The reports one may wish to include in regular analysis include the following:

Segregation of Duties Report – by User

Reports all users who meet the SOD criteria. The report can list all users who have access to each transaction though they do not meet the SOD violation criteria. There is a *Report Parameter* which you can set to filter the output to report only users who meet the SOD *Violation* condition. The advantage of listing all users who can have access to each transaction is that the report can also be used to identify users who have inappropriate access to sensitive transactions. A sample report for SOD by user is shown in Figure 5.9.

Segregation of Duties Report – by Role

Reports all roles that can be assigned to users that could then mean they meet the SOD criteria. The report can list all roles. The advantage of listing all roles means one can quickly determine roles that could be in conflict and require break-out into more finite granularity on a role.

Comparison Reports between Two Time Frames

Support of multiple *Time Period* analysis allows comparison of users, profiles, and authorization values between any two points in time. You can use these reports to identify changes made to authorization data between the two periods of analysis.

Ad Hoc Queries

Ability to generate other forms of analysis is available with an *Ad Hoc* capability. This is critical in allowing more customized perspectives on the analysis and reporting.

Figure 5.9 Sample SOD Report by User

SAMPLE Segregation of Duties Report

Type:	**By User**
Inputs:	
Analysis Starting Date	**Mar-08**
Analysis Completion Date	**8-Jun**
Risk Category Rank	**High**
Analysis Area	**Create Master Record and Post Document**

Line Number	User ID	User Name	Group	Create	Post
1	123456	Paul Jones	AP	FS01	FB01
2	123455	Does Itmatter	Mgr	FS01	FB01
3	341234	Gone Fishin	Super	FS01	FB01
Total Users	3				
Users Analyzed	322				

Tcode	Object	Field	Values
FS01	F_SKA1_BES	ACTVT	1
FS01	F_SKA1_BUK	BUKRS	%
FB01	F_BKPF_BUK	ACTVT	1
FB01	F_BKPF_BUK	BUKRS	%

Profile	Authorization	Object	Field	ValueFrom	ValueTo	Date
123456: Paul Jones						
	ZZ:MCXKDKP12	F_SKA1_BES	ACTVT	1	*	5/1/08
	ZZ:MCXKDKP13	F_BKPF_BUK	BUKRS	*	3	5/1/08
341234: Gone Fishin						
	ZZ:MCXKDKP12	F_SKA1_BES	ACTVT	1	*	5/22/08
	ZZ:MCXKDKP13	F_BKPF_BUK	BUKRS	*	22	5/22/08

Access Control

As SAP points out, "A critical piece of the GRC puzzle, proper segregation of duties (SOD) and access control over key information assets is one of the most effective safeguards against fraud and mistakes, and a prerequisite for sound corporate oversight required by various regulatory mandates around the world, such as the Sarbanes-Oxley Act. It is also one of the most difficult controls to deploy and sustain given the thousands of users, roles, and processes that require access and authorization evaluation, testing, and remediation."[4] User provisioning is provided through Virsa *Access Enforcer*. *Role Management* is provided by Virsa *Role Expert* and *Superuser Privilege Management* comes from Virsa *Firefighter*.

GRC *Access Control* allows *Identity Management* applications and other non-SAP applications to integrate. This means they all benefit from the tightly integrated compliance solution offered in the tool. For environments that are extremely complex, this offers an even greater advantage for minimizing operational complexity in compliance management. Thus, adherence to critical requirements is sufficiently enabled through the tool and with Web service provisioning partners are able to offer a variety of scenarios from SAP's usage type model. Figure 5.10 illustrates the model for GRC Access Control. Users define business rules and policies and these are enforced with provisioned services. The Web services provided by GRC ensure that the users who are set up for given applications do not have specific risks that prevent access to be granted for them.

Figure 5.10 Access Control

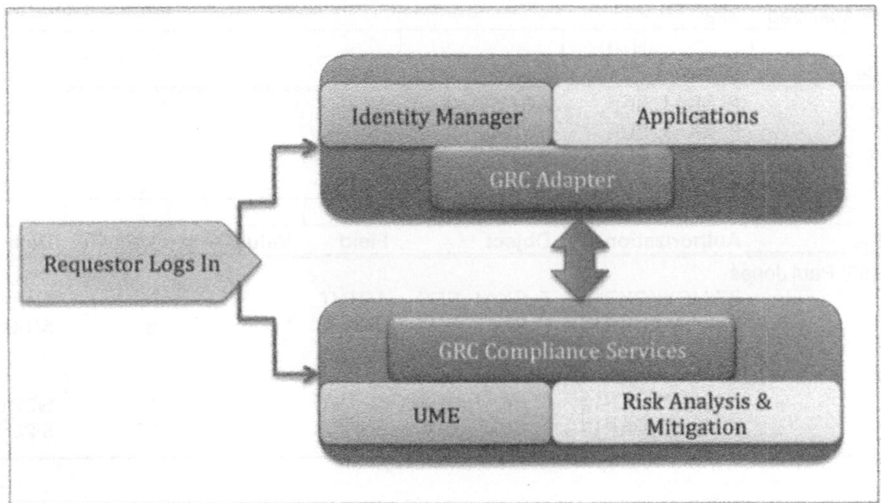

Monitoring is performed in real time with proactive policies that ensure compliance, particularly SOD issues. The tool also anticipates potential SOD conflicts before they arise, and helps prevent assignment of roles within an application, which could compromise appropriate segregation of duties. It also allows the customer to run what-if scenarios for potential role changes. This would indicate if those changes could pose a risk. The services also enable users to provide exceptions but with appropriate mitigation or remediation documentation trails to ensure those acceptations are properly recorded and traceable. The *Key Features/Benefits* include the following:

- Simplified compliance
- Enterprisewide including home grown and non-SAP applications to act as single source for the enterprise

- Duplication and manual efforts eliminated that can introduce or promulgate errors
- Easy to follow best practice methodologies
- Consistent communications unified across the organization so those that have different definitions become integrated and have a single version of the truth
- Strong prevention features
- Easy role creation and comparison for provisioning new users or changes to users
- Proper documentation trail, particularly for temporary changes as well as approval flows
- Automated change management
- Reduced fraud potential
- Audit-enabled reporting

In the overall area of compliance, with the tool one sets up access controls using a comprehensive library of SOD rules in order to jump start the program. This means the initial cleanup process is highly efficient. The library is based on many years of cross enterprise projects. Custom rules are added to the library in an efficient fashion as they are needed. A large benefit to this approach is also in the area of cross-application risks, which aims at stopping future violations before they occur. In addition, with SOD enforced from the start, compliance becomes a part of the initial project and is built in rather than an afterthought. Prevention also keeps violations from recurring as employees change roles. And the business processes are still enabled and able to support emergency changes and exceptions as needed with adequate traceability. Finally, with effective timely access control and management comes the need for oversight and audit capabilities. This is the strong suit for the tool. Managers get comprehensive views of the entire cycle including SOD rules, mitigations, and audit trails covering emergency process changes and exceptions. This enables auditors to comprehensively and more easily validate proper management oversight to ensure the business complies with all policies by making sure all access is properly authorized and by ensuring that SOD risks are appropriately mitigated.

The tools all reside on the SAP NetWeaver Platform. The *Compliance Calibrator* installation contains two parts: the front-end Java package and the real-time agent.

Configuration prerequisites for *Compliance Calibrator* are to define the connectors for all systems for which analysis is expected to be performed and to generate rules by uploading the rules file.

Access Enforcer installation contains two parts: the front-end Java package and the real-time agent. Configuration prerequisites for *Access Enforcer* are to define the connectors for all system in which provisioning will be performed, to define the request conditions and the business flows, and to enter the correct Web services to enable *Compliance Calibrator* to carry out the functions required.

The *Role Expert* contains two parts: the front-end Java package and the real-time agent. Configuration prerequisites for *Role Expert* are to define the landscape and connectors for all systems to be included. Next, one must define the parameters such as processes to be included and then the Web services for both *Access Enforcer* and *Compliance Calibrator*.

The *Superuser Privileges* module, *Firefighter*, also contains two parts: the front-end Java package and the real-time agent. Configuration prerequisites for Firefighter include definition of the connectors for the backend system to be connected, the configuration parameters such as Remote Function Calls (RFCs), and key transaction tables for interaction with *Compliance Calibrator*.

SAP has an install guide and prerequisite guides for installation and service package level requirements. These are available from the marketplace and help pages.

SAP Process Control

With *Process Control*, SAP is ensuring compliance and enabling business process control management by centrally monitoring key controls over cross-enterprise systems. The idea behind process control is to inject automated controls into cross-enterprise business processes and enable improvements in what were formally resource-intense manual control processes. This means that business risk can be automated to ensure key compliance drivers in a timely and cost-efficient manner. The increasing demands on compliance organizations from global and country-specific challenges means any new processes must be developed. With a proper GRC architecture and a method for quickly and efficiently adapting processes with automation, mitigations are quickly and conveniently managed through this tool.

The approach is risk based and spans the IT systems landscape. With streamlined workflows and automated controls there is a breakthrough in compliance management. SAP also offers a model for minimal resource impact to controlled testing to improve delivery time to compliance. And, with real-time monitoring across business processes, the GRC *Process Control* system improves the strategic management across an organization's multiple disparate systems, uniformly achieving policies across the organization.

There are three key facets to this solution as depicted in Figure 5.11.

Figure 5.11 GRC Process Tool

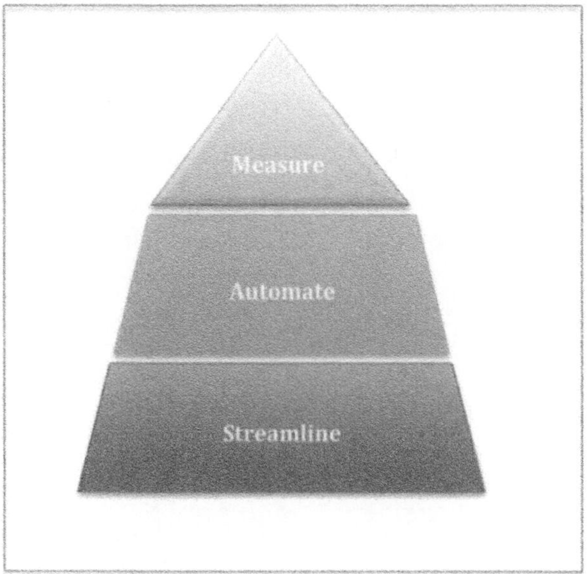

The three facets included are implementing the operational controls to improve business process management, reducing costs without negatively impacting compliance, and enabling lines of business to effectively mitigate risks. These are the foundation of the tool, which I call the *streamline piece*. The focus is on the process aspects under review. The next stage is the *implementation piece*, which relates to the automation of business process control management for streamlining business processes and offers controlled risk management. So, in combination with automated monitoring, controlled testing, and self-assessment, trends and patterns are used to optimize efficient performance. This is the *automation stage*. Reducing costs occurs through reductions in manual and disintegrated activities. By simplification and deployment of predefined scenarios across the organization, businesses can reduce the total number of control processes and their corresponding maintenance. By increasing efficiency and accuracy around processes, together with repeatability, the impact of manual functions is reduced and flaws and control challenges become a thing of the past.

Lastly, by enabling lines of business, there is a view to role-based cockpits for monitoring activities. This stage is *measurement* and is also necessary to ensure the cost impacts to failed controls are understood as a key metric in validating the positive impact from this tool. With this kind of robustness in the tool set, when coupled with the other aspects and considerations of SAP GRC, as well as the Portal Model, an organization has the enablers necessary to achieve their GRC program.

Summary

The biggest challenge in implementing any new program is to determine a retrofit in order to get to a new paradigm. Using GRC is a project in itself, but adding it to a design initiative in order to kick-start the process is worth exploring. Looking at a single application and expanding it is always an approach for success. Achieving senior stakeholder buy-in is critical. In addition, aligning priorities between ongoing projects, senior management, and key stakeholders including compliance and security personnel is also crucial. Once the decision is made and the project gets moving, the use of the tools and the methods can come easily with the right education and planning. It is hoped this book has added value to that process. Once an area is perceived as under governance, the compliance process can benefit from further automation through tools such as SAP's GRC Process Control. The value proposition offers a number of points including:

- Corporate alignment
- Flexibility in responding to market pressures and compliance changes
- Reduced SOD analysis and correction time
- Handling of legal issues within the process without extra overhead costs
- Clean and smooth audit reports and preparation
- Enforced best practices
- Reduced costs of user/role maintenance and compliance

Solutions Fast Track

Architecture

☑ Without an overarching strategy for your GRC program, the tools will not solve your challenges.

☑ Baseline architecture is needed to ensure minimal wasted, redundant efforts on the tools and projects.

☑ The tools from SAP are aimed at enabling this new strategy for a complete architectural vision.

☑ Marrying results and plan yields the overall methodology tailored to the needs and processes of the company and IT.

☑ Each phase of architecture definition delivers requirements to the next phase to yield the overall architecture.

☑ Employees must understand the GRC program is not about compliance but rather a mindset to manage and minimize challenges in the workplace that bar productivity and reduce effectiveness.

Design Considerations

☑ Considerations for design include the model, the tools, the stakeholders, and the project participants.

☑ Communication must be at all levels and targeted for the participants. Education must be considered and consistent.

☑ Team members should come from across the organization.

☑ The project should not be IT driven but IT enabled.

☑ Compliance is not the key driver that requires focus. Rather the focus must be on the results expected from the architecture definition.

☑ Metrics and reporting must be defined and matched to stakeholder requirements.

SAP Tools

☑ Determine tools for enabling the strategy based on design requirements.

☑ Tools to consider include Enterprise Portal, GRC-SCC Virsa Compliance Calibrator, GRC-SAE Virsa Access Enforcer, GRC-SRE Virsa Role Expert, GRC-SFF Virsa Firefighter for SAP, and GRC-SPC GRC Process Control for SAP.

Frequently Asked Questions

Q: What are the key capabilities of GRC platforms?

A: Solutions must establish risk management and oversight of IT-related processes and controls.

Q: What considerations are necessary for an organization to develop the GRC architecture?

A: In order to develop a proper GRC Architecture one must define the goals and scope of the project. It is important to ensure a consistent system of record for enterprise risk and compliance while managing the intricacies and relationships of risk and compliance. Marrying Results and Plan yields the overall methodology tailored to the needs and processes of the company and IT.

Q: How do you design your risk program?

A: The program must manage your compliance initiatives as well as collect and manage the other more significant risks that must be understood and mitigated. These are all parts to the design process.

Q: How should an organization stage their GRC program?

A: A partnership between CFO and CIO organizations is needed and tools from IT are required to enable the requirements established by these strategic roles to implement a new culture of GRC at a high level in an organization.

Q: What methods should be used to understand how to integrate risk and governance activities?

A: One must communicate with all levels of the organization. Surveys of existing projects, security compliance requirements and executive management drivers are all important tools in building this understanding. Partnership with the heads of divisions that span the organization is critical with the development of a cross-functional team to address the priorities and build the program.

Q: What are the key challenges facing security organizations today?

A: There is a communication gap among role owners, security administrators, access approvers, and auditors (the stakeholders). Then there is the pressure of audit compliance that must be cost effective and efficient. There is an endless cycle of role maintenance with a lack of properly integrated tools to enforce best practices. Often security is an afterthought in design processes and seen by management as a low-level necessary evil function rather then an enabler for the business.

Q: How does a company prioritize and integrate?

A: Like any successful program, surveying existing initiatives and requirements into a single listing is critical to starting. Interviewing division heads and high-level executives for their business motivations and individual priorities is key. From this package can come basic recommendations to make at a steering committee-type level. Once a recommendation is made, the right level of participation by a committee to discuss and negotiate priorities is necessary. This should include budget discussions and funding decisions.

Q: Where does IT fit into the GRC program?

A: IT is an enabler to the overall strategy. They have a seat at the prioritization table and heavy involvement in collaborating solutions to prioritized requirements; however, they should not be in the leadership position to appear as dictators to the company priorities, mission, and alignment.

Q: Where does communications and change management fit?

A: It is critical for the culture to adapt to the new GRC mindset, to have a strong program of communications at all levels ready to explain priorities and justify them. When a mission is clear, it is easy to fulfill. Change management teams are often the facilitators to this communications process in helping all levels adapt to new thinking and training on tools and process where needed.

Q: What does SAP offer to solving the GRC challenge?

A: The SAP toolset is poised to solve a great deal of the challenges associated with GRC management. Together with a sound document and policy administration strategy, a bulk of the challenges in GRC are managed through the SAP offerings.

Q: What is the foundation for implementing a GRC culture?

A: Having a common and consistent mission for what is addressed and why is key to the change in culture for a company. Taking GRC seriously through executives walking the walk is a major step forward in ensuring the success for this.

Q: What are the expected results from a comprehensive GRC program?

A: Reduced administration, improved systems management, and successful audits can all be positive results from a GRC program. The key is to enable efficient business.

Q: Who should be involved in GRC challenges?

A: GRC is everyone's challenge at all levels. Successful companies take empowerment seriously and ensure their personnel are leaders regardless of management status. This type of culture engages persons at all levels and can be a positive indicator of success.

Q: How can a company solve the GRC challenges without any SAP Virsa toolsets?

A: While SAP does offer the capabilities in Virsa that can be conveniently integrated into the NetWeaver framework, it is important to recognize alternatives. Firms that are investing in this area would want to include offerings from other firms that can tightly couple their products with SAP. One example of an alternate product would be Approva. Any of the products offered in the SOD space will provide the basic capabilities. Other determining factors include architecture requirements, time to implementation, availability, and price are all considerations. I'm finding that a number of firms are beginning to adapt a homogenous approach to tools and products in relation to SAP. They use SAP products as the default and justify external bolt-ons when an SAP product is found lacking or not aligned with the business requirements.

Notes

1. Roland, H. "Balancing More than Just Books: Transforming the Role of a CFO." 2007. New York: *Business Trends Quarterly Magazine*.
2. Personal communication from French Caldwell, VP of GRC at Gartner.
3. "AMR Research Finds Spending on Governance, Risk Management, and Compliance Will Exceed $32B in 2008 with Spending on Sarbanes-Oxley Compliance to Reach $6.2B." Boston: PR Newswire. March 25, 2008. www.prnewswire.com/cgi-bin/stories.pl?ACCT=104&STORY=/www/story/03-25-2008/0004779692&EDATE
4. SAP GRC Planning Guide, 2007.

Chapter 6

Back End: UNIX/Oracle

Solutions in this chapter:

- Database Security
- Operating System Security

☑ Summary

☑ Solutions Fast Track

☑ Frequently Asked Questions

Introduction

When we speak of SAP security the topics are generally specific to the SAP application and infrequently venture into the database and operating system. In this chapter we will cover some of these other security considerations specific to the underlying database and operating systems. The topic of operating system and database security is very detailed and lengthy so we'll focus specifically on concepts as opposed to product-specific security implementation. Since there are many databases and operating systems supported by SAP, we will focus our examples specifically to the Oracle database and Solaris Operating system.

Database Security

When it comes right down to it, SAP is nothing more than a monster database. Overlooking or skipping database security considerations is nothing but a disregard for a large aspect of the security SAP maze. I'm sure if you speak with your SAP Basis and/or Security Administrators, they would unequivocally agree that database security is important and critical. However, when it comes down to the actual implementation of mitigating controls, from what I've seen, only a minority of SAP installations actually take active measures to secure their SAP database. More companies take risk and control seriously due to regulatory requirements such as the Sarbanes-Oxley Act of 2002. However, if you are not required to abide by the standards, you are less likely to implement the security measures.

When it comes to database security, there are two ideas to explore: (1) denying unauthorized access and use and (2) processing and delivery accurate results. Denying unauthorized access and use has become very well publicized from the multitude of virus alerts flooding the Internet to reports of hackers gaining access to sensitive private information. Put simply, denying unauthorized access is ensuring your data is shared only with those privy to that information. Another aspect of database security is ensuring the accurate processing of data. For example, 1 plus 1 should always equal 2. If it is anything different, we could potentially have a major problem of data integrity. This idea of accuracy is not always labeled as a security threat, but it does directly tie into data integrity and consistency. Having accurately processed data is just as important as keeping people from seeing that data. Producing accurate data results from an SAP database is tremendously important since SAP by default is not an application configurable from the database level. As an SAP application user and developer, one should always expect results from the database to be true.

The topics that we will explore focus on these two ideas. The various database security concepts explained and demonstrated in this section are followed by examples from a WEB AS 7.0 system running on Solaris and an Oracle 10g database.

Patches

Database manufacturers periodically deploy patches to mitigate security risks and deploy big fixes. There are numerous opinions among database administrators regarding the frequency of patch implementation. Regardless of your philosophy and opinion regarding frequency, it makes sense to keep current with patches. Whether right or wrong, the first thing a support technician asks is "Are you patched to the current patch level?" If you're not at the recommended patch level, the call quickly ends with, "Once you're patched up to the required level, we can resume support." Maybe it's not that blunt all the time, but I'm sure you get the picture. Without going into too much detail about this topic, let me answer the following question: How frequently? The frequency of patch implementation is directly related to the amount of time and effort you can spend researching, implementing, and testing prior to productive deployment. So, the answer is, "it depends." Let's wrap this topic up with a few examples; we hope, you can identify with at least one.

Imagine that you're the database administrator of Big Company. Big Company has a team of dedicated database administrators assigned to patch management and a team of SAP application testers devoted to regression testing. Big Company Information Technology policy aims to be patch compliant with a maximum of a one-month delay since patch release. The dedicated technical resources along with the company policy really enable the team to be successful at achieving their patch mandate.

Now imagine that you're the database administrator of Medium Company. Medium Company has a moderate-sized team of database administrators and system and Basis administrators. The company has a patch policy of implementing patches two times a year. Corporate policy supports this endeavor by making resources available to implement, test, and roll out patches.

In the last scenario, you are the one-man shop: database administrator, systems administrator, Basis administrator, and network administrator of Small Startup Company. You have too many hats and not enough time. The company has no policy for patches aside from what you put into motion. You try to patch yearly, but even that is very difficult. You have too many responsibilities and not enough focus and attention to one task. Consequently, patches are implemented irregularly and usually with little testing prior to production rollout. Your situation if far from optimal, but in short, it is what it is.

Patch Implementation

The two methods of patch implementation are via the runinstaller or the opatch utility. Scenario one highlights the implementation of Oracle patch bundle 10.2.0.2 using the runInstaller utility. The second example will show the implementation of the Critical Patch Updates (CPU) using OPatch. CPUs are released quarterly from Oracle. Only SAP-approved CPUs must be applied to the Oracle database. You can research the certification status via http://service.sap.com/notes and search on term "CPU patch."

Patching Procedures: Oracle to 10.2.0.2

1. First download the patches from SAP Service marketplace using the alias URL http://service.sap.com/patches A question that I'm often asked is, "Are the patches available via SAP and Oracle's site the same?" The answer is Yes.
2. Unpack the Patch in a staging area.

   The patch directory has a directory called ***Disk1***.

   Change the working directory into the ***Disk1*** directory.

   Execute runInstaller as UNIX user ora<sid>.
3. Set the location of the inventory of the ORACLE_HOME that is being patched. The inventory location is kept in /var/opt/oracle/oraInst.loc.
4. Install the Patch in a staging area.

   Stop any database using the ORACLE_HOME.

   The patch directory has a directory called ***Disk1***.

   Change the working directory into the ***Disk1*** directory.

   Execute runInstaller as UNIX user ora<sid>.

   Enter the ORACLE_HOME directory and confirm and start the installation.

   After installation of the patch run the script $ORACL_HOME/root.sh as UNIX user root.

   After the ORACLE_HOME is updated to version 10.2.02 you must run a script to upgrade the database.

Start the database using "startup upgrade."

Run the script "$ORACL_HOME/rdbms/admin/catupgrd.sql."

Stop the database using "Shutdown immediate."

Start the database using "startup."

Run the script $ORACLE_HOME/rdbms/admin/utlrp.sql to recompile all PL/SQL packages.

Patching Oracle Security Patch CPU

1. First download the patches from SAP Service marketplace using the alias URL http://service.sap.com/patches.
2. Apply the patch for OPatch. Opatch is the patch installer utility.

   Backup the existing OPatch directory which is generally located in ORACLE_HOME.

   Copy in the new patch.
3. Set the location of the inventory of the ORACLE_HOME that is being patched. The inventory location is kept in /var/opt/oracle/oraInst.loc.
4. Query the patches applied.

   Run the command "perl opatch.pl lsinventory" from inside the OPatch directory.

   The output is the list of all patches applied to the ORACLE_HOME.
5. Apply the patch.

   Stop any database using the ORACLE_HOME.

   Place the copy of the patch in a staging area.

   Change the working directory into the numbered patch directory.

   As UNIX user ora<sid> Issue the command "perl $ORACLE_HOME/OPatch/opatch apply."

Users

SAP is an application that sits on top of the database. Unlike other applications, Oracle users are not associated with SAP users. In fact it makes no sense for a user to have any sort of database access. No one other than the Basis team should have access to the database. I've seen some implementations where the customer used the SAP database to host other applications or allow direct database access to users to "retrieve" data. That is simply not a good idea. Keep SAP's database separate from any other application and limit direct access to the database to the administrators.

Default Passwords

One of the first doors that an unauthorized user will try is the well-documented and published default passwords of standard database users. Keeping the password default is just like leaving the key in your ignition. Needless to say, changing the default passwords is a must. Fortunately SAP's installation program, "sapinst," starting with Web AS 640 includes a section that allows the installer to choose a new password for default Oracle and SAP database users. Unfortunately, if your database was created in earlier versions of SAP, it is possible that your Oracle database users may have the default passwords.

As a point of reference, here are database users in an SAP installation and the default passwords (see Table 6.1). Oracle username and passwords are case insensitive.

Table 6.1 Database Users in an SAP Installation

Database User	Default Password
SAPR3	SAP
SYSTEM	MANAGER
SCOTT	TIGER
OUTLN	OUTLN
SYS	CHANGE_ON_INSTALL
DBSNMP	DBSNMP

We have two tools in our arsenal to change these passwords. We can use SQL or SAP's tool *brconnect* formerly known as *sapdba*. Figure 6.1 shows you an example of how to view all users defined in the database and then changes the password for user SYSTEM to RANGER using SQLPLUS. The same operation is performed using *brconnect* (see Figure 6.2). Use only SAP's *brconnect* tool to change the password for the SAP schema owner and the OPS$ user. SAP uses a table named *sapuser* that stores an encrypted password that is necessary for connection to the database for SAP functions such as *startup*.

Figure 6.1 Select All Users in the Database and Change to Password Ranger

```
usrv01:gb1adm 22% sqlplus "/ as sysdba"
SQL> select username from dba_users;
USERNAME
------------------------------
SYSTEM
SYS
OPS$ORASR3
OPS$SR3ADM
DBSNMP
SAPSR3
OUTLN
SQL> alter user system identified by ranger;
User altered.
```

Figure 6.2 Change Password for User SYSTEM to Ranger

```
usrv01:gb1adm 22% brconnect –u / -c –f chpass –p ranger
BR0801I BRCONNECT 7.00 (30)

BR0280I BRCONNECT time stamp: 2008-05-08 22.42.58
BR0828I Changing password for database user SAPECC
BR0280I BRCONNECT time stamp: 2008-05-08 22.42.59
BR0829I Password changed successfully in database for user SAPSR3
BR0830I Password changed successfully in table OPS$SR3ADM.SAPUSER for user SAPSR3

BR0280I BRCONNECT time stamp: 2008-05-08 22.42.59
BR0802I BRCONNECT completed successfully
```

Download the latest patch set for the BR tools from SAP from http://service.sap.com/patches The packages will be bundled as an SAR file. SAR is the SAP's compression and packaging format uncompressed with the utility SAPCAR. Details regarding the files in the SAR program bundle are listed in Table 6.2.

Table 6.2 BR Tool Details

File name	Installation Location	Suggested UNIX Permissions	UNIX Ownership	Function
brconnect	/sapmnt/<SID>/exe	4755	ora<SID>:dba	SAP Oracle database maintenance utility
brbackup	/sapmnt/<SID>/exe	4755	ora<SID>:dba	SAP Oracle database backup utility

Continued

Table 6.2 Continued. BR Tool Details

File name	Installation Location	Suggested UNIX Permissions	UNIX Ownership	Function
braarchive	/sapmnt/ <SID>/exe	4755	ora<SID>:dba	SAP Oracle database backup utility for Oracle archivelog files
brrecover	/sapmnt/ <SID>/exe	755	ora<SID>:dba	SAP Oracle database recover utility
brrestore	/sapmnt/ <SID>/exe	755	ora<SID>:dba	SAP Oracle database restore utility
libsbt.so	/sapmnt/ <SID>/exe	755	ora<SID>:dba	SAP backup library
init<SID>.sap	$ORACLE_ HOME/dbs	755	ora<SID>:dba	BR tools Configuration file
sapconn_role. sql	$ORACLE_ HOME/dbs	755	ora<SID>:dba	Creates role SAPDBA and assigns to the OPS$<SID>ADM and OPS$ORA<SID> Oracle users
sapdba_role. sql	$ORACLE_ HOME/dbs	755	ora<SID>:dba	Creates role SAPCONN and assigns to the OPS$<SID>ADM and OPS$ORA<SID> Oracle users

Before using *brconnect* or any of the BR tools, make sure to assign the appropriate Oracle roles and UNIX permissions; see Table 6.2 for the specific details. Figure 6.3 shows the commands necessary to assign the correct UNIX permission. Earlier versions of the scripts have different syntax, so check the comments in the beginning lines of the script. See Figure 6.4. After running the scripts, scroll thru the log file. A log file is generated in the current directory as the script with .log extension.

Figure 6.3 Granting UNIX Permissions to BR Files

```
usrv01:gb1adm 22% chmod 4755 brarchive
usrv01:gb1adm 22% chmod 4755 brbackup
usrv01:gb1adm 22% chmod 4755 brconnect
usrv01:gb1adm 22% chmod 755 brrecover
usrv01:gb1adm 22% chmod 755 brrestore
usrv01:gb1adm 22% chmod 4755 brspace
usrv01:gb1adm 22% chmod 4755 brtools
usrv01:gb1adm 22%chmod 755 init<SID>.sap
usrv01:gb1adm 22%chmod 755 libsbt.so
```

Figure 6.4 Viewing the Comment's sapdba_role.sql and Running It against SAP Schema SAPSR3

```
usrv01:gb1adm 22% more sapdba_role.sql
-- @(#) $Id: //bas/700_REL/src/ccm/rsbr/sapdba_role.sql#11 $ SAP
-- Create/update sapdba role
-- This script can only be run on Oracle 9i or higher
-- Calling syntax (sapdba_role.sql in current directory):
-- sqlplus /nolog @sapdba_role <SAPSCHEMA_ID>
-- <SAPSCHEMA_ID>: for owner SAPR3: R3, SAP<SID>: <SID>, SAP<SID>DB: <SID>DB
-- Log file sapdba_role.log will be created in current directory
usrv01:gb1adm 22% sqlplus /nolog @sapdba_role SR3
```

Default Privileges

Oracle security is organized in a logical context to limit data and resource accessibility. Before going into the explanation of how to reduce the vulnerability with the default PUBLIC group, let's talk about the fundamentals of Oracle database security. Oracle database security is based on a hierarchy of object controls. Privileges give the ability to execute given statements on objects. Roles are a logical container of privileges and, if so desired, other roles. The last link in the chain is the user. Users are assigned roles and/or privileges. See Figure 6.5 for a hierarchical illustration of these security principles.

Figure 6.5 Oracle Security Hierarchy

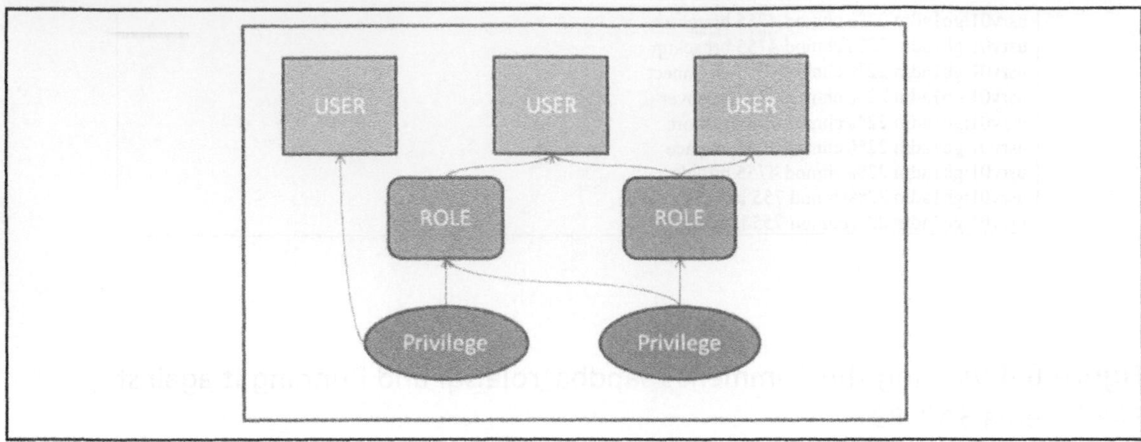

Oracle organizes all users into a group called PUBLIC. By default the group PUBLIC has default-granted privileges. Any user created in the database will automatically have those privileges. Other than the users created by SAP within the database, you probably should avoid creating and allowing users to directly access the database. However, if you must, limiting the privileges assigned to the group PUBLIC will better secure your database. See Figure 6.6 for the SAP's recommendations.

Figure 6.6 SAP Recommendations for Group PUBLIC

```
Revoke execute for:
UTL_SMTP
UTL_TCP
UTL_HTTP
UTL_FILE
UTL_INADDR
DBMS_RANDOM
```

Database links are objects within the database that allow connections between databases. Database links can create potential security risk by opening a tunnel to another database. This allows SQL statements to be executed thru these links. It is a good idea to remove the privileges from users to create database links. Figure 6.7 show the commands to remove the *create database* link privilege from database user SAPSR3 and database role SAPCONN.

Figure 6.7 Remove Create Database Link

```
revoke CREATE DATABASE LINK from SAPSR3;
revoke CREATE DATABASE LINK from SAPCONN;
```

Password Rules

Passwords assigned to Oracle users should have some level of complexity to reduce the possibility of password "guessing" by unauthorized users. Unless absolutely necessary, avoid allowing and creating Oracle database users. You can decide to implement passwords as a mandatory system requirement or more simply as a procedural rule. It is possible to implement password rules using database profiles; unfortunately, SAP does not support or recommend that implementation. The preferred method of password control is via a procedural implementation. Procedural implementation means to set passwords to specific values based on rules and conditions. See Figure 6.8 for some example password rules.

Figure 6.8 Example Password Rules

1. Minimum length = 8 characters
2. Number of special characters = minimum 1
3. Number of numeric characters = minimum 1
4. Number of alphabet characters = minimum 1
5. Maximum password validity = 90 days

Restrict Network Access

Network security for the database is another important aspect of securing the database. The few items that we discuss here limit access via the Oracle listener. The first item is how to prevent unauthorized hosts from establishing *sqlnet* connections to the database. The minimum requirement for SAP is a *sqlnet* connection from all application servers to the database server. Let's use an example to demonstrate this point. Suppose that your SAP production system exists on two physical servers: server1 and server2. Server1 is the database server and server2 is the central instance. In this example, we can limit the *sqlnet* connection from server2 to server1 and from server1 to itself. See Figure 6.9 for the *sqlnet.ora* configuration that limits access to only the necessary hosts.

Figure 6.9 An sqlnet.ora Configuration

```
# IP address for server1=192.168.1.10
# IP address for server2=192.168.1.11
# Once the listener is restarted, this configuration is activated
#
tcp.validnode_checking=yes
tcp.invited_nodes=(192.168.1.10, 192.168.1.11,127.0.0.1)
```

The configuration file *sqlnet.ora* is located in the $ORACLE_HOME/network/admin directory. The configuration takes effect after the restart of the listener. If you are implementing this on a live system, and you are a little timid about pulling the trigger, analyze the listener's log file to see which hosts have been accessing your database via *sqlnet*. I've included a sample script (see Figure 6.10) that parses the listener's log file and outputs the addresses that have been accessing your listener. Run the script as <sid>adm or ora<sid> UNIX user. It will look at all listener logs located in the default location that are named like $ORACLE_HOME/network/log/listener.log*.

The configuration profile *sqlnet.ora* specifies the implementation of specific Oracle Net features. The *sqlnet.ora* is located on both the server and client in the default location of $ORACLE_HOME/network/admin or in a specific location as identified by the environment variable TNS_ADMIN. In an SAP implementation of Oracle, the *sqlnet.ora* file resides on the database server and the application server. See Table 6.3 for Oracle Net features important to SAP.

Table 6.3 sqlnet.ora

Parameter Name	Description
DEFAULT_SDU_SIZE	This parameter specifies the size in bytes of the session data unit (SDU) size. Set this value to 32768 at the client and server side.
TRACE_LEVEL_CLIENT	This parameter implements a client trace. Possible values are 0-16 where 0 is the lowest and 16 is the highest level of trace. The trace level should be set to 0 during normal operations.

Continued

Table 6.3 Continued. sqlnet.ora

Parameter Name	Description
TRACE_UNIQUE_CLIENT	This parameter separates sessions into separate trace files. Set the value to true.
SQLNET.EXPIRE_TIME	This parameter specifies time measured in minutes after which a connection in error state is terminated. Enter a value of 5.0 will deactivate this feature.
SQLNET.INBOUND_CONNECT_ TIMEOUT	This parameter specifies time measured in seconds after which a connection is closed after a logon is not successful. Set the value to 120.
	Sample Web AS 7.0 sqlnet.ora file

Figure 6.10 Sample Script to Parse listener.log File

```
#!/usr/bin/perl
# Sample script that generates a list of hosts accessing the listener on the current host
# Includes the loopback address in the list
@manual_ip=qw/127.0.0.1/;
$LOGS="$ENV{'ORACLE_HOME'}/network/log/listener.log*";
print "Analyzing logs in $LOGS\n";

@list=glob "$LOGS";
for (@list) {
 open (FH, "$_") or die "Err\n";
 @FH=<FH>;
 close(FH);
 for (@FH) {
 /HOST=(\w+)/;
 $hash{ $1 } = 'hostname';
 }
}
for (keys %hash) {
if ($_=~/^$/) {next}
$x=`/usr/sbin/nslookup $_|grep Address`;
@x=split(/\s+/,$x);

$hash{$_}=@x[1];
}

for (keys %hash) {
 if ($hash{$_}=~/^\d{1,3}\.\d{1,3}\.\d{1,3}\.\d{1,3}$/) { $ipp{$hash{$_}}='X' } else {next}
}

for (@manual_ip) { $ipp{$_}='X' };
for (keys %ipp ) { print "$_\n";}
print "\nAdd this to your sqlnet.ora\n";
print "
tcp.validnode_checking=yes
tcp.invited_nodes=(";
$num=keys %ipp;
```

Figure 6.10 Continued. Sample Script to Parse listener.log file

```
for (keys %ipp) {
 $i++;
 if ($i == $num ){
 print "$_";
 } else {
 print "$_,";
 }
}
print ")\n";

sub get_input {
  print "Press Y to continue\n";
  chomp ($response=<>);
  $response=~tr/a-z/A-Z/;
  if ($response ne 'Y' ) { print "OK, bye now\n\n"; exit }
}

Sample execution:
server01:oraabc 32% ./check
Analyzing logs in /oracle/ABC/102_64/network/log/listener.log**
127.0.0.1
10.31.39.13

Add this to your sqlnet.ora

tcp.validnode_checking=yes
tcp.invited_nodes=(127.0.0.1,10.31.39.13)
```

The other item we'll talk about is actually securing the listener. The entries are input into the listener configuration file located in the default location, $ORACLE_HOME/network/admin/listener.ora. In NetWeaver 2004s 10g installations, SAP declares the location of the listener via the TNS_ADMIN environmental variable. The entries shown in Figure 6.11 protect all listener activities via a hashed password "97A82B7E9A8725CD" and mandates that changes to the listener are done to the actual listener.ora file.

Figure 6.11 Protecting the Listener

```
#
#
# Entry in listener.ora file
#
# Password protection for LISTENER
PASSWORDS_LISTENER = 97A82B7E9A8725CD
# Disable runtime modification of listener named LISTENER
ADMIN_RESTRICTIONS_LISTENER = on
```

Operating System Security

The topic of operating system security is a very lengthy discussion owing to not only the vast amount of technical details but also the number of operating systems and versions. Since our focus is SAP, we'll cover items directly relevant to SAP and Solaris operating system security.

Changing Some Defaults

Let's start by addressing system defaults. When the operating system is installed, there are some default configurations that should be changed. Below the Solaris operating systems there is a firmware called Openboot. The Openboot resides on the Programmable Read Only Memory (PROM) and starts every time the systems start and even determines the boot behavior at startup. Needless to say, we must protect the Openboot from unauthorized access. By default the Openboot is without a password and is set at the lowest level of security. Openboot has three levels of security: *none*, *command*, and *full*. The security level *none* requires no password and allows full access to the Openboot commands. The security level *command* requires a password for all commands other than *boot* and *go*. *boot* is the Openboot command to initiate the boot process utilizing any options. *go* resumes processing after halting the system. Security level *full* requires a password for all commands other than *go*. It is best to set the security to command or better with a specified password. See Table 6.4 to set the Openboot security level to *command* and a new password.

Table 6.4 Openboot Security Levels

Security Level	Description
none	The default value which is the lowest level of security. No passwords required.
command	All commands require a password except *go* and *boot*.
full	Highest level of security. All commands require a password except *go*.

Once a security level is set above none, define a password. See Figure 6.12 for an example of setting the Openboot security level to *command* using the command *setenv security-mode* and setting the password using the command *password* via the *Openboot OK* command prompt.

Figure 6.12 Changing the Openboot Defaults

```
OK> setenv security-mode command
OK> password
```

Some other defaults that should be changed are UNIX user passwords. When users are created, either manually or via an installation script, default or standard passwords may be used. These passwords may not be necessarily set by the system but by an unwritten but readily known practice. Change these passwords immediately.

Techniques

After changing some of the riskier defaults there are some techniques that can help secure your system even more. Some are system and others are more procedural. Let's start with the system setup techniques. First off, turn off any unnecessary services on the host. This will improve performance since fewer processes are running on the host but also reduce the possibility of risk associated with these unnecessary services. See Table 6.5 for a list of services that you can consider disabling. We've listed services that are generally activated after a base Solaris 10 install. You can do without these services in an SAP implementation plus documented and published incidents have prompted administrator to disable these services/protocols.

Table 6.5 Some Processes to Disable

Service/Process	Description
telnet	Telnet is an unsecured network protocol for remote connection. Replace telnet with the implementation of the Secure Shell Protocol (SSH).
ftp	Ftp server allows ftp connection to the server. The ftp protocol is unsecured.
Network File System (NFS)	NFS is a protocol for sharing file systems across the network. Unless specifically necessary, turn these services off. NFS process can be another avenue of exploitation.
sendmail	Sendmail is the mail server process. Unless specifically necessary, disable sendmail. Sendmail opens a wide variety of exploitable holes for hackers. Your servers should be within the corporate network and less susceptible, however shut it off if it's not required. It is one less fruit for the intruder to pick.

Continued

Table 6.5 Continued. Some Processes to Disable

Service/Process	Description
rexec	The rexec service that allows the execution of commands on remote hosts. It passes information in the clear. If a host gets compromised, then all other hosts configured to remote login without a password are also compromised. Like in a submarine, you want to contain the leaks to the smallest possible enclosable unit. Enabling rexec is like having a submarine with zero containment chambers.
rlogin, shell	Like rexec, rlogin allows remote access to a remote host via an actual log-in session. Disabling this process will help secure your UNIX submarine in the event of a breach.
finger	The finger protocol queries and retrieves information about users on local or remote hosts. Some security concerns have been identified with finger.
rstat	This process collects performance data from the kernel. This operation is not critical to the operating system. To prevent possible misuse, disable this process.
ruser	The ruser process reports the users on a system. This operation is not critical to the operating system. To prevent possible misuse, disable this process.
ttdbserver	The Common Desktop Environment (CDE) Tool Talk utility has had exploitable vulnerabilities.
SSH X11 forwarding	Disable X11 forwarding to prevent unauthorized X11 sessions. Disable by editing /etc/ssh/sshd_config and setting X11Forwarding no. Restart the ssh service.
X11	Disable the X11 service. Known vulnerabilities have been documented and released.

If you are preventing processes from running, you can do it one of two ways. If you are using the legacy method of starting processes, remove the startup scripts for executing. If you are using Solaris Service Management Facility (SMF), disable that process. See Table 6.6 for examples of disabling with legacy and SMF.

Table 6.6 Disable Services

Action	Legacy	SMF
Disable finger	Comment out lines # FINGERD - finger daemon # finger stream tcp6 nowait nobody /usr/sbin/in.fingerd in.fingerd in inetd configuration file /etc/inet/inetd.conf Comment out lines kill the finger process	Disable and stop service # svcadm disable network/finger:default
Disable nfs client	Move the startup script in the run level script directory # mv S73nfs.client kill. S73nfs.client Stop the nfs client process /etc/init.d/nfs.client stop	Disable and stop service # svcadm disable svc:/network/nfs/client:default

In chess we protect the king; in UNIX it's all about protecting *root*. We can do some things to make it more difficult to get to *root*. For example, we can disable a direct login as *root* rather than the actual console. We can accomplish this by setting the CONSOLE value in /etc/default/login. Figure 6.13 is an example of disabling *root* login from other than the console. The only way to log in as *root* is via the console or executing the *su* command from another user. The benefit of *su* is that it gets logged. Since we are using ssh, you will need to activate the parameter that prevents direct user *root* login. Activate the parameter *PermitRootLogin* with value equal to *no* to disable direct *root* login via ssh. Restart the ssh daemon.

Figure 6.13 Protect Root Login

```
# If CONSOLE is set, root can only login on that device
# Comment this line out to allow login by root
#
CONSOLE=/dev/console
```

Keep the *root* password secret. Be sure only select people know it. Exercise professional skepticism. Malicious users can use it to cause harm, but careless and inexperienced users may unintentionally break your system.

If consultants or special users need access to *root* use an application like *sudo* or Solaris' Role Based Access Control (RBAC). The benefit of these utilities is that users can be configured to only have access to run their particular command. These utilities also have full logging capabilities for any audit purposes. For example, SAP installation programs generally require *root* access. If a sudo or RBAC script is created for this purpose, SAP installations can be run without tying down the UNIX administrator to the Basis administrator. If you end up creating sudo or RBAC scripts, remember to set permissions to disable editing capabilities on those scripts by other than the *root* user. If not, a semiskilled UNIX user can easily get access to *root*.

Some applications require or can be optionally configured with passwords. Where possible, avoid writing passwords into scripts. SAP's backup utility *brbackup* and *brarchive* have a flag for a password *–u*. If you enter the password even within a script that is read only to the user, every time it runs, anyone who lists the processes will see the password in clear text. So, if you are to schedule backups using *brbackup* and *brarchive*, write your script so the *no password* option works. See Figure 6.14 for an example of a *brbackup* command using all defaults with no explicit password typed on the command. RMAN, the Oracle Recovery Manager, needs passwords passed to it. To prevent anyone from greping on the process and seeing the password, implement the rman connect strings in a command file.

Figure 6.14 An Example of brbackup with No Password

```
$ brbackup –u / -c –m all –t offline_force
```

Create a banner that displays every time a user logs into the host. The message should convey the message that only authorized users are welcome. Let your corporate legal team hash out the exact wording. I've read about cases where alleged hackers were given reprise because the language on the banner page was too inviting. First, disable all remote login except ssh. Create a banner page by editing the file /etc/issue. Finally, enable a banner page in the ssh configuration file /etc/ssh/sshd_config and refresh the ssh service. See Figure 6.15 for an example of a sample log-in banner.

Figure 6.15 Enabling a Login Banner

```
# cat /etc/issue

Only authorized user welcome

# cat /etc/ssh/sshd_config| grep issue
Banner /etc/issue
#
#
# svcadm refresh ssh
# ssh hiraoj@localhost

Only authorizeed user welcome

Password:
Last login: Fri Jun  6 16:21:00 2008 from localhost
Sun Microsystems Inc.   SunOS 5.10      Generic January 2005
-bash-3.00$
```

The last item that I'll briefly cover is physical security. All servers should be locked behind closed and monitored doors. This minimizes the chance of your expensive servers from walking out the door, and more importantly, it limits the physical access to the computer. Data protection must be electronic as well as physical. A failure in either case can open a significant amount of risk to your server and data.

Summary

In this chapter we covered the security issues relating to the operating system and the database in an SAP implementation. We covered setting specific details of securing the operating system and database against unauthorized access. Establishing a secure operating systems is one the first foundations to a secure SAP system. Start by securing the Openboot and working up to the operating system. Disabling unsecure defaults help, and setting up system logon messages will help harden your operating system. We've also discussed changing some default configuration such as users and network on the database server to make the database more secure.

Solutions Fast Track

Database Security

☑ Database manufacturers periodically deploy patches to mitigate security risks and deploy big fixes.

☑ The two methods of patch implementation are via the runinstaller or the opatch utility.

☑ SAP's installation program, "sapinst," starting with Web AS 640 includes a section that allows the installer to choose a new password for default Oracle and SAP database users.

Operating System Security

☑ When the operating system is installed, there are some default configurations that should be changed.

☑ If you are preventing processes from running, you can do it one of two ways. If you are using the legacy method of starting processes, remove the startup scripts for executing. If you are using Solaris' Service Management Facility (SMF), disable that process.

☑ Protect root access by disabling a direct login as *root* from points other than the actual console.

☑ Set up log-in messages.

Frequently Asked Questions

Q: How do I install patch bundles on UNIX?

A: Execute the runinstaller program from the patch bundle.

Q: How frequently are Critical Patch Updates issued?

A: CPU patches are released quarterly.

Q: How do I install a Critical Patch Update?

A: Use Opatch.

Q: How do I change default database user passwords?

A: Use SQL or brconnect.

Q: What are the UNIX permissions for brconnect?

A: 4755.

Q: What is the proper ownership of brconnect?

A: ora<sid>:dba.

Q: How do I change the password for the SAP schema owner?

A: brconnect.

Q: What file contains the list of permitted IP addresses that can connect via Oracle net services?

A: sqlner.ora.

Q: How do you password protect the Oracle net listener?

A: Implement a password that is registered in the listener.ora file.

Q: What is the default Openboot security level?

A: "none".

Q: What file in Solaris contains the banner page seen at login?

A: /etc/issue.

Q: Which is a more secure protocol to use: telnet or ssh?

A: ssh.

Chapter 7

Overview of Auditing

Solutions in this chapter:

- SAP Controls
- Master Record Settings
- Transactions and Configuration Related to Business Cycles
- Auditing Configuration Changes
- Auditing Customized Programs
- Auditing Basis
- Auditing Security

☑ Summary

☑ Solutions Fast Track

☑ Frequently Asked Questions

Introduction

Here are some general points about SAP that are helpful in auditing the system. First, SAP is composed of a number of highly integrated modules that can transfer information on a real-time basis. Some common modules are as follows:

- Sales and Distribution (SD)
- Material Management (MM)
- Finance (FI)
- Controlling (CO)

Staff from any department in your organization can have access to information regarding any aspect of the business, provided that information has been entered into SAP. For example, the accounting staff can quickly view the status of a sales order or inventory levels. Access to information in the system is dependent on how user security is set up. Second, SAP allows for a great degree of customization. Some of the customization is done through configuring SAP-delivered settings. These settings are typically easy to review by looking at the tables the settings are recorded in. SAP also allows users to change the programming used for inputting data, updating tables, and displaying information in reports. This is important to note because custom programs can circumvent standard controls in the SAP system.

Third, SAP is composed of five layers. Each layer has a particular task. From an audit perspective individuals working in one layer of the system should not have access to work in another layer of the system. Here are the five layers:

1. **End user** End users create and maintain master data and input transactional data.
2. **Configuration** SAP provides the customer with configurable settings that determine how data is processed in SAP. These settings can be changed to meet the needs of the customer's business. Configuration is done through the IMG that is on transaction code SPRO. Once in SPRO you can choose to go to a custom IMG or the SAP standard IMG. To go to the SAP standard

guide, hit the **SAP reference IMG** button. For the most part the IMG is laid out by module. These changes are typically done in a Development client, transported to a Quality and Assurance client for testing, then moved to Production. This process is referred to as the transport process.

3. **Programming** SAP allows the customer to create ABAP programs used in the system. Through custom programming, the customer can change how data is entered, stored, and reported.
4. **Basis** Basis is the technical core of the SAP installation.
5. **Security** The security layer maintains the user access to the SAP systems.

A good approach in auditing an SAP system is to be sure to perform the following tasks:

- **Document the business process** During this step you will need to do the following:
  - Identify transaction codes and programs used in the process – especially any custom transaction codes and programs.
  - Identify master records used in the process.
  - Identify the configuration relevant to the business process.
  - Review reports used in the business process. Verify the reports pull information in a way that is consistent with what the business process requires.
- **Determine assertions, objectives, and risks regarding the data captured in the business process being audited** Review the data for:
  - Existence or occurrence
  - Completeness
  - Rights and obligations
  - Valuations or allocation
  - Presentation
  - Cutoff

- **Identify key controls** Identify system and nonsystem controls used to mitigate risks.
- **Test of controls** Design tests that will provide evidence that the control structure in place prevents or detects errors in a timely manner and has operated continuously and correctly.
- **Communicate findings and recommendations** After evaluating the test results in the previous step, identify any control weakness and formulate recommendations to address these weaknesses.

SAP Controls

SAP controls can be broken out into four categories: Inherent Controls, Configurable Controls, Security Controls, and Manual Controls.

Inherent Controls are controls that come delivered with the system and cannot be changed via configuration. Some of these controls are as follows:

- All document-level postings record the time, date, and user who entered the document into SAP.
- The debits and credits for all FI postings must be in balance before the document can be saved.
- All document-level postings are given a unique document number.
- SAP provides online data analysis.
- SAP logs and records the history of program changes.
- SAP logs and records the history of the User profile changes and Role changes.

Configurable Controls are controls that can be enabled, disabled, or changed via configuration.

Security Controls are controls that control user access to the system.

Manual Controls are controls outside of the SAP system that are used to complement or compensate for controls in the system.

Master Record Settings

A *master record* contains information regarding a business partner or material. In SAP a master record must be created before any transactions for that business partner or material can be processed. Settings made on the master records drive how transactions are process in SAP. These controls are entered and changed by the end users when master records are maintained. However, the available selections for these controls are often maintained in configuration. Therefore, controls at the master record level are maintained by both the end users and configuration. In auditing master records it is important to verify that only appropriate staff have access to maintain the records and that any configuration changes made to the controls used in the master records were properly approved before being moved to the Production system.

Customer Master Record Settings

Customer master records consist of Company Code Data, General Data, and Sales Area Data. The customer master record is typically accessible by the accounting and sales administration groups.

When a customer master record is created it is assigned to an account group. This account group determines

- If the number assigned to the customer master record is internally or externally assigned.
- What fields on the customer master record are required, optional, or suppressed.

We'll now list controls maintained on the customer master record that are significant for transactions involving the customer master record:

Company Code Data Level

First we'll define controls at the company code data level.

Reconciliation Account in General Ledger

This field determines which general ledger account will be updated when a transaction is posted on the accounts receivable (AR) sub ledger for the customer.

Tolerance Group

This field determines how cash discount and payment difference are processed.

Payment History Record

By selecting this setting the system will record the customer's payment history.

General Data Level

Now we'll define controls at the general data level.

Name

This field has the name of the customer.

Street Address Section

The information in this section can be used for shipping purposes and to determine taxes.

Sales Area Data Level

Finally, we'll define the controls at the sales area data level.

Terms of Payment–Billing Document

This field shows what terms will be used for a sale to the customer.

Taxes Sections–Billing Document

This section shows if a customer is tax exempt or liable for taxes.

Here are some reports that can be used to review the maintenance and completeness of customer master records:

- S_ALR_87012195 - Customer Master Data Comparison – shows incomplete customer master records
- S_ALR_87012182 - Display Changes to Customers

Customer Credit Management Master Record Settings

The *customer credit management master record* cannot be created until the customer master record is created. Here is a list of controls maintained on the customer credit management master record that are significant for transactions involving the customer credit management master record:

Credit Limit

The amount entered here represents a limit for the total receivables and the foreseeable receivables from the customer.

Credit Limit: Total Limit Across All Control Areas

The amount in this field specifies the overall credit limit the customer may receive in all control areas.

Risk Category

The risk category determines the credit checks made for the customer.

Here are some reports that can be used to review the maintenance and completeness of customer credit management master records:

- F.31 – Credit overview
- F.32 – Credit missing data
- FCV3 – Credit Management: Early Warning List
- S_ALR_87012215 – Display changes to credit management
- S_ALR_87012218 – Credit Master Sheet

Vendor Master Record Settings

The *vendor master record* is typically accessible by the Accounting and Purchasing groups. Some of the controls on the vendor master record are similar to the controls on the customer master record.

When a vendor master record is created it is assigned to an account group. This account group determines if:

- The number assigned to the vendor master record is internally or externally assigned
- What fields on the vendor master record are required, optional or suppressed

Here is a list of controls maintained on the vendor master record that are significant for transactions involving the vendor master record:

- ***Name*** This field has the name of the vendor, which is typically the name used on the payment to the vendor.
- ***Street address section*** The information in this section can be used for mailing payment or correspondences to the vendor, and to determine taxes.
- ***Reconciliation account in general ledger*** This field determines which general ledger account will be updated when a transaction is posted on the accounts payable (AP) sub ledger for the vendor.
- ***Check double invoice*** If this setting is selected the system will check if a payment has already been made to the vendor/invoice combination.
- ***Tolerance group*** You can specify how much the actual value of an invoice can differ from the expected value when processing invoices for purchase orders (POs).

Here are some reports that can be used to review the maintenance and completeness of vendor master records:

- F.48 - Purchasing – accounting comparison report
- S_ALR_87012086 - Vendor List
- S_ALR_87012089 - Display Changes to Vendors

General Ledger Account Master Record

General ledger (GL) account master records are typically only accessible by the accounting staff. Here is a list of controls maintained on the general ledger master record that are significant for transactions involving the general ledger master record:

- **GL Account Group** Determines the number range that can be used for the GL account number.
- **Reconciliation Account for Account Type** If an account is set up as a reconciliation account then no direct postings can be made to the account. Posting can only be made via the sub ledger. In this field it is determined which sub ledger can use the GL account.
- **Line Item Display** If this setting is selected then line items can be displayed via account balance transaction codes.

- **Field Status Group** The field status group determines which fields are required, optional, or suppressed when making a posting with the GL account.
- **Post Automatically Only** If this setting is selected then no direct postings can be made to the GL account. The GL account can only be posted to via other modules. For example, a revenue GL account would be set up so only posting generated via a sales order (SD module) can update the GL account.

Here are some reports that can be used to review the maintenance and completeness of GL account master records:

- S_ALR_87012328 – GL Account List
- S_ALR_87012333 – GL Accounts List
- S_ALR_87012308 – Display Changes to GL Accounts

Material Master Records

Because the *material master record* is used in all parts of the logistic system, a number of groups maintain selected portions of the material master. Here is a list of controls maintained on the material master record that are significant for transactions involving the material master record:

- **Sales Org 1 tab (tax data)** Determines how to treat tax when selling the product.
- **MRP1 (MRP type)** Determines how the material is planned.
- **Accounting 1 (valuation class)** Determines what GL account will be posted to for material movements.
- **Price Control** Determines if the material will be valuated using standard or moving average.

Here are some reports that can be used to review the maintenance and completeness of material master records:

- MM04 – Display changes
- MM60 – Material list

Transactions and Configuration Related to Business Cycles

Because of the integrated nature of SAP, it is necessary to consider a complete business cycle when auditing. Controls that appear to be weak at the start of a business cycle might have compensating controls at another point in the cycle. Also, a number of the SAP controls are maintained in Configuration. For that reason it is important to understand which SAP modules are used in the business cycle. The Revenue cycle primarily pulls from the logistic modules SD and MM, as well as the financial modules FI and CO. The Expenditure cycle pulls from the logistic modules MM and PP, as well as the financial modules FI and CO.

Revenue Cycle

The basic steps in the Revenue cycle are:

Sales Order > Pick, Pack and Ship > Customer Invoice-Billing > Customer Payment

Sales Order

In auditing sales orders verify that:

- Only valid sales orders that are created for approved customers with approved credit limits are processed.
- The pricing and terms applied to sales orders are accurate and the pricing conditions used are approved.
- Sales orders are processed completely and timely.

Here are some reports and configuration settings to review to verify sales orders are accurate, complete and timely:

- Verify only authorized staff has access to entering sales orders by looking at security report S_BCE_68001398. Type in the transactions used to maintain sales orders and verify that only authorized staff shows on the report.
- Use the same security report to verify only authorized staff can maintain the customer master record and the credit management master record.
- Review the pricing conditions configuration by using the following menu path:

SPRO > Sales and Distribution > Basic Functions > Pricing > Pricing Control

- User transaction code V/LD to list the prices for materials and verify the prices in the system are correct.
- Review credit configuration by using the following menu path:

  SPRO > Financial Accounting > AR & AP > Credit Management > Credit Control Account
- Use transaction code OVA8 to review how the automatic credit control checks are set up.
- Use transaction code OVAK and OVA7 to verify if the automatic credit check is enabled for selected sales documents and item categories.
- Use transaction code V.00 to list incomplete SD documents. Review the report for any documents that have been on the report for too long.

Pick, Pack, and Ship

In auditing the pick, pack, and ship process verify that:

- The pick list is accurate.
- The system checks if product is available.
- Shipments that are blocked are reviewed and released.
- Verify the GL account determination for material movements are correct.
- Cost of goods sold (COGS) are recorded in the correct period.

Here are some reports and configuration settings to review to verify the pick, pack and ship process is accurate, complete and timely:

- Use transaction code VTLA to verify the pick list is accurate by reviewing the configuration to copy data from the sales order to the pick list.
- Review if and how the system checks to see if a product is available by looking at the availability check on the master data via transaction code MM03 on the **MRP 3** tab. To view the configuration for the available check go to:

  SPRO > Logistics Execution > Shipping > Availability check and Transfers of Requirements > Availability check

- Review the configuration for blocking shipments via menu path:

  SPRO > Logistics Execution > Shipping > Deliveries > Define Reasons for Blocking Shipping
- Review the following reports:
  - Backorders – V.15
  - Delivery Monitor – VL06
- Use transaction code OBYC to review the account determination for material movements. Double click on a transaction key to view what GL accounts are set up for posting for a selected type of transaction.
- Verify the posting periods are maintained so no materials postings can be backdated by looking at transaction code S_ALR_87003642. The account type M should not be open for any past periods. Also, to verify that no postings were made after period end cutoff compare the entry date to the posting period. Use transaction code FBL3N to view any postings to the COGS accounts with an entry date after period end, but with a posting period before period end. Investigate any entries made after period end to the prior period.

Billing

In auditing the billing process verify that:

- All goods shipped have been invoiced in a timely manner.
- Invoices are accurate and the correct GL accounts are updated.
- All billing blocks are reviewed and released in a timely manner.
- Revenue is recorded in the correct period.

Here are some reports and configuration settings to review to verify billing and invoicing is accurate, complete, and timely:

- Use transaction code VTFA to review how data is copied from the sale order to the billing document.
- Use transaction code OVV3 to review billing block configuration.

- Use transaction code VKOA to review GL account determination for the invoice.
- Run transaction code VF04 (Billing Due List) to review documents that have not been invoiced or only partially invoiced.
- Use transaction code S_ALR_87003642 to verify the posting periods are maintained so no Revenue postings can be back dated. The account type K should not be open for any past periods.

Customer Payment

In auditing customer payments verify:

- Customer payments are processed so they are accurate, complete, and timely.
- Cash discounts are correct and post to the correct GL accounts.
- Other payment deductions are correct and post to the correct GL accounts.
- Payments are posted to approved bank GL accounts.

Here are some reports and configuration settings to review to verify billing and invoicing is accurate, complete, and timely:

- Monitor customer accounts by reviewing the following reports:
  - Account Analysis – FD11
  - Customer line item display – FBL5N
  - Due Date Analysis for Open Items – S_ALR_87012168
- Use transaction code FI12 to verify bank accounts are linked to the correct GL accounts.
- Use transaction code OBA4 and OB57 to view tolerance levels for cash discount discrepancies and payment differences.
- Use transaction codes OBXL and OBBE to view the reasons codes for payment differences and what GL accounts the payment differences post to.
- Use transaction code OBA3 to view the settings for the customer tolerances. In OBA3, customer tolerance groups are created and these groups are then assigned to the customer master records.

Expenditure Cycle

The basic steps in the expenditure cycle are:

Purchase Order > Goods Receipt > Invoice Verification > Payment to Vendor

Purchase Order

In auditing purchase orders verify:

- Purchase orders are approved.
- Only approved materials can be purchased from approved vendors.
- Vendor performance is reviewed.

Here are some reports and configuration settings to use to verify purchase orders are accurate, complete, and timely:

- Review the release strategy configuration in order to verify that POs must go through an approval process. The release strategy configuration is on menu path SPRO > Material Management > Purchasing > Purchase order > Release procedures for purchase order.
- Verify if source lists are maintained for materials used in POs. Use transaction code ME0M to run a source list report.
- Verify purchasing info records are maintained. Purchasing info records show information regarding certain materials and the supplier for the materials. Use the following transaction codes to view reports on purchasing info records:
  - ME1L – Source list by vendor
  - ME1M – Source list by material
  - ME1W – Source list by material group
- Through vendor evaluation configuration the system can evaluate vendors based on such items as price, quality, and delivery. To view the vendor evaluation configuration go to SPRO > Material Management > Purchasing > Vendor Evaluation.

Goods Receipt

In auditing the goods receipts process verify:

- Goods receipts are valid and accurate.
- Tolerance for goods receipts is set correctly.
- PO history is updated correctly.
- GL accounts are updated correctly for goods receipts related transactions.

Here are some reports and configuration settings to use to verify goods receipts are accurate, complete, and timely:

- Look at the configuration for reference document for the goods receipt transaction code MIGO. This configuration can be viewed using menu path SPRO> Material Management > Inventory Management and Physical Inventory > Settings for Enjoy Transactions > Settings for Transaction and Reference Documents. The fields on the goods receipt transaction code will pull information from the reference document noted in configuration.
- Use transaction code OMC0 to view the configuration for the goods receipt tolerances. Through this configuration the system will automatically block or issue a warning if the goods receipt varies a certain amount from the purchase order or material master record.
- Use transaction code ME23N to view PO history. The history is noted in the items detail section – Purchase order history tab. Also look at these reports to view PO history:
  - ME2L – Purchase orders by vendor
  - ME2M – Purchase orders by material
  - ME2K – Purchase orders by account assignment
  - ME2C – Purchase orders by material group
  - ME2N – Purchase order by PO number
- Use transaction code OBYC to review the GL account determination for material management transactions.

Invoice Verification

In auditing invoice verification verify:

- A three-way match is done between PO, goods receipt, and invoice.
- Tolerance levels follow approved business requirements.
- Good receipts without invoice receipts are reviewed.

Here are some reports and configuration settings to use to verify invoice verification is accurate, complete, and timely:

- Use transaction code OME9 to review the account assignment configuration. Then look at POs via transaction ME23N to verify POs that require a three way match are set up with the appropriate account assignment. For the account assignment categories used in POs verify the following items are selected/not selected correctly:
  - Goods receipts
  - GR indication binding
  - Invoice receipt
  - IR indicator binding
- Look at transaction code OMR6 and review the configuration for tolerance levels and verify the set up is in line with company policy.
- Run transaction code MR11 - Maintain GR/IR Clearing Account. The report will list out all POs that have a discrepancy between goods receipt and invoice receipts. Review the report for any long outstanding items.

Payment to Vendor

In auditing payment to vendor verify:

- There is proper segregation of duties between creating vendors, entering invoices, creating a payment run, and executing the payment run.
- Payments are made to only approved vendors.
- Payments are not made for duplicate invoices.
- Invoice verification and manual payment blocks are reviewed regularly.

- Payments to vendors are timely.
- Payment terms on AP transactions are correct.

Here are some reports and configuration settings to verify payments to vendors are accurate, complete, and timely:

- Review the security profiles for creating vendors, entering invoices, creating a payment run, and executing the payment run. You can use transaction code PFCG to review the security profile.
- SAP can only make payments to vendors who are set up in the system. However, payments could be made to vendors in the system who are no longer valid vendors. Therefore, it is important to review that invalid vendors are blocked. Look on transaction code XK05 to verify if a vendor is blocked or not blocked.
- Verify that the duplicate invoice check is selected on the vendor master record. This field is located on the Company code – Payment transaction screen.
- Use transaction code MRBR to see a list of invoices that were blocked during the invoice verification process. Review the invoices by entry date to determine if there are any invoices that have been on the blocked report for a long time.
- Use report S_ALR_87101128 - Variance Analysis of Outgoing Payment to analyze when payments were made in comparison to due dates.
- Use report S_ALR_87101129 - Comparison: Payment Terms Document/ Master Record to compare the payment terms used in the vendor line items and the vendor master record.
- Use transaction code OBB8 to review the payment terms configuration to verify the payment terms are configured correctly.

Auditing Configuration Changes

In auditing an SAP system it is necessary to verify that only authorized staff have access to configuration and that appropriate testing of the configuration changes are done prior to changes being moved to the Production client. A number of controls in SAP are maintained in configuration and, for these controls to be effective, any changes to these controls need to monitored. Also, since configuration determines how tables are updated, if changes are not properly tested prior to being moved to Production there could be issues with transactions not working or the database not updating correctly. In auditing configuration changes it is important to verify:

- No configuration changes are allowed in Production. If configuration changes need to be made directly in Production, verify that a special temporary ID is used to make the change. No configuration changes in Production should be made with a regular user ID. The use of temporary IDs in Production should be logged and traced.
- The system logs configuration changes that impact key controls.
- Configuration changes can be made by only approved staff.

Here are some reports and tools that can be used to monitor configuration changes:

- Verify configuration changes are not allowed in Production. Look at transaction SCC4 and verify Changes and Transports for Client-Specific Objects in the Production client are set to "No changes allowed."
- Review the use of all special temporary IDs in Production. Verify the transactions used by the special temporary ID are in line with the purpose of the request for the temporary ID.
- Configuration changes are logged in SAP tables. Transaction code SE13 shows you the technical setting for the table, particularly if the table is flagged for logging of data changes. Logging is enabled by the flag on this table; however, it is activated only when the instance parameter *rec/client* is set to a valid client value or *ALL* for all clients. Transaction code SCU3 is used to view the logs of the changes.
- Use transaction code SE03 to view transports by IMG activities. Identify IMG activities that impact key controls and use those IMG activities as the selection parameter. Once transports that impact key controls have been identified, look at table E070 in Production to verify if the transport has been moved to Production. Verify that all the transports that have been moved to Production followed the company's change control procedures.
- Table E070 notes who created each transport. Look at table E070 in Production and verify that the transports were created only by approved staff.

Auditing Customized Programs

SAP allows a great deal of customization to the system via changes to the data dictionary and ABAP code. In order to track this customization, SAP has established the **S**AP **S**oftware **C**hange **R**egistration (SSCR) procedure that registers all manual changes to ABAP code and the data dictionary. When ABAP code or the data dictionary are changed, the system automatically requests an SSCR key. In auditing customized programs it is important to keep in mind that custom programs can circumvent key controls in the system. Here are some other items to look at when auditing custom programs:

- Verify programs are requested by approved individuals and are adequatly documented.
- Verify that before programs are moved to Production adequate security has been created for the program.
- Verify that only authorozed individuals maintain programs.
- Verify programs cannot be created in the Production enviroment.
- Verify obsolete transaction codes are blocked.

Here are some reports and configuration settings that can be used to review program changes:

- Use transaction code SE16 to look at table TRDIR to review custom programs and verify that:
    - The title of the program sufficiently describes the purpose of the program.
    - Custom programs are assigned to an appropriate authorization group.
    - The person who created the customer program is authorized to created programs.
- Use transaction code SE16 to look at table TSTC to review a list of custom transaction codes, the programs assigned to the transaction code, and a description of the transaction code.
- Use transaction code SM01 to view locked transaction codes. Verify any transaction codes that are no longer used have been blocked.
- Use SE38 review if a custom program was adequately documented. In SE38, type in a custom program and hit the source code button. There should be wording that indicates the purpose for the custom program, when it was

created, who requested the change, and under what logged issue ticket the change was requested.

- Verify ABAP code cannot be updated in Production by disabling repository and client independent changes in table T000, the Client setting table.

Auditing Basis

The *Basis component* in SAP is the technical core of the system. It includes maintaining the databases and the system performance. In auditing Basis it is important to verify:

- The security of SAP application, database, and operating system is monitored and maintained in accordance to company policy.
- The performance of the operating system, network system, and database is monitored.
- Backups of SAP databases and operating systems are performed regularly.
- Database consistency is monitored.
- Application and security patches are current.
- System availability to end users is maintained.
- Only approved changes are moved to Production.

Here are some reports and configuration settings that can be used to review Basis settings:

- Use transaction code RZ20 to review the setup in the Computer Center Management System (CCMS) to verify if they are appropriate. CCMS gives visibility on workloads, databases, and network performance. Thresholds can be set in CCMS to give warnings if the system is having performance issues in any of these areas. Thresholds are set per monitoring property threshold. When thresholds are surpassed, a method is triggered that changes the color of the monitoring CCMS interface for that particular monitoring property. Color coding is Green for *Normal*, Yellow for *Warning*, and Red for *Alert*.
- Use transaction code ST02 to view SAP application server buffer performance. Once in ST02, use Current Parameters to view Profile Parameters for SAP Buffers.
- Use transaction code DB12 to view when database backups have been performed. Look in Backup and Recovery > Backup history to see a history of database backup history.

CTS is the heart of SAP's ABAP change management system. A relatively new tool, called ChaRM (Change and Request Management), gives a consolidated implementation of ABAP change management via Solution Manager. A thorough review of the process and configurations is necessary, whichever tool is being utilized. A sample test that can validate the effective implementation of change management is to select a sample of transports and compare the date and time of importation into the Test and Production system. Another test is to review if any objects originated from other than the development system. Log on to a downstream system such as Production and query the data dictionary table, TADIR, and check if there are any customer objects owned by that system.

Database consistency is critical and must be checked periodically. The *brconnect* utility accessed via UNIX has the facility to check database consistency. Direct Oracle tools such as Oracle's RMAN utility can also verify physical and logical consistency.

Auditing Security

Auditing the actual security mechanism itself is another dimension of an audit. Because security is the mechanism and module that enables user access to data within the system, it is very important to identify the risks and associated controls to mitigate the risks. In auditing security ensure the following points are addressed:

- User ID naming convention
- Password rules
- Locking users
- Validity dates
- Naming convention for Roles
- Critical authorization combinations are not used
- Production client is closed for configuration and development changes

The following reports, transactions, and tables will help determine how the issues are being addressed within the system.

- **User ID naming convention** Transaction code SU01 is the interactive transaction that gives you full visibility to user names; if any convention is utilized. Table USR02 field BNAME is another quick way to look at this data.

- **Password rules** Password rules are controlled by the instance parameters enabled for that particular instance. RZ10 is the interactive transaction to view and change the actual values. Report RSPARAM will give a list of all active and default parameters. Password parameters start with *login/*. Report RSUSR003 is another helpful report that gives a list of only security and password parameters. See Table 7.1 for a list of password parameters and their explanation.

Table 7.1 Password Parameters

Parameter	Explanation
login/min_password_diff	The minimum number of characters that must differ between password instances
login/min_password_digits	The minimum number of digits that must be in a password
login/min_password_letters	The minimum number of letters that must be in a password
login/min_password_lng	The minimum password length
login/min_password_lowercase	The minimum number of lower case characters that must be in a password
login/min_password_specials	The minimum number of special characters that must be in a password
login/min_password_uppercase	The minimum number of upper case characters that must be in a password

- **Locking user rules** Locking user rules are also defined in the instance parameter. Similar to the password parameters, the locking rule parameters also start with *login*; see Table 7.2 for a list of locking rules.

Table 7.2 Locking Rules

Parameter	Description
login/failed_user_auto_unlock	Activates the automatic unlock of users at midnight
login/fails_to_session_end	The number of errored log-in attempts until a user session ends
login/fails_to_user_lock	The number of errored log-in attempts until a user is locked

- **Validity dates** User validity dates are seen and changed in SU01.You can also see this in the security report tree SUIM.
- **Naming convention for Roles** The naming convention is seen in transaction code PFCG and also in the report tree SUIM.
- **Critical authorization combinations are not used** A combination of critical authorizations can potentially jeopardize the system. For a start, SAP has a standard report that looks for combinations of access that can be risky. Run report RSUSR005 for a list of users with critical authorization combinations. The standard profile SAP_ALL (full system access) should not be assigned loosely in the Production client. A deliberate and precise policy should exist in order to safeguard the system.
- **Production client is closed for configuration and development changes** The production client needs to have customizing, client-independent, and repository changes activated. The logic behind this is to enforce a strict change management approval and delivery policy.

Summary

The purpose of auditing is to verify that financial information correctly reflects the economic condition of an organization. An auditor reviews transactional data to verify the data is valid and complete, correctly valued, recorded in the correct period, and presented in a way that would not mislead a user of the financial information. In order to verify the above attributes, the auditor must determine if the controls in place effectively mitigate risks that the financial information in the system does not reflect the economic condition of the organization. An SAP auditor would look at master data setup, configuration settings, controls over custom programs, basis configuration, and security to determine if controls are adequate. There are a variety of tools in SAP for the auditor to review these areas. The above chapter detailed a number of these reports and settings. SAP also provides a list of reports that show information needed to effectively review an SAP system. This list of reports is called Audit Information System (AIS). In earlier releases the reports were located on a single transaction code, which is SECR. This transaction code is still available; however, SAP's new approach to listing useful reports is by assigning audit security profiles to users via transaction code PFCG. SAP note 451960 lists the auditor security profiles. The security profiles group reports by functional areas: accounts receivable, accounts payable, purchasing, etc. This is a great source for viewing reports that can be use to audit an SAP system.

Solutions Fast Track

SAP Controls

- ☑ **Inherent Controls** are controls that come delivered with the system and cannot be changed via configuration.
- ☑ **Configurable Controls** are controls that can be enabled, disabled, or changed via configuration.
- ☑ **Security Controls** are controls that control user access to the system.
- ☑ **Manual Controls** are controls outside of the SAP system that are used to complement or compensate for controls in the system.

Master Record Settings

- ☑ A master record contains information regarding a business partner or material.
- ☑ Settings made on the master record drive how transactions are processed in SAP.
- ☑ The master record settings determine what general ledger account a sale to a customer will post to, if taxes will be calculated for a purchase of supplies, if a material is blocked from purchasing, and so on.

Transactions and Configuration Related to Business Cycles

- ☑ Because of the integrated nature of SAP, it is necessary to consider a complete business cycle when auditing.
- ☑ Controls that appear to be weak at the start of a business cycle might have compensating controls at another point in the cycle.
- ☑ Controls that appear to be weak at the start of a business cycle might have compensating controls at another point in the cycle. Also, in SAP there are a number of ways or transaction codes to do the same thing. For example, to enter a journal entry you can use transaction code F-02 or FB50. In F-02 you can make a straight journal entry to the general ledger or you can make a journal entry to a subledger. In FB50 you can only post to the general ledger. The configuration settings or controls for F-02 and FB50 are different. Knowing which transaction code is used to make journal entries helps in determining what you need to look for in your audit.

Auditing Configuration Changes

- ☑ SAP provides the customer with configurable settings that determine how data is processed in SAP.
- ☑ Configuration is done through the IMG which is on transaction code SPRO.
- ☑ Once in SPRO you can choose to go to a custom IMG or the SAP standard IMG. To go to the SAP standard guide hit the SAP reference IMG button. For the most part the IMG is laid out by module.

Auditing Customized Programs

- ☑ SAP allows a great deal of customization to the system via changes to the data dictionary and ABAP code.
- ☑ In order to track this customization, SAP has established the **S**AP **S**oftware **C**hange **R**egistration (SSCR) procedure that registers all manual changes to ABAP code and the data dictionary.
- ☑ When ABAP code or the data dictionary are changed, the system automatically requests an SSCR key

Auditing Basis

- ☑ Basis is the technical core of the system. It includes maintaining the database and system performance.
- ☑ It is important to have proper control around how the database is maintained since your data is meaningless if the database is corrupted.
- ☑ Poor system performance can adversely impact the end user's ability to do his or her job.

Auditing Security

- ☑ A user ID must be used in order to log on to the system.
- ☑ Each person should have his or her own log-on ID with a security profile that is tailored for the access he or she needs in the system.
- ☑ Password rules are controlled by the instance parameters enabled for that particular instance.

Frequently Asked Questions

Q: What is the difference between master records and transactional data?

A: Master records contain information regarding a business partner or material. Settings made on the master record drive how transactions are processed in SAP. Transactional data is data created from processing business transactions in the system.

Q: Is there a report that shows who created and changed vendor master records?

A: Use the report on transaction code S_ALR_87012089 – Display Changes to Vendors to view changes to vendor master records.

Q: Is there a report that shows who created and change customer master records?

A: Use the report on transaction code S_ALR_87012182 – Display Changes to Customers to view changes to customer master records.

Q: Is there a report that shows who created and changed general ledger master records?

A: Use the report on transaction code S_ALR_87012308 – Display Changes to G/L Accounts to view changes to general ledger master records.

Q: What does the Revenue Cycle include?

A: The basic steps in the Revenue cycle are: Sales Order > Pick, Pack, and Ship > Customer Invoice-Billing > Customer Payment.

Q: What does the Expenditure Cycle include?

A: The basic steps in the Expenditure cycle are: Purchase Order > Goods Receipt > Invoice Verification > Payment to Vendor.

Q: Is there a report tree that shows security-related reports?

A: The security-related reports are located on transaction code SUIM.

Q: What table can I view to see who created configuration changes that were transported into Production?

A: This data is recorded in table E070.

Q: What is the IMG?

A: The IMG is the Implementation Guide for customizing SAP R/3. It lists out the configuration steps needed to implement SAP R/3.

Q: What is AIS?

A: AIS in the SAP Auditing Information System. [In older SAP implementations it a report tree on transaction code SECR that lists out SAP audit reports. In newer releases it is SAP-delivered security profiles that include audit reports.]

Glossary

A

ABAP Advanced Business Application Programming (ABAP) is a programming language for developing applications for the SAP R/3 application.

Access Control List Access Control List (ACL) is a list that specifies which users or system components are allowed to access a resource.

Application Link Enabling (ALE) Application Link Enabling (ALE) technology facilitates the business-driven message exchange between distributed SAP systems using synchronous and asynchronous communications.

Application Programming Interface (API) Application Programming Interface (API) is an interface that is used by application programs to communicate with other systems.

AIS Audit Information System

ALE Application Link Enabled

Authentication The process of confirming the identity of an individual or system component, usually as a prerequisite for allowing the individual or components access to the system. For example, you may authenticate yourself to the SAP system by providing your user ID and password.

Authorization The authority to execute a particular action in the SAP System. You use authorizations to protect the system from unauthorized or unwanted access.

Authorization Concept Each authorization refers to an authorization object and defines one or more permissible values for each authorization field contained in the authorization object. The authorizations are combined into profiles and roles are entered into a user's master record.

B

BizTalk BizTalk is an industry initiative headed by Microsoft to promote Extensible Markup Language (XML) as the common data exchange language for e-commerce and application integration on the Internet. Accepting XML as a platform-neutral way to represent data transmitted between computers, the BizTalk group provides guidelines, referred to as the BizTalk Framework, for how to publish standard data structures in XML and how to use XML messages to integrate software programs.

C

Certificate Authority (CA) A CA is a third-party entity that issues digital public-key certificates for use by other parties. The role of the CA is to guarantee the identity of the certificate owner.

Client/Server Architecture An architecture model that distinguishes client systems from server systems, and that communicates over a computer network. A client-server application is a distributed system composed of both client and server software. Specifically, the SAP graphical user interface (GUI) frontends are the clients and the SAP applications are the servers.

Configtool The offline Java-based administration tool for configuring and administering the Web AS J2EE. The Configtool is started from the *configtool* directory below the J2EE root directory from the server. On Windows the script name is *configtool.bat* and in UNIX it is *configtool.sh.*

Configurable Controls Controls that can be enabled, disabled, or changed via configuration.

Configuration SAP provides the customer with configurable settings that determine how data is processed in SAP. These settings can be changed to meet the needs of the customer.

Cryptography The study and practice of hiding information.

Cryptography algorithm A mathematical algorithm that uses a secret key to transform the original input into a form that is unintelligible without special knowledge of the secret information and the algorithm.

CUA Central User Administration

D

Database Management System (DBMS) A functioning R/3 System must have a database management system (DBMS) to control concurrent access to data to ensure consistency of the data. Some examples of DBMS for the R/3 System include ORACLE Server, INFORMIX-OnLine Dynamic Server, and DB2 Universal Database.

Distinguished Name A hierarchical identifier for an object as specified by the X.500 format. The Distinguished Name (DN) is defined by adding the object's identifier to the Distinguished Name from its predecessor. The X.500 format describes an object in a hierarchical tree.

Digital Certificate This is an electronic *identity card* that establishes a user's credentials when executing transactions on the Internet. It is issued by a Certificate Authority (CA) and contains name, serial number, expiration date, the certificate holder's public key (used for encrypting, decrypting messages, and digital signatures), and the digital signature of the certificate-issuing authority so that a recipient can verify that the certificate is real.

Digital Signature This guarantees that the individual or component that signs a digital document really is who he or she claims to be. It protects the integrity of signed data; if any of the signed data or signature is changed, then the Digital Signature becomes invalid.

Demilitarized Zone (DMZ) Typically a company sets up a Demilitarized Zone (DMZ) between the enterprise's local intranet and the Internet. This is an area that exists between two networks that allows connections between the networks without sacrificing unauthorized access to the systems located within the networks. The DMZ contains the enterprise's firewalls and routers, which allow Internet protocol connections such as HTTP or FTP into the DMZ. Within the DMZ, these connections are controlled and routed so that the enterprise's intranet is not directly accessible to/from the Internet.

Dual Stack An installation of Web AS with both ABAP and J2EE application platforms installed in one system is referred to as a *Dual stack* installation. A Standard Dual stack installation is an installation of Process Integration (PI).

H

HTTP Hypertext Transfer Protocol (HTTP) is the set of rules for transferring files (text, graphic images, sound, video, and other multimedia files) on the Web. This protocol controls the communication between the Web browser (i.e., HTTP client) and the Web server (i.e., HTTP server).

HTTPS Secure Hypertext Transfer Protocol (HTTPS) is a connection that provides for encrypted communications between the client and the server. It supports server-side, client-side, or mutual authentication. You use the prefix HTTPS: in the URL instead of HTTP: when accessing Internet sites that are protected with SSL.

I

IDOC Intermediate Document

Inherent Controls Controls that come delivered with the system and cannot be changed via configuration.

iView A program that retrieves data from content sources in your enterprise and on the Internet to display in the Enterprise Portal content area.

J

Java A general purpose, high-level, object-oriented, cross-platform programming language developed by Sun Microsystems. Java was expressly designed for use in the distributed environment of the Internet.

J2EE Java 2 Platform, Enterprise Edition (J2EE), is a Java platform designed for mainframe-size applications. The application platform for Web AS J2EE is based on J2EE.

J2EE Engine The J2EE Engine is an integral component of the SAP Web Application Server that implements the J2EE standard. It consists of the SAP Java Enterprise Runtime (e.g., class loading, cluster communication, persistent configuration, data management), pluggable components (e.g., programming APIs, interfaces, libraries, and services), and applications that are deployed and run on the J2EE Engine.

JavaBeans JavaBeans is a Java version of a component that is platform independent.

JavaServer Pages (JSP) JavaServer Page is an extension of the Java Servlet technology that provides a simple programming vehicle for displaying dynamic content on a Web page.

Java Virtual Machine A virtual environment responsible for the life-cycle of every Java-based program.

L

LDAP Lightweight Directory Access Protocol (LDAP) is an Internet protocol that applications such as e-mail, address book, and calendar use to look up information from the server. A directory is a set of objects with similar attributes organized in a logical and hierarchical manner (e.g., a telephone directory). Version LDAPv3 is defined in Internet Engineering Task Force-Standard Track Requests for Comments (IETF-RFC) 4510 for accessing directory services.

M

Manual Controls Controls outside the system that are used to complement or compensate controls in the system.

Master record A master record contains information regarding a business partner or material. In SAP a master record must be created before any transactions for that business partner or material can be processed. Settings made on the master records drive how transactions are processed in SAP.

O

OASIS Organization for the Advancement of Structured Information

ODBC Open Database Connectivity (ODBC) is a standard database access methodology. The goal of ODBC is to enable access to any data from any application regardless of the database management system used to handle the data. This is accomplished through a middle layer called a database driver between the application and the database management system. This layer then translates the application's queries into commands understood by the database management system. In order to accomplish this, both the application and the database management system must be ODBC compliant.

OSS Online Service and Support (OSS) is SAP's delivery of problem resolution. The Internet address is http://service.sap.com. Users will need an authorized user name and password.

P

Personal Security Environment (PSE) This is a secure location where a user or component's public-key information is stored. The Personal Security Environment (PSE) for a user or component is located in a protected directory in the file system or on a smart card. It contains both the public information (public-key certificate and private address book) as well as the private information (private key) for its owner so that only the owner of the information should be able to access his or her PSE.

Portal Catalog folders A collection of folders representing the roles, pages, portal objects, and other content available to a specific administrator.

Portal Content Directory (PCD) A repository for objects and relationships, which allows hierarchies and links, supports user personalization, and provides for distributed administration and transport.

Portal layouts The design arrangement or layouts of a portal page.

Portal Role A role defined in a portal.

PI Process Integration

Public-Key Infrastructure (PKI) A system that manages the trust relationships involved with using public-key technology. The role of the Public-Key Infrastructure (PKI) is to make sure that public-key certificates and Certification Authorities (CAs) can be trusted and validated. The collection of services and components involved with establishing and maintaining these trust relationships is known as the PKI.

Public Key Certificate A digital document that contains the necessary information (e.g., serial number, validity period, digital signature, public key, Distinguished Name, and cryptographic algorithm used) to identify its owner and verify his or her digital signatures.

R

Remote Function Call (RFC) RFC is a procedure for data exchange between client and server. It can be used as a function module to call and process predefined procedures/function modules in a remote SAP system. Connections via the RFC interface are possible between different AS ABAP systems, and between an AS ABAP and a non-SAP system. In non-SAP systems, specially programmed functions are called instead of function modules. Connections are distinguished between synchronous, asynchronous, and transactional function calls.

RMI Remote Method Invocation (RMI) provides for remote communication between programs written in the Java programming language. Allows an object running in one Java virtual machine to invoke methods on an object running in another Java virtual machine. The Java world at large is about reuse and minimizing the re-writing of code, often called write-it-once programming. RMI enables use of code everywhere to fulfill the objective of Java.

S

SAProuter This is a SAP program that acts as part of a firewall system. SAProuter simplifies the network security and traffic routing to/from the R/3 System and external networks. You can define which connections are permitted and which connections are protected by password access.

SAP Software Change Registration (SSCR) A procedure that registers all manual changes to ABAP code and the data dictionary.

Security Audit Log An SAP tool that produces a log containing security-related system events such as SAP configuration changes or unsuccessful log-on attempts. The events are recorded based on the settings in the Security Audit Log's configuration, and they provide useful information for monitoring changes and audit tracking on series of events.

Secure Socket Layer (SSL) A protocol for transmitting private documents over the Internet. Secure Socket Layer (SSL) creates a secure connection between a client and a server where data can be sent securely. SSL protects Web sites through encryption, authentication, and verification. SSL communication is meant to provide secure communication between the server and client. The parties involved in the dialog utilize the server's certificate to establish a secure basis for communication.

Security Assertion Markup Language (SAML) Security Assertion Markup Language (SAML) is an XML-based document format used for exchanging security-related information between communicating parties. This format is developed and standardized by the Organization for the Advancement of Structured Information (OASIS).

Security Controls Controls that control user access to the system.

Segregation of Duties (SoD) The concept of having more than one person required to complete a task. A risk is defined when two or more transactions are available to a single user, role, profile, or HR object and it creates the possibility of error or irregularity. As a security practice the main objective is to prevent fraud and errors. These can be systematic or manual business processes. Successful segregation of duties is accomplished by separating tasks among multiple users or departments.

SNC Secure network communications (SNC) is a protocol comparable to SSL that ensures authentication, data integrity, and data privacy. SNC is useful in securing remote function call (RFC) communications.

SOAP... Simple Object Access Protocol (SOAP) is a way for a program running in one kind of operating system to communicate with a program in the same or different kind of an operating system by using HTTP and XML as the mechanisms for information exchange.

SSF Secure store and forward (SSF) mechanisms ensure document security.

SSO Single sign-on (SSO) allows a user to be challenged once then navigate through different authorized applications without having to reauthenticate.

SSO Administration Wizard An SAP System tool (transaction SSO2) to assist you with the configuration of log-on tickets for single sign-on (SSO).

Support Package Manager (SPAM) SPAM is an SAP tool for importing Support Package updates into SAP systems.

U

UDDI Universal Description, Discovery, and Integration (UDDI) is a platform-independent XML-based registry for businesses around the world to list themselves on the Internet.

UME The user management engine (UME) provides central user administration for all Java applications in the SAP Web Application Server. The UME is the source from which the J2EE engine accepts and validates logins.

UME console The user management engine (UME) administration tool accessed via the Visual Administrator.

UNIX Shell The command line interface environment in UNIX. Some different flavors of a Shell are Korn Shell, C Shell, Bourne Shell, and Bash Shell. SAP's default installation shell is C Shell.

URL The technical purpose of a URL, or Uniform Resource Locator, is to designate a specific namespace like *sap.com* which belongs to SAP AG. The common usage is to designate an internet address. Combining a protocol and port, the URL can look something like http://myserver.mycompany.com:50000, which identifies *myserver* at a namespace of *mycompany* thru port *50000* using the HTTP protocol.

User Management Establishment of a user's right to information within an organization. User management involves setting up of user IDs and passwords, defining access levels and assigning authorizations to users, resetting passwords, updating user master records when employees change their job classifications or departments, and deleting users when users leave the enterprise.

User Provisioning The process for setting up users with access to data and technology resources. Provisioning can be a combination of duties of human resources and IT departments in an enterprise where users are allocated access to hardware, applications, systems, databases, and network resources based on the user's unique identity.

V

Visual Administrator The Java-based administration tool for configuring and administering the Web AS J2EE. The Visual Administrator is started from the *admin* directory below the J2EE root directory from the server. On Windows the script name is *go.bat* and in UNIX it is *go*.

W

Web AS Web Application Server (Web AS) is the core server component of SAP NetWeaver products.

Web AS ABAP The Web Application Server based on the ABAP development/ application platform. The ECC product is an example of an SAP product based on the Web AS ABAP server.

Web AS JAVA The official name for all the components of the Web Application Server that relate to the Java technology.

Web AS J2EE The Web Application Server based on the J2EE development/ application platform. The Enterprise Portal is an example of an SAP product based on the Web AS J2EE server.

Web Client Software that enables users to access and browse the Internet.

Web Dynpro A development and runtime environment that is used to create professional user interfaces for business applications powered by SAP NetWeaver.

Workset This is a specific collection of tasks, services, and information that is part of a Portal Role. A workset comprises all the tasks, services, and information for a specific activity area, such as controlling or budgeting.

XML Extensible Markup Language (XML) is a flexible way to create common information formats and share both the format and the data.

Web AS J2EE The Web Application Server based on the J2EE development application platform. The Enterprise Portal is an example of an SAP product based on the Web AS J2EE server.

Web Client Software that enables users to access and browse the Internet.

Web Dynpro A development and runtime environment that is used to create professional user interfaces for business applications powered by SAP NetWeaver.

Workset This is a specific collection of tasks, services, and information that is part of a Portal Role. A workset comprises all the tasks, services, and information for a specific activity area, such as controlling or budgeting.

X

XML Extensible Markup Language (XML) is a flexible way to create common information formats and share both the format and the data.

Index

A

T

U

V

Printed and bound by CPI Group (UK) Ltd, Croydon, CR0 4YY
03/10/2024
01040341-0003